ROSE CHERAMI:
GATHERING FALLEN PETALS

Published 2020 PENIEL UNLIMITED, LLC

PENIEL UNLIMITED, LLC

321 Avalanche Avenue

Georgetown, Texas 78626

http://www.penielunlimited.com

The vision of PENIEL UNLIMITED, LLC, Dr. Michael Glenn Marcades founding President, is to pursue and make available to everyone the truth about his mother Rose Cherami (Melba Christine Youngblood Marcades), her tragic life circumstances and mysterious death on September 4, 1965. Furthermore, PENIEL UNLIMITED, LLC is dedicated to the dissemination of accurate historical information concerning Rose Cherami's efforts to provide advance warning of President John F. Kennedy's impending assassination. All rights reserved. No part of this book may be reproduced or transmitted in any form or by any means, electronic or mechanical, including photocopying, recording, or by any information storage or retrieval system without written permission from the publisher except for the inclusion of brief quotations in a review.

Printed in the United States of America

Copyright © 2016, 2020 Michael Glenn Marcades

1st Printing October 2016 - JFK Lancer Productions & Publications

2nd Printing Revised Edition January 2020 - Peniel Unlimited, LLC

ISBN 978-0-578-64537-7

This book may be purchased for varied purposes. For information regarding Book Club, educational institution, or wholesale orders contact Dr. Michael Marcades: penielunlimited@gmail.com, michaelmarcades@gmail.com, or the Rose Cherami website: rosecherami.com.

Photos for this book are copyrighted by their respective copyright holders and may not be reproduced for any reason or in any format without express permission from the owner or copyright holder.

To find out more about this book and Rose Cherami see http://www.rosecherami.com.

Book Design & Production by John C. Tripp (www.trippomatic.com)

Cover Design by Daniel Whisnant (www.suissemade.com)

10 9 8 7 6 5 4 3 2

ROSE CHERAMI:
Gathering Fallen Petals

By Michael Marcades, Ph.D.

With Norma J. Kirkpatrick

Introduction by J. Gary Shaw

Published by PENIEL UNLIMITED, LLC

Dedication

To my wife Kelly with gratitude for her love,

encouragement and dedication

to bringing to life the Rose Cherami story.

About the Authors

Dr. Michael Marcades completed his Ph.D. in Fine Arts (Choral Conducting) at Texas Tech University in May 1999. His dissertation, Benjamin Britten's Ad majorem Dei gloriam (AMDG): A Musico-poetic Analysis and Performance Guide for the Choral Conductor, was nominated for the 1999 Julius Herford Prize and is housed on request in the Britten-Pears Library, Aldeburgh, England. Throughout his career, Marcades has served on the School of Music faculties at Texas Tech University, Columbus State University Schwob School of Music and Southern Union State Community College.

Additionally, he has devoted extensive time to in-depth research and writing about the tragically, mysterious life and death of his mother Melba Christine Youngblood Marcades. Melba, alias Rose Cherami, is known to the worldwide President John F. Kennedy assassination community as the woman who knew in advance and tried to warn authorities about the pending assassination plot. Her character, depicted in Oliver Stone's landmark film JFK, reveals her struggle with heroin addiction, involvement with nationwide prostitution rings and drug trafficking, association with assassination figures such as Jack Ruby, and her extensive work as an official FBI informant.

After three decades of research and ten years of writing, ROSE CHERAMI: Gathering Fallen Petals, initially published in 2016 by JFK Lancer Publications, revealed his mother's provocative life narrative. A Revised Second Edition is scheduled for publication in late 2019 by PENIEL UNLIMITED, LLC. Information regarding this new edition and Marcades' availability is accessible via penielunlimited@gmail.com, michaelmarcades@gmail.com or rosecherami.com.

Michael is married to Kelly Casey Marcades, a music professional in her own right. Together, they celebrate their seven grown children, four grandchildren and their three wonderful dogs, Molly, Sadie and Lucy. Michael and Kelly are proud residents of Georgetown, Texas.

Norma J. Kirkpatrick is a wordsmith of long tenure in varied categories of the printed word. She is a newspaper columnist, has written teaching materials, collaborated as a ghostwriter, is a partnership novelist and manuscript diva. Her slogan is, "Let me say it for you." She believes the right word at the right time is the key to reaching into the heart and mind of the reader.

It was happenstance that brought Norma and Michael Marcades together, leading them to work as a team on the massive project to capture the true and accurate story of his infamous mother, Rose Cherami, in a form that could be shared with the world. The two of them together felt it was their destiny to do so; now it has come about in the publication of *Rose Cherami: Gathering Fallen Petals (FIRST EDITION, 2016).*

Table of Contents

Introduction, J. Gary Shaw 1

Prologue 15

Chapter 1, Hard Lessons: The First School of Life (1923 - 1938) 17

Chapter 2, Moving Up and Out: Nothing is Free (1939) 37

Chapter 3, Trying It All: Beyond the Boundaries (1939 - 1940) 47

Chapter 4, More Hard Lessons:
The Road to Hell (1941 - 1942) 61

Chapter 5, A Horror Named Angola: Hell on Earth (1942 - 1944) 82

Photo Section 108

Chapter 6, Sensual Sirens Entice: Bourbon Street (1944 - Early 1952) 121

Chapter 7, Search for Normalcy:
Tried and Denied (Late 1952 - Early 1953) 151

Chapter 8, The Beginning of the End:
Houston and The Mafia (Mid 1953 - Early 1960) 171

Chapter 9, Dead End Roads:
Touching Home and Becoming Rose Cherami (Late 1960 - 1963) 219

Chapter 10, Florida: "A Merry Go 'Round"
Montgomery: Tours, Drugs and the FBI (1964 - 1965) 259

Chapter 11, The Final Highway: Pathway to Truth (September 4, 1965) 291

Epilogue, He Who Loves the Rose: A Son's Reflections 311

Acknowledgements 315

References 319

Additional Records 325

Second Edition Documentation 343

When Hummingbirds Do Sleep

For Mother
Melba Christine Youngblood Marcades
~
(Rose Cherami)

Can't help I but imagine, within the foliage deep,
    the care that God provides the hummingbird, seldom as she sleeps.
I wonder if the constant flutter of tail and wings combined,
    stop for e'er one second, as in darkness,
    yesterday unwinds.

If so, now perched on branch so thin, this tiny creature rests,
    surely God around her cups –
His hands, a warmly nest.
    Now engulfed in darkness, God's protective vest,
    its heart can finally now slow down,
    consuming less and less.

Within God's nest her head bows low – inside sweet dreams abound,
    of others who n'er have the time,
    to ever sleep so sound.
For they are still consumed by nothing but themselves to keep,
    oblivious to the truth that warns,
    that what they sow – they'll reap.

Without God's overarching hands, protecting us through all,
    lives will soon be torn apart
    and man will surely fall.
How sad it is that we, so smart,
    a simple truth can't see,
    yet hummingbirds, with God alone, in tandem freely be.

September 13, 2012 – Michael Marcades
Seale, AL
(a.m., on the front porch – watching the hummingbirds feed)

INTRODUCTION

Rose Cherami and the Murder of President Kennedy

BY J. GARY SHAW — (COPYRIGHT 2019)

I first met Michael Marcades, son of the infamous Rose Cherami, in late 1989. My first thought upon meeting him was, my, what a distinguished, pleasant and personable man. He greeted me with a ready smile and firm handshake, important traits in Texas.

My second thought was, knowing what I knew about his mother, how could this be?

Rose Cherami, real name Melba Christine Youngblood Marcades, "Crit" to her family, was everything a mother shouldn't be with very little of what one ought to be. Actually, up until the time of her death at age 41, she had seen her son only on rare occasions. She had been in and out of jails and prisons, and had been hospitalized more than once as mentally ill due to alcohol and drug abuse. She had been a stripper and a prostitute and had been arrested multiple times for various crimes such as vagrancy, car theft, Dyer Act, narcotics, drunkenness, arson and larceny. Her aliases were numerous and varied.

But she also was a valued informant (narcotics) for law enforcement — an important connection that should not be overlooked or ignored. Rose's story is an ugly, heart wrenching one. But I'll let Michael tell you her full life story. My interest in Rose, as I will refer to her in this Introduction, has to do with my lifetime quest to find the real perpetrators of the crime of the century, the murder of President Kennedy.

My interest in Rose began around 1966 when I met and began working with Penn Jones, a gutsy owner/editor of a small town newspaper just outside of Dallas, Texas, the city where President Kennedy had been assassinated. And where the accused assassin, Lee Harvey Oswald, had been gunned down by nightclub owner Jack Ruby while in the custody of the Dallas police.

Penn had begun chronicling in his paper certain stories pertaining to the sudden and suspicious demise of a number of people who were close to events and/or individuals connected in some way to the assassination. One of these people was Michael's mother, who died less than two years after the assassination, and under very mysterious and suspicious circumstances. But, again, I'll let this book tell the whole story about her tragic death. My major interest lies in *WHY* she had to die.

Rose died at age 41, her death sinisterly shrouded in mystery. Many believe she *had* to be silenced because she knew too much and therefore was a threat to the *real* killers of our President.

What did Rose know?

- She knew and had worked for Jack Ruby, assassin of the alleged assassin, Lee Harvey Oswald.
- She had seen Lee Oswald in the company of Jack Ruby, a bothersome circumstance the investigating authorities categorically denied — even in the face of numerous corroborating witnesses.
- She knew first-hand of Ruby's association with men connected to organized crime, again, a disconcerting connection the authorities knew but, knowingly lying to the American people, denied.
- She knew, and had been in company with, two men prior to the assassination and had heard them say that they were on their way to Dallas to kill the President.
- She had expressed her knowledge of these men, their names and their intention. And Rose had done this while in the presence of a law officer and several hospital personnel — two days prior to the assassination.
- She had again warned that the President was going to be killed in Dallas, this time as she was watching the TV account of the beginning of President Kennedy's motorcade — and, as previously, she had done so in the presence of hospital personnel.
- Sometime later, when told of the remarkably quick arrest of Lee Harvey Oswald, she asked hospital personnel if the authorities also had arrested Jack Ruby.

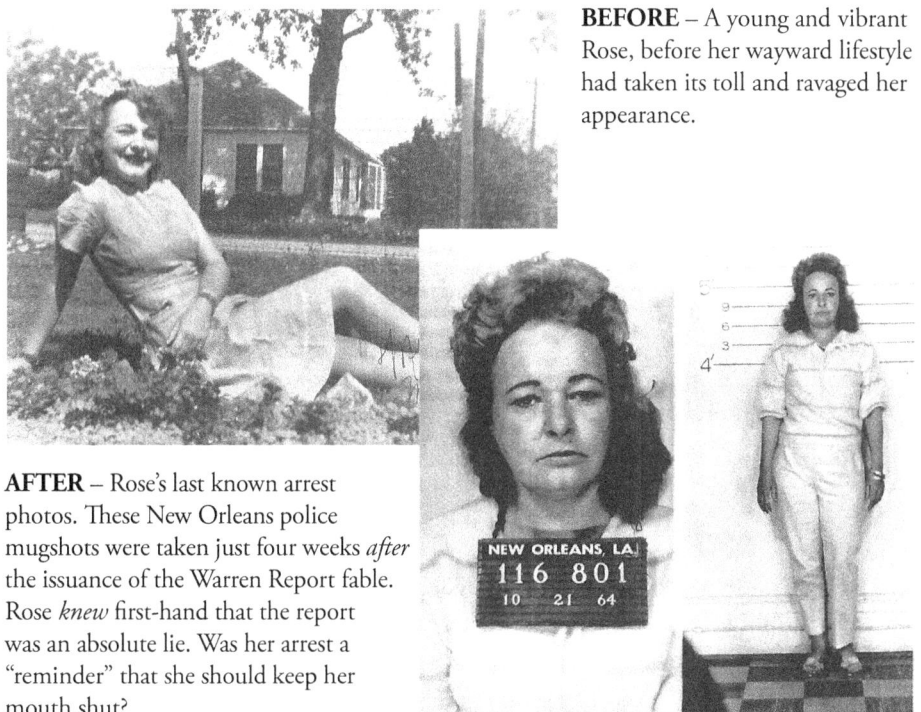

BEFORE – A young and vibrant Rose, before her wayward lifestyle had taken its toll and ravaged her appearance.

AFTER – Rose's last known arrest photos. These New Orleans police mugshots were taken just four weeks *after* the issuance of the Warren Report fable. Rose *knew* first-hand that the report was an absolute lie. Was her arrest a "reminder" that she should keep her mouth shut?

Rose possessed prior knowledge of the murder, prior knowledge of the identities of possible assassins, knowledge of an association between Oswald (*The Lone Assassin*) and Ruby (*The Lone Avenger*), and first-hand knowledge of Ruby's ties to known members of organized crime. This kind of information could get a person killed. Especially if one's behavior was as erratic and uncontrollable as Rose's.

The authorities ignored and tried to bury Rose's dire warning of the President's assassination, and the vital information regarding the identities of possible assassins or accomplices.

As we've learned, Rose was not the only one with prior knowledge of the assassination, there were several others. I'll mention only a couple with which I have some personal knowledge.

Two Men Who Also Knew

Just weeks before the President's Dallas trip, a Kennedy-hating Georgia man had been surreptitiously recorded predicting that Kennedy would be assassinated by a rifleman shooting from the window of a tall building. Though the recording of this threat was passed on to authorities, Kennedy's secret service detail (we are told?) never received the information.

About the same time, a Dallas independent oilman angrily told a Texas businessman and his wife that Kennedy would be killed when he came to Dallas. He said there were three oilmen who would put up the money. I have met with and interviewed the man who was told of the threat. Now deceased, he was a well respected businessman known for his integrity.

As it turns out, this same oilman had purchased a high caliber rifle in downtown Dallas on the morning of the assassination and purportedly had been seen by at least two witnesses carrying the rifle west on Elm Street toward Dealey Plaza and the Texas School Book Depository (TSBD).

Interestingly, a few years after the assassination, the oilman purchased a ranch in Texas's hill country located a short distance from the LBJ Ranch, home of President and Mrs. Lyndon B. Johnson. Available records reveal that the Johnsons are known to have flown by helicopter to the oilman's ranch on occasion for dinner.

The oilman was questioned by the FBI regarding the threats, which he denied. He was never asked about his whereabouts or actions at the time of the President's murder.

A Little Bit Like Rose — But Different

Additionally, there was another witness whose knowledge seemed to correspond and lend credence to that of Rose's. One cannot talk about Jack Ruby, Lee Oswald, strippers and possible prior knowledge of the assassination without bringing up the name "Little Lynn."

Karen "Little Lynn" Carlin was a stripper for Jack Ruby at his Carousel Club in downtown Dallas. According to Karen's sister, she was also "arm candy" for some of Ruby's mysterious trips and was privy to some of his criminal and gunrunning activities and associates.

On the morning before he shot Oswald, Ruby had sent a $25 money order to Karen in Fort Worth, an act seen by many (including some in law enforcement) as an attempt to establish that his murderous act was not premeditated.

Late on the evening of Ruby's shooting of Oswald, a Secret Service Agent interviewed Karen in her Fort Worth apartment.

Left - Karen "Little Lynn" Carlin, stripper at Jack Ruby's Carousel Club in Dallas.
Center - A jailbreak occurred during Karen's first appearance at Ruby's trial. Scared out of her wits, Karen kept repeating, "He's got a gun! - He's got a gun! - He's after me! - He's after me!"
Right - Karen attempts to hide behind her fur collar and dark glasses while being searched prior to entering the courtroom for Ruby's bond hearing. The search revealed a pistol and she was arrested for carrying a concealed weapon.

Karen, the agent reported, was "highly agitated," "...twisted in her chair, stammered in her speech, and seemed on the point of hysteria," and was "reluctant to make any statement."

More significantly, Karen further told the agent that she thought that *"...Lee Harvey Oswald, Jack Ruby and other individuals unknown to her, were involved in a plot to kill President Kennedy and that she would be killed if she gave any information to the authorities."*

Apparently Karen, like Rose, had some prior knowledge of Oswald, Ruby and the assassination.

Within a year, Carlin seemed to have disappeared and was rumored to be dead.

When I finally located the very much alive Karen "Little Lynn" Carlin, some 30 years later, she was living (under a different name) in a house with barred windows and black curtains, and several dogs. The home was just outside of a small town in a far northern part of the United States. She had finally settled there — after, as her long-haul truck-driver son would laughingly say — "we moved around a lot and had lived in more states than I passed through on my truck routes across the U.S."

Karen's son, as well as her sister, also confirmed to me that Karen had been placed under some kind of government protection. While the current Witness Protection Program did not come into official existence until around 1970 or 71, there WAS some type of protective custody program in place in 1964. It was utilized during that period of time for mafia henchman turned government informant, Joe Valachi, as he loudly and grandiosely spewed out organized crime secrets to a government committee.

Following a number of phone conversations, and mail correspondence through an intermediary, and — for reasons she never explained — my assurance that Florida mafia chief Santo Trafficante was dead, Karen finally agreed to a face-to-face meeting with me.

Karen, now in her sixties, surrounded by her children and grandchildren.

After agreeing on time and place I flew up north and stayed all night in a near-the-airport motel. My room opened onto a restaurant area with an indoor pool surrounded by tables and chairs. On the morning of our planned meeting, as agreed, I sat at one of the tables near my room. While awaiting Karen's arrival two well dressed men came into the pool area and took nearby tables. Neither of the men ever looked my way. Though they increased my awareness, I thought little about them at the time.

Karen did not show at our scheduled time. I had continued waiting an hour or so when the restaurant hostess announced on the intercom that I had a phone call at the front desk. The caller, in a woman's voice I did not recognize, told me that Karen said she could not meet me, that her car had " broken down," and to tell me she was sorry. I told the caller it was OK and that I could wait, even overnight if I had to. The caller then said, "you don't understand, she can't meet," and hung up. Returning to my table I noted the two men were now gone.

I attempted to call Karen several times with no answer and finally flew home disappointed. It was years later that I learned from Karen's sister that the reason Karen couldn't meet me that day was that someone had shot at her while she was driving to our meeting.

In the end, the "protection" provided for Karen "Little Lynn" Carlin was successful. She eventually died in 2010 at age 65 — a plump little grandmother — taking her secrets with her.

Back To Rose - Protection Unsuccessful?

I now suspect that, like Karen Carlin, Rose too was placed into some type of protection program. If so, Rose's apparently hadn't worked out as well. She didn't make it to 65. The wild and erratic Rose was fearless and probably couldn't be controlled. And, undoubtedly, she knew too much and perhaps talked too much.

It does, however, seem as if Rose had attempted to settle down. About 6 months after the assassination, in a letter dated May 12, 1964, she had written her mother:

> "Well like the old saying goes, the bad penny has turned up again. But it isn't quite like it was before this time. I am married, & that's the truth."

She went on to write that she was married to a retired Navy man named Gene and that they both were receiving monthly government checks. It seems curious that Rose, at the age of 40, would have been receiving a government check. The only possibility that comes to mind is that she had worked for the government — which she had. But only clandestinely.

The letter is lengthy and Rose writes beautifully and quite eloquently, unlike what one would expect from someone with her background and history. Interestingly, the letter contains no names except "Gene" and her nickname, "Crit." And while the envelope is postmarked Cape Canaveral, Florida, it bears no return address. Within a month of the letter Rose was arrested twice within a two month period in Florida. Five weeks later, on October 21, 1964, she was arrested for a third time, this time it was back in her old haunt, New Orleans.

Nothing further is heard from Rose for almost a year. Then, on August 4, 1965, seemingly out of the blue and for reasons yet unknown to this writer, she suddenly contacts — or is contacted by — the FBI.

> **PHYSICAL EXAMINATION**
>
> Family Name: **Mercades, Mrs. Melba Christine** Attending Physician: **Dr. McKenzie** Room No: **211** Hosp. No: **208-30**
>
> Date: **9/4/65**
>
> This is an adult WF who was brought to the ER of the hospital comatose and unresponsive. She has deep punctate stellate type laceration noted over the right side of the forehead. There is a deep extensive 15+ cm. laceration extending completely around the left posterior scalp area, extending down to the underlying cranium and effectively lifting the scalp from the underlying skull. The external auditory canal on the left is filled with blood and the entire left ear is swollen and contused in appearance. The pupils are large and unresponsive to light. There is blood in the pharynx and mouth. There is the odor of alcohol to the breath. The pt.'s breathing is regular and essentially normal. She is swollen and contused over the entire left side of the face. The neck is supple, but each time the pt.'s head is turned toward the right side she apparently has occlusion of her airway and becomes slightly cyanotic and has vomiting. She has open airway and normal respiratory exchange and no vomiting occurs when she is lying with her head to the left side. She is contused over the left shoulder and there is crepitation of bones in the left forearm with deformity. Portable X-Ray was performed, which revealed fracture of both bones of the forearm. There are scattered rales over both lung fields and markedly impaired breath sounds. The skin is cold and clammy to palpation. The abdomen is soft and flaccid and no specific organomegaly or evidence of internal injury to the abdomen is noted. There are contusions over both lower extremities, but there are no deformities noted. The lacerations of the scalp were cleansed and sutured and dressings applied. There was closed reduction of the left forearm with application of a cast, and there was a cutdown with a venous catheter applied to the left leg, and the pt. is being transferred to her room in very poor condition.
>
> IMPRESSION: Accident victim apparently struck by an automobile, who is in shock with intracranial damage, lacerations of the forehead and scalp, fracture of the left forearm, and pulmonary edema.

There appears to be some skepticism among the "lone-nut" fanciers concerning the veracity of Rose having had a punctuate stellate type wound to her head, indicating the possibility of her having been shot. This is a page from the multi-page Gladewater (TX) Municipal Hospital records which references the *"deep punctuate stellate type laceration"* over the right side of Rose's forehead.

Exactly one month later, on September 4, 1965, Rose Cherami was dead, allegedly struck by a car as she hitchhiked along a small and remote Texas Farm-to-Market Road. And, like Little Lynn, Rose took to her grave perhaps some of the more important secrets about who really killed JFK.

But the mysteries surrounding Rose Cherami did not end there. After meeting Rose's son, Michael — and on his behalf — I and a Houston, Texas private investigator began to look into all aspects surrounding Rose's background and her untimely, suspicious death.

By early 1990, we had obtained Rose's hospital records. What we quickly discovered was that while her Death Certificate declared she was DOA, (Dead On Arrival), her hospital records detailed eight hours of medical treatment. *More importantly, the records also indicated the possibility of a gunshot wound to her forehead.*

We also interviewed (and recorded) the man who was thought to have hit Rose with his car while she lay beside the remote highway in east Texas. Further suspicious elements were revealed in his story and are told in detail in this book.

And we learned from the DPS officer who investigated the incident that:

> "…although he had some doubts as to the authenticity of the information he received, due to the fact that the relatives of the victim did not pursue the investigation, I closed it as accidental death."

Intriguing; mysterious and highly suspicious circumstances — questions never asked — and questionable conclusions reached without proof. And no one had seemed to notice or care.

We asked ourselves, "What is going on here?"

Perhaps, we thought, her autopsy, which her death certificate denotes was performed, will shed some light on all this. It didn't. It had disappeared, either lost or destroyed.

But, as we soon discovered, there was more to come.

An Ominous Phone Call

By spring, 1990 — as we continued our quest — we had contacted Rose's sister, Mozelle (Mrs. Morris) Wall, who lived just south of Dallas, and had arranged a meeting with her for sometime in April.

A real surprise awaited us at the Mozelle Wall home. The Houston investigator and I arrived at the Wall residence on April 21, 1990, and were shocked to discover that someone had gotten there before us. Obviously, it appeared, word of our snooping around the Cherami issue had gotten around.

After our first contact with Mozelle, and two weeks before our scheduled visit, Mozelle had received a sinister, somewhat demanding, and to her, very disturbing phone call.

Rose's sister, Mozelle Wall, who received a foreboding and adamant phone call from a "former CIA Agent." This "Agent" informed Mozelle that he needed to provide her with "vital information" about Rose and "certain events" which occurred prior to the assassination. This information, he said, was for her own "protection and foreknowledge," and that he was also attempting to contact four other families — one in Houston, two in Louisiana, and one in Florida.

When we arrived, Mozelle and Morris Wall, and Rose's son, Michael, were there and waiting. After the usual introductions and greetings, Mozelle immediately began relating, from her notes, the telephone conversation she had had on April 8, 1990 with a man introducing himself as "Eli Swartzen," a "*former* member of the Central Intelligence Agency."

Swartzen, carefully spelling for Mozelle his last name, proceeded to assure her that he was indeed an agency man and that he would furnish her with a phone number she could call to verify his present association with the CIA.

The reason for his call, Swartzen said, was to request a meeting with Mozelle for the purpose of providing her with, "vital information concerning her sister, Melba Christine Youngblood Marcades, aka Rose Cherami."

The "vital information," according to Swartzen, had to do with Marcades/Cherami, and "certain events" pertaining to her "prior to her hospitalization in Eunice, Louisiana on November 20, 1963" (two days before the assassination).

Swartzen continued, saying that the information he wanted to pass on to her was, "for her own protection and foreknowledge," and that he was attempting to contact five families — two in Louisiana, one in Houston, one in Florida, and one in Dallas (meaning Mozelle's family).

Mozelle refused to see Swartzen, and declined his subsequent attempt to meet with her five days later.

We left the Wall home with Mozelle's signed, witnessed and notarized statement regarding Swartzen's foreboding phone call.

Who was this self-identified representative of the CIA? I've been unable to find anyone with the name Eli Swartzen and all of my efforts to discover who and what he is have been futile.

And, more intriguing, what "vital information" did he wish to convey to Mozelle for her "protection." More importantly, why did she need protection? And from whom and/or what did she need to be protected?

Since some in the CIA, it appears, have become the official conservators and promoters of the *myth:* "*Oswald did it alone and unaided — and so did Ruby;*" and with their history of disinformation, misinformation, deceit and deception regarding the assassination, it's not unreasonable to think that they were still actively involved in clandestine "mopping-up operations" as late as 1990.

And perhaps, with the mysterious Swartzen, they were being proactive because of the movie *JFK,* which was rumored to be in the works at that time, and soon would began filming in Dallas. This film, which was to become a powerful and disturbing movie pointing to conspiracy in the President's tragic death, would feature the sinisterly significant and highly problematical Rose Cherami incident in its opening scene.

It was surely the myth-maker's and myth-propagator's nightmare — a myth which was now believed to require another fresh coat of whitewash.

Rose had to keep quiet — or, they would keep her quiet. She had seen and heard far too much, and, apparently, had shown herself to be incapable of keeping her mouth shut.

She had been in all the wrong places and seen too many of the right faces.

She could actually identify some of the people who were participants in the President's murder. To an astute and honest person, her death was no accident — Rose was murdered!

Shakedown?

Shakedown is a common word used to describe the obtaining of goods or services through the means of force, threats, *intimidation* or abuse of power.

With regard to these two important witnesses the term "intimidation" certainly seems applicable. The lone assassin myth would be destroyed if what they had seen and heard was ever revealed. Consider the following chronology of events in the lives of Rose and Karen:

On **November 21, 1963,** Rose is in a Louisiana hospital after being roughed up by two men who told her they were going to Dallas to kill the president She made these statements before several witnesses.

The next day, **November 22, 1963,** while watching TV coverage of the President's arrival in Dallas, Rose reiterates before witnesses that the President was going to be killed, a story later relayed to Dallas authorities who said they didn't need her.

Later that **same day,** an almost hysterical Karen told the Secret Service that she thought Oswald, Ruby and others were involved in a plot to kill JFK.

While at court for Jack Ruby's bond hearing on **December 23, 1963,** Karen is arrested for carrying a concealed weapon.

On **January 10, 1964,** a missing person report is filed on Karen. Later, when located, she tells authorities that her grandfather knew where she was.

On **January 30, 1964,** Rose is arrested in Fort Worth for investigation and released the same day.

After the Ruby trial, Karen fades out of sight and only the FBI and Dallas district attorney's office knows her whereabouts.

She later resurfaces, appearing at the Skyliner Ballroom in Fort Worth where she is arrested on **September 6, 1964,** and charged with indecent exposure. Shortly afterward, she seems to disappear for good and is rumored to be dead.

Three weeks later, on **September 27, 1964,** the Warren Report, the government's fictional account of the assassination, is released to the public.

On **October 21, 1964,** about four weeks after publication of the Report, Rose Cherami is once again arrested in New Orleans. Afterward she seems to disappear for almost a year. She reappears on August 4, 1965, and, for reasons still unclear, reconnects with the FBI.

One month later, on **September 4, 1965,** Rose was dead. She was only 41 years of age.

Many years later, in **1992,** I learned that Karen was alive and well, living just outside a small town in Michigan; under "protective custody," and with a different last name. She died in **2010** at the age of 65.

Two questions which beg answers come to mind: (1) Did Karen do as she was told — had she shut up and lived? And (2), had poor Rose continued to talk, as she previously, and so openly, had done on November 21-22, 1963 — and, therefore, had to be eliminated?

In my opinion, the answers seem crystal clear!

J. Gary Shaw

November 4, 2019

Michael Marcades with J. Gary Shaw, 2019

Prologue

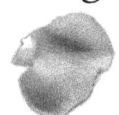

It was September 4, 1965, when the Chevy sped down the familiar stretch of East Texas Highway 80, on the way to Dallas. Rose was physically and emotionally exhausted. She leaned back against the padded headrest of the front seat, staring at the road ahead as the headlights cut through the heavy night mist. Though she was used to staying up all night, the constant hum of the engine made it hard for her to stay awake.

Rose glanced over at the driver. He had driven her on other late night excursions, but she didn't know much about him. She could sense he was not interested in carrying on a conversation. If she said anything to him, he would reply with one or two words, or a shrug. That made her uncomfortable because men always wanted to talk to Rose, her mature sensuality drawing out the maleness in them.

Not a kid anymore, Rose had experienced everything anyone could imagine about the dark side of life. After all of these years, the things that she used to think were dangerously exciting and fun, were just a job now. Rose was in her forties and some would consider her used up and worn out ahead of her time. Once a stunner and a charmer, she had tried it all, done it all and had it all.

Rose was riding along, mesmerized by monotony while thinking about her life. By the time she reached twelve years of age back on the farm where everyone called her "Crit" short for her real name "Christine," she had started throwing away and destroying anything that tied her down, or tried to set a boundary. Rules did not apply to her. Fences could be climbed and restrictions trampled. Freedom to do as she pleased was the lodestone that constantly lured her, no matter the outcome.

What a dumb ass I have been. I threw away the chance to get to know my baby boy, my Michael. Having him was the only good thing I ever did. He was a little doll, those dark eyes and wavy hair right from the day he was born. Rose wiped a tear from the corner of her eye. What is he now twelve years old?

I pray to God this is my last job working both sides of the trafficking fence. I know I'm playing with fire and have got to get out while I still can, before one side or the other takes me out. Maybe I will have a chance to set things right back at home, and be a real, honest to goodness mother to Mike, if it's not too late.

Rose tried to think of something else, as she stared out the window on her side of the car. The litany of the towns ahead seemed endless: Gladewater, Mineola, Terrell, Forney and Mesquite, before they would reach Dallas. She planned to get a few hours of sleep there in a pre-reserved hotel room before making her assigned drug delivery the next day. Once that was done, she would be told what to do next before being whisked quickly out of Dallas. The trusted runners like Rose were kept on the move and as low profile as possible.

Gladewater was only a couple of miles away as she succumbed to sleep. When they neared the edge of town, the car slowed slightly. Suddenly the driver made a hard right turn off of Highway 80 onto North FM 155.

Partially wakened by the quick change of direction, Rose lifted her chin and looked around at the darkness of the area. "What, where are we going? Why did you leave the highway? This isn't the road to Gladewater!" Suddenly wide-awake, she sat up in the seat, trying to see where they were going.

"Short cut," the driver said, without emotion.

"Short cut, my ass! Where in the hell are you taking me? Stop now, damn you, stop!" Rose screamed, her heart pounding. She tried to grab the steering wheel while clawing at the driver with her long fingernails.

He roughly hit her under the chin with his elbow, brutally throwing her against the far side of the car. Almost unconscious, Rose knew this was life or death.

CHAPTER 1

Hard Lessons:
The First School of Life
(1923 - 1938)

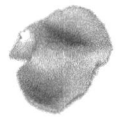

Melba Christine Youngblood stood up on the railing of the pigpen, throwing corncobs as hard as she could at the big sow. Squeals from the pig soon brought her mother to the back door of the old farmhouse, wiping her hands on her apron in exasperation.

"Melba Christine Youngblood!! Stop that this minute. How many times do you have to be told not to trouble that old sow? Do you want a whippin'?"

"No ma'am."

"Then don't do it, and I mean it. You don't want me to tell your papa, do you Crit?"

Everyone called her Crit. The only time her real name was used was if her parents were mad at her or the schoolteacher was calling roll.

"No ma'am. I'd just as soon you didn't."

She held an extra corncob behind her back and threw it at the sow as soon as she heard the creaky screen door shut, and then ran as fast as she could to the barn. Crit knew for sure she did not want her papa to spank her. "Spare the rod and spoil the child, Minnie." She could hear him say it in her head, and see her mother nodding in agreement. Climbing up into the hayloft, Crit dangled her feet over the edge because it was dangerous, but mostly because her parents had forbidden her to do so. She sat there swinging her legs and daydreaming about her approaching birthday. At least it was something to look forward to. As the child of a tenant farmer, life was hard and sparse.

Crit thought to herself, "I'll probably get a pair of dumb socks again, not that I couldn't use them. My old ones have been darned so many times they are damned to hell. Socks ain't much of a present." Ever the optimist she still hoped, "Who knows, I might get some hard candy. If I get candy, I ain't sharin', no matter how much Mozelle whines."

"Crit! Where are you?" Minnie yelled. "Get yourself in this house right now and get your chores done. You won't like it if I have to call you again! You know it's your morning to watch the biscuits and your papa don't like them burnt." Minnie did not wait for a reply as the screen door slammed shut forcefully behind her.

The gangly, long-legged girl hopped down the ladder rungs two at a time. She knew her father would be coming back from the far horse lot and she didn't want to get caught in the hayloft. Hay and dust fell into her blonde disheveled hair while she was descending. She gave herself a quick brush off with her hands. Crit refused to tie up her hair or plait it into pigtails as her two sisters did. She wanted it free to blow in the wind like the mane of a horse. There was plenty of wind in Texas.

Pausing on the back porch, she looked at herself in the mirror hanging above her papa's shaving stand, his leather razor strop beside it. Dipping the tips of her fingers into the enamel wash pan, she flicked the water on her face and patted it off.

"Did you wash your hands after playin' around the pig sty?" Her mother's cheeks were rosy red from the heat of the cast iron cook stove.

"Yes, Mama."

Grace Geneva rolled her eyes at Crit and tossed her an apron. "You didn't, you dirty little pig," Grace whispered into her ear. "And is that hay in your hair?" Crit gave her a shove and Grace staggered backward, plopping down on the stack of wood beside the cook stove. Crit snickered, looking to see if her mother had seen the incident. Crit wasn't allowed to hate Grace, but she didn't have to like her. In Crit's mind, there was a mile between hating and liking. Not only did she have to wear all of Grace's hand me downs, but Grace was four years older and had titties already. That was something Crit often daydreamed about in her hoped-for future. Someday, hers would be bigger than Grace's and Mozelle's. She just knew it.

"Check those biscuits, Crit. Take them out careful like and don't burn yourself. Mozelle, have you got the table set?"

The younger of the three girls, Mozelle was more gentle and reserved, and her papa's little girl. "Yes, Mama. I did it. But I didn't move the coal-oil lamp off the table."

"That's good, baby girl. Let one of your big sisters do that. Crit."

"I'm tendin' the biscuits. I can't do everything."

Minnie stopped and wiped the sweat off of her forehead with the tail of her apron. "Well, Crit, I figured since you had time to shove Grace onto the woodpile, you could probably find time to move that lamp. I expect I can find some other things for you to do today, too."

Crit obeyed quickly, becoming agreeable and helpful. "Can I do anything else to help you, Mama?" Minnie looked at the angelic face of her golden-haired daughter with the winsome smile. Crit's mother knew she was manipulative and strong-willed, and only a firm hand was going to keep her under control.

~

Minnie Bell Stroud and Thomas Jefferson Youngblood had married in 1916 when she was seventeen and he was twenty. Tom had grown up in the home of a successful farmer and knew almost everything about farming. He was good at what he did, having already gotten enough money together before they married to buy a used Model-T Ford. He paid $550 dollars for it, which was no small amount of money.

Minnie felt attracted to Tom the first time they met at the Baptist church. He had a confident Texas "gentleman-farmer" air about him. Like her, he had a sixth-grade education and she knew he would be a good provider. Everyone thought they would make a great match. Minnie didn't have a lazy bone in her body and her apple pies were the first choice at any picnic. Tom didn't mind that she was also pretty.

Soon after they married, Tom struck a deal with a local big time farm owner to manage and run one of his properties outside the county seat town of Fairfield, Texas. There was a big barn, animal pens, and acres of rich, loamy soil where massive cotton crops were grown. The bonus for the newly-weds was that it also had a three-room tenant farmhouse where they would live.

Their first baby was born there, with the help of a midwife and Minnie's mother. It was a boy they named Harvey Lee. Minnie had complications and he was born prematurely, his body was very frail. His little, thin neck connected a severely underdeveloped head that had a slight hint of hair. He had ten fingers and ten toes with no nails, but silk-like coverings instead. His face was sweet to see with thin, reddish lips, two dark searching eyes, and a nose like Tom's.

The despondent family members stood watch over him as baby Harvey Lee struggled for every breath. In their hearts, Tom and Minnie hoped against what they knew already in their heads. Less than four months later, Tom and Minnie were talking in whispers in the darkened front room of the house where they had his little crib. Then suddenly, something happened that they would tell others about for years to come. Harvey Lee's crib was suddenly enveloped in a soft, yet radiant light. In a few seconds, the glow above the crib intensified slightly then vanished as mysteriously as it had appeared. Tom and Minnie knew immediately what had happened. Their little son, Harvey Lee, was gone.

In times of reflection, Minnie would think of the experience sadly and wonder how it had affected Tom. He'd dreamed of passing on his love of the land to his son. He could be a teacher, as his father had been to him. That was something most men wanted. As each girl was born, Minnie searched Tom's face for any sign of disappointment, but he always seemed to be happy when they came healthy and whole. By the time Mozelle was born, Tom had accepted that it was just going to be girls and took to her with enthusiasm.

As Mozelle got older, he gave her rides on his shoulders, let her sit on the saddle in front of him, or lifted her up off of the ground by one arm as she reached up. Eventually, Tom began to call Mozelle, "Boy," and that was her nickname for years to come.

Somewhere in all of that, Crit was stuck in the middle; squeezed from both sides. She wasn't old enough to do what she wanted, nor young enough to get away with it if she did.

~

Eventually one glaring sore spot began to grow and fester in the marriage of Minnie and Tom. After all of the girls were born and in school, Tom started taking periodic trips out of town in his well-kept Model-T Ford. He would come in from the field, bathe, put on his nicest dungarees and western shirt, and pack a few things in a small leather bag. With his best hat in one hand, Tom would pull a clean handkerchief out of his pocket with the other to flick the dust off of his Sunday boots. He would then take money out of the sugar bowl.

The first time he did it, Minnie stood in the kitchen watching him. "Where are you going?"

"Business."

"Why are you taking the egg money? I need that for groceries."

"Gas money."

"When are you comin' back?"

"Whenever I get ready. You tend to your business, and I'll tend to mine."

As he put on his hat, he turned towards Minnie with a hard look she didn't recognize. "And Minnie, don't ever ask me again what I am doing and where I am going." He stomped out the door, pausing on the back porch to look at himself in the shaving mirror. In a couple of minutes, Minnie heard the engine of the T-Model Ford and the crunch of the tires as he pulled away. He didn't come back for five days.

His absences had become a habit that could no longer be ignored. One night as the girls were sitting around the dinner table with their mother, Grace asked, "Mama, where does Papa go when he just ups and leaves?"

"Let's not talk about that," Minnie replied.

"Why not?" Crit asked. "What gives him the right to go off and leave us here on the farm. He sure wouldn't let none of us pull a trick like that. It ain't fair to us."

"Ain't fair," Mozelle echoed.

"Life isn't always fair," Minnie said. "It seems that men can do just as they please, and women can't do nothin' about it."

"If he was my husband, I'd show him how the cow ate the cabbage." Crit energetically pounded her fist into the palm of her hand. "I bet then he would straighten up." At the age of twelve, Crit was starting to exercise her own opinions.

"Crit, don't be disrespectful of your father," Minnie said softly.

"Well, he's disrespecting us and ought to treat us right."

"Don't any of you girls tell anyone about this, or say anything to your papa. I don't want to hear talk of it in this house again. Do you understand?"

The three girls all nodded as they looked at their distraught mother and the pain on her face. They never mentioned it in her presence again, but often talked about it when she wasn't around.

~

A few months after that discussion, Minnie shook Tom out of a deep sleep. "Tom, get up now! Crit is really sick, and burning up hot. Her eyes are rolling back in her head. None of the girls have ever been this sick before."

"Aw, that's just Crit pulling one of her tricks, Minnie. Get back in the bed."

"Damn it, Tom, get up and I mean now. Get your clothes on!"

In all of their years of marriage, Tom had never heard Minnie curse before. He knew it must be serious. He obeyed quickly while Minnie wet a sheet in a bucket of water in the kitchen to wrap around their sick child, trying to control her fever. Crit was lethargic as Minnie picked her up with twice her normal strength.

Grace had heard her mother calling for her and came running barefoot out onto the screen porch. "Mama! What's wrong?"

"Crit is bad sick and we're on our way to the hospital in Dallas. Hold that screen door open. Take care of Mozelle. You two girls go to grandma's house when the sun comes up. I'll get in touch with you there!"

Grace followed her mother to the car and held open the door as Tom started the engine. "Mama, is Crit going to die?"

Minnie stopped and looked into the eyes of her oldest daughter. "I don't know

Grace, I don't know. I'm leaving you in charge now."

The car lurched forward as Grace stood in her nightgown watching them drive out of sight, leaving her feeling all alone. She had never seen her mother look so scared and that frightened her.

"God, please don't let Crit die," she prayed aloud.

Since Tom went to Dallas on "business" quite often, the side bonus at this time was that he knew his way around the city and drove directly to the hospital. It was rare for Minnie to go to Dallas, with three children and multiple farm duties that had to be done daily. She would not have been able to find the way without him.

Tom and Minnie sat side by side in the waiting area, holding hands. They were stony silent. The hospital staff had whisked Crit away for immediate care and notified the doctor on call to attend the deathly ill Crit. Tom was trying to be manly and not show his emotions. He was thinking about the day they had buried Harvey Lee and the hell it was to put a child into the ground.

It seemed an eternity before they saw the doctor coming up the hall toward them carrying a chart. Tom and Minnie sprang up and met him halfway. "Are you Mr. and Mrs. Youngblood?" They nodded. "Daughter, Christine Youngblood, age twelve?" They nodded again. "It's a mighty sick girl you have brought to us."

"What's wrong with her," Minnie interrupted.

"We have diagnosed her with encephalitis. Encephalitis is an infection of the brain itself. Of course, you know how important the brain is. People can have a variety of symptoms, and side effects. Because of the seriousness of this, we will need to keep Christine here at the hospital with professional care. We have also called in a specialist to take her case."

"We never heard of that before, Doc. Can you tell us more what to expect?" Tom knew this was out of the arena of their knowledge. "Is it contagious?"

"No, you don't need to worry about that. Let's go to the seating area." The doctor knew they were not prepared to hear what he was going to tell them, and should probably be sitting down.

The couple followed him back to where they had been sitting; the doctor took a chair across from them. "I'm going to be honest with you that while every case is different, depending on the severity and length of the infection, Christine could be left with headaches, eye problems, and there could be changes in her behavior. We've even seen personality changes. She is nearing puberty and her hormones could aggravate this situation."

Minnie gasped, leaning her head against the back of the chair as she looked at Tom in relief. She knew he was thinking the same thing as her, even with those problems; they wouldn't have to put another child in the ground.

"Christine seems to be in good health otherwise, and has a fair chance to come through this okay. I just want to be frank with you so you'll understand there is a long road ahead to recovery. This illness could seriously impact the rest of her life and the choices she makes. You should warn her not to drink alcohol and never take medicine of any type, unless under the care of a doctor."

After Christine had been in the hospital for almost a month combating the infection and taking therapies to help her toward physical recovery, she came home weak and not exactly the same girl. The community of Fairfield was supportive and encouraging with kind acts, as was their church, relatives, and friends. But, as is the way of life, time moves on to the next important thing and the past is just a memory, no longer supported in a tangible way.

Grace and Mozelle had stepped up by taking over her chores, which Crit was happy to let them do. Now they were beginning to grumble and complain. It was healthy for Crit to slowly move back into the normal family flow, but she had truly enjoyed being the center of attention for so long, even if she had to be sick to do it.

Grace didn't go to school anymore because she had finished eighth grade. That made Crit guardian and overseer of her younger sister Mozelle while at school, a responsibility she did not want. During recess she was to watch out for her so she wouldn't get hurt.

"Let's seesaw Crit." Mozelle looked up at her older sister.

"I don't want to. You just sit on the steps and don't move. I want to play tag with my friends." School was a reprieve from the monotony of isolated farm life and daily chores for Crit. She wished every day was a school day.

"I'll cry."

"So, who cares? You big baby."

"Papa does, and the teacher will tell him."

Crit eyed the sugar cookie Mozelle was holding in her chubby hand.

"Oh…okay. Let me hold your cookie so you won't drop it. Now, go get on the other end of the seesaw."

Mozelle gleefully handed over the cookie and straddled the board opposite Crit. "Are you holding on good 'cause here you go up in the air!" Crit yelled.

Mozelle squealed as Crit raised the board higher and sat on the lower end, holding her suspended. "Up and down, Crit!"

"I don't think so. I just think I will sit here and eat this good sugar cookie."

"No, no, Crit! That's my cookie." Mozelle reached out with both arms in protest.

In response, Crit laughed and jumped up off of the board, letting it crash to the ground on the opposite end with Mozelle violently flying through the air.

Mozelle's broken arm was in a cast for weeks. The red welts on Crit's back and buttocks made by Tom's leather razor strop lasted almost that long. After the whipping experience, Crit avoided her father as often as possible. Mozelle also avoided Crit. That was just fine with her.

~

Saturdays were a day of additional activity for Minnie who oversaw the process of the weekend meal. The daily chores were hectic enough, but Saturday included chasing down two fat hens, wringing their necks, and gutting them before a quick plunge into a big pot of boiling water. That made it easier to pluck off their feathers. The clean carcasses were cut into pieces; dredged through an egg and milk wash, rolled in flour, and deep-fried in lard. After the chicken cooled, it was plated and covered with a tea towel, waiting to be eaten for Sunday lunch. Needless to say, Minnie thanked God when Grace and Crit were old enough to help her with that task.

In the afternoon, they also helped by bringing in the washtub from outside and pumping buckets of water to pour into the tub sitting in the middle of the kitchen floor. That's where everyone would bathe after supper.

Every family member knew what they had to do, and when to do it. Getting ready for Sunday took everyone pulling together, except for Tom. He always had work to do outside around the barn. After all of the girls had taken their baths and gone to bed, Minnie would pump clean water for his late night bath, pouring in a kettle of boiling water to warm it.

While Tom bathed, Minnie flat ironed clothes in the dim light of the coal oil lantern, wrapping a pad around the handle to keep from burning her hand. When the iron got too cool, she alternated with the other iron heating on the stove. She then put out what everyone was to wear the next day. The mantle clock rhythmically ticking was the only sound in the kitchen. Tom would stand up in the tub to dry off, step out of the water, and go straight to bed. He slept nude. Minnie would drop her work clothes on the floor and step into the water he left behind, holding back the moans of her one luxurious moment of the day.

When he was younger, Tom would wait and look at her. Aroused, he would lift her out of the tub dripping wet and take her to bed with him. Now, they never even touched. Minnie sat in the chilly bath water Tom had left for her. She could hear him snoring, barely able to see his fading wet footprints leading to the bed.

The next morning, the Youngblood family would sit erect and properly dressed in the T-Model Ford, as Tom drove them to Sunday morning worship service at the Baptist Church in Fairfield. They always sat together in a row on the same pew. Tom was often called on to take up the offering or to lead the morning prayer. Everyone knew where he hung his fine Stetson hat on the back wall. The other men would never use his hanging peg. Tom saw the Sunday excursion as evidence to the world of his success as a farm manager who also owned his own car and had a well-turned-out family, even if they were all girls.

Minnie had a great deal of pride herself. The way she held her head high and her shoulders back, sitting on the pew with her family, gave the impression that the whole production was no effort at all, though it had taken super human drive and determination. The girls sat beside her, neat and perfectly groomed, ribbons in their hair, shoes buffed. The youngest, Mozelle, was required to sit next to her mother on the pew. Minnie was willing to overlook that she swung her feet, because they didn't touch the floor. Grace, the oldest, could feel her heart pound under her gingham dress as she saw Jackson Stewart glance at her out of the corner of her eye. Since there was to be a picnic after the service, she was certain they would manage some way to hold hands, and perhaps steal a secret kiss.

Crit was probably the only one of them who was listening to the sermon. She believed in God. It was okay that God had rules, but he was fair. Most of all, he loved everybody. "Ye shall know the truth, and the truth shall make you free," the preacher read out of the Bible. "That sounds good to me," Crit thought. "That's what I want to be. I want to be free." Crit always felt good sitting in the church house, like she was safe and God was putting his arms around her.

Crit also liked singing as Miss Deaton played on the pump organ. She knew a lot of the old hymns by heart. Miss Deaton was an old maid who wore wire-rimmed glasses pinched on her nose and looked like a little sparrow sitting up on the organ bench, rocking back and forth as she pumped the pedals. God probably thinks she is beautiful, but I guess the men don't. Maybe if she'd fix herself up, some man would want her. Crit mused the thought for a moment, "I don't know. It might be too late."

Crit sat in the backseat of the car daydreaming about getting to have her own life and doing whatever she wanted to do. She started thinking about running away, and never having to live on the farm, ever again.

"I wonder how far it is to Teague? Ginny Houston moved there last year. I'll bet I could walk that far, or maybe find a ride."

Though she seldom spoke to her father without being spoken to first, the question was out of her mouth before she could stop it. "Papa, which road goes to Teague?"

"Why, Crit? Are you going on a trip?" Everyone in the car laughed, except Crit.

"Whenever you get ready to leave, take the road going out of town in front of the courthouse. You ought to be able to remember that."

Minnie heard the rumble of the old wagon coming up the rutted dirt trail and going out to the barn. She knew it was Mr. Butrum from the feed, seed and fertilizer store. It was the annual time for him to deliver one of Tom's standing orders. She took off her apron and patted her hair in place before going out to meet him. "Howdy, Mr. Butrum. How's Mrs. Butrum doin?"

"Kinda poorly, Minnie Bell." He and his wife had known Minnie since she was a girl; knew her parents as well. "How's your folks? I ain't seen them much lately. Sometimes your pa stops by the store after he goes to the Post Office. Guess they is like me and Mable, just doin' the best they can. Where's Tom at today?"

"He's gone on business, Mr. Butrum. Your hired hand came on ahead of you and is waitin' in the barn. I'll send Crit out with some water for both of you, I know you are thirsty."

"That'd be mighty kind, Minnie Bell." He touched his hat, driving the wagon on into the barn where the hired hand had a chain and lift ready to pick up the palates and swing them into place. Tom was neat, organized and ready, which always made deliveries to his place less of a pain.

"Get two quart mason jars of water and take out to Mr. Butrum and his hired hand, Crit. Stand way back because they are swingin' those big palates."

"Where is Papa, Mama? He is always here when these big orders come."

"Well, he isn't this time, Crit. You know how it is, so I guess it's up to us women." Minnie showed obvious disgust on her face, no longer trying to hide her disapproval of Tom's escapades. "I'm going to take a rest now; I didn't sleep much last night. When Mr. Butrum is finished, gather the eggs. You might need to go up to see about the mule, too. She could probably use some feed and water."

"I will, Mama." Crit felt a pride like she had never felt before. Her Mother had said "us women." She had never been called a woman before.

Crit suddenly realized this was the moment she had been waiting for. She got the water ready, then gathered up some of her clothes and put them into a pillowcase. When she saw the hired hand about ready to get on his horse, she ran out with his water. "Just sit your jar on the fence post. I'll get it later."

"Thank you kindly, ma'am." He touched his hat, tossing down the water in a few gulps.

Crit ran back into the house, picked up her bundle and the water for Mr. Butrum. He was turning the big wagon around after making a stop at the watering trough for his horses.

Crit made her move with a bewitching smile, "Here's your water, Mr. Butrum. Mama wanted to know if you could do her a favor and give me a ride into town." Lowering her eyes demurely as a damsel in distress, she added, "Since Papa isn't home yet? I've already got my things with me."

Enchanted, he handed the empty water jar back to Crit, looking down at her from the wagon seat. "Why sure, little dolly. I'd enjoy the company."

She sat the empty jar beside the barn door. "Mama will get it later. I don't want to hold you up."

The old man gave the horses a pop of the reins as they leaned forward, pulling their load. "You needn't worry about that, Crit. Going to see your Grandma and Grandpa, are you?"

"Yes, sir. Mama thinks I might could give them a hand," Crit lied.

"I know they'll be mighty proud to see you."

The kind old friend told stories to Crit about her mother when she was a girl and how many changes he had seen at Fairfield in his day. He was very hard of hearing, so Crit gave up yelling at him and left him to his storytelling. She was so excited with this new adventure she actually felt a little faint. There was no remorse in her heart about leaving her home and family behind. In her own way, she did love her family, but she loved herself more. Crit knew she had to do everything just right to get away with what she was doing. Well-practiced in shrewdness, tricking other people and taking chances was exciting to her. She was good at it.

"We're gettin' close to town now, Crit. Where do you want me to take you?"

"Oh, just let me off at the Post Office. I'll walk on to PaPaw and MaMaw's house. It's not far from there."

"Gonna git their mail for 'em?"

"Yes, sir. It's hard for them to get down here," she said, turning to Mr. Butrum with the disarming smile she used when lying.

"You are a sweet girl, Crit. We need more like you." He stopped the wagon and let her off. "Be careful now. Bring your PaPaw by the store while you're in town."

She waved at him as he snapped the reins, pulling slowly away.

Crit had been spotted half way to Teague by an old couple working in the garden beside their shack of a house. They talked her into taking a rest on their front porch, where she gladly accepted a cup of milk and a molasses teacake. When they asked her why she was walking to Teague, she replied, "Business."

Minnie was out of her mind with fear, dragging Mozelle by the hand as she frantically searched for Crit every place possible. She had run to the barn to be sure Crit had not fallen out of the hayloft, or been kicked by the horse, trying to think of any calamity that could have befallen her. She then saddled the horse and sent Grace racing into town to tell the sheriff, and her ma and pa that Crit was missing.

The part-time sheriff of Fairfield questioned Mr. Butrum and his hired hand, as they were the last two people to see Melba Christine Youngblood. He was especially suspicious of the young Mexican hired hand. Mr. Butrum vouched for the young man with his life, having half raised him since he was a teen.

After the sheriff and a group of men searched thoroughly around the Youngblood place, and finding no trace of Crit, he suggested that Minnie and Mozelle should ride back to town with him and stay the night with her ma and pa. He had already sent Grace on to his house. It was his opinion they should not be out there on the farm that night with Tom away.

The little town of Fairfield was in an uproar as they looked en masse for one of their own lost children. Minnie Bell's middle girl had disappeared. Grace happened to remember Crit had asked where the road to Teague was and reminded her mother.

The sheriff took his volunteer deputy with him as they slowly drove the road to Teague in the arc-light of the old Ford, stopping to look in ditches and around trees. They knocked on the doors of a few scattered houses visible from the road.

"Let's check with these folks here. If they haven't seen Crit, we will have to go back to town and wait until the morning. We're not doing much good feeling around in the dark. I'll get word to the sheriff in Teague tomorrow."

"Hope Crit didn't get in the car with somebody," the deputy said.

They stood on the porch of the old shack. "It's the sheriff and deputy from Fairfield. We're looking for a lost child." The sheriff spoke as loudly as possible.

After some shuffling noises inside, they saw the glow of a coal oil lantern around the sides of the door. "I'm comin'. Hold on."

The elderly man opened the door a crack. "What did you say?"

"We're looking for a young girl with blonde hair, about fourteen or so. Have you seen her?"

"Sure have. She's asleep over there on a pallet we put down for her. We didn't have no way to take her anywheres with night time comin'."

Crit was returned to Minnie at her parent's home. They were all so glad to see her, and so exhausted, there was no thought of retribution at the time. Crit knew there would be later. The next afternoon, Minnie and her girls were returned to the farm. Everyone in Fairfield knew Crit had run away, that she had lied and tricked Mr. Butram into being her accomplice.

~

Minnie was glad Tom didn't come back home for two days. That gave her time to mull over what Crit had done. It was not a normal thing to do and with no regard for her family or anyone else. Minnie thought about the heartless act of Crit that broke little Mozelle's arm. She also remembered what the doctor had told them when Crit was in the hospital. She could not ignore the facts. Minnie would have to keep a watch on her middle child, maybe for the rest of her life.

Minnie heard Tom toot the horn to warn the dog as he drove up the drive. The Ford sputtered and came to a stop.

"Girls, go outside and speak to your papa. Then go to the barn." They timidly obeyed, acting stiff and reserved. They were afraid to even think about what was going to happen next, especially to Crit.

Tom stepped up on the back porch. "What's gotten into them girls?" he asked quizzically, looking at Minnie.

"I've got something to tell you, Tom." She reiterated the things that Crit had done, not sparing a single detail. "Since no one knew where you were on your 'business,' you weren't around to help me, or to see about your family."

The girls could hear Tom yelling and cursing from the barn. This was one time Grace and Mozelle were not happy that Crit was in trouble. Crit climbed up into the hayloft, putting her hands over her ears.

Tom shoved past Minnie to grab for the razor strop, but it wasn't there. He whirled back around to face her menacingly.

"No more, Tom. Not now. Not ever. You are never goin' to whip Christine again."

"And why not?" Tom's face was red with rage. "First Crit and now Minnie?" he thought. No one in this house ever defied him.

"That child has been through a lot and we are lucky she has lived through it. Crit will be startin' her monthly bleed pretty soon and I don't think it is fittin' that you should treat her like she's a child. I will take care of her discipline from now on. That is something a woman should do."

Tom was speechless, confused at the thought of Crit nearing her womanhood. He didn't know how to confront the logic of Minnie's words.

"What about Boy? I guess you think you're gonna take her over too?" he asked sarcastically.

"I might as well, since you are away on 'business' so much. That will just be one more thing you don't have to fret about."

"Damn to hell," Tom yelled as he slammed his hat back on his head. He stormed angrily out to the car and drove away. He would be disgraced in Fairfield because of what Crit had done. The whole town knew about it by now. In the early hours of the morning, Tom crawled into bed with Minnie. She could smell the stench of liquor and stale tobacco on him. He hadn't been to church, that was for sure.

~

The tension and uneasiness within the Youngblood family slowly faded away as the routine of life took over. Tom was staying home now because the massive cotton fields under his management were exploding with the promise of a bumper crop.

The white cotton bolls were huge and top quality, as long as it didn't rain on them before they were picked. He wanted the crop picked and taken to the cotton gin ahead of everybody else, bringing in top dollar.

Minnie and the girls spent long hours in the kitchen, getting food ready to feed the hands when they came to work. "If you don't feed them, they can't work," Tom always said. He had a quirky compassion that functioned spasmodically, depending upon the climate.

Just before daybreak, three wagon loads of itinerant pickers rolled up the road toward the edge of the cotton field with men, women and children; mostly blacks and Mexicans. They each carried a croaker sack longer than they were tall, with a wide shoulder strap. Some of the teenage girls carried a baby held on their back by a swaddling wrap, freeing their arms to work. Laughing and talking with one another, work was their social life, as well as their livelihood.

Slowly they waded out into the cotton, starting on one edge of the field. Bent over all day, dragging the sack behind them, their hands were a blur that picked several bolls at a time and deftly put them into the bag. Some wore cotton gloves with half of each finger cut out to try to save their flesh from the pricks and cuts. That helped some, but didn't do much good against the dried, razor sharp pods.

When each sack was full, it was picked up and weighed on a swinging scale, the picker anxiously looking at the needle to see how much they had picked. At the end of the day, that weight would be translated into money. The cotton was then poured out into the high-wired walls of the cotton wagon slowly following them through the fields, so they could return to their work with the empty sack and continue to pick. The teenage boys, younger and stronger, bragged about being the fastest pickers as they competed with one another.

Grace and Crit put rough boards on saw horses out under the cottonwood trees, returning to the kitchen to help Minnie and Mozelle bring baskets and bowls full of food for the workers. Water buckets with ladles were by the hand pump to hold drinking water. As the workers made their way to the cottonwood grove, some stopped at the pump to get water in their hands and splash their faces, wetting the bandana they wore around their neck or forehead.

Crit could tell some of the boys were cautiously taking a look at her. Her blondness and fairness attracted their attention as she went back and forth to the house replenishing the food. Her tittie buds were growing at last and her limbs were long and lithe. Though Grace had a beauty of her own, it was Crit, nearly as tall as her older sister, and definitely more sensual, who took everyone's eye.

A girl didn't grow up on a farm full of animals without knowing about copulation. She liked the empowering feeling that the boys were looking at her each day at lunch, and wanted her. It made Crit laugh.

The same group of pickers had continued to return until the work was completed, moving across the acres and acres of cotton like a hoard of locusts stripping the white bolls. When they had finished, the fields looked tired and deserted, having served their purpose. Perhaps it was an omen of things to come.

Financially, the Youngbloods, as well as cotton farmers all across Texas, had suffered a steady decline in income due greatly to federal programs limiting cotton acreage. Increased cotton competition from foreign countries had also glutted the market, eroding the profit margins of the past.

Rural life was changing drastically as America was slowly becoming urbanized. The Rural Electric Association was beginning to get electricity out into the countryside and cars were much more common on the roads leading into the big cities where there was work. Tom tried to keep up his limited farming opportunities, but that no longer brought in enough money to support his family and held no promise of a better future. He was still struggling to pay Crit's medical bills.

Tom was a good farmer. It was what he knew best and had done all of his life, but now he had to pick up any kind of job he could do on the side to make extra money. He did random construction work, cement finishing, plastering and the like in the small surrounding towns. Minnie used fewer of their eggs for the family and sold more of them to help buy staples.

As the family sat around the supper table that night, Tom led in a short blessing of the food, as he always did. "Amen."

"Amen," Minnie said. It had been their custom since the day they had married.

Saying grace at meals was one of the rituals Minnie and Tom exhibited before their daughters, along with faithful attendance at the Baptist Church. The girls were often versed in the benefits of heaven and what you did to get there. Hell, fire and brimstone — where people went if they were bad — received equal time.

Bowls of food were passed around the table, followed by a plate of biscuits left over from breakfast. Casual conversation was not encouraged while the family ate. The sound of forks and spoons clicking on the tin plates was magnified by the silence. The methodic tick of the mantle clock played a duet with dying embers snapping in the cook stove. The soft glow of light from the coal oil lantern sitting in the middle of the table cast flickering shadows on their faces.

When Tom finished eating, he shoved his chair back from the table. "Minnie, I have somethin' to tell you. I've got a new job on a construction project in Dallas. I'll be leavin' in the mornin'."

Tom's wife and daughters looked at him in shock and disbelief at the unexpected announcement. What was that going to mean for them?

CHAPTER 2

Moving Up and Out: Nothing is Free (1939)

With every passing month, being able to stay on at the Fairfield tenant house became less hopeful. The property owner was losing money on all of his massive farm investments and allowed much of the acreage to lie fallow, no longer needing a manager on site. It was obvious to Tom that he had to find another place for his family to live right away.

In spite of Tom's failings, he was not lazy and always had an eye out for making a living, no matter what that required. He also maintained the admirable, manly trait of feeling responsible for his family. He would have never deserted them.

Through word of mouth at his temporary work site in Dallas, he heard there could tentatively be an opening at a large family owned farm down in the little town of Aldine, Texas. It was in Harris County, close to Houston. Tom knew that even if it didn't pay much, there would be a tenant house, and he could pick up extra work in Houston. Not only was he an experienced farmer, but out of necessity he had also become a cement finisher and a budding plastering expert.

Tom immediately got in touch with the farm owners. After hearing about his years of experience and success as a farm manager, it was evident he was a good fit for their needs, and Tom knew it was a good fit for him and his family. His primary responsibility would be to run the Aldine farm and free the farm owners of that responsibility, just the way he liked to do things.

As they traveled toward their new home, Minnie, Grace, and Mozelle were a mixture of feelings. They were nervous about leaving the familiar behind and didn't want to leave their relatives and friends. Along the way, they would alternately burst into tears for no reason. Crit, who would be sixteen in a few months, with a different point of view, saw it as a great adventure to be leaving that farm forever and moving a few miles from Houston. The door of opportunity had opened for her at last.

The small group of family and friends from Fairfield who were helping with the move formed a caravan of cars and trucks with furniture, possessions, and livestock in tow. As they approached Aldine on Farm Road 525 on the outskirts of Houston, they saw a couple of general stores, a fig preserve, and some small poultry breeders and dairies. Fairfield was a metropolis compared to this. The large Aldine Farm, named after a local family, was just about all that was holding Aldine together.

Though the little town was disappointing, the Aldine Farm definitely was not. The living conditions far surpassed the Fairfield experience. The house was quite a bit larger, better accommodating the needs of their family of five. Electricity had recently been installed, totally revolutionizing their way of living. Additionally, they discovered that there were hired hands to do some of the menial tasks the three girls and their mother had been expected to do for years. Their chores had been cut in half.

Undoubtedly, the most significant difference was the nearby Houston affiliated school system, known for its excellence. That opportunity would immediately change the lives of the Youngblood siblings, as Grace reentered school for more education. Mozelle, who tested below her grade level, had no problem catching up. Crit was quickly known as the beautiful, voluptuous new girl and the subject of wolf whistles from the boys, jealousy from the girls.

Tom could not have chosen a better time or place to relocate as he busily worked in two productive worlds, the farming world of Aldine and the skyrocketing construction world of Houston, the largest city in Texas in the 1930s. Though not immune to many of the adverse effects of the 1929 Great Depression, Houston managed to maintain an upward surge in productivity, unlike most of the nation. Downtown Houston was booming with record-setting high rise construction, along with numerous other forms of industry.

League and professional baseball, a developing enterprise of its own, was still America's favorite pastime, in spite of the Depression and a looming world war. There was no time to think of bad days, or to be afraid of storm clouds on the horizon, as Houston propelled baseball into the limelight as the thing to do for entertainment and escape.

Tom sat at the breakfast table, looking at *The Houston Chronicle*. With two jobs, he and Minnie didn't have much time for conversation, so they had begun to have their breakfast together before the girls were awake. The new move had helped to improve their relationship. They weren't rich but much better off with Tom having two jobs. It wasn't necessary for Tom to be away on 'business' anymore since he worked in Houston. Now he was home every night.

"Looks like we're headed for another war, Minnie Bell," Tom said, as he folded the newspaper. He only called her "Minnie Bell," when it was just the two of them.

"Thank God you weren't in The Great War. I couldn't have stood that."

"Nope. I missed that one because I was married with a family. If we have another one, I'll probably have to register, but they won't call me up for the same reason. But I'm willing to fight anytime my country needs me if they want me."

"I know you would Tom." She patted his shoulder.

"How's Crit doin'?"

Minnie paused. "Nobody ever knows that for sure, do they? There's no tellin' what wild thing she might do next." She shook her head. "I try not to stay on pins and needles about Crit. I just want her to be a good girl; I don't want something bad to happen to her."

"We might as well face it, Minnie Bell. Crit is the black sheep of this family. She's nothing like any of us. She seems to always be pulled over to the dark side." Tom looked down at the floor, well acquainted with the dark side himself.

"I know, Tom. She's a troubled child." It upset Minnie to have a constant concern for Crit because she felt helpless to do anything about it. "She's missed school some, and tardy a lot. I think she is in with the wrong crowd."

"How about the girls' grades?"

"They are all doin' real good. You know every one of them is smart."

"Crit's makin' good grades, too?" Tom couldn't help feeling pride that they were smart.

"She is. Even on her tests."

"Well, that's hard to figure." Tom picked up his tool bag. "I'm just afraid she's goin' to get a bad reputation around here."

"She may already have one," Minnie thought.

Crit stood at the kitchen door, listening. She knew what they thought about her, all of them. She wasn't like them and was proud of it. But it still hurt to be called a "black sheep." What Mama and Papa would say that about their child? She wanted to love and be loved by her family, but it just seemed they couldn't work it out.

Crit had hitched a ride several times into Houston, which only fed the fire of her discontent. On her latest ride, a well-groomed young man, obviously aroused, had reached over and gripped her creamy white thigh, while he looked straight ahead driving his Tin Lizzie. Unafraid, she lifted his hand and laughed.

"How much?" he asked.

"Nothin', cause you ain't gettin' nothin' today."

"Then why were you hitching?" He looked at her in irritation.

"I just wanted a ride, at least you got a feel for free." She looked over at him coyly. "Let me out here."

He slowed the car to let her get out. "You're going to get into trouble, playing 'let's pretend'."

Crit laughed her delightful laugh. "I might decide to please you some other time." She had known how to flirt for years, using it as a skill to get into and out of trouble. So far it had worked.

Men, older men, not schoolboys, openly looked her up and down with flushed faces on the streets of Houston. She knew they would give her anything she wanted if she would provide what they wanted. All she had to do was just show them the "come on." She had seen the art of that by watching movies.

She loved going to the movies and being absorbed into the fantasy world she saw on the screen. The tipping point was seeing Vivian Leigh in the movie "Gone With the Wind." Crit understood Scarlett O'Hara; cinched waist, bosom on display, getting her way with men by lying and cheating, being in control of her own property and even being a heroine while wicked at the same time.

Crit felt she was like Scarlett. Women who were smart had to learn to use their seductive gifts to get ahead, to have fun and thrills; to be free. Clods like Grace and Mozelle were going to be like slaves, married to some farmer and milking cows.

And not like her mother. That comparison made Crit feel guilty.

Minnie kept her voice low. "Grace, wake up, do you know where Crit went? She's not in her bed."

"What is it, Mama? Is it time to get up for school?"

"No, Grace; it's early. Did Crit talk to you about leaving?"

Grace was still half asleep. "Leaving? Going somewhere?"

"Yes. She isn't anywhere on the place."

By now, Mozelle was awake. "What's wrong, Mama?"

"Crit is missing."

"Again?"

"I'm afraid so."

The girls followed Minnie into the kitchen where Tom sat at the table, his head in his hands. It was dark outside. He and Minnie had seen Crit's bed empty before they began the day or ate breakfast. Having searched the house and all of the out buildings, they knew she was gone and must have left during the night. The four of them sat there in silence for a while.

"Where do you think she is?" Mozelle finally asked.

"I have no idea," Tom said.

"Are we going to look for her?" Grace asked.

"I wouldn't know where to begin," Minnie said.

"Mama and Papa, I guess you know she hitch-hikes sometimes to go to Houston, instead of going to school," Grace said timidly.

The parents looked at one another, not in shock, but with dismay. "She does?" Mozelle asked in disbelief. "I wouldn't do that!"

"I know you wouldn't and we are glad." Tom put his arm around the youngest daughter he had nicknamed "Boy."

"If she got a ride, she could be anywhere. She could have headed for Dallas or Galveston. I pray it was just Houston, so she can come back home if she changes her mind." Minnie talked out her worries while she stirred up a breakfast and put on the coffee.

"No use to go lookin' for her. This isn't Fairfield this time," Tom said, in sad resignation.

"What in the world is a sixteen-year-old girl going to do out there all by herself?"

"Minnie…we have to let her go this time and get on with our lives. We have to think about Grace and Mozelle now. We've done every single thing we knew how to do; in spite of all the trouble she has caused us. No matter what happens to her, it will be her own doin' and not ours." Tom picked up his tool bag and gave Minnie a rare kiss on the cheek.

The four remaining family members knew things were forever changed and their only recourse was to move on as if they were not.

~

The milk truck driver had stopped at the neighborhood diner just outside of Houston when he spotted a young woman walking through the fog. It wasn't yet dawn, but with the light of the diner sign, he could tell she was out of place wearing overalls, stained and worn likely from doing chores. He thought she must be from one of the neighboring farm communities.

"Do you have any spare milk in that truck for me?" Crit asked with a hopeful smile.

The driver was reminded of his young granddaughter. This one looked tired but determined. "How about breakfast instead, missy? On me," the man replied.

Sitting at a table, Crit told him she had a job waiting in Houston and didn't have a way to get there. That was why she was hitchhiking in the early hours of the morning. An older man, he warned her of the danger of being out in the dark alone like that, especially since she was so young and beautiful. He couldn't help but notice the hint of womanly shape hidden under the overalls. As Crit ate, he saw her raw beauty and wondered if she was aware of it.

He went out of his way to drop her off on a major downtown thoroughfare of her choice. As she stepped down from the truck, he handed her the small leather bag she had packed, the one her Papa used when going away on "business."

"Now you be careful out there. Do you have any money to get you started until a payday?"

Crit pushed her hair back from her eyes. "I have a little," she said demurely.

He reached into his pocket and gave her two dollars. "At least you won't go hungry."

Crit stepped back up into the truck and gave him a hug. As he shifted gears and pulled away, she suddenly felt very alone. Now everything was up to her. She quickly adjusted her attitude into survival mode.

There were lights and advertisements all up and down the busy street. Traffic had picked up already as Houston awoke from a short nap and sprang into action. Crit went into a café and sat on a stool at the counter. She ordered a cup of coffee, which wasn't her favorite thing, but seemed more grown up. The waitress was friendly and out-going.

"Here you go, pretty lady, your coffee with cream. The sugar is there in front of you."

"Thank you," Crit responded. "Do you know where I could find a room around here?"

The waitress made a couple of suggestions. "They're not fancy, but as least it's a bed while you are looking for something better."

Crit had the money the milkman had given her, and some she had gotten together at home for being paid to do extra chores. The first rooming place had the price listed outside and seemed too much to her. The second place was upstairs, and crummy looking, but for less money. She took that one on a day-to-day rate. There was a common bathroom down the hall. It was moderately clean, but smelled awful.

"I won't stay here long, just while I look for a job." Crit dared not let herself get discouraged. She had always wanted to be on her own, and now she was. So, Crit spent the rest of the day getting better acquainted with the new surroundings and trying to get an idea for a future job. She saw a few "Help Wanted" signs, but they were mostly for men.

She arose early the next morning to beat the rest of the residents to the bathroom, cupping her hands under the faucet for a drink of water. It smelled and tasted strange to her, not accustomed to anything but well water. Before long, someone pounded on the bathroom door. "Hey, you're not the only person here who's got to piss!"

Crit quickly gathered up her things and hurried back to the squalid room. There, she groomed herself, smoothing her blonde hair into a sleeker style. She applied red lipstick and blotted her lips just as she had seen actresses do in the movies.

Stepping back to see herself better in the long mirror on the back of the door, she liked what she saw. She carefully examined her reflection. Pulling the belt in tightly at her already slender waist, she stood tall with her shoulder's back. She was beautiful, confident and intelligent, and she knew it. Crit planned to use all of that to her best advantage to find a job.

Sitting in the privacy of a booth at the diner, Crit had toast and coffee, while looking through the classifieds of the *Houston Chronicle* for a job. Most all of the listings had restrictions. There was a limited offering for single women and none for married women. At least that was on her side.

Wanted: waitress, minimum age, 16

Wanted: secretary

Wanted: sales clerk

Wanted: nurse, state certification required

Wanted: performer, no experience required, minimum age, 16

Crit decided the best choice for a temporary job, which she needed quickly, would be a waitress. There were cafés and coffee shops scattered all up and down the streets. Within a few hours, her beauty and irresistible charm had secured such a job, uniform and all. She would draw a small salary, could eat free, and keep her tips, which would keep her afloat until she could find something better.

Days turned into weeks, and weeks into months. Crit began to call home "collect" to hear the voices of her family. She missed her mother and her past life as a child, having grown up far too quickly by choice. Ever restless, life and the routine of work was no longer fun. Minnie was relieved each time she called; reassured that her middle daughter was still alive.

Eventually, Crit returned home for short visits. Sometimes, she brought friends who were not suitable to her parents, especially the men. Most of them were in their twenties, fool-hardy and rough. Crit was attracted to dangerous liaisons. She never stayed long with her Papa and Mama as it just reminded her why she had left in the first place and made her anxious to get back to Houston.

At the end of one call back home, Crit almost let the truth slip out. "Mama, I'm so tired. Did I tell you how tired I am all the time?" Minnie sucked in a breath, waiting for Crit to explain. "I'm gettin' tired of being a dumb waitress." The silence continued for longer than Minnie wished. Not that Crit said much anyway, and Minnie tried not to ask too much, not wanting to discourage contact.

Crit finally exclaimed, "Oh, Mama, I'm just saying that because I'm bored. I didn't mean that at all."

"What did ya'll talk about Minnie?" Tom asked later that night.

Minnie looked right into the eyes of her husband, "Nothing. Nothing at all," she said with resignation.

Crit's calls became shorter, and further apart, and she didn't reveal much about herself when she and Minnie talked. For some reason, she just wanted her mother to know that she still had a job and was relatively safe.

She was growing increasingly bored in her job as a waitress, having expected her life to be much better than it was. Some of the men who frequented the café were way out of line in their behavior toward her, even for Crit. The upside was that some of the regulars were more than just customers and became friends beyond the café.

After pulling her shift at work each day, Crit began to party most of the night, sometimes in her room or the apartment of friends. She caroused around at bars, picking up men, and drinking. Though underage, she never had a problem acquiring a drink, but she had big problems with drinking. Alcohol was new to Crit, and once she moved past beer to hard liquor, she turned into another person when drunk. Anything could happen.

She began to lose control of her judgment, as she partied away her money. Her overwhelming desire to party with friends superseded paying the back rent or buying food. On weekends or other stretches of free time, she started going to Galveston for parties on the beach, where she flaunted her body and drank herself into a stupor. She didn't remember who, or how many fondled her or anything else she might have done.

During one of her sober periods, Crit realized she had been living in Houston for two years and her life was on the skids. She was on the verge of losing her job at the café because of her drinking, and she was so far behind on her rent, she would never be able to pay it. Only by lying had she been able to hang on to everything as long as she had.

Crit weighed her options. She could run away from Houston and leave the situation she had created by going to another big city. Or she could go back home.

CHAPTER 3

Trying It All: Beyond the Boundaries (1939 - 1940)

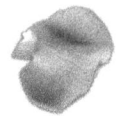

The thought of going home passed through Crit's mind as quickly as it had entered. On her few visits back to Aldine, she had conjured up glorious stories of how well she was doing on her own in Houston, a free and independent woman in charge of her own future. She had bragged to Grace and Mozelle about how much better off she was in the city than they were on a farm, savoring the envy she saw in their eyes.

Crit chose to ignore the disbelief on the faces of her parents as they listened to her grandiose pretense. They were totally jaded by all of the disappointing experiences they had with her in the past and knew she could not be trusted. She was their child by birth, but that was where the commonality ended. Crit was a stranger who had no sense of the form of ethos the other four of her family members shared.

The truth was, Crit was broke and in debt. No one who had dealings with her in Houston believed anything she said because she had lied to them so often, manipulating them for money, food, and lodging. Now she had to find a way to run away from all of that and get a new start somewhere else. The last thing she wanted to do was go back home in humiliation and have to face her family, especially after all of that bragging. She searched for some other way out of her predicament.

Crit stood on the shoulder of U. S. Highway 80. As she held her thumb out, the wind whipped at her golden hair and blew her skirt up in billows.

She had talked a deliveryman on his coffee break into bringing her that far out of Houston, so she would have a better chance of hitching a ride to San Antonio. She was thinking of some of her party trips to San Antonio in the past, with good-time friends from Houston. All the money that was thrown around by older men in classy cars who took her and other young women for wild nights in high-end hotels. They ate elaborate meals, and the wine flowed freely as they danced all night. Everyone was drunk, erasing any shame for all sorts of open sexual acts, as the girls were passed around granting their favors.

The *ooogah* of the Tin Lizzie horn of a passing car brought her back to the present. A gust of wind blew her skirt almost over her head, revealing her best pair of black panties with nylon hose held in place by a matching black lace garter belt. Crit would go without food before going without lacy underwear.

The car slid to a stop on the rock shoulder, slowly backing up toward her. A man's arm appeared out the driver's side window, motioning her to get into the car. Crit picked up her only case, the one belonging to Tom, and clutched her purse. She strolled nonchalantly toward the car, not wanting to appear desperate or anxious to run away from the debt and issues she was leaving behind in Houston.

Crit leaned over looking through the window at the driver, "Can you take me to San Antonio?" To her pleasure and in contrast to some of her unpleasant experiences with hitchhiking, the young man leaning forward to see her was clean-cut and handsomely dressed.

"That's just where I'm going!" the driver exclaimed. "Hop in. Just sit your bag on the back seat."

Crit complied, smoothing her dress into place as she sat down. She straightened her hair that had been twirled about in the wind.

The driver looked over his shoulder as he pulled out onto the highway. "I'm sorry about running by you like that, but I couldn't believe you were hitchhiking, at first." The vision of a breath-taking, beautiful blonde with long silken legs standing beside the road was not something he commonly saw when driving down the highway. "You looked kind of lonely out there all by yourself."

It struck Crit that she did feel lonely. She didn't have anyone who stayed in her life for any length of time. As the young man looked at Crit, she smiled, her red lips turning up at the corners. "Thank you for picking me up."

"It's my pleasure, believe me." He returned the smile, glancing back and forth at her and the road. Crit tried to size him up, thinking he might be military because of his close haircut.

"Where are you from?" he asked.

"Up until the minute you stopped to pick me up, I was from Houston," she said. Her playful laughter charmed her new male acquaintance. "But now, I am headed for Alamo City."

"That's right," he said, beginning to feel more comfortable in her presence.

"I am feeling better every mile we go. It's complicated, but I'm turning over a new leaf, getting a new start. Does that make sense?"

"I understand that completely. All of us need a chance just to start over every now and then. I sure hope 'San Antone' will treat you better than Houston did, doll."

"Hey, who you callin' doll?" Crit lifted her shoulder and looked at him playfully.

"No offense meant! Okay? I didn't mean to be fresh." The young man blushed slightly, cueing Crit that she had the upper hand. "So, if you don't mind me asking, what's your name... ma'am?"

Without hesitation, Crit answered, "Patsy. It's Patsy Sue Allen from East Texas." The name came out as smoothly as if she had used it all of her life, instead of for the first time at this moment.

"Okay, Patsy Sue, East Texas girl, it's nice to meet you. I'm Bill from San Antone."

Crit thought it strange he did not offer his last name. She suspiciously wondered if he was telling the truth since she wasn't.

"Well, to be honest, I'm fairly new to San Antone. Just lived there a short while, courtesy of the U. S. Air Force."

"Uh huh. One of Uncle Sam's finest and best, no less," Crit answered back, keeping her smile in place.

Bill glanced over at his passenger. "Well, I don't know about that, but with all that's going on over in Europe, construction has heated up at Kelly Field over the last few months. Scuttlebutt is that within a year or so, it's going to be one of the top-notch airbases." He sounded proud, almost boastful.

Crit, now Patsy Sue, was relieved to hear these things about Bill unfold. It helped to know she was riding with a decent man, though she held that opinion with reservation. She had learned from experience that just because a man seemed to be decent, it often was not true.

"So, Patsy Sue, when we get to San Antone, where do you want me to drop you off? What's your plan? It's a good-sized city. Do you have a place to stay? Apartment? Room?" Bill pressed.

"Whoa. Slow down, fly boy. You're gettin' a little nosy, aren't you?" Her demeanor was playfully familiar, not a put-down.

By now, Bill was relaxed and greatly enamored with the luscious young woman who had fallen into his presence by surprise. He had a hard time keeping his mind on his driving as he stole glances at her. He could smell the scent of her, her femininity. Bill noticed she had no ring on her wedding ring finger; that was good. "I was just tryin' to be helpful," Bill said, reassuringly.

"Okay. I'm just not fond of people I don't know asking me too many questions or wanting to know my business."

"I can understand that. I'm just curious about you, so beautiful and everything, out here by yourself. Not everybody you meet will be a nice person and respect you like they should. I mean, all you've got is a little suitcase. You'll have to look out for yourself. If somebody picks up on the fact you are alone, they could try to hurt you," Bill warned.

"Thanks, Bill. I will be careful." She was touched by the sincere concern in his voice. He could not have imagined the worldly experience of the young woman riding in his car.

Patsy Sue grew excited, thinking about the new life waiting a few miles ahead. Nearly eighteen now, she was going to start all over again. She knew a room, food, and a job would be first on the list since she had little money, less than when she went to Houston at sixteen.

"You haven't told me where to drop you off, yet. There's a couple of pretty nice hotels downtown. The Gunter? The Menger?" Bill interrupted her thoughts. "They are being renovated. The Great Depression was tough, but I think the city is starting to pull out of it. People are starting to come back here to work and especially military personnel are moving in from all over the place." Bill was trying to be upbeat and helpful.

"Oh, just drop me off at the Menger. At least I've heard of that one."

Patsy Sue knew she would not be spending the night at the Menger. She had partied there before, and no way had that kind of money but pretended it was her plan as Bill pulled his car up to the curb in front of the hotel. He jumped out of the car and beat the doorman to the passenger side door, opening it politely and helping Crit out.

"Well, Patsy Sue from East Texas, good luck here in San Antone." He tried to give her an encouraging smile as he handed her the lone leather case. Bill knew the guys at Kelly Field were never going to believe this story.

Playing the charade as Patsy Sue, Crit stepped up on the sidewalk in front of the Menger. She remembered how she felt two years before as the milkman, who had given her a ride, let her out of his truck in downtown Houston. That day she had been naively filled with the dreams of an adolescent who was leaving farm life forever. Today was very different. Former giddy feelings of freedom were now displaced by an undertow of doubt, as she recalled how hard it had been for her to survive on her own in Houston.

Once again, Crit reached down into her well of determination and held her chin high. "Nothin' but good times comin'!" she said, as her goodbye to Bill. As she stepped toward the hotel's revolving door, Bill returned to his car and pulled away. Once he was out of sight, she made an about face and never looked back toward the hotel. Instead, she headed up the street toward flashing neon lights. They indicated the front entrances of a variety of inexpensive rooms and short-term apartments.

As Crit looked up and down the street, the garish lights were cheap and gaudy, and none of them provided much promise. Knowing that, she just picked one at random, entering the stale, dingy lobby. A gaunt man wearing a green visor sat behind a caged-off desk where he had propped up his feet. When he spoke, she jumped, because he had acted as if he didn't know she was there.

"Need a room?" He put his feet down and stood up with a bored sigh.

"Uh, I guess so. Yeah. How much is it?" The answer mattered greatly to Crit.

"Single room, no bath, is $1.35 a night, common bath down the hall, clean linens.

Pay in advance and $6.00 a week covers it all. Not many left. You interested?" He rattled off the information as if it had worn a rut in his memory.

"Yeah, that's fine. I'll take a week up front." Crit reached into her purse and counted out six one-dollar bills from her money pouch. She had been given four of them her last day of work at the café by a man who said he would give her a dollar for every time she would lean over the counter and let him look at her breasts while she was serving him. Paying for the room left her practically broke again. She looked at the pittance of coins left in her purse and tried not to be nervous about being so penniless.

The jaded desk clerk turned the register around for her to sign. As if it were a usual thing for her to do, she quickly scribbled Patsy Sue Allen on the indicated line.

"Room 202, one flight up, end of the hall." He took a key off a hook and slid it out for her to retrieve.

Dry from her time on the road, Crit asked, "Say, could I have a piece of that gum you're chewin'?"

The desk clerk reached into his pocket and slid a piece out to her, but said nothing, as if he did not have a spoken response to any unfamiliar request. With a deep sigh, he returned to his chair, putting his feet back up on the desk.

Crit sat on the edge of the bed looking around at the decrepit room. It was Houston all over again. She had gone down to the common toilet; it was as gross as she expected it to be. No one ever wanted to clean a toilet, even if it was their job. She put her things in one of the dresser drawers and slid the empty suitcase under the bed.

Her stomach was growling from hunger. All she had eaten that day was the coffee and toast the deliveryman bought for her before taking her out to the highway. Now she wished she had hit Bill up for a meal. He would surely have been delighted to buy her one, but she knew he would want something in return and then she wouldn't be able to get rid of him.

Shaking off the downside of her surroundings and feelings, she freshened up, renewed her red lipstick, and took the wooden stairs down to the first floor. Crit purposefully avoided the ancient lift. It was common for drunks to urinate in the elevator of a low-end hotel like this, or men expose themselves, drunk or not. Stopping by the front desk, she asked the clerk if there were any restaurants nearby. He sighed, as if her question was a huge imposition, and pointed to the right.

Crit left the dingy lobby, happy to join the foot traffic on the sidewalk as it made her feel less alone. She walked past several restaurants to see what her chances might be to get a meal, and maybe find a job. She had seen a couple of "Help Wanted" signs; restaurants always needed employees. Crit retraced her steps back to one she had passed where the sign said "Waitress Wanted." Looking through the window, she saw several waitresses in nice aprons busily serving platters of burgers with piles of fries to tables of young military men.

She went in and sat at the counter. All of the young men turned around and looked at her, elbowing one another. "Want to see a menu, honey?" The middle-aged waitress was warm and friendly, obviously in her comfort zone.

"How much is a hamburger?" Crit asked. "I'm a little down on my luck right now, lookin' for work."

The seasoned waitress sized her up, evaluating her youthfulness. "Tell you what, baby doll. I've been there myself a time or two. I'm gonna cover you for a burger and fries; you can pay me back when you get a job. How does that sound?"

"That sounds swell. I will pay you back. I promise," Crit added.

"What kind of work are you lookin' for?"

"Well, I saw the waitress wanted sign in the window. Is that taken yet?"

"Are you over sixteen?"

"I'm almost eighteen." Crit looked up at her with needy eyes.

"Got any experience?"

"Lots."

"Oh, well then, you're a regular woman now. When I turn in this order for your burger and fries, I'll tell our manager about you. I know Al is in a hiring mood because he just had to let two of our girls go. They wouldn't show up for work when they were supposed to. That's one thing Al don't put up with. You're not like that, are you?"

"No. I keep my word."

"I'll tell Al you said that. He might want to talk to you."

"Thank you," Crit said, with sincerity.

"No problem, honey. We girls have to stick together. Al will probably come out to meet you once he's caught up on the orders." She tore the order slip off her pad.

"Just in case we end up working together, my name is Rosa. Do you want to trade me yours?"

"Patsy. I'm Patsy Sue Allen." Crit used her beautiful lying smile that always served her well. The new name felt more natural every time she used it.

In a few minutes, Rosa sat the plate of food down in front of Crit. "Here you go, Patsy Sue. Al said he would be out after you finish eating. I told him you were hungry, and no one who works around all this food wants to hear that from a pretty young lady like you."

Rosa glanced around before leaning over the counter to share a confidence with Crit.

"In the way of a little tip, Al does appreciate some visual stimulation, if you know what I mean. It could go a long way toward you gettin' that job, 'cause you've got plenty to show him."

The two women smiled knowingly at one another, as Crit sat up straight and unbuttoned the top three buttons of her blouse. "Is that enough?"

"Just right. Always leave them wanting more." Rosa gave Crit a wink.

"Hi, I'm Al, owner and manager of this café. Rosa tells me you might be interested in a job as waitress? Is that right?"

"That's right, and I've got plenty of experience." Crit gave the middle-aged man a demure look.

"That's good. Do you have a name, honey?" Al was very relaxed with himself.

"Absolutely, I do! I'm sorry. My name is Patsy Sue Allen. I just came from Houston, and I'm desperate for a job. According to Rosa, you need me as much as I need you."

He laughed at her forward manner. "Rosa, bring me a cup of coffee and get Patsy Sue whatever she wants to drink. We're going to go over and sit in a booth."

"What'll it be Patsy?" Rosa asked, familiarly.

"I would really love to have a Coca-Cola."

Al nodded at Rosa as he and Crit went over and slid into a booth. "Rosa was right that I do need a waitress. I had to let a couple of girls go who just couldn't stay out of trouble."

"Here I am! Ready, willing and more than able. And I guarantee you won't be disappointed."

Al had only just met Crit, but he knew already that all of those things were true. He felt like a teenager again, reading a sensual meaning into everything she said.

Rosa sat the drinks in front of them and rolled her eyes at Crit. "Okay, that's just swell. When can you start?" Al asked.

"Tomorrow is fine with me, or is that too soon?"

"No…no, let me get you to fill out an application, just for my files, and we'll talk about a schedule for you. By the way, you can see from Rosa's clothes, I don't have my girls wear a uniform or anything like that. Just dress nice. Tomorrow I'll give you an apron, and I'm having new nametags made. That covers everything you need to know to start to work."

While he was gone, Rosa sidled over to the booth with a glass of reddish brown liquid. "Want me to add a little excitement to that Coca-Cola?"

"Sure, half and half." Rum and Coca-Cola was one of Crit's favorite drinks.

"Looks like you've hit a home run, Patsy Sue." Rosa covered the empty rum glass with a napkin and took it behind the counter.

Al hurried back with the application form. Crit could hear the excitement in his voice as he shared with her. "Just fill it out and give it to Rosa. I've got to get back to the kitchen now, but I'll see you first thing tomorrow morning, bright and sunny, for the 6 a.m. breakfast shift!" He paused to see her reaction to being assigned to the shift that no one wanted. Well versed in body language, Crit did not flinch, but sipped her rum laced Coca-Cola without a hint of the displeasure she was feeling.

Having the rest of the evening free, and no money to spend, Crit lolled on the faded slipcover of the broken down couch. She turned the dial of the old radio beside her, trying to find some music. Only one station was clear of static as the well-trained voice of the announcer covered the news and then read the police roster of crimes committed in San Antonio. She listened while winding up the old alarm clock beside the bed, setting the alarm for 5:00 AM. Crit didn't like the 6:00 AM shift, but she needed money right now more than sleep.

"Oh, that's shitty," she complained, aloud. "I hope they're not reading my name on the radio in Houston for leavin' town without paying my bills." Then she laughed.

"Oh, that's right. I'm Patsy Sue Allen. She doesn't have a record anywhere because she is a brand new person. Now how many people can claim that? Just me!"

As the news program ended, music began to play, introducing an hour of entertainment by The King of Swing himself, Benny Goodman, and his quartet. No one played a sweeter clarinet than Benny Goodman did. It could be hot, or it could be sensuous, as he played a slow glide up the scale.

Crit stood up and began to sway with the music, her eyes closed to the grubby room she had rented by the week. The rum had helped take the edge off any worries she might have had. She started trying some of the moves she had seen a stripper do in the back of a private club in Galveston when going there with a group from Houston two years before. She was sixteen then.

Tentative at first, she slowly became more uninhibited, interpreting every nuance of the music with a response from her body. As she slowly took off her clothes one piece at a time, she twirled it around before tossing it into the air. She slowly ran her hands seductively up and down her naked body, striking poses from one piece of furniture to the other and throwing her head back and forth in abandon. Ending in a wild frenzy and panting, she opened her eyes to see herself in the dresser mirror, naked, her blonde curls hanging in her face.

"I wish those people from the Baptist church in Fairfield could see me now. Little Crit, dancing her way to hell. That would keep the party line buzzing. Mama and Papa thought everything I did or wanted to do was a sin. So did Grace and Mozelle. I never could please any of them. Of course, Papa's 'business' was okay. What a bunch of hypocrites!"

There was a mixture of melancholy and abandon in her thoughts. At last, she had the freedom she always wanted but had rejected her family in exchange. She saw the glaring imperfection in both her family and the price of her freedom. Crit fell across the broken down mattress of the bed with exhaustion, dropping off into merciful sleep.

At five o'clock, the irritating sound of the alarm clock snatched Crit from her deep sleep. Disoriented for a second, she began slapping at the clock, knocking it off the table onto the bare floor, where it continued to clang and bounce around.

"Damn, damn!" She rolled out of bed and grabbed the unfamiliar clock, trying to turn it off. It finally ran down as she threw it across the room. "I hate you, you stupid jackass!"

She fell back into the bed, her head aching and fuzzy mouthed. "God, I need a drink or at least a cup of coffee. Guess I'll have to go to work to get that."

Crit gathered up her clothes and make-up. Cracking open the door and seeing no one in the hall, she started toward the common bath to get ready for the day. A man stepped out of a door slightly ahead of her. She started running down the hall to beat him to the bathroom, slamming the door and locking it just as he touched the doorknob.

He hit the door with his fist. "Bitch," he said.

She leaned against the door, listening as he went back to his room. Crit laughed, now feeling wide-awake.

The new Patsy Sue Allen stepped out onto the sidewalks of San Antonio on the first day of starting all over again. Her bright red lips accented by the abundant blonde hair piled high above her face. The activity on the sidewalks and streets was just beginning to stir, and she already felt as if she belonged there.

As she strolled energetically into Al's Place, Rosa cheerfully greeted her. "Hey, Patsy! I see you made it this morning, and on time. Good girl." Rosa gave her a motherly hug. She poured a cup of coffee and handed it to Crit. "Here, drink this before you start to work. It will help clear out the cobwebs." She gave Crit one of her knowing winks.

From the noises and smells coming from the kitchen, the food would be ready soon. Hearing Al's voice, Crit walked back and leaned her head in the kitchen door. "Mornin', Al." Her smile was a ray of sunshine. She disappeared before he could reply.

Patsy Sue tied on the stiffly starched apron while finishing the cup of coffee. "You'll get a break to eat later, after the first rush slows down," Rosa whispered.

Crit nodded and went to work taking orders and refilling cups of coffee as if she had worked there for years. Charming and chatty, she knew pleasing the men customers would pay dividends in bigger tips and would bring them back to the café.

During her morning break, she sat at a table in the kitchen as Al served her breakfast personally. His face flushed red when she put her hand on top of his and thanked him for being so sweet. "You are an excellent cook, Al. No wonder you have so much business."

"I like to give people their money's worth. One thing people have to do is eat. You know your meals here are free when you are at work, I think I forgot to tell you that."

"I appreciate that, Al. And I will do my best to give you your money's worth." A merciless master of the double entendre, she could leave a man guessing without even trying.

Things that started well with Crit never seemed to end well. Within a few months, she had fallen back into her old lifestyle. Going out with low-life new friends to clubs and bars, she was descending into depths she had not experienced before. Added to her growing need for alcohol was the gradual introduction of various drugs, recreational at first but accelerating far past. As her needs grew, so did the prices required by her suppliers who had started out as friends.

Her paycheck and tips, once adequate to support her, were now spent on drugs and liquor. She stayed up all night, going to work late or not at all. Her personal grooming was lacking and her speech slurred. Al might have been flattered by her attention, but he was a businessman first, and nobody's fool. Not only did he let her go, but warned other café owners not to give her a job.

Alone in San Antonio, the brand new Patsy Sue Allen was just the same old Crit, roaming the streets with no place to stay. Thinking back, she recalled the warnings from her parents not to drink or use drugs since her serious bout with encephalitis, but she never took advice from anyone. Carrying her leather case around with her, she tried to get with anybody who would buy her a drink or share drugs.

After having a few beers, she called home on Thanksgiving Day of 1941. On the other end of the line, Minnie Bell listened intently. "I have a collect call from Christine; will you accept the charges?"

"Yes…yes, I'll pay the charges," her mother said, with emotion. "Crit? Where are you? Are you okay? I thought for sure you would call on your eighteenth birthday!" Her voice was filled with fear and relief. "I waited all day."

"Sorry, Mama, but it's me, your black sheep callin' you. I keep turnin' up like a bad penny, don't I, Mama?" Her speech was slurred indicating her condition.

"Crit, you've been drinkin'. What in the name of God are you doin' to yourself?"

"Oh, Mama, I'm fine. I just had a few beers. That's nothin'. I just wanted to call and wish you and Papa a happy Thanksgivin'!" Uninhibited, Crit yelled out the greeting. People near the pay phone looked around at her. It was rare to see a woman publicly drunk, especially one so young and attractive.

"Crit, listen to me. Come home. Please come home. We'll try to help you any way we can, you know that." Minnie's voice was pleading.

"Oh, Mama, I can't do it. That's why I called to say happy Thanksgivin'. Eat some turkey for me. You know I love your turkey."

By this point, Minnie struggled to speak through her tears. "Oh, Crit…"

Crit interrupted. "Mama, I love you, and tell Papa and the girls that I love 'em, too. I gotta go now." She abruptly hung up the phone.

CHAPTER 4

More Hard Lessons: The Road to Hell (1941 - 1942)

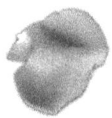

Crit became a ghost-like figure roaming the streets of San Antonio as the cold nights of December came. She wandered from bar to bar, seeking someone to buy her a drink: having strange men enter her mind, soul, and body for the favor of a meal, or mostly for liquor and drugs. When she was drunk, she became uncontrollable and loud, with blackouts of memory.

She slept any place she could find: doorways, cars, under stairwells and bridges. She didn't know when Christmas came and went, while her mother hoped she might call home again since it was a holiday.

On Valentine's Day, 1941, she was arrested in San Antonio for vagrancy. Having lost her way along the path of life, Crit was strangely relieved to be incarcerated. She was jailed with an assortment of tramps, wanderers, gamblers, beggars and other varieties of people who were void of a moral compass. The good part was that she was provided with momentary shelter, plus a bed and food.

While Crit was in jail, she didn't have any alcohol, had some decent food, and plenty of time to think. Looking at the kind of people who were sitting in jail with her, she realized that she was one of them, and was no longer the person she imagined. Taking stock, Crit had to face that she was in jail and now had an arrest record. She was drinking and falling deeper into drugs; neither of that was good for her and often got her into trouble, causing her to lose two jobs. She was estranged from her family, and no home, being evicted twice for lack of payment. She didn't have any money, no possessions. All of that before barely turning eighteen! While her head was clear, Crit vowed to change her life and stay away from the dangerous way she had been living. For a lucid, sober moment, she feared for her safety because of the things she had been doing.

Unable to pay the fines associated with vagrancy, Crit remained jailed for several days. Once released, she had no option but to return to the street life she had been living. Sleeping in the back seat of an unlocked car, hungry, cold and thirsty, Crit stumbled into a small bar. Going straight to the restroom, she washed her face, brushed her hair and put on the small amount of makeup left in her purse. Her hand was shaking, but she still managed to draw a perfect red bow on her lips, though the lipstick was almost gone.

As she left the restroom, Crit took a deep breath and held herself erect to accentuate her bosom. She strolled over to the expansive wooden counter of the bar and took a seat right in the middle. As she expected, everyone looked at her. Living on the street, staying in jail, and living a careless lifestyle had not been able to erase her natural eighteen-year-old beauty; she was still quite a presence.

As the bartender approached her, Crit looked up at him and slid her tongue over her red lips to moisten them. He had seen plenty of pretty girls, but none so soft and creamy looking as this petite blonde. There wasn't a blemish on her skin anywhere.

"Well?" She held his eyes with hers. "Don't you want to know what I want?"

"Uh yeah. What'll you have?" His face reddened at the surprise repartee.

She only paused a second, her new resolve already dismissed. "How about a cold one?"

"What kind?"

"It doesn't matter. Anything frosty with a long neck will meet my needs. This has been some day for me. In fact, it has been a damned to hell year," she added, under her breath.

"Yeah, I know what you mean, darlin'." He sat a cold bottle of beer on the bar in front of her. His eyes didn't miss one curve or niche of her. Crit was used to it. Men found her irresistible, siren-like. It wasn't just her looks, though they were phenomenal, everything about her was sensual, the way she talked, the way she crossed her legs and held her body. Without even trying, she was a deadly lure that appealed to lust; men sensed the danger but couldn't help being drawn to the excitement.

"So you understand what I'm sayin', huh?" Crit picked up the beer, taking a gulp.

"Sure, I've been there myself, lots of times." He was experienced in the art of deceit himself, searching for her weakness. That was part of the art of being a bartender.

"Oh, really?" She gave him a flirtatious look, before throwing her head back to finish emptying the bottle of beer. "I think I'll have another one." She moved her leather bag closer to the bar stool as if planning to stay for a while. "Hell, just keep bringin' them. I'm dry as a desert."

"Comin' right up, babe. I'll open 'em, you drink 'em."

Any form of alcohol was rapidly intoxicating to Crit, even beer. The recent promise to herself to change her life was discarded, along with any remaining inhibitions, as the second and third beer flooded her bloodstream. She was considering how she might hit this bartender up for a hot meal and a warm bed, though she had just met him. Crit didn't think she could stand another night without a place to sleep. A bowl of hot soup would be good, too. She signaled him to bring her another beer. He opened the bottle and sat it in front of her, removing the empty one. The two of them chatted between customers as he walked up and down behind the bar making flirtatious small talk. As the hour grew late, patrons slowly left, and the bar was becoming quiet, almost intimate.

"So, hey look, we might as well get better acquainted since you've been here a while tonight. I'm Johnny Delano." The bartender wiped moisture off the wooden bar. "Why don't you tell me something about yourself, like your name?"

Crit was holding a bottle of beer in one hand and had propped her head up with the other as she teetered precariously on the barstool. "Uh, Patsy," Crit mumbled, before lifting the beer bottle to her lips.

"That's Patsy Sue Allen, from Houston." She belched loudly. "'Scuse me."

He laughed. "You're excused, Patsy Sue. Do you live somewhere around here?"

"Nope. I used to before I lost my job. Then I couldn't pay the rent. I told you it has been a damned to hell year for me. I'm just a lost black sheep with no place to sleep or eat." She laughed loudly at her own rhyming words, slapping her hand on the bar as if it were incredibly funny.

"It sounds like you've had a long streak of bad luck. Where do you plan to sleep tonight?" He reached over and took the beer bottle out of her hand then lifted her hand to his lips and kissed it.

She looked at Johnny's smiling face through her drunken haze. "You're just a regular gentleman who knows how to treat a lady right. Say, Johnny, do you think you could cover my tab tonight until my next paycheck?" He picked up her bar tab and slipped it into his pocket before returning to polishing glasses and preparing to close for the night.

As he removed his uniform vest and turned off the overhead light, she watched him curiously. "What are you doin', Johnny boy? Are you goin' to leave me here all by myself?"

"It's time to close. Can I give you a ride somewhere? You didn't tell me where you're going to sleep tonight."

"Probably on a park bench, if the dirty bums haven't taken all of them by now."

"Come on, darlin', let me help you get off that stool before you fall off," Johnny said, as he picked up her leather bag and thin jacket. Putting an arm around Crit to keep her steady on her wobbly legs, he guided her toward the back door and out to his car. "It's a little cold out here to sleep on a park bench tonight."

"I know that! Do you think I'm too dumb to know that?"

Opening the front door of his car, he manipulated her drunken body into the front seat before throwing her things into the back seat. Hurrying around the car, Johnny slid under the steering wheel and started the engine.

"Do you think I'm dumb, Johnny boy?" Crit reached over and slid a finger down his cheek. "My Mama says I do dumb things."

"No, Patsy Sue, I don't think you're dumb," he said. "But I'm sure your Mama thinks so," he thought.

"Who's Patsy Sue?" Crit was almost incoherent.

"That's you. You've had so much to drink you don't even know your own name."

She put an unsteady finger in front of her lips. "Shhh, don't tell." Her head fell forward with her chin against her chest.

Johnny turned on the radio, filling the car with Big Band music. He reached over, and pulled her into a more comfortable position against his shoulder, trying to look at her and drive at the same time. Her long eyelashes swept upward as she opened her eyes and looked at him.

"I like that music. I know how to dance real good. You're so sweet, Johnny boy. I'll dance for you sometime." Her eyes closed as quickly as they had opened as she fell into a deep sleep.

Johnny's emotions were all over the place. He fought the impulse to stop the car and ravage her in her drunken stupor. Her provocative manner and body was asking too much of any ordinary man to resist. However, he also felt a strange sort of sympathy for her, like an innocent little girl who needed his protection. Crit, whom Johnny knew only as Patsy Sue, appealed to his wantonness and his nobility at the same time. It was maddening.

Johnny picked the sleeping Crit up into his arms, kicking the car door closed with his foot. Even though it was past midnight, there were a few people around as he carried her into the small foyer of the apartment building where he lived. Some people stopped and stared, and a man exiting the elevator as Johnny stepped on smirked knowingly and jealously. Johnny threw him a scathing look before pressing the button with his elbow.

In front of his apartment door, Johnny threw Crit over his shoulder. She hung as limp as a rag doll while he fumbled in his pocket for his key to open the door. Flipping on a light, he carried her over to the sofa where he laid her down as carefully as possible. Putting a small pillow under her head, he then removed her shoes and covered her with a little blanket. She was sleeping peacefully, looking like a beautiful, vulnerable child of innocence. He knelt down and kissed her on the cheek.

"Sweet dreams, Patsy Sue, you gorgeous doll," he whispered.

~

Crit woke up in strange surroundings, blinking her eyes as she tried to focus. She slowly sat up, holding her throbbing head, a reminder of a night of drinking. With her bare feet on the carpet, she leaned her head back against the couch where she could slowly rotate it for a look at the apartment. It was much nicer than any place she had awakened in for many months. It wasn't anything fancy. Small, sort of new furniture, and best of all, clean. It even smelled clean. She had forgotten a room could smell clean. Johnny had been up for a while and had retrieved her bag and jacket from the car. They were placed at the end of the couch, which helped Crit remember who she was, a sense of identity.

Johnny had cooked breakfast for himself, his custom. He was hungry since he never ate anything at night. The smell of food made Crit feel a little nauseous; she wanted a drink. She lifted her head up and moaned. Johnny, having finished eating, stuck his head out of the kitchen door when he heard her waking noises. Seeing him, she remembered he was the bartender.

"Where the hell am I?" she asked, with a dry mouth.

Johnny walked out of the little kitchen with a huge mug of black coffee and two aspirin in his hand. "You're in my apartment. Here…this will help. I'm sure you feel rotten."

"Pour some vodka in my coffee."

"Nope, you don't need that."

"What kind of damn bartender are you?"

"The kind that is not at the bar today, but is trying to help a lady in distress. Just be glad it was me and not some weirdo that brought you home with him."

"I don't remember anything. What did you do to me last night?" She looked at Johnny suspiciously.

"Not a damn thing, but that doesn't mean I didn't think about it. Now, get that aspirin and coffee down so you can start feelin' better." He sat beside her on the couch, helping her to take small sips until the mug was empty.

"Ohhh, God. I feel awful. Johnny, right? Your name is Johnny?" He nodded. "Yeah, now I remember, you're Johnny boy. Well, Johnny boy, do you have a bathroom, 'cause I sure do need to pee."

"Right down that little hallway on your left."

Crit looked at herself in the mirror over the sink, still feeling disoriented with hardly any memory of the evening before. She washed out her mouth and splashed water on her face. Noticing a new bar of soap on the sink, she picked it up and ran her hand over the white bar imprinted with "Ivory Soap," and then she smelled it. Running the water until it was warm, she washed her hands and up her arms with the new soap, feeling tearful at the luxury and the reminder of loss in her life, like warm water and a clean bathroom.

Regaining her composure, she finger combed her hair to look as presentable as possible. It needed to be washed badly, so did her whole body. "Maybe Johnny boy will let me take a bath," Crit silently hoped.

Johnny encouraged Crit to sit at the small table in the kitchen and eat some breakfast. He sat another big mug of coffee beside her plate. "I know you don't feel hungry, but you need to try to eat, at least the dry toast. You haven't had any food in a long time." Johnny was glad he worked at night so that he could have this morning with Patsy Sue. She picked at the food as he sat across the table from her.

"How come you're bein' so nice to me? You don't really know nothin' about me."

"I don't know, Patsy Sue. This is sure not something I usually do. It's like you just fell into my lap and I had to catch you." He laughed at himself. "I'm a pretty good guy, but I'm not normally this good!"

As experienced as Crit was with men, she knew they only wanted one thing from her, and most of them weren't shy or polite about it. This man was a paradox to her, and she didn't trust him. The majority of men didn't try to hurt her, but there were those who did, acting like animals. A girl on her own had to be careful. She also knew that nothing in life was free; there was a price of some kind for everything, especially for a beautiful woman.

After an uncomfortable silence, Johnny said, "So, look, I have an offer for you."

"Here it comes," she thought. "Oh yeah? What kind of offer?"

"The way I see it, there's no reason why a beautiful woman like you should have to be sleeping out in the cold, just anywhere you can find. That's just not right. It looks like we ought to be able to work something out here. You could help me out some keeping the apartment clean, not overly much, and then you could sleep and eat here. I might even be able to get my boss to put you on doing something at the bar, at least part time, so you could make a little spendin' money."

Never shy, Crit jumped right in. "Now, look Johnny, I appreciate what you have done for me. I really do. We hardly know each other; I don't know you, and you don't know me. Believe me, I can be a handful and pretty much live life as I damn well please whether other people like it or not. I'm not a woman who lets a man tell her what to do!" Crit openly clarified the situation, not willing to do anything that would put her freedom at risk.

Johnny's response surprised her. "Look, Patsy Sue, take it or leave it. I'm just trying to turn you a good deed here. Besides, I kinda have feelins' for you, and I think we could be good for each other, without either one of us givin' up anything."

They stood faced off on an equal playing field where Crit's manipulative style had been neutralized. "Well…maybe it's worth thinking about," she said, hesitantly.

"I tell you what, you don't have to decide anything right now. Hell, take a few days to make up your mind. It's not like we're gettin' married or anything."

"That's for damn sure," Crit said emphatically.

"Just remember, little darlin', you're the one that's sleepin' on the couch and it doesn't seem to me that you've got a lot of choices to pick from. I looked in your purse and I know you are dead broke. In fact, when I go back to work, I'm goin' to have to pay your bar tab for those five beers you swigged down last night."

Disconcerted and angry that what he said was true, she pounced again. "It's not that I'm not grateful for what you've done for me, but I'm not gonna be your whore, and you damn well know what I mean. Hell, I'd rather sleep on the ground in a cold alley than to have a man think he owns me!"

"Relax, Patsy Sue. This is all gonna be fine," Johnny reassured. With that, he opened a dresser drawer in his bedroom, emptied the things on a chair, and gave it to Crit. "Here; take this. Put your stuff in here and just sit it over in the corner of the front room, close to the couch. Put any of your things you want to in the bathroom to make it easier on you."

Johnny's calm manner disarmed her, turning off her fight or flight mechanism. She put her things into the empty drawer and placed the few grooming items she had left on a shelf in the bathroom. Crit had not been able to do that for months. She stood looking at the powder, rouge, and brow pencil. She removed the diminishing tube of lipstick from the shelf and put it back into her purse.

When she returned to the kitchen, Johnny was cleaning up. Crit had never seen a man clean up a kitchen in her life; in a restaurant, maybe, but not at home. This Johnny boy was so different she didn't know where to put him in her mind.

By the end of the fourth month after the original arrangement, things had changed. Crit's clothes were still in a dresser drawer, but now back in Johnny's bedroom dresser. The sheets and pillow she had used on the couch were folded and stored away, no longer needed as she had gone to Johnny's bed a week after settling in. The cataclysmic sex of the first couple of months had soon waned in the drudge of familiarity; all of the excitement of a new experience was gone. They each had cracks in their façade that were soon exposed distinctly to one another.

With each passing day, Crit saw more and more of a hidden darkness in Johnny that wasn't there in their initial encounter, when he first rescued her from living on the street. They partied together after he got off from work at the bar, often staying up all night, and sleeping late the next day. He began to include wild new friends with questionable connections in their activities. With no obvious source of income, the men had plenty of money to throw around and cheap looking prostitutes for their dates. Crit sensed that Johnny was beginning to make some kind of deals with them and was tapping into their money source. He started having wads of money in rolls lying out on his dresser, more than he could make all year as a bartender.

Johnny became less satisfied with Crit, growing belligerent when she didn't please him. When he was unable to perform sexually, he blamed her and wouldn't talk to her for hours. She was dependent upon him for liquor and drugs, giving him leverage to control and manipulate her. He had first lured her in by using her dependence on him for food and shelter but now kept her by fueling her addictions. She would do anything to feed the dragon of addiction that had become her master.

Johnny began to use Crit to run secretive errands at night for him in his car, while he stayed visible working at the bar. She made deliveries of drugs, liquor, and cigarettes to soldiers on post in Texas and Louisiana. On one of those runs, a new contact was waiting and hid two young soldiers in the back end of the car. They had swapped their uniforms for street clothes and were sweaty, looking very nervous.

"Just drop them off on the street in San Antonio. The rest is up to them," the contact said gruffly, before he slammed down the lid of the trunk. He locked the trunk and handed the keys back to Crit. A beautiful blonde in a nice car was never stopped by the military police, making Crit a perfect accomplice to carry out the illegal activities forced on her by Johnny.

There was always plenty of money, and Johnny dressed her well, picking out her seductive clothes and sending her to the beauty salon for upswept sophisticated coiffures and make-up that made her look much more mature than she was. He created her image and told her what to do. No longer Crit, she was Johnny Delano's woman at the age of eighteen. He would give her as a "date" to a few high-ranking military officers but threatened to kill her, or any philanderer, if she ever had a liaison without his permission. She was his!

Every time she went on one of those nighttime errands, Crit wanted to run away. Then she would weaken at the thought of having no place to go, with no way to get the things she needed. There was part of this new lifestyle that excited her, the clothes and makeup, a nice car to drive, all of the alcohol and drugs she wanted. However, she had no freedom to do as she pleased. Johnny was her benefactor and her captor. Crit had become just another one of his possessions. She was the beautiful moth caught in the spider's web, with little hope of escape.

Each time Crit lay in the bed beside Johnny after one of their nights of carousing, she found him more and more disgusting. That repulsion and disgust was slowly overcoming her fear of him, as she thought more and more of a way she might be able to escape. She had run away before, and she could do it again. Crit had to get away from San Antonio and create a new identity.

After so many months of obedience and usefulness, proving her dependability with each delivery and secreting of AWOL soldiers and flyboys, Johnny was beginning to take Crit's reliability for granted. He was no longer antsy when she left in the car. She dropped him off at the bar as she had done many times before, giving him a kiss before he got out of the car. Crit flashed Johnny a charming smile and mouthed, "I'll see you later," as she drove away. "So long and good riddance, you jackass," she said aloud, with contempt.

Driving hurriedly back to the apartment, Crit gathered up her belongings, cramming them into the leather bag she had always used. Rushing back out to the car, she threw the bag into the back seat and headed for the nearest filling station.

"Fill 'er up and make it snappy," she instructed the attendant. Crit pulled the payment out of the stack of money she had been skimming off the rolls Johnny left lying around the apartment. Her hands were shaking. She started the engine and headed northwardly out of San Antonio. With no exact destination, she decided just to follow her instinct. All that mattered right now was to get out of town as quickly as she could. Crit knew if Johnny caught her, he would kill her. No doubt about it.

With each mile marker she passed, Crit began to feel more secure. By the time Johnny got off from work that night, she would be several hundred miles away.

~

Johnny stood outside the bar, looking up and down the dark street. Crit was always waiting for him at the front door when he locked up. Something didn't feel right about this. After waiting half an hour, Johnny went back inside and called the apartment, letting the phone ring multiple times. He slammed down the receiver. "Where the hell is that bitch!"

He went back outside, looking up and down the street again. A familiar patrol car pulled up in front of him. "Hey, Johnny. Is something wrong?"

"Hello, George, I don't know. Say, could you give me a ride to my apartment?" George had driven the night patrol on the streets around the bar for years. The two men were accustomed to seeing one another.

"Sure thing, hop in buddy."

"I owe you a drink for this." Johnny was trying to control his feelings.

"Aw, forget it. Glad I can help you out."

When they arrived at the apartment building, Johnny could see that the car was not in its parking place. Somehow, his gut told him it wouldn't be there. As the police car pulled away, he raced into the foyer. Not waiting for the elevator, he ran up the stairs two at a time. Fumbling with his key, he finally unlocked the door.

"Patsy Sue, are you here?" He ran through the small apartment calling her. Going into the bathroom, he saw there was nothing on Crit's shelf. Facing the reality of the situation, he walked more slowly back to the bedroom and opened her drawer. It was empty.

Johnny sat at the little kitchen table smoking one cigarette after the other, mulling over what he should do. He was hesitant to involve the police, considering the types of business ventures he had been pursuing. What if Patsy Sue had turned him in? No, she was too smart to do that, because she would be implicated, too. Maybe she had a wreck, or decided to make a run without him knowing it? Johnny nor Patsy Sue had any scruples, so they didn't have a basis of trust with one another.

Johnny made a pot of coffee, drinking all of it by the time daylight began to dawn. He took a bath and shaved, dressing in fresh clothes. After pacing around the apartment, conflicted in his decision-making, he picked up the telephone and called the police.

"San Antonio Police Department, Sergeant Alderson, here," answered the duty officer on the other end.

Johnny cleared his throat. "Uh, yeah. Uh…I think my car's been stolen." He couldn't believe those words were coming out of his mouth. People didn't dare steal from him because they were afraid of the consequences. But, a woman? A damn woman?

"Well sir, has your car been stolen or not?"

"Yes, it has. What do I need to do to get you to look for the bitch that stole it? I want her to be arrested and thrown into the slammer! I want my car back!"

"Take it easy, there. You're going to have to come down to the station and do some paperwork. We've got to have some information and a signature before we can put out an all-points bulletin with the Texas Highway Patrol. We'll get the San Antonio PD looking as well."

"Alright."

"My advice is that you get down here as fast as you can. That car is probably getting farther and farther away the longer you wait since you seem to know the perpetrator."

~

Johnny hitched a ride with a friend and did the paperwork as required. He also took a snapshot of Patsy Sue in a black bathing suit with him to help with identification. Johnny knew the police wouldn't believe her description unless they saw her.

As Johnny left the station, the policeman who took the information showed the snapshot to the officer sitting next to his desk. "I'd say he's a damn lucky man."

The other officer laughed. "Not if she stole his car!"

Having driven all night and into the next day, Crit moved around in the seat trying to stretch her muscles while driving at the same time. She had stopped twice to buy gas and get a quick bite to eat. An empty Coca-Cola bottle rolled around on the passenger side floorboard. She had driven through numerous towns along the way seeing local police as well as highway patrol, but no one had noticed her as anything out of the ordinary.

Crit had no idea what kind of action Johnny might have taken against her. He wouldn't know what direction to go if he hired people to spread out and look for her. She didn't think he would involve the police because he would want them to stay away from all of his risky businesses.

She had almost decided to stop and disappear in Lubbock as she drove through the decent-sized city, but she would have had to ditch the car, and she wasn't ready to do that. She was planning eventually to get somebody to paint the car a different color and steal another tag so she could keep it, however, it would take just the right person to do that for her. Crit pressed on, planning to keep driving until she couldn't stand it anymore, still heading north.

As Crit continued up the highway towards Amarillo, the sun had almost set in the West. She turned on the headlights ahead of the approaching night sky. She sang and wiggled her toes to keep from getting drowsy, now feeling more assured that she had gotten away with her escape.

Casually glancing into her rearview mirror, she saw an approaching sheriff's car coming up behind her. "Oh, damn it to hell. Stay calm, Crit," she said aloud. "Maybe he'll go around." She could feel her heart pounding as she remembered the drugs from some of her deliveries for Johnny were stashed in her purse for her own use. Crit jumped when the officer turned on the blaring siren and flashing red light on the car roof. She thought about floor boarding the accelerator, but knew that would be dumb.

Gradually slowing down, she turned on the right blinker and pulled over to a stop on the bumpy right shoulder, then turned off the engine. Crit propped her left elbow in the window opening and leaned back against the seat, drawing on her courage to face what was about to happen.

The sheriff's car sat behind her, red light flashing, for what seemed like an eternity. Then the front doors opened on each side as two men stepped out and turned on their flashlights. They moved slowly, leaning over to see each side of her car before moving forward on both sides. As one officer looked through the window on the passenger side, the other walked up to Crit's window, addressing her sternly.

"Lady, put both of your hands on the steering wheel so I can see them."

Immediately, Crit sat up in the seat and complied with his command. "Is there something wrong, officer?" She innately knew this was not the time to flirt.

He shined the flashlight into her face as she squinted, while the officer on the other side used his light to see the floorboard and back seat. "Uh, yes ma'am, we do believe there is a problem here. I need to see your driver's license and car registration."

Crit put her head over on the steering wheel in resignation. She knew there was no point in pretending they were in the glove box or left at home. Always the con artist, Crit knew it was different this time, and she had been caught red-handed. She looked respectfully up at the man in uniform.

"Officer, I don't have them," she said so softly, he could barely hear her.

"You don't have either one?"

"No sir."

"Ma'am, do you have any form of identification on you at all?"

"No, officer, I don't."

"Well then, ma'am, I'm going to ask you to step out of the car and keep both of your hands where my deputy or I can see them at all times." The second officer had come back around the car. As Crit got out of the car, he stepped beside her and asked her to put her hands on the fender and lean over, spreading her legs apart.

The sheriff stood straight, as he spoke in an official manner. "Ma'am, it is my duty to inform you that we have been notified that the vehicle you are now driving, belonging to one Johnny Delano, was found missing late last evening and formally reported stolen this morning by the San Antonio Police Department."

Crit was stunned. Johnny had snitched on her, using the police as his bloodhounds.

"Furthermore, Mr. Delano provided a full detailed description of the suspected perpetrator, and you fit the description." Both men ran their lights up and down her body, looking at her hair, and into her face. "Therefore, I need to inform you that you are being held pending arrest for car theft."

The deputy pulled her hands behind her, handcuffing her wrists. She had experienced plenty of scrapes with the law, but this was the first time Crit had ever been handcuffed. As she was put into the back seat of the Canyon City Patrol car, she never felt more vulnerable. As the car door locked behind her, she saw the wire mesh divider between the back seat and the driver in front. No amount of kicking or screaming would set her free. She felt fearful as never before. The sheriff started the patrol car and pulled out onto the highway, the deputy following behind in Johnny's car.

It was a short drive to the city sheriff's office in the small town of Canyon, Texas, population 2500. After the sheriff parked in his reserved spot, he went into the building, leaving Crit alone in the car. The deputy pulled Johnny's car into the next parking place and turned off the engine. He was holding Crit's purse when he stepped out, then reached into the back seat and picked up her leather case before locking the car. He walked around the sheriff's car to unlock the rear door where Crit was seated. She sighed with relief to get out of the cage that held her. The deputy courteously assisted Crit in getting out of the car and held on to her arm leading her into the station as she walked with her hands cuffed behind her. Crit could feel the intense gravity of her situation.

They stopped at a desk for some rudimentary processing, before the deputy took her directly to a holding cell. As the steel door was slammed and locked behind her, she shuffled over to a musty steel cot. Crit, still handcuffed, sat down, and fell over on her side, consumed by exhaustion. As she lay there, she could hear the sheriff making a phone call to the Amarillo Police Station.

"Uh, yeah, this is Simpson in Canyon. I need to speak to the Captain. I think I have a package that will be of interest to him."

"Captain Harris here," the head police officer answered bluntly.

"Captain, this is Sheriff Simpson here from over at the Canyon City station." He sounded boastful and somewhat smug. "I'm callin' to let you know my deputy and me just caught us a live one you'd want to know about, namely, the car reported stolen out of San Antonio and the female driver." It was rare for a sheriff in a small station like Canyon to have dealings with the big city boys in Amarillo or Lubbock, and Sheriff Simpson felt as if he had won the grand prize.

"No kiddin'? So you guys caughta big one, did you?" Captain Harris sounded surprised.

"Yeah. What are the chances on that, and at night?" He marveled at the unlikely event himself. "What we got here is a black, late model Chevy reported in the early mornin' APB, driven by a young, Caucasian female, preliminarily identified as Patsy Sue Allen. Suspect is in her late teens, maybe early twenties, blonde hair, and mostly blue eyes."

"Mostly?"

"Yeah, they got some kind of gold flecks in them. That's what the report said, and seein' them under the flashlight, that's the way they looked to me, too."

Captain Harris laughed. "Okay, Simpson. Let's just call them blue to keep things simple. Has she got any ID?"

"Not a shred, that don't help any. I'm gettin' ready to question her, but that don't mean she'll tell the truth. I'll get everything for you I can tonight."

As the conversation continued, the two law officers negotiated an early morning transfer of the suspect from the Canyon City Sheriff's Police Station to the Amarillo PD for formal processing. As Sheriff Simpson grabbed a questioning form, Crit called to him from the holding cell.

"Please sir, Sheriff Simpson, take these handcuffs off of me, they hurt so bad." Crit was almost in tears. He walked into the holding cell and stood her up.

"Turn around." He quickly removed the handcuffs. "Sit down in this chair." He dragged two straight back chairs into the small cell, one for each of them. "Now if I think you're jerkin' me around, or not tellin' me the truth, I'm gonna put them back on you for the rest of the night. Understand?"

She nodded, submissively.

"Now, little lady, I've just talked to the Amarillo PD. Tomorrow morning, you will be transferred there for a formal arrest process, but tonight, you and me need to talk about some things to make life easier for everybody, since we are just holdin' you. Do you get my meaning?"

She nodded, wiping her hands over her face. Crit looked directly into the eyes of the man across from her, determined to do what he asked. She didn't want to do anything that would get her into more trouble than she was already.

As he began to ask questions about her identity and past, all of her answers would have to be lies, even her relationship with Johnny and how she came to steal his car. She held back tears.

"Look, let's just set the record straight right now," she blurted out suddenly. Patsy Sue Allen isn't my real name. I just made that up when I moved to San Antonio, you know, kind of an alias. The truth is my name is Melba. Melba Christine Youngblood."

"Alright, Miss Youngblood, that's a start. I need your birth date, city, last place of residence, and the name and address of your parents or the nearest kin. Are you ready to give me that information now, please ma'am?"

She reached deep down inside herself to find the strength to comply, having had no sleep and very little to eat, plus the shock of her arrest. Crit felt light headed as if she was going to faint.

"I was born in Dallas, October 14, 1923. My parents are Tom and Minnie Bell Youngblood, and right now, they live in Aldine. You already know I left San Antonio over twenty-four hours ago. I lived there for a few months if you want to call that livin'."

"Okay…I have that. Just to be clear, the car you were drivin' isn't yours, is it Miss Youngblood?" The sheriff was probing for everything he could get, to share with the Amarillo PD the next morning.

She hesitated. Crit knew that Johnny would be in the middle of everything very soon and would identify her as having stolen his car. There was no place for her to run or get out of this one. It was bad, and it was going to get worse. She felt sad, seeing all of her plans collapsing around her.

"Look, Sheriff, let's just call a spade a spade. We both know I stole that car yesterday from Johnny Delano of San Antonio. He and me met at a bar and shacked up together for a few months at his place. To tell you the truth, I'm afraid of him and what he might do to me. I made a plan over a few weeks how to get away from him, and I used his car to do it."

She let out a big sigh, from having told the whole truth about herself in such a short time. "Now, can I please have a damn glass of water?"

He chuckled. "I think we pretty much have the story now, Miss Youngblood. I'll have the deputy bring you some water and some food to eat, too. In the meantime, if you need something, just let us know."

The sheriff left for his office, and Crit stretched out on the bed in her cell, completely exhausted. By the time the deputy came with a plate of food, she had already fallen asleep. He couldn't help but stare at her through the bars. Then he quietly slid the food tray under the door and turned out most of the lights. He was assigned night duty to guard her and had hoped she might talk to him, a beautiful young woman like that, but she didn't make a sound until sunrise.

When he checked on her the next morning, she was sitting on the side of the bed, picking through the cold food he had slid under the door the night before. "Hey, ma'am, you don't have to eat that cold food; there's a hot breakfast comin' anytime now."

"Oh…okay. Hell, I'm about to starve to death. What about some black coffee?"

"I can get that right now." He hurried back and handed it to her through an opening in the door.

Crit took a sip. "That's the best damn coffee I ever tasted."

"I'll be back in a minute with your food and you will need to eat it pretty fast, the sheriff said the Amarillo police are supposed to be here in about fifteen minutes."

As he left, Crit pulled the chair the sheriff left in the holding cell the night before over to the corner of the room where the commode stood. She hung her blanket over it to give her privacy while she relieved herself. Grimacing, she thought, "What a hell hole for a lady to have to stay in. I deserve better than this."

The Amarillo black and white pulled up in front of the sheriff's office. Two officers had been assigned the task of transporting one Melba Christine Youngblood to Amarillo for official processing, arrest and arraignment. They took her paperwork, belongings, and the key to Johnny's car. One of the officers handcuffed her and placed her in the back seat of the Amarillo police car, the other followed along behind, driving Johnny's car.

She put her face against the wire cage. "Sir, can I have my purse?"

"No, it is sealed for evidence."

"What will I be charged for? Stealing?"

"Most likely it'll be larceny, maybe other charges, too. It's not my place to make those calls. You sit back and be quiet now. It's against the rules for us to talk."

She leaned back as well as she could with her wrists handcuffed behind her back. Larceny…that sounded a lot more serious than vagrancy. Crit shifted around and looked through the wire mesh of the rear window. She could see Johnny's car following at a safe distance. She was disgruntled to know that car came close to belonging to her. Maybe it would have if she had picked another road of escape. Fate was fickle and cruel.

In less than thirty minutes, the squad car entered the parking lot of the Amarillo PD. Following close behind, Johnny's car turned right and disappeared into a fenced holding area. Crit's silent driver turned left toward a guarded rear entrance for unloading prisoners where she was quickly removed from the back seat and led inside to the station's processing desk.

The receiving officer double-checked the papers, verifying her name and description. She was then taken to the desk of another officer who finalized the official arrest.

Her handcuffs where removed, her picture taken, and she was fingerprinted. That was a new experience for Crit. For the first time, she felt like a criminal.

Her case was opened and all of her personal items put into a box. The contents of her purse were dumped into a container, along with the wad of money that was once going to help pay to have the car painted and provide Crit with a totally new life. Each thing was listed for her verification and she signed a form that said these items belonged to her, having been noted correctly. The items from her purse were sealed in her presence. Her name and arrest number were indicated on the front before it was removed to secure storage as evidence. The amount of drugs and money would be key among her charges.

Next, she was led briskly to a private room where a female attendant instructed her to disrobe completely, and then told to put on a drab prison dress. The woman stared at her during the process, making Crit very uncomfortable. The attendant then opened the door and motioned for the officer standing guard to take Crit. He escorted her directly to a jail cell, locking the door behind her. She was told she would be held there until her arraignment before the municipal judge.

During the process, no one had smiled at her, only speaking to give her instructions or to ask questions. It was all very impersonal, business-like. No one acted as if she was unusual or special. All of her well-developed survival tactics were useless in this setting; she was just another person under arrest. The experience was so demeaning and belittling that tears silently rolled down her cheeks.

Less than an hour later, two officers approached her cell door. One of them called her by name and barked a terse set of instructions. "Youngblood. Step forward. Arraignment." The other officer motioned for her to come forward. Her arms were pulled behind her back, and Crit was handcuffed again.

The two officers, each with a pistol in leather holsters on their hip, walked Crit down the wide hallway toward the courtroom. No one said a word. The three of them stopped outside a set of double doors leading into the courtroom. Within seconds, the doors opened, and she was directed to a designated table directly in front of the judge. To her left, a lone man sat at another table. She learned that he was the prosecuting attorney for the State of Texas.

As she sat down at her table, a nicely dressed man came and sat beside her. He was the public-provided defender.

"Miss Youngblood, I have been assigned to your arraignment process today. Basically, the judge will ask you only one question: 'Do you plead guilty or not guilty?' I am advising you not to lie, just tell the truth and don't hem-haw around about it. Do you understand me?" It was the rote advice he had given dozens of times as a court-appointed attorney. Only after he completed his statement, did he pause and truly look at Crit. He tried not to show he was taken by surprise to see this beautiful young woman looking back into his eyes for help, her eyes crystalline blue. Crit nodded her head that she understood the part about telling the truth.

Within seconds, the judge entered the room, announced by the bailiff. "All rise for the honorable Judge David J. Allen, presiding over the Amarillo Municipal Court."

Everyone stood to their feet as the judge strolled in casually and climbed a few steps up to his bench. Once he was seated, the bailiff motioned for all to be seated and the judge slammed down his gavel indicating court was in session. "This court will now come to order," he said, adjusting his wire rimmed glasses; looking over the top of them. "Bailiff, are we set to move forward with the first case on today's docket?"

"We are, your honor," the bailiff said.

"Very well. Does the prosecution have an opening statement regarding charges against the first defendant?" The judge sounded bored and nonchalant.

As the proceedings moved forward, Crit began to tremble. She didn't understand the jargon of law as statements flew back and forth between the lawyers and the judge. She was then ordered to take the stand and sworn under solemn oath to tell the truth and nothing but the truth. She was afraid she might not remember the truth as she was asked lengthy questions about a series of topics and her involvement in each of them. The focus finally funneled down to the particulars about Johnny's car and the drugs in her purse. As she answered, Crit was panting for breath, her heart pounding, and the veins on her neck were distended and pulsating.

Crit struggled to keep up and focus on everything as they began to talk about Johnny. Suddenly he was more important to the State in this hearing then she was, as it was revealed by the prosecution that Johnny Delano was little more than a temporary resident of San Antonio. His permanent, legal residence was his parent's house in Shreveport, Louisiana. Furthermore, the prosecution informed the court that Mr. Johnny Delano, now formally represented by Louisiana counsel, had requested that the defendant, Melba Christine Youngblood, aka Patsy Sue Allen, be extradited to Louisiana for prosecution.

"Case closed. Bailiff, remove the defendant and announce the next case on today's docket," the judge said decisively.

Crit looked around, not understanding what had happened. Nothing was making any sense to her. The two officers who had escorted her to court appeared by her side as her legal representative thumbed through papers for the next trial.

She pulled on his sleeve. "What happened? What does that mean? Is it over?"

He looked at her matter of factly. "You're going to Shreveport to be tried. Now get up girl and go with these officers, we've got a busy docket today."

Crit was returned to her cell where she was kept for almost two months before extradition details were finalized. As she waited, she weighed all of her options, trying to imagine what might be ahead. She was seething with anger that Johnny had reported her to the police, criminal that he was. Of course, that wasn't brought out in the hearing since she was the defendant in this case.

During the painfully lonely nights, locked behind bars, Crit hoped beyond hope Johnny might get over her taking his car and out of some inexplicable sense of love for her drop the charges.

In late August, she was told the extradition plans had been completed. Her relocation, coordinated between the Dallas Sheriff's Department and various Shreveport authorities, was to take place via a two-step process, requiring several days of travel under guard. During the first week of September 1942, she was received and processed by the police department in Shreveport. Once again, she experienced the entire process of formal booking, finger printing, and mug shot. It was even more sobering than the first time.

As before, Crit was assigned public counsel and a court date was established. On September 6, 1942, she in essence repeated the process already experienced in the court at Amarillo. Crit realized no one was going to come forward to rescue her and Johnny had not dropped the charges. Her assigned counsel encouraged her to get it over with and admit guilt. All that remained was the declaration of a final verdict and associated sentencing.

Shortly before her nineteenth birthday, Crit sat in court experiencing child-like fear as she faced the ominous prospects.

"Will the defendant please rise for the pronouncement of verdict and sentence?"

As asked, Crit stood with the assistance of counsel. She was trembling while she held her breath.

"Melba Christine Youngblood, this court finds you guilty on the charges brought against you. On the count of larceny, you are sentenced to one year imprisonment and on the count of possession of an illegal drug and large sums of money indicative of trafficking in drugs, you are sentenced to one year imprisonment."

"In accordance with the laws of the State of Louisiana, you are hereby sentenced to a total of two years imprisonment at the Louisiana State Penitentiary in Angola."

Counsel put his arm around Crit to hold her up as her knees buckled. He knew she had been sentenced to the maximum security hellhole of Louisiana.

CHAPTER 5

A Horror Named Angola: Hell on Earth (1942 - 1944)

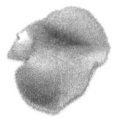

"**M**ama, it's Crit, your black sheep again." The somber tone in her voice flagged Minnie that something was different this time; something grossly and terrifyingly wrong.

"Oh my Lord, Crit…where are you? We haven't heard from you in months, and I have been out of my mind with worry." The anguish in Minnie's voice was heart-rending.

"Mama, I'm really in bad trouble this time, the worst ever. It's not good, Mama. Not good at all," Crit whimpered, sniffling back the tears. She struggled to find the words to explain what lay out before her. How could she tell her parents she had been convicted of a serious crime and was facing prison?

"What Crit? Tell me what is it now?" Minnie put a hand over her mouth as fear filled her heart. She listened.

"It's a long story, Mama, but mainly I just got mixed up with the wrong man in San Antonio." Crit sniffed, then wiped her nose on her arm.

"Oh, God…did he hurt you, Crit?" Minnie raised her voice as Tom came in from the other room and stood beside her. He pressed his ear against the phone as the two of them shared the receiver.

"No, ma'am, but I knew he was going to if I didn't run away where he couldn't find me. That's why I had to steal his car."

"You stole his car!!" The middle-aged couple stood in an embrace as they listened. "Yes, ma'am. They caught me with drugs, too, and heroin."

"Just go on and tell me everything, Crit, and tell me the truth this time," Minnie said, firmly. Crit had lied to her parents so often they knew her words could not be trusted.

"After I took the car, I got stopped the next day by the police in Canyon, Texas, and they put me in jail." Crit heard her mother gasp, as she continued with the story. "The next day they moved me to the jail in Amarillo and booked me while I waited for a hearing. But then, damn it to hell, I was extradited all the way to Shreveport for the trial!!"

Crit's voice had morphed over the course of the call, from the Youngblood's little girl, to the crude words of a worldly woman. "I didn't even know that asshole I had taken up with was from Louisiana. He had me shipped back here to stand trial."

"Have you been tried yet? Me and Papa will come to help you!"

"It's too late, Mama. They already found me guilty and charged me with a felony." Minnie began to sob. "Oh no, Crit! Are you in jail now?"

"Yes, here in Shreveport. But I will be moved in a few weeks."

"Where to? We want to come see about you. Maybe we can do something about all of this."

"Listen to me, Mama, I love you and Papa, but you can't do nothin' about this. I was sentenced to two years at Angola. I'm going to prison, Mama."

Everybody had heard of the infamous Angola Prison in Louisiana, rife with implications of depravity and cruelty. It was no place for a young girl. Crit would be ruined for life.

Minnie sagged against Tom as he took the phone. "Crit, this is Papa."

"Time's up, Youngblood!" The supervising officer drew a finger across his throat to signal the end of the call.

"I have to go, Papa. I can't talk no more. Please try to come see me!!"

"Crit! Wait, we love you!!" Crit heard Tom's voice faintly, as the officer snatched the phone out of her hand before she could reply.

Tom helped Minnie into the kitchen and pulled a chair out for her at the table. She was sobbing uncontrollably, her head in her hands. He brought her a glass of water and patted her back; trying to offer some comfort.

"What did we do wrong, Tom?"

He shook his head. "I don't know, Minnie Bell." One tear slid silently down his cheek. "But I think we did the best we knew how."

~

While being held in jail in Shreveport, Crit faced frequent questioning by various investigators. Though worldly savvy, Crit was naïve about law enforcement or any rights she might have claimed. Normally, brash by nature, she felt subdued and fearful that if she did the wrong thing, her situation could worsen and get her into more trouble. She obeyed each command and cooperated as much as possible during every interrogation.

However, as the interim time in the Shreveport jail lengthened beyond what would seem to be normal limits, she grew aware that the questioning periods were not about her present case. They never brought up Johnny Delano, but wanted to know about events far beyond the fact that she had stolen a car and sold heroin.

Crit soon realized her extended detention in Shreveport was because she had been implicated in some situations involving soldiers who were missing from Barksdale Air-Force Base in Bossier City. In the back of her mind, she knew full well that some of her assigned errands, while under Johnny's thumb, had been directly connected to Barksdale.

Fortunately for Crit, those who did the questioning about the Barksdale fly boys never seemed to have a clear picture themselves regarding those who were AWOL. Eventually, the questioning stopped. The Shreveport authorities then made arrangements to have Crit transferred to the state penitentiary by Louisiana State Troopers.

By the time the details to transfer Crit to Angola had been finalized, it was early November of 1942. On November the ninth, the day she was transported to Angola by the State Police, there was a slight chill in the early morning air. Nighttime temperatures would be slowly dropping. The subsequent cold was the type that could chill a person right down to the core.

After being handcuffed by the Sheriff's deputy, Crit was led to a State Police car parked immediately outside under a protective awning. Though wearing a light jacket provided by the authorities, Crit was shuddering and clinched her jaw to keep her teeth from chattering. Once situated in the vehicle, a different kind of chill wracked Crit's body with alarming fear of the unknown, as she faced the terror of being taken to Angola. She knew nothing about Angola or any other maximum-security facility.

During the trip of more than two-hundred miles from Shreveport to Angola, few words were exchanged between Crit and the officer in the driver's seat. As she looked out the window, the scenes she took in were drawing her closer and closer to the prison located in the deeply secluded Louisiana parish of West Feliciana. Trying to remember what she was seeing, Crit was acutely aware she would not be seeing anything like this again for a long time.

The prison Angola was named after one of the prominent southeastern countries of Africa. By the 19th century, the country of Angola had become one of the largest, if not the largest source of slaves shipped to Brazil and the Americas, including the United States. Co-incidentally, Louisiana's state penitentiary had been relocated to an 8,000-acre plantation by the same name, Angola. Eventually, this individual tract of land was expanded to include four contiguous plantations: Panola, Belle View, Killarney, and Angola.

The final result was an 18,000 acre, maximum-security prison, bordered externally on three sides by the vast and treacherous Mississippi River, and on the remaining side by the more than 2000 acre northern parcel of the Tunica Hills Wilderness. The wilderness encompassed extremely rugged hills, densely entangling brush, ravines and an overrunning contingent of venomous snakes, along with alligators. Consequently, escape efforts were rare.

By the 1930's and early 1940's, at the hands of the politically corrupt, Angola had evolved into a deviant correctional facility. There, thousands of convicted men and women were subjected to widespread deprivation, relentless beatings, sexual slavery and other indescribable perversions. For decades, such conditions, none of which could be remotely akin to logical and humane rehabilitation, were ignored and exploited by many Louisiana politicians and influential persons.

Crit, as a nineteen-year-old girl, could never have imagined what awaited her. Her participation up to this point in a perverted lifestyle would look like a church picnic compared to Angola. The security and comfort of the trooper's car was the last she would take for granted for many months. She was soon to become one of the dispossessed.

They had driven deep into nowhere when the car suddenly made a hard left turn onto LA 66, a rough, poorly paved, meandering road. To her right was a dirty sign: Louisiana State Penitentiary – 22 miles. Crit shifted nervously in her seat, rubber necking to take in whatever she could see. There was nothing, just miles and miles of rugged, God-forsaken terrain. Later she learned it was called the Tunica Hills Wilderness.

At this moment, she would have been content to be on one of the old farms where she had lived as a girl, walking the dusty path back to the house from the barn. She had planned to have a life better than that, but now she was on her way to a prison hidden away from the rest of the world.

"Just about there, Youngblood!" Crit jumped as the officer called to her in the backseat.

"Uh, okay." Up ahead, Crit saw what appeared to be the front entrance of the prison. There was a small gatehouse and a clearly marked entrance.

"You're just about at your new home now." The officer chuckled. "They're really gonna like you here. They don't get many pretty ones like you."

Crit's skin crawled at the obvious innuendo. She felt exposed.

The trooper's car turned into the graveled driveway of the prison entrance. As he stopped, Crit looked left and right. She saw nothing but section after section of secure fencing, an ominous preview of her new world.

As an Angola gatekeeper approached the car, the trooper rolled down his window. "Afternoon; LSP here, delivering one Melba Christine Youngblood, Shreveport SO #4535. How should I proceed?" asked the trooper.

With a simple nod of the head, the gatekeeper reversed his steps and returned to the gatehouse. Once inside, he picked up the phone and notified prison authorities of Crit's arrival. When he returned to the car, he instructed the trooper.

"All clear. Just follow the winding road to the processing house up ahead. Don't stop along the way for any reason, go directly to the house. You can't miss it. It's that big white one," he explained, as he pointed directly to the house standing off in the distance.

As the car pulled away from the front gate, both Crit and the trooper gazed at the expansive farming acreage peppered with patches of heavily guarded male prisoners; each dressed in wide-striped, black and white uniforms.

They slowly grew closer to the palatial white house ahead. The benign exterior belied the things that took place there. Though the house served as the Warden's primary residence, it also contained offices for a limited number of elite prison personnel, as well as the processing center for newly arriving convicts.

As the trooper's car pulled up to the house, a trustee, dressed in prison black and white, motioned for the car to continue around to the side of the house. Once there, another trustee told the trooper to stop near the door marked: PRISONER RECEIVING. After parking, the officer stepped out and was immediately met by the acting warden who appeared to be an ordinary, civilized individual. He carried a document-filled clipboard holding Crit's pertinent data and nodded at her in the backseat as the two men talked.

"Officer, welcome to Angola. I see here that you have a package for us?"

"Uh, yes sir, I do." The trooper touched the brim of his hat in respect.

"Well, let's get her out of there and into processing."

"Yes, sir." The trooper opened the back door where Crit was sitting. As he helped her out of the car, an additional prison employee came forward to take Crit by the arm. He led her into the side entrance door, the warden and state trooper following behind.

Once inside the house, the trooper signed some papers, removed Crit's handcuffs and shook the warden's hand, before returning to his vehicle for the trip back to Shreveport. Crit was immediately led down a set of stairs by a black female trustee; followed by the warden.

The base of the stairs opened into a large receiving room that held a reception desk and a couple of wooden benches. Seated at the desk was a stern-faced, well-dressed woman, whom Crit assumed was a prison employee. Within seconds, Crit was instructed about new prisoner admission proceedings.

"Are you Youngblood, Melba Christine, SO #4535, convicted of larceny, possession and sale of heroin, sentenced to two years on the Angola farm?" the woman sternly asked.

"Yes, ma'am," Christine answered.

"Okay, Youngblood, over here." As the woman spoke, she motioned for Crit to follow her behind a small, portable privacy divider, where she gave Crit her next set of instructions.

"I need your clothes, and I mean everything. Strip and hand `em to me. They'll be stored in a box with your name on the outside. Who knows if they'll be here when you walk back out the front gate in two years," the woman continued with little empathy.

With some reluctance, Crit complied with the woman's orders. As she undressed, she carefully folded each item of clothing and stacked them on the bench behind the room divider. Once Crit was totally naked, the woman continued.

"Our policies require cavity searches for all new prisoners, male or female. Do you need to pee?"

Crit nodded. She was about to burst from the long car ride. "Bring the slop jar," the woman said to the trustee. "Are you having your monthly?" she asked. Crit shook her head "no". "That's good. Are you pregnant?" Crit shook her head "no" again. "That's good, too." She looked away casually while Crit squatted over the receptacle. Crit sighed with relief as she finished emptying her bladder.

"Now, young lady, spread your legs and put your elbows on the table so we can be done with this," the woman said, as she pulled on a rubber glove. Crit sensed an ever-so-slight feeling of understanding and concern from the prison employee, making her compliance easier as the woman invaded her body with probing fingers. Little did Crit realize she had only begun the imminent loss of all personal privacy for the next two years.

With that humiliating experience over, Crit was then handed a set of prison garb that included a drably colored cotton dress and a sweater. Shoes, socks and underwear were not issued. Next, Crit was taken to a sink and told to wash off all make-up, as inmates were not allowed to wear such unless doing so facilitated some aspect of their assigned duties. She had not been allowed make-up since being jailed in Shreveport, but she complied anyway. No make-up accented how young and beautiful Crit truly was.

"This way, Youngblood," the woman barked. Whatever shred of empathy Crit sensed before had vanished.

The two women headed back upstairs. Emerging into a hall, they turned right, into an adjoining room where the warden and an armed male prison guard waited for Crit.

"Alright, Youngblood, today marks the beginning of your time here at Angola. My advice is that you do what you are told, and when you're told to do it. Hell, make the best of it, and who knows, maybe being here will drive some sense into your head. You might just want to give up your life of crime and return to society completely rehabilitated."

Though Crit found the warden's lecture rambling and pointless, she listened intently and responded respectfully. "Yes, sir." As she answered, Crit looked directly into the warden's eyes. What she saw in there gave her a chill.

~

"This way," directed the guard, as he pushed Crit forward and through a door out into the expansive prison grounds. As they walked, he blurted out a seemingly routine set of facts about Angola life, particularly as it related to female inmates.

"Youngblood, as you can see, there's almost no end to Angola. Shit, it includes thousands of acres, mostly for farming. But, Angola has a cannery and a sugar refinery, too. If you're lucky, you'll spend most of your time at the cannery."

As Crit listened, her eyes roamed the prison grounds. It was almost too much for her to take in at one time. If she was going to survive at Angola, Crit knew she had to learn the lay of the land and learn it quickly. The word "cannery" imbedded in her brain as a lucky place to be.

As the guard continued the brisk walking tour, he pointed out some of the vast acreages and listed the crops that were rotated there. He pointed to a good-sized lake, the main house where she had just been processed, and an outwardly dilapidated wooden barrack or dormitory for prisoners, known as Camp A. She later learned there were many of these buildings in various states of disrepair scattered about the property, where hundreds of prisoners were housed.

Off in the distance, Crit saw a grouping of male prisoners still working in a field, though the sun barely hovered above the western horizon. Suddenly, the man guarding them began to yell at the top of his lungs at one of the workers. The guard showing Crit around stopped abruptly to listen.

"Get up, you lazy nigger! Get up and get your sorry ass back to work before I beat the livin' hell out of you!" The guard's unrestrained rage was terrifying to Crit.

"You see that, don't you Youngblood? That's what happens around here when you don't do what you're told," her guard said in a casual, disengaged manner.

Crit didn't reply as she kept walking while continuing to stare at the surreal, inhumane sight before her. Without warning, the irate guard pulled out a leather strap and started flogging the prisoner who was struggling to regain his footing and get back to work. The guard continued to curse and berate the pitiful man at the top of his voice.

All of the other prisoners kept their heads down, with both hands buried in their work. Had they dared to stop and watch they would have met the same fate.

Crit shuddered as she thought about her Papa's razor strop lashing her back and buttocks; how much it hurt, and stung and humiliated her. How her mother spread lard on the whelps to help them heal, but she never protected Crit from the lashes as her father beat her. It turned her heart to stone to think of it.

"Keep walking, woman," demanded the guard. He led her deeper into this place called "Angola" that Crit now knew was actually hell on earth. They emerged into a clearing. "There's your new home, Youngblood. Ain't it grand?" The guard sounded sadistic and calloused as he pointed to Camp D, a singular wooden shack of a place that housed both Negro and white female inmates.

As they drew closer, Crit saw a few women loitering around the only door leading into the Camp D dormitory. Covered with dust and dirt, they seemed listless and exhausted, their hair matted and full of debris. Crit thought it strange that not one of them looked at her, ignoring her and the guard as they walked up to the building. She began to sense that the only way to stay out of trouble at Angola was to pretend you didn't see or hear anything and never to speak without permission.

The deplorable exterior of the dormitory was nothing compared to what awaited Crit inside. She followed the guard up a short set of steps leading into the building, as he shouted a warning to the women housed there.

"Guard on deck!" Those were the only three words required as a signal whenever a man entered any of the female facilities at Angola.

Dutifully, Crit followed the guard up the steps and into the place she would call "home" for the next two years. Immediately, she saw dozens of women: Negroes and whites, young and old, dressed and half-dressed. Though a male guard had entered their living space, none of the women seemed remotely concerned about their varied stages of physical exposure. Modesty and self-respect were only memories of their past life.

As Crit and the guard entered the interior of the dormitory, several women unabashedly surveyed Crit's slender body, curly blonde hair, fair skin and blue eyes. All of her life, men had stared openly at her, but this was a different feeling. These were women.

"Alright, you bitches, listen up. Make room somewhere for Youngblood!" And with that, the guard turned around to leave the dormitory, as he chuckled slightly under his breath. Scattered throughout the room there was a wave of sardonic laughter.

"Over here, Youngblood," called one of the inmates, as she pointed to a vacant, upper bunk bed.

As Crit walked to the bed, half-a-dozen women followed. They gathered around her, introducing themselves and firing a flurry of questions.

"What 'cha in for girl?" asked one of the women.

"Met the wrong man and stole his car!" Crit knew this was no time to be timid, as she expressed herself with confidence. She knew how to bluff her way through and never had a problem with unexpected situations or meeting new people. Crit seldom felt fear, but on the rare occasion when she did, she knew how to cover it up. This was one of those times.

Some of the women groaned. "We women are damn fools. It's always some man," one of the older women said. "I solved that problem. I shot mine between the eyes," she added, as the women gathered around cheered and laughed.

After talking for a few minutes with the women, Crit climbed to the top bunk and sat on the mattress with her legs dangling over the side. The mattress was a thin pad stuffed with straw; covered with a soiled sheet and a couple of worn blankets. There was no pillow, which had probably already been claimed by another inmate. Physically and emotionally exhausted, Crit fell over and stretched out, feeling fortunate to be on an upper bunk lifted above the women milling around the room.

Looking at the ceiling, she saw a series of electrical cords with bare light bulbs hanging from exposed rafters.

Crit sighed deeply, daring to close her eyes for a split second.

Her moment of mental escape did not last long as a trustee hollered, "On your feet, you bunch of sluts. Supper time!"

Crit hopped down off of the bunk and joined in with the women who were pushing and shoving as they formed a line two abreast, facing the exterior door. She was starving and couldn't remember when she had eaten last. Her stomach growled with emptiness.

They marched out silently, knowing any disobedience would mean no food. Crit learned that supper was served in shifts in the prison's crude dining hall housed in a portion of the prison cannery. It was a good distance from Camp D, down a well-worn path and skirting a large field.

As the women entered the cannery, they were directed to wooden tables and benches. Sparse food servings awaited them on worn metal trays. After getting to the table, Crit followed the leading of her new dormitory mates by standing at attention, waiting for permission to sit down.

"Sit!" barked the trustee from a nearby corner.

All of the women sat down obediently and began to devour the food, shoveling it into their mouths with spoons held crudely in their fist. There was no conversation, just the sounds of spoons hitting the metal trays. Crit looked down at the tray before her. As hungry as she was, she was repulsed by what she saw. Cold, overcooked red beans and rice looked like mush, cornbread was burned black on the bottom, and the one slice of white bread was the most recognizable item on the tray.

As Crit picked up the slice of bread and began to nibble at it, one of the inmates at the table spoke in her direction. "Welcome to Angola, darlin'. Bon appetite," she spoke in a whisper, so as not to be heard by the attending guard. It was dangerous to be caught talking during meals.

Less than fifteen minutes later, the same voice that had commanded the inmates to sit, ordered them to stand. Supper was over, and Crit had barely enough time to choke down the dry piece of white bread and drink the glass of water at her place.

She noticed the other women folded their paper napkin and hid it in their hand before standing, so she did the same.

After that initial meal, she learned to close her eyes and eat fast if she didn't want to starve to death, not allowing herself to smell, look at, or taste the slop before her. She also learned to save and hide the paper napkin. It was the only toilet paper she would ever have.

Like trained animals, everyone stood and headed back to their respective camps. Crit cautiously glanced around at as much of the cannery as she could see, with hopes it might be her assigned place to work. Recalling the words of the guard who first pointed it out to her, if this was the best option, the others must be hell.

Once back to Camp D, all inmates were allowed fifteen minutes of relaxation outside, strolling around the front of the dormitory or sitting on the ground to chat with one another. Some were in groups, some in isolated pairings; they headed left and right like children on a playground. Only the anti-social, the mentally unstable, or the brand new prisoners were left to spend that time alone.

In isolation, Crit tried to warm herself in the night's chilling air by wrapping her own arms around herself, while staring off into the thickening darkness. She stood quietly in this moment of limbo, not wanting to remember the past, and not daring to imagine the two years ahead of her. Nothing seemed real on either side of this moment.

The moment of reverie was broken as the women were gathered and herded into the dormitory. The surroundings were squalid, the stench of body odor, urine, and menstruation hung in the air. There was a large wood stove standing in the middle of the room, unlit because winter wasn't official yet. Crit was bone cold from damp air and shattered nerves.

Women were scurrying around, making preparation for the impending bedtime. Crit climbed up into her bunk, the flimsy frame swaying and squeaking as she lifted her weight. She rolled up in the one blanket and drew her knees up close to her body. The woman, who had pointed out the available bunk to her, walked over and poked her with a finger.

"If you plan to pee tonight, Cinderella, you better get your butt into the toilet right now, or wish you had later," she said with some urgency.

Crit sat up quickly, swinging her legs over the bed and dropping to the floor. She had been waiting until most of the women started getting into bed, hoping for a minute of privacy. She held her nose as she entered the horror of horrors. The stench overwhelming. There were four filthy sinks, stained with rust and years of use. A small polished metal mirror was secured to the wall, having little polish left, it distorted any image beyond recognition. Most demeaning were the three, fully open, and dirty toilets without seats, for the use of more than 200 women.

Crit half bent her knees as she tried to relieve herself without touching the filthy toilet, holding the tail of her dress up around her waist at the same time. She had stayed in some run-down, low-end flophouses and hotels in her day, but nothing could compare to this.

Prison yard bells began to clang loudly, alerting inmates to prepare for bed count. The woman who had warned Crit to go to the toilet stuck her head around the corner. "Youngblood! Get the hell in your bunk before you get busted on your first night here."

Crit ran across the bare wooden planks of the floor and scaled the swaying frame as she rolled into the top bunk. "Hey girls, we got a squirrel done moved in with us," one of the women yelled, as others laughed. In some crazy sort of way, the levity made Crit feel more at ease.

The trustee yelled, "Lights out!" heralding in the first of 730 nights Crit would spend in Angola. As she lay on her back, she could see that some of the bare bulbs hanging above the beds were left on.

A kind voice whispered in the semi-darkness. "You'll get used to it, kid. Hell, you're gonna be so tired at night it won't matter to you if the sun is hanging over your head. There ain't nothin' gonna keep you awake."

Crit nodded at the woman, then stretched out and rolled on her side, hoping to go to sleep quickly. In a short period of time, some of the women wandered from their own beds to that of others, seeking companionship and intimacy. They were entirely overt with their unabashed behavior and noises as if they were the only people in the whole dorm.

From the looks some of the women had given her, she considered the fact there could be a nighttime attack on her as the new girl in the dorm; possibly a group thing. She had already psyched herself up to be ready to fight if need be. If anyone tried anything on her in any way, she planned to gouge out their eyes and spring like a tiger.

Throughout the night, Crit tossed and turned on her primitive mattress, the bunk frame squeaking and creaking with every motion. There was the constant irritation of light from the dusty, overhead light bulbs. The incessant rotation of searchlights mounted on top of the guard towers continually flashed through her eyelids, a nuisance she would grow to accept. With the 200 plus women in the facility, it seemed there was a constant shuffling of bare feet across the wooden floor, accompanied by an undercurrent of snores, coughs, and whispers.

The time for rest seemed far too short as the early morning routine began each day. Crit had pretty much accepted the opportunity for personal hygiene as a regular part of life in the past, except when she was struggling as a vagrant out on the streets. But even then, she could find a service station or a restaurant for private time to clean up in their public restroom. That did not exist at Angola, not even for women. There was no privacy, fresh clothes were exchanged for dirty ones, once a week and only ten-second showers in cold water were allowed three times weekly. It was impossible to do more than run water through your hair, if one could stand it at all. There were a few towels hanging in the shower area for everyone to use.

With chattering teeth and purple lips, Crit would run back to her bunk and dry off with the sheet, spreading it to dry some before she had to make up the bunk. She learned to ignore the brazen eyes that openly stared at her young body, as she stood nude, trying to hurriedly dress. There was not another woman in the dormitory as young and lovely as she or like her in any other way. Like a beautiful butterfly trapped against a windowpane, she was vulnerable and helpless. She was intended to be free.

Then there was the relentless, slave-like labor that started from "can see" and ended with "can't see." Those assigned to the cotton fields were primarily males but females were not excluded, and it was not unusual to see them in the work contingent. It was tough work, taking a serious toll on the hands since no gloves were provided. Between the crude hoe handles, the razor sharp cotton bolls, and the constant onslaught of biting pests in the Louisiana river bottoms, the workers always had open sores, painfully blistered and festering. Sockless, ill-fitting leather shoes fostered the same on aching, bleeding feet.

Though Angola women were assigned a variety of tasks, often including arduous field work right alongside their male counterparts, they were also used in vegetable processing in the prison cannery, running the sugar cane refinery, and also in specialized cleaning and cooking assignments in the main house.

During the first few days of imprisonment, Crit was placed in various venues. In each work location, she cautiously had snatches of conversation with other female inmates and became privy to the way the prison surreptitiously used some women, especially those who most men would describe as pretty or attractive. Periodically, those who fell into such physical categories were selected for short-term or extended servitude in the big white house near the main entrance to the prison. Occasionally, they were assigned to work in the homes of important Louisiana politicians far and away from the main grounds of the prison.

"Girl, you won't be out here in this cold field long. You be headed to the big house real soon, honey." The black woman working beside Crit had befriended her early on after she moved into Camp D.

"What do you mean?" Crit asked, her back hunched over as she pulled weeds.

"You too purty for the fields, girl. You'll see." She put her hand over her mouth and laughed. Crit looked at her curiously, unsure of the implications. At the moment, all Crit could think of was trying to endure her sentence, get out of Angola, and move on with starting a new life.

Within a few months, Crit began to understand what had been shared by the friendly inmate in the field that day. As she stood with the group from Camp D to leave the dining hall after the evening meal, a guard approached, grabbing her arm as he pulled her out of line. The women in line with her cut their eyes around but said nothing as they marched dutifully back to their dormitory and the few minutes of break time awaiting them.

"Is something wrong?" Crit asked.

"No talking," he replied, as he led her outside into the approaching nightfall and around the side of the dining hall where they could not be seen. He pressed her up against the building, sliding his hands intimately over her body, then up her dress. He smelled of sweat and body odor, his breath vile.

"I'll scream," Crit said, trying to shove his hand and probing fingers away.

"Oh, no you won't, blondie." He put his hand over her mouth. "If you do, you'll never scream again when I get through with you."

Crit tried to act calm although his threat filled her with fear as he pressed her so hard against the boards she could barely breathe.

"Carter!" a voice yelled out in the dark. "Where the hell are you, man?"

The guard let Crit go and quickly zipped up his pants. She took the opportunity to escape as she ran back around the corner of the building and onto the path back to Camp D. She was panting as she finally caught up with her group just before they arrived at the clearing.

"Did he peg you?" one of the women asked, in a whisper. Crit shook her head, "no."

"Oh, he will. He's just waitin' for a chance. The only hope for you Youngblood is to get on the party list. I can't believe they hasn't put you there by now before your purtiness gets all messed up working out in the field. If the men here is goin' to start screwin' you, you can do a lot better than the guards, and get some perks along with it. Bein' young and purty is your ticket! Ain't many of us that lucky."

Crit had already experienced having some of the guards coming into the dormitory at unexpected times for a surprise "inspection." It was obvious they were trying to catch her at bath time so they could leer at her naked body. One did a "body search" of Crit after she had gotten into her bunk for lights out. When she first went to Angola, she was afraid of being gang raped by the women in her dorm, but now she feared that one day it would be the guards, and she would have no way to protect herself.

~

After the episode at the dining hall, Crit knew she had to save herself before she was seriously hurt or killed. She began to ask about the party list, and found that select women and men inmates were chosen by the prison administration to be used in the big house to serve at high society events and dinners. The occasions were frequent and extravagant, with gourmet meals, a variety of entertainment, plus well-known musical groups and dancing.

Attendees were politicians and other powerful state government officials, hand-picked toward maintaining a flow of funding, while blind toward the accounting of those funds at the Louisiana State Penitentiary. They ignored reports of cruelty, depravity, and unexplained deaths. Privilege and debauchery had won a place high above any concern for the lives of the human beings enslaved in the endless torment of Angola.

Their wives, or girlfriends, often accompanied these powerful men to the opulent affairs. Should their eyes fall favorably upon one of the luscious maids or waitresses on the party list, they had but to let their host know, and the girl would be awaiting them in their guest bedroom. If she was especially winsome, she had the chance of becoming a man's favorite and might join him for the festivities and be his companion each time he visited the great house. His needs could also be met if he preferred one of the waiters. The guests had no fear of their behavior being exposed beyond the big house, as they were all cohorts in crime.

The multi-course dinners were prepared and served by freshly bathed, meticulously groomed and dressed waiters and waitresses, butlers and cooks. White shirts, bowties, and black jackets accentuated the good looks of the waiters and butlers who were often effeminate male prostitutes within the confines of the prison. Draped with serving napkins over their forearm, they coordinated with the starched, form-fitting dresses worn by the comely waitresses and maids who also attended the guests.

Attractive, savvy inmates vied for the opportunity of getting on the party list. It meant a hot bath in a clean bathroom with soap and fluffy cotton towels. Benefits also included temporary clean clothes, nice shoes, haircuts, and grooming, with beauticians employed to coif the women and apply makeup. Best of all, they were allowed their fill of the best food and delicacies they could ever hope to eat after each party, albeit they were not allowed any alcohol.

On the serious side, the inmates also knew if they made any error, or broke any rules while serving in the big house, they would meet with severe punishment beyond anything they had experienced before.

However, if they excelled in the ability to maintain the desired image and degree of service expected, they could occasionally be borrowed for work opportunities in elegant homes beyond the confines of Angola. That was also a common practice for large-scale projects at the homes of some politicians who were given male inmates "on loan" for their labor and construction skills. They could be borrowed for days or weeks at no cost. Once the off-site project ended, they were returned to the labor gangs back at Angola.

Crit made contact with one of the inmates who had been on the party list for several years. She told Crit to ask for a session with the Guard Supervisor. All she had to do was tell him she wanted a meeting about the party list with the woman who had admitted her to prison; the contact referred to her as "The Cavity Search" woman. Though Crit was afraid, she followed through and was astonished the next day after placing her request with the Guard Supervisor, to be called to the admitting office beneath the big house.

"What's your gripe, Youngblood? It better be good." In a strange way, Crit liked the admitting woman, and she seemed to find Crit interesting. Crit had never met a woman with authority and position; this woman was an example that it was possible. The woman over female admissions never received a young, beautiful inmate at Angola, especially one with a fire still burning in her eyes. That made Crit unusual.

After Crit had made her request to be placed on the party list, the woman shrugged. "I thought you would have been called in for that a long time ago. Guess the guards wanted to keep you for themselves. By the way, the real name for this placement is the Cordiality Crew, but it means the same thing. Go up those stairs to the Warden's office. The secretary will tell you what to do, and explain everything; I do mean everything. You're young, you do know what the men at the parties will want from you, don't you?"

"Yes, ma'am. I've known that all of my life. They want to fuck me."

~

As Crit headed for the stairs, the woman called to her, "Youngblood, the guards, and trustees can't bother you anymore when you are put on the Cordiality Crew. They will be flogged, or worse if they do. It is one of the rules. Under the circumstances, that is one way your life will be better."

The intermittent big house events gave Crit a reprieve from work and the filth of the camp. For two or three days every few weeks, she could be human again, in some ways she felt it saved her life. She was also given less arduous daily assignments to preserve her beauty. Crit was not given field assignments out in the grueling sun, picking cotton and hoeing, nothing that would give her blisters and callouses.

Work in the cannery was a frequent task. Though no tea party, it was much better than other options. Some of the women in Camp D quit associating with Crit because of the favoritism she was shown as a party girl. She didn't care. Crit learned as a young teen that a girl had to do whatever it took to survive, and by damn she was going to survive this hellhole.

Crit had only worked on the Cordiality Crew for a few weeks before one of the guests reserved her for the night. She didn't know who he might be until she tapped lightly on his door and he stood before her. He was very tall, wore glasses and exuded the self-confidence of a man in his late thirties.

"Come in," he said, opening the door wider. He closed and locked the door behind her, loosening his necktie at the same time. "You're gorgeous. I could barely eat my dinner for looking at you tonight."

"She's even smaller than I thought, tiny, but everything about her is perfectly proportioned," he thought. He wanted to touch her, but it wasn't time yet. As a doctor, he touched patients all of the time. It was rarely sexual as he planned this night to be, although at times he did become stimulated. In reality, he was something of a bore, full of self-doubt. Getting to come to the Big House was the perfect set up for him to play the dominant male as he was in this bedroom.

"What's your name?"

"Just call me Crit, that's my nickname." She was looking straight up as he towered over her. "What's your name?" she asked.

He laughed. "Just call me 'Dr. B.'"

"Well, Dr. B, I haven't seen you around before."

"No, you haven't. I'm a visitor, a guest."

"What do you do? All of the men who come here are important. Are you important?" He laughed again. "More important to some than to others."

Crit sat down on the sofa and kicked off the high-heel shoes she was wearing. "Oh… I've been standing up all night. My feet hurt. I never wear heels except when I'm here at the Big House." She slowly peeled off her nylons and draped them across the back of the sofa. The act made her somewhat nostalgic. Sure wish I had my lacy black garter belt. I miss it; my red lace panties, too."

The doctor had watched her during cocktails, dinner and dessert as she floated around the room in her snugly fitted waitress uniform. Hands down she was the most beautiful woman there. He had said something about her to the man seated next to him and was told he could reserve her for the night if he had the hots for her.

"How do I do that?" he asked, as his interest soared.

"Go around that corner; there's a guy there taking reservations," his seat mate said as he nodded toward a partially hidden hallway.

Leaving his dessert unfinished, the doctor hurriedly left the table and made the arrangements immediately with a desk clerk seated in a reclusive alcove.

"I was told to come over here and talk to you. This is my first time to come to The Big House. I'm a guest." The doctor had perspiration on the top of his lip and wiped it on his coat sleeve. "Lots of humidity here," he explained.

"That's true. It's our pleasure to have you as our guest. What bedroom are you in this evening?" The clerk never looked at him directly, as if his presence was a well-kept secret.

"I'm in the Old Hickory room."

"Do you have a preference for a companion tonight?"

"Yes."

"Waiter or waitress?"

He momentarily flinched. "Waitress."

The clerk flipped open an album. "Would you choose her picture please?"

"There, that's her."

"Very good choice. This one is probably our youngest girl and has only been serving here for a few weeks. If you aren't pleased, just let me know. She will come to your door about an hour from now. Does that sound okay?"

"That would be perfect," the doctor responded with a nod.

"Help yourself to any of the items there in the basket if you think you might have use for them tonight."

The doctor picked up a condom and slipped it into his pocket.

Now, she lay before him, stretched out on the satin sofa like Cleopatra, his for the taking. "How old are you?"

His voice made Crit jump, as she had been thinking about her past. She could see he was looking at her silky legs and tiny feet. He sat opposite her head on the end of the sofa and took her feet into his lap. Her toenails had been painted bright red by the beautician, to match her fingernails. He caressed her feet, and slid his hand up and down her smooth legs and up under her short skirt.

"I'm twenty…almost."

"Does that feel good?"

Crit was enjoying being caressed by a man who wasn't crude, for a change. "It feels splendid."

"Do you want a drink?"

"We're not supposed to drink, but you won't tell on me, will you? We drink whenever we can snitch something while we are serving, even what's left in the glasses we pick up."

"Well, you get your own glass tonight, and as much as you want to drink." Putting her feet down gently on the sofa, he went over to the well-stocked bar. "Ice?"

"A little, maybe one cube. I don't want it to get watery." She sat up and put her feet on the floor. "You didn't tell me what you do to make a livin'."

"I do research."

"What kind of job is that?"

"I'm doing a special project for the government."

"What kind of project?"

He smiled at her innocent probing. "It's complicated, something you wouldn't know anything about. Very few people do." He handed her the drink and sat down beside her, touching her hair; feeling the softness of it.

"Well, where do you work?" She took a sip, waiting for his answer.

"East Louisiana State Hospital, over at Jackson."

"Where is that? I never heard of it."

"It's about a forty-minute drive from here, real close."

"Hmm, I didn't know that."

Her new suitor put his arm around her, putting his tongue in her ear. "That tickles." A shiver went through her as he kissed the nape of her neck.

"I need another drink." Crit played him along to get as many drinks as possible.

He got up and took her glass. "Maybe you could come over to the hospital to see me soon? I have a room there in the doctor's wing. I could show you around."

"Sure. I would love that if you can work it out. I know what you want, but that's better than being at Angola."

"If I ask for you, they will bring you."

"See. I knew you were important."

He laughed again, an easy, relaxing laugh, as he brought the second drink over to her. "Here, swallow this little pill and wash it down with this drink." He held the pill before her in his opened hand.

"What is it?" The drugs she used when she could get them were not pills.

"I know you have used before, maybe smoked a little pot, snorted some horse?"

"Why do you think I'm here? I sold heroin. I stole a car, too."

He raised his eyebrows. "You are experienced, aren't you, for a girl your age? Sounds like you've been around the block a few times."

"Well…what is it?" She took the drink he extended to her.

"It's LSD."

"I've never heard of LSD."

"It's something new. Try it. I guarantee you will like it. I'll get some more for you, as long as you belong to me when I come to these parties."

Crit popped the tiny pill into her mouth and washed it down with the drink, looking at this man she did not know as she took his dare.

"Now take off all of your clothes." He reached into his pocket for the condom he had picked up off of the desk when he reserved Crit for the evening. He knew these prison inmates were risky sex, but this mere slip of a girl he could not resist, as his lust overrode caution.

Crit stood up and began slowly dropping her garments one by one, as one of the strippers she had seen in Galveston. Dr. B was obviously enjoying the show; his eyes riveted on every newly revealed part of her body.

During the process, she began to feel dizzy and cold. By the time she was naked, her teeth were chattering, and she was shivering wildly. Then Crit started to giggle and laugh. "Look at that funny door; it's round. How did it do that?"

"Okay, you are on your way to LSD land." The doctor stepped out of his clothes and threw them on a chair. "Just give into it. Let the feelings have you."

Leaning against his naked body, she put her hands over her ears. "Why are you talking so loud? You don't have to shout at me. Quit changing shapes. You look so silly."

Crit was giggling as she rocked back and forth, then she threw back her head, laughing uncontrollably, while she tried to keep her balance. "Did you know I can fly? High!"

Her paramour for the evening picked her up and took her over to the luxurious bed. "Who are you?" she asked him. "Are you God?" Her speech was slurred, her head rolling around.

"That's one thing I'm not." Crit could smell the seductive scent of alcohol on his breath.

"I feel so sad. Why do I feel so sad that it hurts me?" Crit sobbed. She saw his flushed face over her as he held her wrists against the pillow before she started giggling again, without being able to stop.

During the following months, Dr. B visited the Big House whenever invited, reserving Crit each time. He took her gifts of candy, perfume, and drugs of all sorts. She liked LSD. She didn't go through a physical withdrawal from it, but mentally she wanted it desperately, a whole new driving addiction. But it was alcohol and heroin she craved most of all.

The doctor also sent for her often to stay for several nights at a time in his room at the hospital, where she willingly submitted to his sexual commands. To justify her presence at the hospital, he also performed the same tests on her that he was doing on some of the hospital patients, and a few inmates from Angola as well. The Army and the CIA had a keen interest in the use of LSD as a path to mind control. Not only would that possibility be useful during interrogation, but the manipulation of the will through the power of suggestion could create assassins with no regard for their own lives.

Crit was fortunate that Dr. B transferred before he got around to trying shock therapy on her. The downside of his leaving was that the sudden withdrawal of all drugs and alcohol left Crit without a supplier. For days she lay babbling, tied to a bed in Angola's inmate infirmary, fighting the demons of withdrawal.

As the months slowly passed by, the despair and abandonment of the women around Crit was written like a story upon their faces. Angry and forsaken, they didn't bother to count the days until their release from Angola. When they got out, most of them had no place to go anyway. With no social life or work skills, in all probability they would commit another crime and return to this place, where old inmate friends would welcome them back. Right back to the only familiar place they knew. Contrary to that way of thinking, Crit was hanging on, trying to survive and hold it all together, marking the days until she would be free.

No matter how tough she was she still felt a sense of isolation. Being surrounded by hundreds of people was no comfort. There were a hand full of women who had become superficial friends, a group where she could chat and exchange tales, but there was no way she shared anything in common with them. She also received an occasional letter from home, written in pencil on a piece of lined paper. Crit was glad to get them, though they were filled with a discouraging mix of conditional love, finger wagging, and condemnation. She would fold each letter and return it to the envelope, smelling the paper. It bore the unique scent of her mother.

Before November 9, 1942, Crit had no idea how negatively seven-hundred-thirty days and nights at a place called Angola could impact her mind and body. Not yet twenty-one years old, she had seen and experienced a Pandora's box of inhumane deprivation, cruelty, and debauchery. Still amazingly young and beautiful on the outside, within she was hardened, and as experienced in all things degenerate as an older woman more than twice her age. As if seared upon her forehead by a branding iron, she would ever be a convicted felon, as well as an ex-inmate of the Louisiana State Penitentiary at Angola.

Crit walked out the front gate of Angola on October 9, 1944, carrying a small amount of cash and wearing the complimentary, distinguishable dress issued to each woman when released from the Louisiana State Penitentiary. It hung on her like a sack.

A dust covered taxi awaited, pre-paid and pre-assigned to take Crit to the nearest bus station. Before entering the car, she stood a moment breathing in the air of freedom and staring at the vehicle. No shiny black limousine could have looked better.

Crit climbed into the back seat, sitting erect and holding her head high. She could barely remember who she had been two years before, but today, she was a free woman. As the taxi pulled away from the hated prison and onto the dusty gravel drive, Crit did not look back. Angola no longer held entitlement over her, not even a last glance.

In a short period, the taxi slowly pulled out onto LA Highway 66, and Crit was on her way to becoming…whoever she wanted to be.

Little "Crit" and her younger sister Mozelle (Photo Copyright Michael Marcades)

Christine, early incarceration, c. 1941 (Photo Copyright Michael Marcades)

Mr. and Mrs. Robert Rodman
(Photo Copyright Michael Marcades)

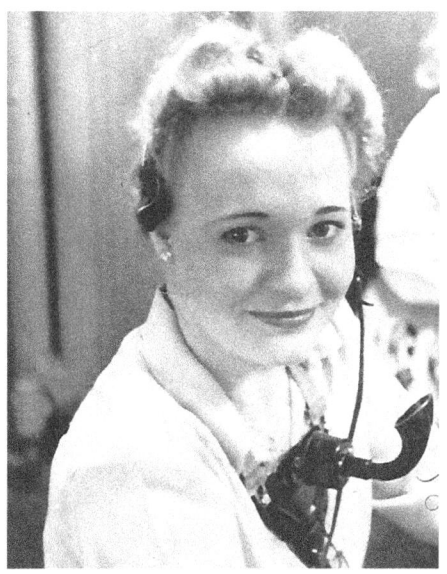
Christine, post-Angola c. 1944
(Photo Copyright Michael Marcades)

Mr. and Mrs. Robert Rodman
(Photo Copyright Michael Marcades)

Christine, visiting New Orleans
(Photo Copyright Michael Marcades)

Left to right: Grace, Minnie Bell, Mozelle, Christine
(Photo Copyright Michael Marcades)

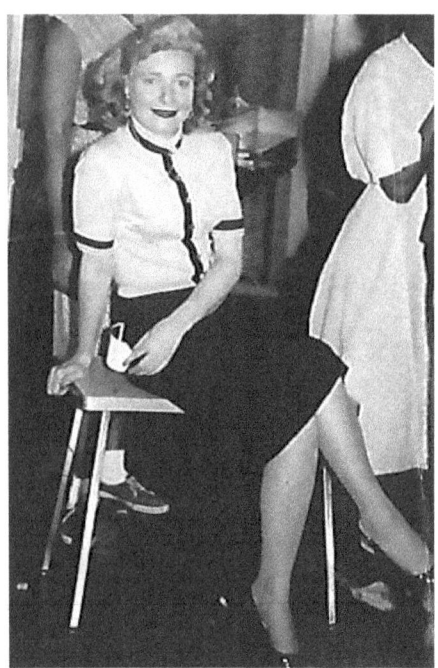

Left to right: Mozelle, Grace, Christine
(Photo Copyright Michael Marcades)

Christine c. 1952, New Orleans (Photo Copyright Michael Marcades)

Edward Joseph Marcades' home on Veteran's Boulevard, c. 1953 (Photo Copyright Michael Marcades)

Edward Joseph Marcades, U. S. Navy, c. 1946
(Photo Copyright Michael Marcades)

Christine with Michael at his christening, 1953 (Photo Copyright Michael Marcades)

Uncle Malcolm Guidry and paternal grandmother Jenny Guidry with Michael c. 1954.
(Photo Copyright Michael Marcades)

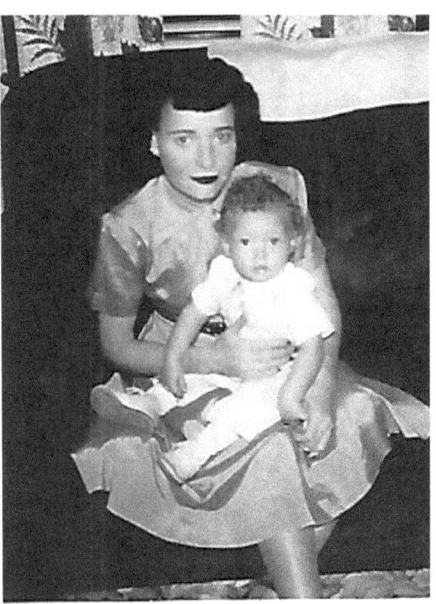

Christine with young Michael in New Orleans
(Photo Copyright Michael Marcades)

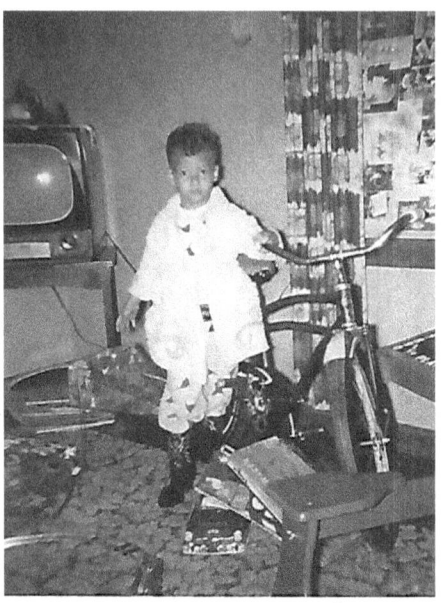

Michael's first Christmas with guardian grandparents in Houston (Photo Copyright Michael Marcades)

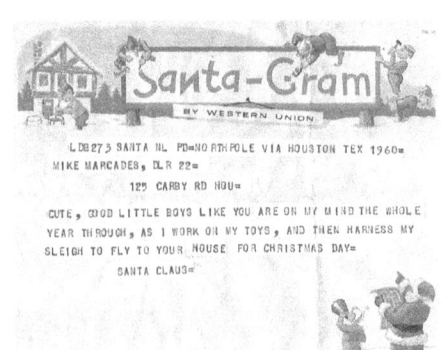

Santa Claus Gram to Michael, 1960
(Photo Copyright Michael Marcades)

Michael at Miss Connie's Playland, Houston
(Photo Copyright Michael Marcades)

Michael and his mother on Easter Sunday, 1959 (Photo Copyright Michael Marcades)

Michael and his maternal grandparents on Easter Sunday, 1959 (Photo Copyright Michael Marcades)

Christine, Sandy Lake c. 1962 (Photo Copyright Michael Marcades)

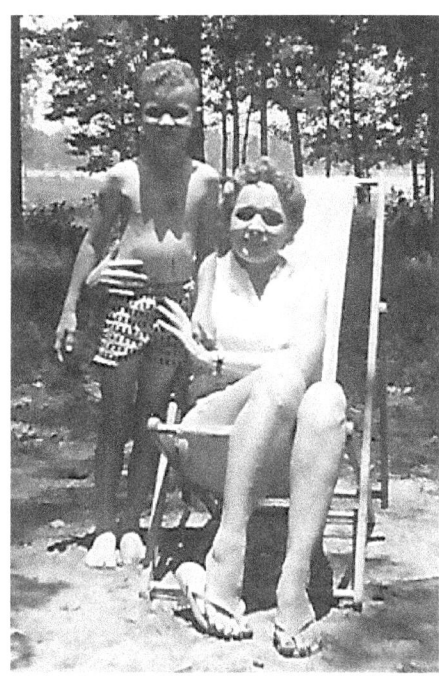
Michael and his mother at Sandy Lake (Photo Copyright Michael Marcades)

East Louisiana State Hospital (Courtesy of Joan Mellen A FAREWELL TO JUSTICE)

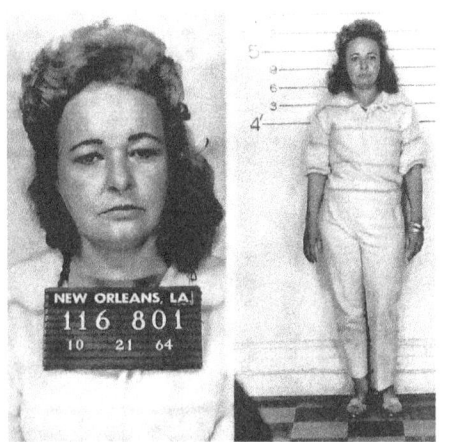 

Rose Cherami's final arrest mug shot,
New Orleans, 1964 (Photo Copyright Michael Marcades)

Melba Christine Youngblood Marcades funeral casket and headstone, Wheatland Cemetary, Duncanville, September 1965 (Photo Copyright Michael Marcades)

Michael with his maternal grandparents, Thomas Jefferson Youngblood and Minnie Bell Stroud Youngblood
(Photo Copyright Michael Marcades)

Michael's first visit with his father,
Edward Joseph Marcades, Metairie c. 1989
(Photo Copyright Michael Marcades)

Letter from Christine to her mother Minnie Bell, 1952
(Photo Copyright Michael Marcades)

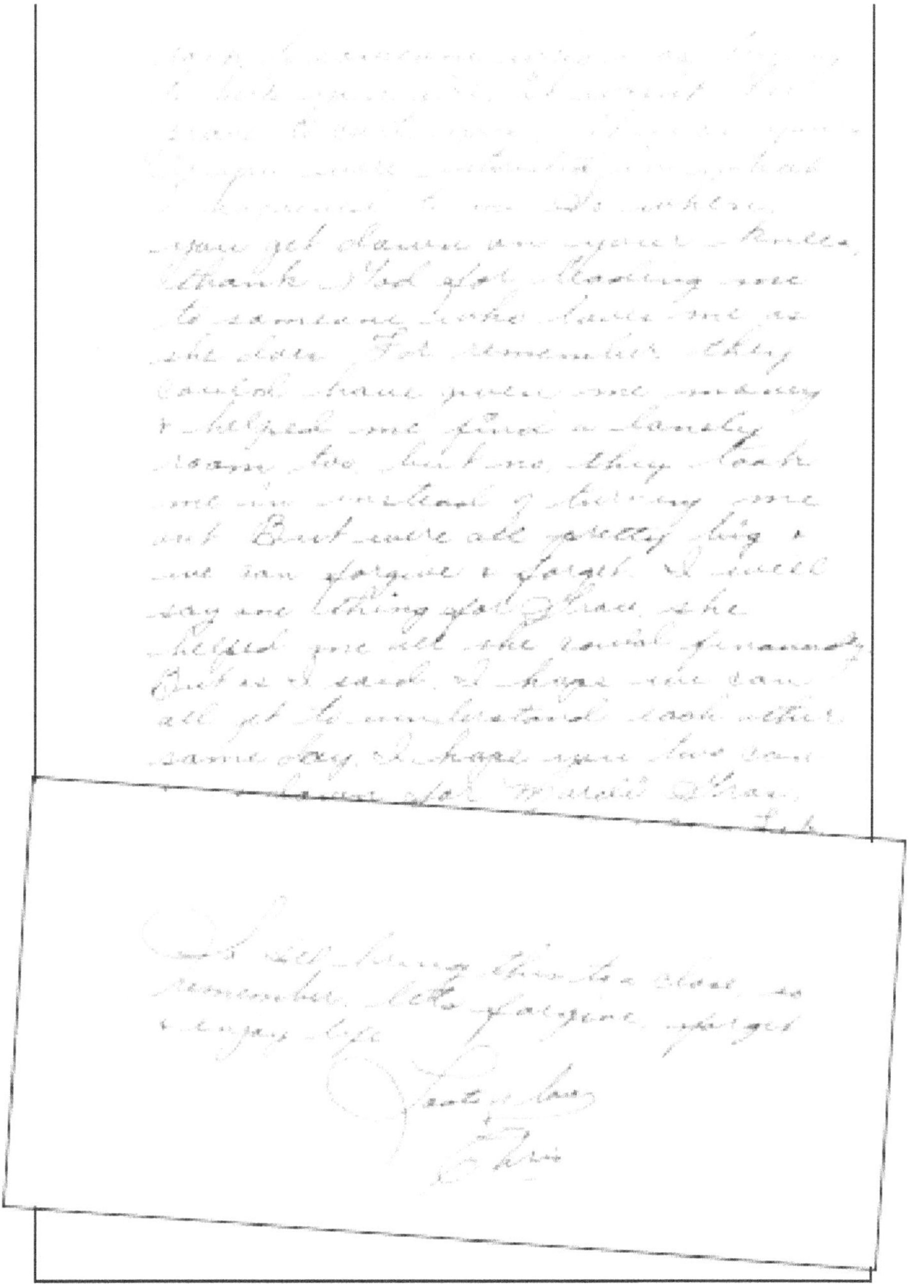

[illegible]

... happened to me. So when
you get down on your knees,
thank God for leading me
to someone who loves me as
she does. For remember they
could have given me money
& helped me find a lonely
room to but no they took
me in instead of letting me
out. But we're all pretty big &
we can forgive & forget. I will
say one thing for Grace, she
helped me all she could financially.
But as I said I hope we can
all get to understand each other
some day. I hope you two can
[illegible] for [illegible] Grace,
[illegible]

I [illegible] bring this to a close [illegible]
remember let's forgive & forget
& enjoy life.

Lots of love
&
Chris

CHAPTER 6

Sensual Sirens Entice: Bourbon Street (1944 - Early 1952)

Crit made her way from Angola to Aldine, Texas, a small town located just a few miles north of Houston. Her parents lived and labored there on a small tenant farm. Not knowing exactly where to go or what to do, she had called collect from the bus station after leaving prison. She wanted to tell them she had been released, and asked if she could come home. As she stepped down off of the Greyhound bus wearing the sack dress she had been given at Angola, Crit clutched a paper bag for a purse. It contained fifty cents in small change and one-half of a stale donut. At this time, that was her total worldly possessions. None of the things that were sealed in the cardboard box upon admission to Angola had been returned to her.

The bus roared as it accelerated back on to the highway, having dropped her off on the gravel shoulder. She stood for a moment, taking in the surroundings. It was the familiar place where she stood to hitchhike as a high school girl. Crit started walking the narrow blacktop road leading to the Aldine Farm, when she saw the old faded red pickup coming toward her. Her father made a U-turn and pulled up beside her as he leaned over and opened the door.

"Hello, Papa." Crit stepped up on the running board and slid into the seat.

"I guess I'm a little late. Can't never depend on that bus comin' when it says. You probably remember that, don't you Crit?"

"I remember a lot of things, Papa." They sat stiffly, not speaking.

Crit broke the silence. "I appreciate you and Mama lettin' me come back home until I can get on my feet and find some place to work." She spoke formally, almost as if her father was a stranger. The two of them were alien to one another in many ways.

"You know you can always come home, Crit, as long as you behave yourself and don't upset your Mama. Her nerves ain't too good since you was put in prison."

"I won't stay long."

As they pulled up into the yard of the well-kept farmhouse, Crit saw her mother standing out on the front porch. When she got out of the truck and started toward her, Minnie put her hands over her mouth and started crying.

"Crit, oh my baby, I didn't think I would ever see you alive again. You look so skinny and pale. What's that awful dress you're wearin'? Ain't you got no pride?"

"It's all I've got, Mama. This is what they give all of the women when they leave Angola." Crit looked down, speaking softly. She was trying to be patient with the lack of understanding from her parents.

Minnie reached out her arms as Crit stepped up on to the porch and into her embrace. Crit smelled dirty and stale. Minnie held back her judgmental nature and didn't comment to her daughter about that. "You're so thin and bony, like a chicken raised on the poor farm."

"I'm fine, Mama. I just wanted to come see you and Papa, and have a chance to clean myself up. Maybe there are still some clothes left in the closet from one of us girls."

"I didn't tell nobody you was comin', since you've been in prison and all. I didn't know what to say, anyway."

"I know, Mama."

"Crit ain't stayin' long, Minnie. She wants to look for a job." Tom stepped up on the porch, wincing from pain in his bad knee.

"A job? That's a good thing. Let's get in the house."

"Mama, I'm hungry."

Tom and Minnie looked at one another with great sadness to know their middle daughter, Melba Christine, had no food or clothes. They managed to forget themselves, all of the heartbreak, displeasure and worry Crit had brought into their lives, as they hovered over her with compassion. Their prodigal had come home.

Though Crit was young, it was weeks before she began to recover from her two-year imprisonment at Angola. She slowly began to function more normally. Undisturbed sleep, good meals, hot baths, peace and privacy were the balms she desperately needed; that and a new tube of bright red lipstick. She was starting to smile again.

Minnie was an excellent seamstress and made Crit a new dress, as her feet rocked back and forth on the treadle of the old Singer sewing machine. The dress was plain, but it fit. For decoration, Minnie had embroidered a rose on one shoulder along with Crit's initials: MCY. Tom threw the prison dress on the trash pile in the back lot and burned it with other refuse.

Herself again, vivacious, well-groomed and smiling, Crit found a job as a switchboard operator with a small phone company that serviced several rural communities. She had become a normal, regular person with a set routine and her own money. The rift between Crit and the rest of her family began to heal, as her parents, her sisters, and their families as well, cautiously let her back into their lives.

During that healing time, Crit met and married a fine young Army Air Force man, Robert E. Rodman. Everyone called him "Boy Bobby," a carry-over from his childhood. Of course he was smitten by Crit's beauty and fell head over heels in love with her. She had told him about her stent at Angola, it made no difference as far as he was concerned.

For the first time ever, Crit seemed satisfied and happy with the life they made together, as she went to her job at the telephone switchboard. For over two years, Crit did not drink or use drugs. She stayed out of trouble completely. It seemed that her stay at Angola was a lesson that took and her marriage to Robert had been what she needed.

Then, growing restless with the sameness of everything, the routine and lack of excitement made her begin to feel as if her job at the switchboard was a pretense and her marriage was a frustrating limitation. She wanted to go back to where the real Crit waited.

One day she walked out to the highway with a suitcase and hitchhiked into Dallas. She could no longer resist the call of her addictions and the pleasure of being with men. She felt empty without the highs from drugs, the sedating freeing of herself with alcohol, and the seductive admiration of men. Drugs, alcohol, and men; to Crit, life meant nothing without those three elements together and at the same time. She needed them all.

One month before Crit's 25th birthday, she was arrested twice in New Orleans, two weeks apart. Once under the name Melba Christina Youngblood, changing her name to Melba Christina Nichols the second time. The first charge was for Obscene Language, with a notation on the charges: Believed to be insane. The second arrest was related to the Dyer Act for acts crossing state lines.

A little more than five months later, she was arrested in Houston as part of an investigation, with the charges dismissed. As Crit's situation continued to deteriorate, she wandered from place to place, engaging in a variety of questionable activities, enslaved by her addictions. Within three years, she resurfaced in New Orleans, where once again she was arrested, this time for suspicion of theft of $100, and under the alias Rosa Lee Stewart.

Crit was not yet thirty years old as she looked at herself in the mirror of the women's restroom at the Greyhound bus station. She wasn't going on a trip, but with people always coming and going, she could hang around for periods of time without notice. Crit liked being back in New Orleans and was especially fond of the French Quarter. It did bother her to be in the same state with Angola. She hoped that her having no legal identification, being a good liar, and continuing to create new aliases, could keep her ahead of the law.

She washed her hair in the sink with cold water, using the bar of soap for public use. Crit leaned forward, tousling her wet hair into curls that would dry into place. She had been able to panhandle a cup of black coffee for breakfast, but would have preferred a stiff drink. The coffee and the cold water had helped to clear her foggy brain and awaken her self-respect.

Crit wiped the mirror off with a paper towel, and carefully applied the bright red lipstick, using a little on her finger to blush her cheeks. Her good looks and alluring smile had been both a boon and a bane in her life. Her history with spells of drunkenness and drug use, her term at Angola, through some miracle of nature had not taken that major asset away from her.

Done with her makeshift grooming, she glanced around craftily. She noted that a woman had gone into a toilet and locked the swinging door, leaving her leather bag outside the crowded stall. Crit turned the water on full force and made noise with the trashcan, before picking up the bag and walking confidently out the door and away from the bus station. Heading toward the French Quarter, she had already decided to see if she could find a steady job. Tired of working the streets, while trying to avoid arrest at the same time, Crit needed something more dependable.

The Storyville Red Light District of New Orleans lay adjacent to the French Quarter, on Basin Street. In the hay day of the district, patrons could find plenty to drink and every sort of entertainment the mind could conjure. Suggestive vaudeville acts, illegal gambling venues, houses of prostitution, and the strip tease of burlesque were all available in this jambalaya of experiences, designed to satisfy any lust of the flesh one might envision. The raucous sound of the hottest music in the land rolled out the doors of bars and brothels all through Storyville, as talents like King Oliver and Jelly Roll Morton belted out notes that made it impossible to listen and sit still at the same time.

Like most things that tease and titillate, the experience Storyville had offered in its day ran out of life and tolerance. The new generation of seekers for flesh-pleasures simply moved on to Bourbon Street. There, in the heart of the French Quarter, they brashly yelled to one another: *Laissez les bon temps rouler,* "Let the good times roll."

By the mid-twentieth century, "The Quarter," covering thirteen blocks from Canal Street to Esplanade Avenue, could still be identified by the influence of a centuries-old French Creole culture, and its inherent fondness for freewheeling morals. Uninhibited and self-indulgent, it had resisted Americanization by maintaining a unique lifestyle while adamantly protecting the distinctive architecture from the claws of change.

During the 1950's, over fifty adult clubs were thriving on Bourbon Street. Extravagant burlesque shows had taken the place of the outdated vaudeville acts once so popular in Storyville. Erotic striptease shows now had queues of exotic dancers in training, vying for the attention and benefits of making it to center stage burlesque. Among those clubs was The Blue Angel. It was at the top of the list for having the sexiest, most gorgeous strippers on Bourbon Street; this exclusive list included Melba Christine Youngblood.

The live music was so loud, talking was impossible, and no one was there for conversation anyway. Two young men strolled comfortably into The Blue Angel, hoping to find a seat at the bar. Edward Joseph Marcades, known to everyone as Eddie, was tall and handsome with a smile that would stop a streetcar. Malcolm, his somewhat shy half-brother, let Eddie lead the way through the crowd of men who were coming and going.

Eddie and Malcolm lived in New Orleans. The French Quarter was a normal part of life to them, as were the clubs on Bourbon Street. Unlike the out-of-town tourists who made fools of themselves in over indulgence and lewdness, the brothers saw the environment as a relaxing evening out on the town.

The darkness and smoke added mystery and a sense of the surreal to the scantily clad women undulating, bumping and grinding. The brothers wanted a seat up at the bar where they could watch the show reflected in the mirror that reached to the ceiling behind the bartender. The place was crowded as the heavy low mumble of male voices played undercurrent to the music and palpable sexuality in the atmosphere.

Isolated couples sat in dark corners, kissing passionately as a prelude to overt fondling, while groups of men sat around small circular tables, drinking and eating peanuts. They nudged one another, ogling the waitresses who would allow extra intimacies for a good tip. The servers knew how to increase the bar tab, and their tip as well, by flirting and teasing as they moved among the tables in their provocative outfits.

One of the crowd favorite strippers, dressed in fur, feathers and ornate jewelry, had taken her time, dancing and slowly removing items. Nearing the end of her show, the crowd grew more attentive. In four-inch glittery high heels, and little else, her figure was enhanced by her studied posture and stride. Turning her back to the gawkers, she removed her sequined bra, throwing it to the crowd over her shoulder.

A roar went up. "Come on, Celestine, take it all off and let us see what you got!!"
"Yeah! Come on, don't play around no longer!!"

She turned around as the stage lights blinked on and off rapidly, giving the impression of an old silent movie. Celestine took three long strides stage right, untied her G-string and hurled it through the air before disappearing. Men shoved and scrambled to claim the trophy, while onlookers laughed and talked about Celestine's "knockers." And then they lied about their female conquests of grandiose proportions.

"Hey boys, I'm Iris," the hostess said, approaching Eddie and Malcolm, with a warm smile. "I didn't want you to miss seeing Celestine's finale. Can I find a seat for you?"

"Hey beautiful, do you have something over there at the bar?" Eddie never met a stranger; women especially found him charming. Malcolm envied Eddie that he found it so easy to talk to people.

"Since you two guys are so handsome, I'm sure I can find a couple of spaces at the bar for you. You don't mind squeezing in, do you?" She winked flirtatiously. "I'll bet you two boys know all about squeezing."

They both laughed as they followed her to the popular bar area. She asked a couple of men standing at the bar talking to the bartender to move over, and pulled out two stools where there seemed to be none.

"Thanks for taking care of us, Iris." Eddie gave her a tip.

"Anything, anytime for you, Eddie baby," she said, pressing against his chest and kissing his cheek.

"You're a lucky SOB, Eddie. No chick would give me a kiss with a little tittie rubbing at the same time." Malcolm's cheeks were flushed.

Eddie laughed and slapped Malcolm on the back as they sat down on the stools. "You should have tipped her, tight wad."

As the bartender looked their way, Eddie held up two fingers and pointed toward his choice of beer. The bartender pulled two tall bottles out of a bin of crushed ice. Removing the caps and wiping the bottles off with a bar towel, he then slide them expertly down the bar to stop in front of Eddie and Malcolm.

"How the hell does he do that?" No matter how many times he had seen the feat before, Malcolm still found it amazing.

"Practice." Eddie licked the foam off of the top of the bottle before lifting the cold, refreshing beer to his lips.

Eddie liked to spend time down in the Quarter. The camaraderie was infectious among those who were accustomed to crawling the clubs in the French Quarter. A couple of old friends called out his name from one of the tables, as he responded with a nod. Eddie was muscular and well built, muscles hardened by his time in the Navy and still well developed from his civilian job of heavy labor in the railroad yard. He was a stand out in a crowd with jet-black wavy hair, dark eyes, Greek features and olive complexion. His disarming, infectious smile drew people to him, as did his approachable manner.

He and Malcolm sat sipping their beer, watching the total action of the room reflected in the mirror behind the bar. They didn't talk much; it wasn't worth the effort above the deafening noise in the club. The center stage lights lifted, then turned into a soft blue haze as the band changed cadence into a sensuous number that drew all eyes to the venue.

Out of the mist emerged a slender, petite woman wearing elevated emerald green high heels, holding two large fans made of flowing white feathers held tantalizingly in front of her nude body. Her blonde curls were held up on her head by a jeweled clip that matched her shoes, her flawless skin like cream.

That was the first time Eddie saw her, Melba Christine Youngblood. He turned around on the bar stool so he could see her more completely, the bar mirror no longer adequate. His heart was pounding from a surge of testosterone.

As she started moving sensually to the music, Crit was carried back to the memory of that night so long ago in Houston, when she had returned to her rented room, tired and disgusted. The sounds of Benny Goodman playing his sweet clarinet over the old radio had drawn her up from the bed in the isolation and seclusion of the bedroom as she began to free herself, moving to her feelings. Timid and hesitantly at first, she had gradually evolved into a state of total abandon and loss of inhibitions. That was the same true freedom she felt every time she took the stage at The Blue Angel.

Unlike others who had enticed the male patrons with manipulative, self-serving, flirtatious glances and peeks, Crit's sensual disinterest in those who watched her on stage, made her all the more alluring. Her aloof manner was maddening to the male onlookers as they stared at the unobtainable.

With slow, flowing motions, Crit allowed the gift of casual glances at her body and exposed skin as she skillfully changed positions with the feathered fans. Malcolm and Eddie were drawn deeper into Crit's artistically seductive web. They sat motionless, held in place by silent stares.

As the music stopped, Crit stood before the onlookers like a perfect, porcelain doll. Breathing heavily from the emotional display, her breasts were heaving up and down.

Applause, hoots and hollers erupted throughout the club from dozens of half-sober patrons who were characteristically oblivious to the soulful, erotic art that had been created before their eyes. Even they knew this had been something special, but only knew how to react to the carnal part of her dance, and not the artistic overtones.

Such an unbridled and unique display of emotion left some in the room discomfited, which included Eddie and Malcolm. As the stage lighting faded away, they looked at one another with mingled embarrassment and awe.

"Oh, my God. What was that?" Eddie put his hands on his head.

"I've never seen anything like that before, and that's the truth," Malcolm said.

"Malcolm, I've got to meet that girl tonight before we leave here!"

"Oh yeah, sure thing, Eddie. No problem," Malcolm responded sarcastically. He and Eddie had picked up girls before, but nothing like this publically known bombshell. She was out of their league.

No sooner than he had that thought, out of the corner of his eye, Malcolm saw Crit as she walked through the crowd. Passing the elevator that led to the elite second floor where the high rollers had a private playground, she greeted a few friends at the other end of the bar before heading toward Eddie and Malcolm. As she neared, Malcolm grabbed Eddie's shoulders and spun him around so he could see her approach.

She was even more beautiful off stage than on. The subdued lighting of the room cast shadows on her face, enhancing her exquisite facial features. Her hair was down and the blonde curls bounced around her face as her petite and perfectly proportioned form glided closer. She was definitely a presence. To men, and to women who were secure enough to admit it, the entire package was hallucinogenic.

Confidently, though not a surprise to Malcolm, Eddie shifted his body directly into Crit's oncoming path. Smiling flirtatiously, he placed his piercingly dark eyes squarely on hers.

This was not the first time a patron had approached Crit after one of her shows. She had learned how to handle all kinds of customers, ranging from those who had too much to drink, to those who aggressively tried to proposition sex. As a last resort, she could always give the bouncer a nod and he would take care of it.

As Crit neared Eddie, she took inventory; handsome, dark, great body, jet-black wavy hair, and eyes that wouldn't let go of hers. She felt something as she drew closer to him, while pretending to be disinterested. He had a very sensual aura.

"Excuse me, babe. Do you have a minute?" There was a dense, masculine softness and slight sound of Greek accent in the way he spoke. Crit was enamored of the sound and was unable to hold back a smile.

His head was spinning that the beautiful showgirl he had just watched on stage was now standing right in front of him, so close he could reach out and touch her, if he dared. "I've, uh, we've never seen anything like that routine you just did." Eddie returned her smile.

"Yeah," Malcolm barely mumbled. "Nothin' like it."

Crit responded demurely, "Thanks guys. You're sweet to say that."

The two men thought her voice sounded like music from the portals of the gods. "Any chance I could buy you a drink?" Eddie asked, as he motioned for Crit to claim his bar stool next to Malcolm.

"Why not? My shift just ended and I'm off the clock." Crit crawled up on to the bar stool and crossed her legs. Eddie could see her exposed thighs and quickly looked away, his face flushing.

"What can I order for you?" Eddie was cautious with his choice of words as he tried to make a good impression.

"He knows what I like." Crit nodded toward the bartender.

Eddie lifted a finger to catch the bartender's eye. He walked over and stood in front of them with a toothy grin.

"Uh, yeah, we'll have two cold ones, and whatever this lady likes," Eddie said.

"Comin' right up." He looked at Crit. "Christine, you were on fire tonight! Hell of a show, baby. It's hard for me to keep my mind on my work when you're on stage."

Feeling jealous of the familiarity between Christine and the bartender, Eddie swelled out his chest and stood erect to accentuate his full height as he extended his hand to Crit.

"Hi, I'm Eddie. Eddie Marcades. This here's my brother, Malcolm. And, if I heard the bartender right, your name is Christine, right?"

"Yes…Christine, Melba Christine. Most people just call me Crit."

As they shook hands, Eddie was intensely aware of the softness of her skin, and how her hand was dwarfed in his. "Christine…that's a pretty name," said Eddie as they shook hands. "We're both from N'Awlins, just out on the town for a little fun after work. Lucky for us, we dropped by the Angel tonight just in time to see you." The two brothers took a deep swig out of their beer bottles, as Crit took a sip from her glass.

"You were something else up there, heck, you were just plain beautiful. Those feathers floatin' around in front of you." Eddie was starting to get carried away, as Malcolm looked at him and lifted his eyebrows in warning.

The three of them made small talk as the two men started on their third beer. Crit wanted to drink more, lots more, but had been working at more self-control when it came to liquor and drugs. It was hard for her.

She studied Eddie. Now in her late twenties, Crit had encountered and been involved with lots of men since leaving home at the age of sixteen. She knew what made men tick and how to manipulate their weaknesses to her gain. Men found her attractive, irresistible, so finding a man was never an issue. However, finding a good man infused with enduring sensuality always seemed to be out of her reach.

Throughout the conversation, Crit cautiously answered questions without revealing too much about her present or past. She seldom talked about Angola with anyone after the day she left that hellhole. Mostly, she studied Eddie, trying to figure him out. He seemed a combination of things; suppressed fury, inner strength, and an unusual compassion coupled with total masculinity. She maintained her emotional and physical distance from Eddie, having been burned before by trusting too much and too soon.

Crit drained her glass and sat it decisively down on the bar. She wheeled around on the bar stool, standing up quickly as if she planned to leave.

"Hey, where you goin', Crit? The night's young," pressed Eddie.

"Look, it's been a long day, I'm exhausted," Crit responded firmly, but with kind directness.

"Well, when can I see you again?" Eddie asked, as if he had known her longer than just an hour.

"Uh, I'm workin' tomorrow night, same time. Maybe I'll see both of you then." Crit's response left the door open, giving Eddie hope.

"Christine, I'll be here," Eddie confirmed, as he and Malcolm stood like gentlemen and shook Crit's hand.

"Okay, Eddie. I'll see you then." She smiled up at him as an indication of her expectancy that he would be there.

As Crit walked away from the bar, down the crowded aisle, and headed toward a set of stairs leading to the employee dressing room, she could feel Eddie's eyes following her. As she reached the stairs opening, she glanced back over her shoulder toward the bar, and their eyes met.

Through the dim light and smoky haze, Crit gave Eddie one more smile before disappearing down the stairs. That look said more to Eddie than spoken words; they both wanted to see one another again.

With each downward step, Crit continued to think about all that had just transpired. Everything had happened so quickly, and so naturally. She felt anxious that Eddie might not come back and she would never see him again. If he does come back, what then?

"What in the hell are you doing, Crit?" she asked herself aloud. She reminded herself that men were seldom anything more than on the prowl, thinking only of their own sexual desires. It was easy for them to use a woman and throw her away. This time, she was determined she was not going to be consumed, chewed up and spat out in emotionally and physically abused pieces. That had happened every time she allowed herself to begin to care about a man. Even if Eddie was immensely attractive to her, she determined not to go there again.

As Crit entered the dressing area to get her purse and a sweater stashed under her personal make-up table, she could see some of the other women in the room reflected in the mirror that was encircled with lightbulbs. The top burlesque stars shared the space, separated from the bevy of ingénues serving tables who hoped to take their place some day at the top of the list. In different stages of dress and undress, they were whispering, while throwing glances her way.

"Hey, girls! What's up? I think I heard my name as I was coming down the stairs." She looked at them in a way that demanded an answer.

Now discovered, the women shuffled around and glanced sheepishly at one another.

After an uncomfortable pause, one of the more outgoing dancers spoke up. "We weren't being gossips, Crit, but couldn't help noticing you at the bar with those two heart throbs. The really handsome one was staring you up and down like he couldn't decide where he wanted to start first."

The tension in the room relaxed as they all laughed. "Yeah, Crit. You don' need two of them anyway. Give us one," another woman said, as they all laughed again. "Who are they?"

Normally, Crit would have been right in the middle of the buzzing hive of chatter, but her feelings felt more personal this time.

"Look, ladies. We all know how it is around here. After every show, some guy is so wound up from watching us dance that they'll do anything to meet us. That's what our routines are all about. These guys didn't seem any different, maybe a little sweeter than most. That's it. As for the one doing all the talking, we'll see if he's like all of the rest who are just in it for what they can get, and ready to pay for it. You all know about that."

They laughed again. "We sure do. A girl has to make a livin', so get it up and pull it out, but show me the money first!" one yelled. Another said, "Yeah, and from the looks of you buster, you better have plenty of money!"

Generally, The Blue Angel clientele were well-heeled and came expecting to pay top dollar for time with the top performers. It was not uncommon for middle-aged and older men, near a drunken stupor and already spent by the end of a stripper's routine, to have nothing left in their quiver but groping and fondling, but they still paid big anyway. The weren't above taking money off of a man who wasn't going to remember any of it the next day anyway.

Crit picked up her belongings to leave. "See you later, girls. *Laissez les bon temps rouler!*"

Weary of the conversation, Crit headed out the secret passageway reserved for the women in her dressing room. Leading up to street level, it was much easier for them to get out unnoticed by tourists and obnoxious customers who felt they were public property. The women had not sensed Crit was holding back her true feelings regarding

Edward Marcades, Eddie. She did not think of him as a customer. Crit stepped out on Bourbon Street, where the swarming mass of humanity seldom slept, and where she could disappear.

~

Though Crit was one of the best paid dancers at The Blue Angel and something of a star in the Quarter, she was not able to afford one of the nicer residential apartments on Bourbon Street. She lived in a cramped apartment with limited comforts. Every time she went there after work, she vowed that someday she would dance her way into something better and there was a promising future ahead. Her self-confidence and self-reliance never wavered, though her lack of self-discipline repeatedly destroyed each opportunity to reach her dreams.

~

Crit was looking forward to getting back to the club to prepare for her night shift. With a few personal items in a paper sack, she left the apartment and bought a praline from a street vendor. The distinctively New Orleans sugar treat would give her the energy lift she was going to need to carry her into the unpredictable late hours. All she could think about was Eddie. Would he really be there, as he said? Would she catch sight of him from the stage as she had done the night before?

~

"Oh God, please let him be there," Crit whispered. She walked with a bounce as she imagined they might meet again.

As she reached the club, Crit entered the private side door leading down to the hidden passageway, and straight to the dressing room. She greeted the girls who had arrived before her, but didn't stop for pre-show chatter as usual. All she could think of was Eddie and how she wanted to look irresistible for him.

Crit was more meticulous than usual with her choice of costume and cosmetics. Putting on a silky dressing robe, she leaned forward into the mirror. Deciding to leave her hair down, she pulled it over to one side across her brow with a jeweled clip. She carefully applied foundation and blush, gently patting silken powder over her face, somewhat Geisha style. The paleness accented her large eyes as she attached long false black eyelashes, with tiny zircon jewels glued in a row at the roots. She drew a line outside her natural lips to emphasize them, filling in with the purest red color she could find, it was the color she had chosen since the first day she wore lipstick.

Crit finished up with bright blue eye shadow, and coal black eyebrows drawn to perfection, just like Greta Garbo.

She stood up and removed the silk robe. Standing nude before the mirror, Crit attached red sequined pasties with a tassel over her nipples, and tied on a matching G-string. Her teasing props were two large red fake fur muffs. She struck a few poses and practiced moves with the muffs so as not to reveal everything too early in the routine.

"Five minutes, baby! You're on in five!" shouted the stage manager.

She took a deep breath and whispered under her breath, "This is for you, Eddie." Looking at herself one more time, Crit went up the steps in her red satin high heels and struck a pose on a glittery swing as she was lifted into the air. The adrenaline surge she felt before each performance was better than a drug high; Crit knew she totally owned the moment.

"Ladies and gentlemen, but mostly gentlemen," barked the announcer as the crowd laughed, "The Blue Angel proudly presents tonight's center-stage delight, the lovely Melba Christine!"

Before he completed announcing her name, the room erupted into wolf whistles and cat calls. The band slid into music that would have charmed a snake as the spotlight beam was thrown on Crit, where she stood on the swing above the stage. Surprised, the crowd cheered again. She stood there provocatively as the swing was slowly lowered to touch the floor. Crit then stepped forward in her red satin heels and black fishnet stockings.

It was a cleverly contrived routine to draw the eyes of everyone seated around their drinks. Crit was especially good at coming up with fresh new ideas and the patrons were never bored. Her routine was always sophisticated and womanly, with a confident sensuality, unlike the bawdy, front on display of the young girls. While everyone was staring at her, she was scanning the crowd, searching for a pair of dark eyes she wanted to see again.

She glided gracefully toward the front of the stage as coins were being tossed by her admirers. A few men, with folded money, were able to slip the bills into her muffs as she leaned over toward them. As they looked up at her, Crit gave them a satisfying view of everything the muffs had been hiding, especially a good look at the tiny red pasties with dangling tassels and the voluptuous breast they decorated.

A large bouncer stood on the floor, keeping control of the men who surged forward, wanting to get next to the stage. Her ability to tease the men in ways like this drove them wild, and greatly increased her income for the week. She always tipped the bouncer who gathered up the coins and protected her.

As Crit turned her back to the crowd, holding a red muff over her derriere, she looked provocatively over her right shoulder toward the bar, and there he sat in exactly the same place he had been the night before. It was Eddie, as he had promised.

Though the room was dark, Eddie's outline was unmistakable. She turned back around and vamped toward that side of the stage. Eddie stood up as their eyes met, making sure she could see him. For a brief moment, Crit forgot what she was doing, until the familiar notes of the band grew louder as an introduction to the end of her routine.

She blinked and looked away, turning her back again and undulating to the music as she returned to the swing now lifted above the floor. She took a seat with her back to the onlookers. As it rose into the air, colored mist fogged the stage. Crit had a muff pulled up on each arm as she leaned backward and pointed her fishnet covered legs and red satin heels into the air, revealing the full length of her body before the spotlight darkened. The place broke into applause, whistles and yells.

Crit raced down the stairs to her dressing room and kicked off the uncomfortable red satin heels. She could think of nothing but Eddie. "I hope he liked it," she thought. She was ecstatic that he had come back and was waiting for her at the bar. "What's wrong with me? I feel like I'm sixteen again." She carefully removed the glued on pasties and pulled off the G-string that had ridden up into her crotch.

As Crit was putting on street clothes and shoes, she was trying to resist the thought that she had felt like this before, many times. Each time, it ended in disappointment and disaster.

All of the men she had ever known, even her own father, were capricious and selfish. They had used her to meet their physical desires. Totally uncaring and unfeeling about her as a woman with her own needs, who wanted to be loved and treasured, they had exploited her instead.

"It's different this time," she thought.

Crit took her paper sack of personal items with her so she wouldn't need to go back to the dressing room. As she walked the length of the bar, she and Eddie saw one another. He flashed his captivating smile as she drew closer, making her feel warm and safe. Looking into his eyes, she smiled back. Eddie reached out his arms toward Crit and she walked into them as if it were the most normal thing in the world.

Her blonde curls covered his face as he whispered into her ear. "You are so beautiful, Crit. You were just great up there. I wouldn't have missed seeing you again for anything in the world!" He kissed her cheek before she stepped back to look at him. He took the paper sack out of her hands and sat it under his bar stool.

"Eddie, you're sweet. I danced for you tonight. I pretended you were the only man here."

His face flushed as his desire for her was hard to control. "Can I buy you a drink?" "Sure, you know I'm off the clock now," she replied, with twinkling eyes and a slight smile. "Where's Malcolm?"

"He wasn't invited tonight." Eddie laughed. "I want you all to myself."

As Crit sat on the stool, sipping her drink, Eddie stood protectively beside her, his arm around her shoulders. They were whispering and laughing as if they had been a couple for years.

"Christine, why don't you let me get you out of this noisy place. We could go somewhere else where it's easier to talk and we could have a nice dinner together. Would you like that?" Eddie, tall and standing above her, put his hand gently under her chin to lift her face so he could look into her eyes.

She lit up with delight. "I would love it, but I need to go to the bathroom first."

"Okay, I'll pay the tab and wait here for you. I haven't finished my beer anyway. I'll get your things."

"I'll hurry."

"I'll be here when you come back." He leaned down and kissed her on the cheek again.

Eddie stood watching her as she left. He sat back down on the stool and emptied his bottle of beer before paying the tab, putting Crit's paper bag under his arm so he wouldn't forget it. "I can't believe it," he thought. "Not me, not in a million years. Not with a woman like that!"

It felt like forever to Eddie, but Crit returned in a few minutes. "I'm ready," she yelled above the loud music.

"God, you're beautiful," he yelled back.

"What?"

"Later." He mouthed the word.

Crit smiled up at him as he took her hand and guided her through the crowd. Some of the patrons gave them a nod, or a smile of recognition as they were leaving. Crit could never remember feeling so safe and secure in all of her life as she did now, with her hand held by such a man as this.

Once out the front door, Eddie led Crit to his car and let her choose where she wanted to go for dinner. He treated her like a man should treat a lady who was his date, with gentleness and respect. That was something she had not experienced for many years.

Eddie was a charmer all throughout the evening, as they dined on the marvelous New Orleans cuisine served at one of the Quarter's finest restaurants. Sitting in an intimate circular booth, they sat side by side sharing a piece of bourbon cheesecake and having dark roast coffee to top off their delicious dinner.

Eddie looked around. "You know, Crit, we're the last people here. Maybe we should leave now so these people can go home."

"Oh, my gosh, you're right, Eddie. I didn't realize we had been here so long. I could talk with you forever."

"Same here." He slid out of the booth and took her hand. "Is it okay if I take you home now?"

"Yeah. It's not far from here."

"Good thing we had some coffee. I've had a lot to drink tonight," Eddie said, as he opened the car door for Crit.

"Me, too."

As Eddie got in on the other side, he motioned for her to slide over beside him. Crit scooted across the seat and put her head on his shoulder, he kissed her forehead. She told him where to turn, what streets to take and pointed out a parking place when they arrived at her residential apartment.

As they got out of the car, Eddie noticed there were no street lights on the side street where she lived. "Crit, are you okay here? This can be a rough place, especially after dark." Alert and on guard, he glanced around cautiously.

"Oh, I'm makin' it okay. When I get rich and famous, I'll move to a mansion." She giggled, silly from food, drinks, and the late hour. "For now it will do; hell, I've seen and lived in worse than this. Lot's worse."

The teasing didn't make Eddie feel any better. He was concerned for Crit's safety, feeling protective of her. "I'm going to walk you to your apartment door so I won't be worried about you," he said.

Crit took Eddie's hand and led him up the stairs to her small apartment. As they stood in front of her door, Eddie slid his arm around Crit's tiny waist and pulled her close for a goodnight kiss.

"Thank you for a wonderful night, Eddie. You are such a sweet man."

"How can I reach you when you're not at work? Do you have a phone?"

Crit nodded and gave him her phone number. He repeated it several times so he wouldn't forget it. Crit stood on her tiptoes, pulling his head down for another kiss.

"Get some sleep now, Crit. I'll call you before you go to work, okay?"

"Please do." Crit unlocked and opened her apartment door, smiling at Eddie through the crack before she closed it. The lock clicked.

Eddie walked to his car, whistling. He would pay the price of going to work in a few hours without much sleep, but he didn't care. "Christine, Christine, what a beautiful name. What a beautiful woman."

The coming weeks were filled with similar times together, as Crit and Eddie became inseparable. As Crit's sense of love and trust grew, she began sharing more and more about her past with Eddie. She told him about her childhood, her running away to Houston and Amarillo. She tentatively told him about Angola, and serving two years there on the larceny charge. No matter what she told him, he remained steadfast and steady in her life. It was a catharsis for Crit.

It was still a struggle for her to continue to be so open about all of the things she had done. Her life read like a rap sheet, arrests for vagrancy, automobile theft, aiding armed force soldiers to go AWOL, petty theft, public obscenity, and other outbursts that caused her to be labeled as insane. And then, there were also charges for prostitution.

Her deepest fear was that she would lose Eddie. He was one of the few wonderful things that had happened to her since she left home and went out on her own. It was extraordinary to know that the majority of men would have run away from any woman with a life story like Crit, but Eddie did just the opposite. His empathy and passionate love seemed indestructible, no matter what she told him. It was amazing to Crit, and brought tears to her eyes, having never encountered such forgiveness.

When they weren't working, Eddie and Crit were together, usually all night until sunrise. They often fell asleep in one another's arms at his place, her place, and sometimes in Eddie's car. He continued to work at his heavy labor job in the railroad yard, she as a stripper at The Blue Angel.

Eddie had talked with Crit about moving in with him, and also about going with him to meet his mother. Crit had already met Malcolm at the club. For the first time ever, Eddie seemed to offer a normal life to Crit, stability and lasting contentment.

Eddie had left for work and Crit was sleeping in after an unusually long night at the club. Oddly, she awoke with her mother on her mind. For some reason, she never quit longing for love and acceptance from her family, and for their elusive approval. Crit wanted to share her new found happiness with Eddie, and wanted her family to be happy for her.

She had not talked with her mother for many months, nor told her what she was doing, except that she was in New Orleans. Courageously, Crit picked up the phone and called Minnie collect again; she always prayed her father wouldn't answer.

Crit could hear the phone ring, and her mother pick up. "Hello? Will you accept a collect call from Christine Youngblood?"

"Yes, I will." Her mother replied with poorly disguised disgust.

"Mama?"

"Crit, is that you? Where are you this time? I guess you're in trouble again, or I wouldn't be hearin' from you."

"Mama, I'm fine. It's just been a long time and I decided I would call."

"Where are you?"

"I'm in New Orleans, been here for months."

"I guess that's a long time for you to stay in one place."

"Everything is good, Mama. I'm workin' steady at a big club on Bourbon Street, and Mama, I've met a wonderful man, he's not like the others. His name is Eddie, Eddie Marcades."

"I never heard a name like that before. I guess he's some kind of foreigner."

"No, he's not. He lives here in New Orleans. He really loves me, Mama, and wants me to meet his mother. He's told her about me."

"Oh, Crit, are you sleepin' with him?"

"Mama, are you listening to me? I said he loves me! I've told him everything I've done and he still loves me!"

"If you keep sleepin' with every man you meet, you're goin' to get some bad disease."

"Look, I just thought I'd call and let you know I'm okay, and happy. I gotta go now, Eddie's pickin' me up for a late breakfast. Tell Papa I said hello, and Mama, I love you. I hope you can meet Eddie some day and see what a nice man he is. Goodbye."

Click.

When Eddie came by on his morning break to take Crit for beignets and café au lait, he found her crying uncontrollably. "What's wrong, baby?" He took her into his arms, holding her tightly.

She just shook her head, so grateful to have Eddie's comfort. "Nothin'."

He lifted her chin. "It must be somethin' that would make you cry like this. I've never seen you cry before. Come on, let's go down to the French Market and talk about it together."

She nodded and dabbed at her eyes with a tissue. "Okay."

As they sat in the open air market with their coffee and beignets, she shared about the phone call to her mother.

"Eddie, I tried to tell her about you and it hurt me so bad that she wouldn't even listen to how much we love each other. I thought maybe she would be happy for me. All she does is criticize me and belittle everything I do, that's what she always does even if we haven't seen each other or talked in months! She's my mother! You would think she could find a little love in her heart for me somewhere." Crit blew her nose.

Eddie reached over and patted her hand. "I'm sorry Crit. I know you are all alone here with no family and that is hard on you."

"I have you."

"You sure do, baby. You've always got me." He looked at her tenderly. "Do you have any other family, we really haven't talked about that."

"I have two sisters. My baby sister, Mozelle, lives in North Dallas with her husband Morris. She has a deaf daughter, Dianne, and a little boy, Dennis. I haven't seen them in a long, long time, or even talked on the phone."

Eddie sat quietly, trying to think of some way to cheer Crit and show his love for her. "Why don't you go to see her and her family?"

"I can't do that," Crit said dejectedly.

"Why not? You need some time off from your job anyway, and I will pay for your bus ticket."

"You would?" Crit looked at Eddie with disbelief, hardly knowing how to act that anyone should care so much about her feelings and her needs.

"Sure. I have a good job. Why not? Of course I would miss you awful, but I think it would be a good thing for you."

"It's a long way, but maybe," Crit said pensively.

"Just think about it, baby doll. I've got to get back to work now. Don't cry anymore, Crit. I can't stand to see you unhappy, not if I can do anything about it." Eddie looked at her with a pained expression.

As he drove back to her apartment, Crit snuggled close under his arm. He was always struck by how tiny and fragile she seemed. "I love you, Eddie. You are the most wonderful man in the world. No one has ever loved me like you." He kissed her forehead.

Crit tentatively put through a call to Mozelle. When she answered, the conversation was immediately stilted as Mozelle spoke coldly to her sister. One polite phone call was not going to eradicate the years of hurt, disappointment, suspicion and outright anger between the two women.

"Mo, things are different now. I have a good job, and though I know it's hard for you to believe, I have a good man. His name is Eddie, Eddie Marcades."

There was a pause on the other end of the line. "Oh, really? A job and a man, huh? I've heard that before, Crit."

Mozelle's judgmental tone grated on Crit as she fought against the urge to hang up. Crit spat out, "I guess I had that comin' from you, baby sister, but I'm tellin' you Eddie is one hell of a man and nothin' like the other men I've known."

Mozelle hated Crit's cursing and crudeness. "Come on, Crit, stop talking that way. No need to cuss. You know we don't talk like that at our house," she scolded.

Crit reluctantly broached the subject of her phone call. "Look, let's not fight. I want to come see you, Morris and the kids. I love Dallas and it would really be wonderful if I could stay at your house. I won't be any trouble, and if I want to go somewhere, I will take a cab. So, what do you think? Can I come?"

"Well, you know I'm not going to turn you away, Crit. We'll do what we can to help you, so come on. What are your plans?" Mozelle sighed and sounded resigned.

"Eddie is going to buy my ticket. I think I can get a bus early in the morning and should be there by supper time, if that's okay. I will check the time and give you a call later." "Okay. Well, let us know so we can make plans to pick you up at the bus station tomorrow evening."

Mozelle's voice was not filled with the happy anticipation Crit had hoped, but the plans were made for the next morning and it was final, she was going to Dallas. As the bus driver loaded Crit's suitcase onto the Greyhound bus, Crit wrapped her arms around Eddie and buried her face into his chest.

He leaned down and whispered in her ear, "I love you, Christine. Have a good trip and call me any time you want. Call collect and don't worry about the money. We will work that out some way. Hurry back, I miss you already." He then kissed her firmly on the mouth and brushed away the tears trickling down her cheeks.

"All aboard!" shouted the driver.

"I love you, Eddie. I will come back to you soon."

They had spent at least part of every single day together since the first day they met. This separation, though temporary, was not going to be easy. Crit sat by the window, looking at Eddie waving at her until the bus pulled away from the station.

As the bus neared Dallas, Crit started feeling apprehensive. She had not been in direct contact with Mozelle for over a year and since Crit's imprisonment at Angola, their relationship had been unpredictable. She could see the familiar Dallas skyline in the distance and in a short while the bus pulled into the Greyhound station. Out the window, Crit saw Mozelle, Morris and the two children waiting for her. She felt relieved that the entire family had come.

Crit quickly gathered up her belongings and bounced off of the bus. Running toward the children and squealing their names, the two children met her with open arms, hugging her around the waist. The kids adored Crit, nicknamed "Aunt Pippy" by Dianne, Mozelle's deaf daughter. Their parents approached slowly and gave Crit reserved hugs.

"I'll get your bag," Morris said. "Nice to see you, Crit." Unlike Mozelle, he was willing to accept Crit for who she was and always treated her kindly.

"Long time no see," Crit said to Mozelle.

"That's true. Come on Dianne and Dennis, leave Aunt Pippy alone. She's been on a long bus ride." The children were looking at Crit's unusual earrings and bright red lips, twirling her blonde curls around a finger. She looked like a fairy princess to them as they talked non-stop. Mozelle grabbed them by the hand, leading them to the car as the entourage followed Morris with the bag.

"How long do you plan to stay, Crit? What's your reason for coming to Dallas?" Mozelle asked before they reached the car.

Though Crit felt offended, she held herself in check. "I just wanted to see all of you again. I figured to stay a few days, unless that doesn't work."

Mozelle nodded and instructed the children to get into the back seat of the car. They immediately began to argue over who would sit next to Crit, so she solved the problem by sitting between them.

For almost a week there had been no major incidents between Crit and Mozelle. Crit showered her sister with compliments regarding her seemingly picture-perfect life, often biting her tongue to do so. Perhaps it was her own insecurity that made her feel as though Mozelle was flaunting all of her accomplishments as she bragged about her husband, two lovely children, a mortgage on a new (albeit small) frame house, their many friends and neighborhood get-togethers. Morris tried to keep things jovial in the midst of the tension between the two sisters. That was always his role when the two of them were in the same space.

At every meal, Crit and Mozelle entertained Dennis and Dianne with stories about their childhood back on the farm in east Texas, including the time Crit caused Mozelle to break her arm by letting her fly off of the seesaw at school, and how awful it was to use the outhouse in the dead of winter. The two children giggled through the stories and found it great fun to have Aunt Pippy with them.

Mozelle somewhat jealously struggled with the fact that her children were drawn to Crit and that she adored them. She wanted to believe Crit was capable of being inappropriate when with them by using bad language or telling lewd stories, although she knew in her heart that wasn't true. Mozelle didn't want anyone to like Crit because she didn't believe Crit deserved to be liked.

Crit was waiting for an opportunity to tell Mozelle and Morris about Eddie. Though she had mentioned his name to Mozelle on the phone, her sister had not brought it up. Crit felt conflicted that she wanted them to know and in some way was seeking their approval. She wanted them to understand the genuinely true love she and Eddie had for one another.

Then, an unexpected phone call from Eddie catapulted all three adults into the middle of Crit's reality. "Eddie!" Christine squealed with excitement as she heard his voice.

"Hey, baby. How's Dallas? I miss you and couldn't wait any longer to talk to you."

"Oh, it's alright, honey. But I miss you so much, too!" Crit exclaimed in front of everyone.

As the conversation continued, Crit decided to let Eddie meet her sister over the phone. Rather sheepishly, Mozelle took the phone from Crit, stretching the cord as far as it would reach into the adjoining bedroom. She put her hand over the receiver, saying to Crit and her family, "We can hear better this way." Then she closed the door.

Crit was disconcerted by Mozelle's actions but didn't know what to do about it, so she took the children into the living room to play a game. Crit wasn't worried, completely trusting Eddie to do the right thing. Quite a while later, Mozelle exited the bedroom and called Crit to take the phone. The silent glances between the two of them were daggers and far from pleasant, as Crit grabbed the phone, taking it into the bedroom and closing the door for privacy, as Mozelle had done.

After a long time, Crit came out and hung up the phone.

"My God, Crit. You must have talked for over an hour!" exclaimed Mozelle.

"What's it to you, Mo? He called me and it isn't going to cost you one dime, and while we're at it, I didn't appreciate you taking the phone into the bedroom so I couldn't hear whatever you said to him."

Unspoken rage erupted between the two women as they raised their voices. The two children, unsure as to what they should do when the sisters began to argue and shout, retreated to their bedrooms. Since marrying into the family, Morris was fully aware of the longtime, simmering strife between the two of them. Trying to restore peace, he walked between Crit and Mozelle, stretching out his arms and pushing them apart.

"You girls need to stop this right now, you're frightening the children," Morris said, calmly.

Mozelle stormed out and went to visit her next door neighbor, where Crit was sure she was spilling her guts. Crit sat alone at the kitchen table, facing the fact that to her family she would never be anything more than an alcoholic, car-stealing felon, jailbird, and prostituting, exotic dancer whore.

Crit knew this visit had been a big mistake. It was time for her to go home to Eddie who loved her unconditionally. She went into the bedroom where she had been staying and pulled her bag out from under the bed. She began to throw her things into it, while cursing under her breath.

Crit heard Mozelle come back in the outside door to the kitchen, sobbing and crying loudly. "Mattie wasn't home," she heard her say to Morris.

"Maybe that's a good thing, Mozelle. You probably should keep your family problems to yourself." Morris was not easily ruffled.

"Why do you take Crit's side all of the time, Morris? You always have and I'm sick of it!"

"I'm not on a side, Mozelle. This issue has nothing to do with me."

Unable to wait any longer, Crit walked out into the kitchen where she saw Morris leaning against the sink counter. Mozelle sat on a wooden kitchen table chair. Knees up and her feet on the edge, she clutched a cigarette in her shaking hand, looking distraught and inconsolable.

Crit had her suitcase in her hand. When Mozelle saw her, she jumped up and left the room. "Crit," Morris said.

"Morris, I'm sorry," Crit interrupted, before he could say more. "You have always been kind to me, and I appreciate that so much. Just know that I never meant for all of this trouble to happen and upset your family. Out of everyone, you have always stuck with me no matter what, and of all people, you shouldn't have to put up with this thing between me and Mozelle."

Looking at his sad face, Crit put her hand on his arm. "It's been like that since we were little girls, Morris, and I guess it's not ever goin' to change."

He nodded and looked down at the floor. "I know." Morris looked back up at Crit. "I see you have your bag."

"Will you take me to the bus station?"

"Of course. Do you need help with your ticket?" Morris asked, ever thoughtful.

"No. I'm fine. Eddie took care of everything. You would really like him, Morris, he is a good man like you. Not like the others I've been involved with."

"I hope so, Crit. Let me tell the children you are leaving, they are going to be upset about that."

She handed her bag to Morris. "Let me tell them." She went into the living room where they were playing Pick-Up Sticks. Sitting on the floor with them, she put her arm around Dennis and looked into Dianne's eyes. Unable to hear, Dianne watched Crit's mouth as she explained that it was time for her to go back home. The children began to cry, putting their arms around her as she showered them with kisses.

The children trailed behind Crit as she went back into the kitchen. Mozelle was standing ashen-faced beside the refrigerator. The sisters looked into one another's eyes, and felt the pain between them for all the years of hurt. Morris picked up Crit's bag and kissed Mozelle on the cheek. "Time for us to go," he said.

"Mo," Crit said softly to her baby sister.

They hugged without speaking. As Crit walked out the back door, she felt this could well be the last time she would see any of them.

The trip to the bus station was uncomfortable, not the normal, humor-filled banter that usually occurred between Morris and Crit. Arriving there, Morris took her bag out of the back seat of the car and went with Crit into the station. She checked in at the counter and made the necessary arrangements while Morris waited.

"Okay, Morris. Everything is set. Thanks for bringing me on such short notice, and for your patience."

He gave her a fatherly hug and headed for the door. Before taking the exit, he looked back at Crit and gave her a wave. Then he disappeared.

Crit went over to the pay phone and placed a collect call to Eddie. Since it was Saturday, she was pretty sure he would be home. After two rings, she heard his voice on the other end.

"Yeah. Hello."

"Will you accept a collect call from Christine Youngblood?" the operator intoned.

"Hell, yes!"

"Baby, it's me! It's Crit! Eddie, I'm comin' home and I'll be there late tonight. Can you get me? You'll need to check the bus schedule, sweetheart."

"You bet, baby. I'll be there! Are you okay?"

"I'm fine now that I can hear your voice. I just couldn't stay away from you any longer."

"Well, I'm glad about that. I've missed you awful bad and I'm not gonna let you go off without me anymore."

Crit was going back to Eddie, where she was loved, wanted and belonged.

CHAPTER 7

Search for Normalcy: Tried and Denied (Late 1952 - Early 1953)

"**B**aby, I have an idea." Eddie brushed Crit's curls away from her face.

"You do?" She sat up, looking at him with interest.

"Look, it's Saturday evening, and there's no reason for you to go back to that awful apartment where you live. I want to take you to my house, and I don't just mean for the night. I want you there for good."

"Oh, Eddie! For real? You mean it? What about your mother? How is she gonna feel about that?"

"Look, Mama will be okay. Trust me. Everything will be okay." Eddie put his hands on Crit's shoulders, looking into her eyes with reassurance.

With the vision of a secure future floating in her head, Crit threw her arms around Eddie's neck and leaned against his chest. "Oh, Eddie, let's do it! Take me home with you. I don't want to be alone anymore."

Excited about the prospects ahead, Eddie and Crit headed downtown to her shabby apartment. Once there, they gathered up the total of her personal items, piled them in the backseat and trunk of the car, and headed off, planning to return later to terminate Crit's weekly lease arrangement.

As they drove to Metairie, a suburb of New Orleans, Crit's stomach churned. She felt nervous. Crit had been out on her own for a long time; managing to get by. The times she let a man pay for everything, the relationship always ended in disaster and regrets. Crit doubted Eddie's mother would be all right with her, a Bourbon Street burlesque artist moving into their house, and more particularly, into Eddie's bedroom.

She was quietly weighing the situation when Eddie turned off the road onto a driveway, and up to the shotgun-style framed white house where he lived. It was home to him, his half-brother, Malcolm, and their mother, Jenny. Eddie's biological father had moved out long ago. His step-father, Ray Guidry, was gone as well leaving the tightly knit Marcades-Guidry, Italian-Argentinean-Greek, Catholic household.

As the car came to a stop, Crit exposed her lingering fears about Eddie's mother. "Eddie, tell me again that this is going to be okay. I mean okay…with everyone?"

"Honey, you can take my word for it. Hell, it'll be better than okay. You'll see." He gave her a boyish grin.

Once out of the car, Eddie took Crit's hand and led her up to the porch. Before they could get further, Eddie's mother, Jenny, came out the front door with a pleasant smile.

"You must be Crit." She held out her hand, taking Crit's hand in both of hers. "Eddie talks about you all the time. Malcolm, too. You're just as beautiful as the boys said you were. You can call me Jenny."

She was so sincerely kind and welcoming Crit began to relax, though her face flushed as she wondered if Jenny knew how she made her living. "My real name is Christine Youngblood, but my family and friends just call me Crit."

"Oh, I know. My real name is Jennifer, but I like Jenny. Come on in, Crit." She held open the screen door for Crit while turning to hug and kiss her son. "How's my boy?"

"I'm good, Mama. Real good."

"Oh, I can see that." She pinched Eddie's cheek making him blush.

Crit would soon learn the affection shown her by Eddie was an extension of that shared in his home, though it took her a while to adjust. The Marcades-Guidry family was unapologetic about their overt expression of love to family members, and also friends of the family. Hugs and kisses offered to anyone leaving or coming into the house was just part of the process of welcome into their clan. Ignoring the affectionate ritual, even when some disagreement had arisen, would be considered an insult.

As the evening progressed, a pleasant and relaxing conversation was their natural way to share time together. Unabashed, Eddie and Malcolm talked openly about Crit's spell-binding work at The Blue Angel. Though Crit was flattered by their adoring ravings, she worried that Jenny might be offended. Eddie had brought home a burlesque dancer, not someone he met at a church picnic!

Jenny, a strong Catholic woman, known for her history of active compassion for the down and out by receiving them into her home and giving them food, listened without any outward sign of judgment. Though Jenny might have had doubts about Crit's nature and background, to her, the happiness of her son mattered most of all.

Following supper, they all sat on the front porch. Eddie and Crit were swinging rhythmically back and forth to the creaking sounds of the swing. As the night grew dark, Malcolm stood up and stretched. "That's it for me. I've got to get up early in the morning."

"And I've got to wash them dishes," Jenny said, as she headed for the kitchen. "Should I help her?" Crit whispered to Eddie.

"Not this time." He stopped the swing. "I'll be right back."

Eddie went to the car and unloaded Crit's belongings. "Hold open the screen," he said to Crit as he came up the steps, "now, come on in." He confidently carried her things into his bedroom. She wondered if she was just another woman who had slept with Eddie in his family home. It was evident they were all fully aware of his plans.

"Is this okay?" she whispered.

"What?"

"Me. Here?"

"This is my bedroom. I can do anything I want in here. If Mama and Malcolm don't know I'm a normal man by now, they never will."

Eddie closed the bedroom door. He picked Crit up and sat her on the edge of the bed, before kneeling down on the floor directly in front of her. "Baby, I love you, and I want to take care of you." He brushed his lips softly across her cheek.

"Oh, Eddie." Crit's eyes filled with tears. His tenderness was overwhelming to her.

"I'm just now beginning to understand the problems you mentioned before between you, your sister, and some of your family. Your trip to Dallas was an eye opener for me. That was a bad deal." He picked up her hand and kissed her fingers. "I don't want to hurt you, baby, but I've got to tell you something."

Crit sat still trying not to imagine what he was going to say. Eddie kept holding her hand gently in his. "Crit, the conversation I had with your sister while you were in Dallas at her house was not good. What the hell is the problem with that bitch, Mozelle? She spewed out horrible things about you to me! I stood it as long as I could before I told her to shut up and get you back on the phone. I was mad as hell. Don't have anything else to do with her, Crit. She's a devil."

Crit paled to hear this revelation as tears of anger filled her eyes. Though Crit was tough and independent, it pained her to the core to know Mozelle had turned on her, not caring a gnat's eyelash about her feelings. To think Mozelle would stab her in the back and try to take away the most important thing in her life, her relationship with Eddie! No wonder she couldn't wait for Crit to leave, after Eddie had shut her up.

"Mozelle was trying to hurt me any way she could, Eddie. It's like this was her last chance to destroy something remarkable in my life. She couldn't stand that I was finally happy. Her own sister! What a low down dog!" Crit was rocking back and forth trying to keep her voice down so Jenny and Malcolm wouldn't hear.

"I'm sorry I had to tell you, Crit, but you needed to know that you can't trust Mozelle." He climbed beside Crit, pulling her up on the pillows of the bed without turning back the covers. Cradling her in his arms, he whispered, "Baby, you've got a home now, a real home where you're safe and loved. Shhh, just go to sleep." He wiped the tears from her cheeks with his workman's hands. Her tensed muscles slowly relaxed as she soon fell into a deep sleep.

~

The new day arrived with the early morning rays of the sun peeking around the window shade. A hot shower, breakfast and several cups of coffee filled Eddie and Crit with a renewed sense of hope and love. It was the most wonderful sense of togetherness either of them had ever experienced. The emotional storm of the night before could have upset all of that, but instead just drew them closer together. It was new to Crit to have a confidant.

Crit had not been around people with traditional lives for many years. She was captivated by the display of trust within the family gathered around the kitchen table as they shared breakfast. It was both winsome and naïve. She knew she was not trustworthy. She didn't even trust herself. How could they innocently accept a stripper from Bourbon Street as if she was an ordinary person?

Eddie kissed her goodbye and headed to the railroad yard where he worked as a foreman. Malcolm gave her a hug, following behind Eddie to share a ride. Jenny had some early morning errands to run and drove away within an hour of her two boys. In spite of the fact that Jenny was acquainted with some of Crit's criminal record, she showed no concern about leaving this new resident alone in her home.

Crit thought of her own family in comparison. "I ought to tell Mama about Eddie and his warm family so she will know what a low-down rat Mozelle turned out to be. Oh, I want everybody in the family to know what Mozelle did. Thank goodness Eddie loves me so much he didn't believe her made up lies about me!" Truthfully, some of the stories weren't lies.

Crit started rummaging around in drawers, looking for paper and a pen. "I'm gonna put this in writing so they can all pass it around. No way am I lettin' Mozelle, 'Miss Perfect,' get away with that secret phone conversation with Eddie! What a mistake to think I could visit her and things would be different. She's always been so jealous of me she can't see straight. She never wanted me to be happy for a single minute." Crit was stomping around angrily, opening drawers and slamming them shut as she talked aloud to herself.

Finally locating a sheet of paper and a pen, she cleared a place on the metal kitchen table and sat down to write:

> *Hi, folks. Well, here's the prodigal sitting down at long last to write you a letter. I've been intending to for quite a while, but haven't felt too good, so I just put it off. But, here goes, hope you can read it. I just returned from a short visit to Mozelle's. After I got there, a little time passed before I knew I couldn't stay in Dallas for very long. You know, Mother, when you go to Fairfield, you have sisters that are glad to see you and aren't afraid of how long you're going to stay; they're happy you are there. But I can truthfully say the only ones glad to see me were Dennis and Dianne. From the minute I got off the bus, even before we got to the car, Mozelle and Morris wanted to know what my plans were. Guess they were afraid I'd stay too long. And, while I was there, I called Eddie, the man I love here in New Orleans. I know you won't believe it, but he's a wonderful man. He took the charges for the phone call. No telling how high the bill is going to be. We must*

of talked about an hour and a half. I guess it will be around thirty or thirty-five dollars. I'm hoping it's no more than that. Anyway, during the call, I let Mozelle talk to Eddie. I thought it would be a good idea; maybe she'd see what a good man he is. When I got back to New Orleans, Eddie told me that Mozelle had said lots of awful things about me. Is this the chance she and Morris have been looking for all their lives, to be able to say there's not Christine in the family? It hurts me. I can't say it doesn't. But thank goodness, God has given me someone to fill in the gap of lost love. *(Letter excerpt: January 12, 1952)

For now, Crit was secure in the Guidry-Marcades household. Jenny had voiced some serious concerns about Crit working at The Blue Angel, yet Crit still felt loved and accepted in a way her own mother had not been able to accept her. Eddie had been involved with other women before, but it was different this time. He had never brought a woman home with the intention of her staying; living in the house as one family. Jenny knew Crit filled Eddie with happiness, and that was good enough for her.

Eddie drove Crit to The Blue Angel after his shift each day and picked her up later according to her schedule. He found it hard to accept that strange men were looking at Crit in the same way he had looked at her; with desire and lust. She assured Eddie it was just a job she enjoyed, feeding both ego and pocketbook.

When they got back home together in the early morning hours, the private intimacies they shared allayed any fears Eddie might have had. Though Crit stripped for other men, her bed was his alone. Sex was exciting and frequent. Crit knew all of the moves to arouse and satisfy a man, unlike the inexperienced women of Eddie's past encounters. What followed in the ensuing weeks was not surprising.

As always, Crit and Eddie awoke early to the welcomed smell of bacon sizzling on the stove. But this morning, the smell was repulsive to Crit as she sat up quickly and hunched over, clutching her stomach.

"Baby, are you okay?" Eddie was still half asleep.

Without a reply, Crit stood up quickly and headed for the bathroom down the hall. Eddie pulled on his shorts and followed her. Through the open door, he saw Crit kneeling in front of the toilet with the lid up, holding her hair in her hands and retching.

"Crit, are you sick? Can I help?"

She shook her head "no" and moaned.

Eddie headed for the kitchen. "Mother, Crit's stomach is upset. She's upchucking in the bathroom, and I think she's sick. What can we do?" he asked anxiously.

Jenny set the skillet off of the stove and headed for the bathroom. She could hear the water running in the sink. "Are you okay, dear?" Jenny asked kindly.

Crit smiled weakly and mumbled, "Just a little nauseated. Jenny put her arm around Crit's waist and led her back to the bedroom. "Son, get a wet wash cloth."

Eddie, slightly confused, followed his mother's command. Jenny sat on the bed next to Crit, looking her squarely in the eyes. It was her style to get straight to the point. "Christine, when was your last period?"

"Ummm, I missed last month." Crit dropped her head, putting her hands over her face. "Looks like I've missed this one, too."

"Here now, get under the covers and let me prop you up on the pillows. I'll get you some bicarbonate of soda to help settle your stomach. You're goin' to be okay, honey. I'll be right back."

As Jenny left the bedroom, she met Eddie in the hall. "Son, take that wet cloth and put it on her forehead. It will make her feel better. I'm getting something to settle her stomach."

Eddie sat on the edge of the bed and folded the washcloth, putting it on Crit's forehead. She rested her head on the pillows, looking at him with concern. "What's goin' on Baby? Are you sick? Do you hurt anywhere?" He felt clumsy and inept, as he patted her hand.

"What do you think, Eddie? A woman vomiting in the morning usually means one of two things; she either has a stomach bug, or…" Crit paused, waiting for a reaction.

He stared at her blankly for a moment, until the light dawned. "Oh, my God, Crit! Do you think you're pregnant?" Eddie ran his hands through his thick wavy hair.

"Well, we both certainly know it's possible, don't we?" Crit murmured, as she turned over in the bed and faced the wall. She had no idea how Eddie would react to that probability.

They were both quiet, letting the idea sink in. Eddie reached out and gently pulled her over to look at him. "Baby, is there a chance you could be wrong?"

"Sure, there's a chance; but I am late, Eddie…real late."

Wrapping his arms around her, he whispered into her ear, "We're going to work this out, Crit. Everything's gonna be okay, no matter what."

Jenny reappeared with the bicarbonate of soda, giving Crit a couple of sips. "Just be still and rest for a while, Crit. I expect your emotions are getting the best of you right now." She fluffed the pillows and straightened the covers over Crit as if she were a child. It felt comforting to Crit to have someone fuss over her that way.

"Come on, Eddie, and eat your breakfast so she can rest."

He followed his mother down the familiar, narrow hallway, and took his chair at the kitchen table where his breakfast was waiting. Jenny poured him a cup of coffee, and one for herself, before sitting across from him. They sat silently for a few minutes.

"Eddie, do you love her?"

"Mother, you know I do," Eddie answered without hesitation. "I would never have brought her home to stay with me if I didn't love her."

"Well, then, if Crit is pregnant, there's only one thing to do, marry her. Give the baby a name, and the mother a husband." Jenny took a sip of coffee.

Eddie finished his coffee and walked around the table to hug his mother before going to the bedroom to dress for work. "It was a good breakfast, Mama."

"Thank you, Son."

Jenny breathed a sigh as she remembered another young woman so many years ago. She, like Crit, had been young and in love, but not so fortunate. That man had not felt the need to be a father to Eddie. Eddie would not be like that. He would do better.

~

As Eddie worked at the railroad yard that morning, his body was there, but his mind was somewhere else. He thought of the things that would need to be done. He needed to marry Crit right away. He wanted to take her to a first-rate doctor.

Together, they needed to call her mother. And also on the list, Crit had to quit working at The Blue Angel.

The shift seemed to drag by before he was finally free to return home. Tired from work, and determined to make things right for Crit, their baby, and himself as well, Eddie hurried in the back door. Jenny was standing in her usual place at the stove, finishing up supper. After he kissed his mother hello, he asked about Crit.

"Mother, does Crit still feel sick?"

"No, son, morning sickness passes and doesn't last all day. She felt much better by lunch time and wanted to go on into work to get ready for her routine tonight."

"Went to work! How did she get there?"

"She was determined to go, so I drove her in. She went early to meet a friend. You'll need to go back and get her like you usually do tonight. You know it's her job, Eddie."

"I'm gonna take a quick shower and head on over to the Quarter. I'm bringin' her back home."

"Son, why don't you sit down and eat a good meal with me and Malcolm, while it's hot?"

"No, Mama. I'll eat when I get back. Go ahead without me." He started taking off his clothes as he headed for the bathroom.

Malcolm came in the back door, washed his hands at the kitchen sink, and sat at his usual place at the table. "I cleaned up that wisteria vine that was takin' everything over on the back fence. Where's Eddie? I saw him pull up a few minutes ago."

Jenny took her chair at the table. "We're eating without him. He wants to go get Crit and bring her back home first. Your brother is determined to get her off of Bourbon Street."

A cautious man, Malcolm's only comment was, "Oh."

Eddie, in clean clothes, raced back through the kitchen. He gave Malcolm a slap on the shoulder. "Be back soon. Save me and Crit a plate of that good food."

They heard him scratch off in his car as he hurried away. Jenny shook her head. "That boy."

Though he knew his place, Malcolm adored Crit. In his mind, she was a feminine specimen almost defying explanation. He wasn't surprised about Eddie's protective run to the Quarter to see about Crit. If she was his, he would have done the same thing.

"Mother, what'd you expect? Eddie loves her."

"I know, and there's no cure for that."

Eddie maneuvered through the streets of the Quarter. Finding a rare parking place, he started walking briskly in the direction of The Blue Angel. Bourbon Street was only slightly crowded since it was still early. In a few hours the sidewalks would be crawling with pleasure seekers as they followed the music calling them into the clubs and bars.

He walked into The Angel through the front door, frantically looking left and right through the semi-darkness and flashing lights. The club staff was already working the early arrivals and a couple of them gave him a wave. One of the hostesses put her hand on his arm. "Hey, Eddie. Do I have anything you need?"

It all felt so different to him now. He was completely distracted and preoccupied with his mission. "Have you seen Crit?"

She quit flirting and dropped her hand. "Yeah, I have. She's here somewhere. Want me to help you look for her?"

"Naw, I got this, but thanks."

Eddie scanned the room, squinting as he adjusted to the lighting. He knew Crit would probably be sitting at one of the small tables for two, at the lower end of the bar. Spotting curly blonde hair, he headed in that direction. Crit was sitting alone, sipping a drink. He walked resolutely in that direction with the intent of taking her home. She gave him a smile as their eyes met, surprised he was there so early. Crit would be going to the dressing room soon to get ready for her routine.

"Baby, what are you doin' here?" Eddie asked.

"I was goin' to ask you the same thing. You don't usually come over this early. I haven't even been on yet but I have my staging ready. You knew I had to work tonight, didn't you, Eddie?"

He leaned over to kiss her. "You're not going to work tonight, Baby. Not tonight, tomorrow night, or ever again, please," Eddie pleaded as he cradled her small, soft hands in his that were rough and calloused by hard work.

"I have to work, Eddie. I want to pay my way as long as I can, and not live off of you, Jenny and Malcolm. I don't want the reputation of being a free-loader," she said, with a serious look.

For a rough, tough looking man, Eddie could be amazingly tender. "Christine, if you're pregnant, and even if you're not, you can't be a stripper anymore. Let me take care of you, that's what a husband does, isn't it?"

"Husband? What do you mean 'husband?'"

He let go of Crit's hand and pulled a chair up beside her. "Baby, we got lots to talk about, but we need to get out of here first."

"Eddie, what do I do about the Club…the money?"

"Let me handle that with the boss man. Will you let me do that this time, please?"

"I don't know, Eddie. I just can't lose this job. I've worked so hard to get here. Hell, I'm a star attraction, I've got a big following." Though logic had the answer, Crit was always weak at being realistic.

"You are a star, Crit, but just put it on me. I don't want you on that stage tonight with all these men lookin' at you. And if you are pregnant, I am damn sure not gonna have you and our baby on display in a place like this!" Though Eddie had lowered his voice, there was no doubt at all that he meant what he had just said.

Crit sat very still, her blue eyes with their gold flecks wide and unblinking. Eddie was what she had longed to find in a man all of her life. She was not just a sexual object to him. He cared about her as a person, a woman with a different set of needs from a man.

Eddie stood up. "Go downstairs and get your purse now. I'll wait right here for you."

Crit did as he told her. Eddie picked her empty glass up off of the table and sniffed it. Walking over to the bar, he handed it to the bartender.

Eddie looked like a madman. "If you ever serve Crit anything but Coca-Cola again, I will come back in here and pull your tongue out by the roots. Get it?"

"Hey, sure Eddie, whatever you say. I just gave Crit what she ordered. Cool down, buddy."

Eddie met Crit at the top of the stairs and led her across the room. The club manager was standing by the front exit. "Hey, Booger. Crit isn't going on tonight."

"Oh…okay. Are you alright, Crit?" Booger looked at her with concern.

"Oh, yeah, Big 'B.' I'll call you tomorrow and explain." She and Eddie smiled cordially at the manager as they stepped out the door and into the fresh air awaiting them.

Eddie and Crit sat across from one another at the French Market Café having coffee and a pastry. Walking away from The Blue Angel so decisively had left both of them untethered. Neither of them was necessarily against marriage, but they had never talked about getting married. The thought of pregnancy brought a whole new feel to their relationship.

"Are you sick anymore?"

"No. That went away after a couple of hours, but I felt real yucky this morning. It was something about smelling that bacon cooking." Crit shuddered at the memory.

"Yeah, you were poorly. Mama said you met a friend earlier today. Who was that?"

"You don't know them."

"Man or woman?" Eddie asked, anxiously.

"I've got something to tell you, Eddie. One of the girls from the club took me to see a doctor this afternoon. A lot of the girls use him."

"And?" He twisted his napkin nervously.

"I'm pregnant for sure, Eddie."

"That nails it! Crit, you know I love you out of my mind. I want to do the right thing by you and our baby." Eddie searched for words to explain his feelings. "Christine, if you'll have me, I want to marry you and make my home your home where the three of us will be together from now on. I want you to know I'm not runnin' away from this. No way!"

"Eddie, are you proposing to me? You don't have to marry me just because I'm pregnant. Being married is a lot more serious than just living together."

"That's the point. This is a lot more serious, and yes, I am sure this is what we ought to do."

"Do you mean now, or sometime in the future?"

"As soon as possible, and that's not all. Mama is going to be so excited. She doesn't have any grandchildren. This will be the first! Plus, she loves you, too."

Crit was looking down at her coffee while Eddie waited. "So, what do you think, Baby? Will you marry me?"

Crit's tears were dropping into her cup of coffee that had grown cold. Unknown to Eddie, Crit had drifted away to the past she wanted to forget. It was a past few people knew about. She had already heard proposals of marriage before from Glenn Claywell, and also Bobby Rodman. Their images whirled in her memory. She had said yes to both of them and had already been married twice since Angola. If Eddie knew about that, everything would be ruined. She couldn't marry him for fear he might find out…but she was carrying his baby.

"Crit, why are you crying?" Eddie sounded distressed.

"Can't talk." She picked up the napkin and blew her nose before looking at Eddie. "Yes. Yes, yes, yes, I will marry you. I would be crazy not to marry you and get to be a regular person like other women with a husband and a baby."

Once parked beside the house, Eddie and Crit headed straight for the front door and into the living room where Jenny sat in front of the television. She looked up at them with surprise because the family usually came in the back door. Eddie was smiling broadly as he held Crit by the hand, pulling her along. She looked hesitant, almost timid.

"Mother, can I turn off the TV? We want to tell you something. It's good news."

He turned the knob to "off" before she could answer. Jenny sat up on the edge of the sofa where she had stretched out, half asleep.

"Good news, huh? What have you two been up to today? You both look mighty happy to me so whatever it is will make me happy too."

Eddie put his arm around Crit. "See, I told you everything was gonna be alright. Crit went to see a doctor today. She is pregnant, Mama! You're gonna be a grandmother!"

Jenny stood up, opening her arms wide. "Okay, now, Eddie. It's my turn to hug Crit." She held her as warmly as if she were her own daughter, cooing into her ear. "Now don't you worry, child. This is a wonderful thing, and you are part of this family now. We will stand beside you and take care of you." She gave Crit a pat on the back.

"I hope you went to see a good doctor, Crit. We might want to go to one I know over here in Metairie. And Eddie, we have got to get Crit out of The Blue Angel. That's no place for a pregnant woman. It's just not a good thing for her to be around that anymore."

"We're already workin' on that, Mama."

"I'm glad to hear it." Jenny nodded her approval. "Real glad."

For a moment, Crit felt a pang of loss. She knew Jenny was right, but Crit was also proud of her independence and the progress she had made at The Blue Angel. It was against Crit's nature to let other people take over and make her decisions. It wasn't going to be easy to stand still while that happened as she had fought it since she was a child. She could sense right away that becoming a wife, mother, and daughter-in-law had strings attached.

"Let's deal with that over the next few days. Right now Crit needs some rest. She's had a big day," Eddie said, sympathetically. "I'm pretty tired myself." He led Crit to their bedroom and closed the door. It would be their refuge for the days ahead.

Morning dawned and with it, plans. Crit's pregnancy and the wedding were the topics of talk at the breakfast table. They all decided there was no time to plan a formal wedding ceremony at a church, nor one held at the house. It should be something short and sweet at the parish courthouse, and as soon as possible. Jenny, Eddie, and Malcolm all thought it was the only logical alternative. Looking at Crit who sat listening, they paused, waiting for her agreement. Crit slightly nodded an affirmative.

Once again, that strange feeling emerged in Crit's gut as she listened to them make decisions about her, and for her, not once asking what she wanted. And more unsettling was the fact that she didn't know what she wanted, even if they had asked.

Within two days, Crit and Eddie stood before a Justice of the Peace at the musty old courthouse in Metairie. Jenny and Malcolm stood with them as witnesses. Eddie had bought Crit a corsage, and she wore one of Jenny's hats. It wasn't the Catholic wedding Jenny would have wanted, nor as romantic as Crit had imagined, but at least it was legal.

After a few months of living a life decided by the circumstances of her pregnancy and dictated by the choices others made on her behalf, Crit became jittery and irritable, pacing around the house like a caged animal. The days were dull and so routine, she couldn't believe people in their right minds chose to live like that forever. The sameness was stifling. She sat staring at the bulge in her stomach trying to imagine a child growing inside of her like a watermelon. But it wasn't a watermelon that made little fluttering feelings, it was life.

~

Crit wanted a drink and a cigarette and all of the other things she used that made it possible for her to deal with her own existence; transporting her to ethereal places of perfection that she had never been able to find without them. Crit gradually began to give in to the siren call again by drinking the beer Eddie had in the refrigerator, all the while her mother-in-law protesting by reminding her that she was pregnant. Eddie and Jenny tried to reason with Crit which only led to arguments and upsetting confrontations.

Eddie entered the back door missing the familiar smells of his mother cooking supper. Jenny wasn't in the kitchen. Crit's presence had become so disruptive that even Malcolm would come home late and leave early. For the first time in Eddie's life, suppertime around the kitchen table was no longer a family ritual. He opened the refrigerator door for a cold bottle of beer.

"Crit! Where did all of the beer go?" He sat down in a kitchen chair to unlace his shoes. "Crit? Where the hell are you?" Maybe she went with mother, but I doubt it.

"Crit!" he yelled, on his way to the living room. "Shut up, Eddie! You're making my head hurt!"

He found her sprawled in an easy chair, her hair disheveled and her bathrobe partially open exposing her rounded belly. She was holding a beer bottle with several empties lying around her on the floor.

"Damn it, Crit, what are you doing? Haven't you even gotten dressed today?"

"What's it to you? You're not the boss of me," Crit replied, her speech slurred.

"Are you high? You've had more than beer, that's for sure! Where are you gettin' dope?" Eddie tried to wrest the near empty beer bottle out of her hand as she slapped and kicked at him, screaming at the top of her voice.

"Stop it, Crit! People will think I'm tryin' to kill you." As he tried to pull her up on her feet, she drew back and hit him over the head as hard as she could with the beer bottle.

Eddie staggered backward. He felt a trickle of blood run down his forehead. Jenny appeared in the door at the same time. "Oh, my God, Eddie." She ran to the bathroom and came back with a wet towel. "I never thought I would see something like this in my home!" She helped Eddie into the kitchen where she cleaned the wound on his forehead before applying a bandage.

Eddie put his head in his hands and sobbed. "Mama, what else can I do? I love Crit so much, and I'm afraid for our baby."

She put her hand on his shoulder. "This isn't your fault, son. You've done everything you could do. All of us have. But Crit has got the demon of drugs and alcohol controlling her and she can't hear anything else no matter how much love you give her."

Crit came waddling out of the bedroom, carrying her leather bag. She was eight months pregnant, appearing as a swollen image of her original self. It had been a while since the episode with the beer bottle had sealed the fate of her marriage to Eddie.

"I need a ride to the bus depot." She looked around the room. Jenny, Eddie, and Malcolm looked back at her with surprised expressions.

"Do you think a trip is wise with the baby coming soon?" Jenny tried to say the words lovingly as she was genuinely worried for her unborn grandchild.

"I'm going home to be with my Mama in Houston. I miss her. My sister Grace and her husband, Jack, are there, too."

"Couldn't you just wait until after the baby comes?" Eddie's face showed his concern.

"No, I can't wait. I want my baby to be born in Texas, not New Orleans. I'll come back sometimes, so you can see it. Well, do I need to call a cab?"

"If your mind is made up, I'll take you." Eddie pulled on his shoes and went to get his keys and wallet.

Jenny walked over and put her arm around Crit's shoulders. "I hope you know how much I care about you and the baby, Crit."

"You've been really good to me, Jenny. None of this is your fault. It's all on me. I'm just different."

"This is your home anytime you want to come back."

Crit believed her and gently smiled as she nodded at Jenny before going out the door.

Crit and Eddie rode silently to the Greyhound Bus Depot in New Orleans. As they pulled into a parking place, Crit looked over at Eddie.

"I'm goin' to have to ask you to spot me for the bus ticket since I haven't been able to work, bein' pregnant and everything."

"I will, but you don't have to go. You know that."

"Eddie, I'm just not the marryin' type of woman, I guess."

They got out of the old car, Eddie carrying Crit's worn leather bag. She sat on a bench while he bought the ticket and walked slowly back to her. He helped her lift her own weight as she stood up. "Crit, don't do nothin' dumb now, and take care of yourself. Stay off of that booze and dope. It's gonna kill you."

"I'll try, Eddie." She stuck out her hand as if she wanted to shake hands. He took her hand and lifted it to his lips. "I could have loved you for the rest of your life, Crit, if you would of just let me."

He walked her to the waiting bus and helped her get into a seat. "Bring our baby back for me to hold, Crit. You've gotta promise me that." He leaned over and kissed her on the forehead.

"I will Eddie, but it might be a while before I can do that."

The bus driver had taken his seat, holding the door open so Eddie could get off. Crit could see Eddie's slumped shoulders as he headed for the car without looking back. As soon as the engine revved and the bus moved forward, Crit opened her purse and took out her little compact, quickly sniffing a pinch of white powder up her nose. She was hoping being at home would help her to get clean before the baby came.

Crit was also very afraid. She didn't know how to have a baby.

At Jefferson Davis Hospital in Houston, Texas, on February 13, 1953, Melba Christine Youngblood Marcades, age 29, held her newborn little boy in her arms. She kissed his tiny hands and traced his rose bud mouth with her finger. "You cute little thing. You were almost a Valentine; weren't you? You will always be my own special Valentine."

Minnie Bell leaned over the bed, looking at her new grandson. "Mama, I didn't know it could hurt so damn bad to have a baby," Crit said. Minnie flinched. She detested cursing.

"Life don't come without a price, Crit. Look at that curly blonde hair."

"Just like me. Too bad Eddie isn't here to see what a pretty baby he is," Crit cooed.

"That rat. Oh, don't bring up his name. I've never seen him and don't want to."

"I showed you his picture. Besides, he didn't leave me, Mama. I left him. We didn't stay together long."

"Just long enough to get pregnant…but I don't mean I'm not glad you have a fine son. Have you made up your mind about his name yet?"

"Michael. Michael Glenn Marcades. That's what I put on the birth certificate."

Minnie unwrapped his blanket. "Look at those long legs and arms. He's gonna be tall, this one is. He looks kinda swarthy."

"That's from Eddie," Crit said. Minnie played deaf.

As the baby became fretful, Minnie rewrapped the blanket to make him feel more secure. "Well, Mr. Michael, I had three girls, so I guess you are going to be the big man to me and Papa when we get you and your mama back to our house."

"Mama, I put that I was a 'homemaker' on Michael's birth certificate, but after I get over having him, I promise I will go to work and pay you and Papa back for the hospital bill. I didn't have any place to go but back home with you."

"Don't worry about it now, Crit. You're our daughter and Michael is our grandson. Papa and me will work it out some way or the other. I expect Jack and your sister Grace will help us out, too. Jack got a promotion in the Army. They say it was a big pay raise."

~

When Michael was almost two months old, he was christened in Houston at a Catholic Church. Crit's entire family was Protestant, so they were all taken aback, not understanding the decision Crit had made. For complex, unspoken reasons, she held respect for Eddie, Jenny and Malcolm, and their Catholic faith over the stern faith of her childhood memories.

Tom and Minnie, Grace, Jack and their four-year-old daughter, Jaxie, along with Godparents Sadie and Lucien Spinella – all joined Crit and Michael for the significant and joyous event. Everyone was dressed in their finest, with particular attention to Michael's traditional baptism gown. Lots of pictures were taken to keep the memories of the day when a new baby made everyone forget the differences of church affiliation. However, it didn't make them forget everything. Eddie knew about the occasion, but he was forbidden by Crit's family to come to the christening of his own son.

Crit put on the persona of the model mother and daughter. Like a chameleon, she changed and blended in with ordinary people who had babies and loved them as she took care of every meticulous detail of mothering Michael. His babbling sounds and the way he cuddled against her were the closest she ever came to experiencing pure love. She soon found a job there in Houston, as family members took turns driving her back and forth to work. Minnie Bell and Tom took care of their new grandson, delighted to have a baby in the house again, and also to see Crit taking on a normal lifestyle for the first time in her life.

"I think Crit has finally growed up," Minnie said to Tom over morning coffee.

"Well, we're just gonna hope that be so." Tom added more sugar to his coffee.

CHAPTER 8

The Beginning of the End: Houston and The Mafia (Mid 1953 - Early 1960)

Houston, like other developing Texas cities, was booming with opportunity for the best and worst of society. It did not take long for Crit to find her place among those enslaved by their own private addictions. Formerly a user of petty drugs and alcohol, she now found herself in one of the nation's largest drug ports. Daily, her situation deteriorated and it was in Houston that she learned the perilous control of heroin. The peace and sense of identity that she sought during her marriage to Eddie had vanished. Often, her reclaimed life of illicit drug use, excessive alcohol consumption and promiscuous behavior with men brought her into conflict with the Houston Police Department, which was now under clandestine investigation by the Federal Bureau of Narcotics for alleged connection to organized crime and the heroin enterprise.

"Hey, easy on the arm Mr. Bigshot!" Crit yelled and squirmed, albeit unsuccessfully, to get away from the man who had a firm grip on her left wrist and a rigid right hand and strong arm pressed up against her shoulder blades, forcing her in the direction of a black vehicle parked around the corner.

As Crit drew closer to the vehicle, she saw Houston PD emblazoned on the car doors. With the assistance of another officer, Crit was loaded into the back seat. As the door slammed shut, she stared ahead through a metal meshed divider. The view was all-to-familiar; it reminded her of many days and nights behind bars and the hell of Angola.

As the car pulled into the Houston PD rear parking lot, Crit remained oddly silent and followed the oral directions that led her through the station's back door and into a rather small holding room. As the holding room door slammed shut, Crit surveyed the situation…and waited. She pondered what lay ahead. For months, she had done whatever it took to support her heroin habit and provide food and shelter for her son Michael. She worried about what would happen to Michael were she to be locked up today.

Then, two officers and a female attendant abruptly entered the room. The woman instructed Crit to stand behind a makeshift privacy screen for a cursory body search; the officer that removed her from the street tossed a file folder onto the table and took a seat. The other officer stood near the door and lit up a cigarette.

Crit raised both arms above her head so the attendant could continue her discrete search. Almost immediately, she felt a small bulge sequestered below the left side panel of Crit's bra. As ordered, Crit removed the vial and handed it to the woman who offered it to the seated officer and left the room. He placed it in the center of the table; clearly, the vial was filled to the brim with white powder.

Now alone with the two officers, Crit took a big breath. As was the custom, everything in the room was being observed by Houston PD higher-ups through two-way mirrors and recorded for future reference.

"Ma'am, I am Detective Martin Billnitzer. I'm sorry to inform you that I am placing you under arrest for the possession and distribution of heroin and public solicitation."

Immediately, he began reading Crit her rights; curiously and probably due to a lack of funds, she turned down access to a lawyer. As she had been for most of her life: she was alone.

Billnitzer, whose formidable service to the Houston PD system warranted his quick promotion from policeman to detective, had a reputation for being a "to the point" kind of law enforcement officer. For years, he fought against the rise and destructive consequences of the illegal dope industry. He hated drugs and did everything in his power, with enviable success, to eradicate the product and the supplier. Clearly, his record spoke for itself. By 1949, he had been a pivotal figure in undercover drug stings, including the simultaneous arrest of several dozen heroin traffickers allegedly associated with major mafia figures such as Carlos Marcello, Santo Trafficante and Charles Luciano.

Billnitzer had his own way of doing things. Across the years, he skillfully formulated and maintained a reliable bevy of undercover informants whose newly commissioned mission in life was to assist Martin with the apprehension, charging and incarceration of heroin traffickers throughout Houston and the Port of Galveston.

Crit, who frequently had a way of disrupting the moment, sat in relative silence as Billnitzer shuffled through a stack of papers; Crit squinted at the papers hoping to get a clue about what the detective knew about her past and present.

"Why don't we start with your name, ma'am. I see that you have used a number of aliases. Who are you today?"

Without hesitation, Crit rolled out a list of aliases that would choke a horse.

"Well, let's see," smirked Crit.

"How about Rosa Lee Stewart, or Melba Christine Nichols, or Zada Rodman? Then there's Patsy Allen, Roselle Cherami and Penny Sue Marcades." Crit, who moments ago was in complete silence, had morphed into a cocky comedian making light of her long list of fake names. She continued as if it were all a game.

"Enough," quipped Billnitzer. "Well, why don't you tell me who you really are? I have some names in my file that you haven't spoken….Can you even remember?"

Billnitzer's words hung in the air and for a split second, Crit realized that she had all but forgotten who she really was. Then…

"Fine, Officer, how about Melba Christine Youngblood Marcades? That's what my mama would say if she were here. And God knows I'm glad she ain't. Anyway, I'm somewhat partial to Patsy Allen."

Seconds ago Crit's tone was full of sarcasm; now it was as if she were melting down off of a heroin-induced courage.

Looking Billnitzer square the face, this petite bombshell issued her final command: "Yeah, just call me Patsy."

"Okay, Patsy," responded Billnitzer as he fingered the heroin vial. "As I see it, you have two choices. You can shoot straight with me about everything we are about to discuss…or," holding the vial up in front of her face, "we can save a lot of time and I'll book you now. Prostitution. Possession of an illegal substance, and if I think long enough, I can come up with more. Either way, you're goin' up for a long time. What's your pleasure?"

Instantly, Michael's tiny face flashed before her mind.

She realized that unlike the many men in her free-wheeling past, the officer sitting across the table wasn't going to tolerate her manipulative shit. The time had come for her to tell the truth.

Haltingly, in curt, hushed phrases, Patsy started speaking to Billnitzer.

"What do I have to do?" It was as if she were walking through a mine field. One misstep could place her behind bars, again, for God only knows how long. And, Michael…

"Well, for starters, Patsy, you're gonna tell where you got this powder. I want to know who, when, how, where. You name it; you're gonna spill it all, cause if you don't, you're going on an extended vacation, all paid for by the state!"

Billnitzer's sobering tone shook Patsy; her emotional tension and nervousness escalated. Her voice cracked slightly as she struggled to get the words out.

"They're mean sons-of-bitches; they'll kill me," pleaded Patsy.

"Look, if you don't head down a different road, you and everything dear to you is going to vanish in the wind. Every day, you're walking toward death. You're going to have to trust me," reassured Billnitzer. "Surely, after all this time on the Houston streets, you've run into someone who knows that I'm a man of my word. You'll get protection. You're gonna come through or pay the price. And be clear, I won't tolerate any lying bullshit. We've had you watched for a while. You hang out with… interesting people. Wanna tell me about 'em?"

Little by little, Patsy regurgitated a short list of names, all of whom already seemed to own her; dope suppliers and any man who offered to buy her booze and heroin in exchange for sex. She did not mention the big time mob guys who tapped into her natural beauty and poise. She was often on the arm of some of the biggest names in the underworld.

"That's a start, Patsy. But it's not nearly enough to keep you free today."

Patsy leaned back in her chair and gave Billnitzer a smoldering look of contempt and sarcasm. Then, she spoke in the most saccharine-sweet tone she could muster. "Free. What is free? And jail is a relative concept. There are other kinds of jails…some you can't even see the bars." As she took a deep breath, she concluded with, "I can avoid the jail," indicating the four walls around her. Then, she leaned forward to get Billnitzer's full attention. "By agreeing to live in 'your' jail. Hmm. That's great."

Billnitzer, too, leaned back in his seat. He considered her words and knew that he had the upper hand. Yet, she seemed different from most of the others; straightforward, smart. Some heeded his warnings, others didn't. In his gut, he felt as if this was one who was going to make the right choice; supply him with inside information that would help him wage his private war against the drug madness that had engulfed his city. For this she'd stay out of jail.

Billnitzer and Patsy talked for several hours. Layer by layer, the detective probed her mind and extracted piece after piece of valuable information. As was his habit, everything was scribbled into a notebook. And when it was all over, he stood up and placed the small vial in his pocket.

"Patsy, for now, this stays in my care. What gets done with it is completely in your hands. Do you understand me?"

Patsy nodded as she looked squarely into his confrontational eyes.

Alone, Billnitzer calmly escorted Patsy to the front door, issued a final word of warning, clarified her initial orders, and sent her home. This was to be the first of many meetings between these two over the coming months.

"There you go, Patsy. Go to your son; he's waiting."

Exhausted, Patsy walked out the Houston PD front door and down the steps into the early evening fading light. As she walked away from the police department, she glanced back at Billnitzer. His ultimatum lingered in her thoughts. She couldn't help but be unnerved and jumpy. Her eyes darted left and right looking for any signs of danger. She knew what it was like to be watched by eyes sequestered in the night. All she wanted right now was to get to Michael, and to take a hit.

~

Days, nights and months passed. As instructed and agreed, Patsy – as one of Billnitzer's most reliable and trusted eyes and ears – tip-toed down the precariously thin line between the law and the lawless. Oddly, with each passing, successful, secret arrangement between Billnitzer and her, she felt safer. However, except for the times when Patsy could leave Michael under the safe, loving care of Tom and Minnie, he was frequently subjected to squalid living conditions and the inept care of strangers.

Gradually, tensions escalated in the city between traffickers and those on mission to shut them down. Billnitzer's relentless pursuit of those on the wrong side of the law stunned Patsy. At times, she wished he'd just lay low. Word was on the street that many wanted to bring his tirade to a swift end.

As one who walked through life being both seen and unseen, Patsy frequently witnessed and overheard things that really were not any of her business. As a *fille de joie*, she and others took money from men of all walks of life; mostly those in shinny suits. In almost every situation, drugs, particularly heroin – Patsy's favorite pastime – passed from dirty to clean hands and vice versa.

Sometimes, when Patsy was at or near the Houston PD, as required by Billnitzer, she observed and heard things. Nevertheless, it was clear to her that she was a woman of little consequence, except to Billnitzer.

As a heavy user, Patsy was always looking for an easy score. Sometimes she even observed heroin, collected from arrested traffickers by Houston's finest, walk through the station's front door and then right out the back door for a handy profit. She knew better than to get involved; and, she wondered whether or not Billnitzer was aware. Under normal circumstances, she knew that he wouldn't tolerate it; his mission seemed pure and she imagined that no one was immune from his scrutiny.

~

Throughout the end of 1953 and the early part of 1954, Billnitzer met regularly with Patsy at designated safe locations. At each meeting, Patsy shared with him every known shred of trafficking information, which the detective evaluated. Regardless of its deemed importance at the time, every detail was recorded in Billnitzer's notebook.

Occasionally, Patsy passed on all kinds of information that she hoped Billnitzer would use to stay safe; alive. Far too often, she had seen how simple situations turned bad could end a life in a matter of seconds and she hoped that something like that would not happen to Billnitzer. Over time, she came to understand him as a really good man, one who cared deeply about humanity and the horrible manner in which drugs ravaged lives.

Yet, Patsy still fought against her own demons and her destructive associations beyond Billnitzer. Her everyday life was still spent with pimps, johns, and serious drug traffickers who would not think twice of punishing her for missteps.

In early June, 1954, Patsy, as she had done many times before, reported to Billnitzer's designated meeting spot. In the past, he was always on time, never late. His promptness made Patsy feel as if she were of value, worth something to somebody. But that day everything changed. Billnitzer never showed.

After waiting for well over an hour, Patsy started walking home. It was all she could do to fight off utter panic. Her steps were uncertain. Whatever sense of security she felt in recent months, while linked to Billnitzer, seemed to falter.

Again, she felt alone.

Even worse, she felt watched. Physical safety was always a concern, her's, Michael's, and now Billnitzer's. As she had observed, those in power in the world of prostitution, illicit drug acquisition and trafficking clearly knew their priority: money. Business was business; and sometimes there was collateral damage…it was inevitable.

She wondered if Billnitzer would contact her tomorrow and everything would be as before. As she walked to the place where Michael was staying while she worked, she prayed. Praying; that was something she hadn't done in a very long time.

The night passed painfully slow. Unlike normal, rather than placing Michael in his bassinette, she held him closely in the security of her own bed.

~

The next day, Patsy didn't hear anything from Billnitzer. In spite of her fear, her first inclination was to walk straight into the Houston PD front door and demand to see Billnitzer. Yet, she knew better. So, she waited and went about her day.

At the agreed time, Patsy strolled down the sidewalk toward her assigned location. As she approached a street corner near downtown, she heard a young boy hocking the daily rag. From a distance away, his words ran together in the wind. But as she got closer, she could hardly believe her ears.

"Detective found dead in his office! Read all about it. Policeman shoots himself!"

In utter disbelief, Patsy scampered to the corner and paid for a copy of the Houston Post, June 4, 1954. She scanned front page quickly, looking for any words about Billnitzer. There it was in black and white; written confirmation of her deepest fear.

"2 Relieved of Duty As Officer Kills Self: Melton Out in Big Police Shake-Up; Suicide Blows Probe Wide Open"

Capt. Foy D. Melton, head of the police vice squad, and another policeman were relieved from duty Thursday afternoon less than three hours after a veteran narcotics officer shot himself to death in an office at the Police Station.

The death of Detective Martin Albert Billnitzer, 45, blew wide open a heretofore super secret investigation into alleged "irregularities" in the handling of narcotics cases.

The other policeman relieved of duty was Sidney B. Smith, who was assigned to the vice squad until he was transferred to the burglary and theft squad about nine months ago...Chief of Police L. D. Morrison announced the reliefs from duty after conferences with the two officers and the City Atty Will Sears...

"Pending further investigation of the necessity for disciplinary action for failure to perform his duties in a competent manner, Capt Foy D. Melton is relieved from duty immediately," the chief's brief announcement said.

A different reason was given for Detective Smith's relief. "Pending further investigation of the necessity for disciplinary action for official misconduct, Detective Sidney Smith is relieved of duty immediately," the announcement said...

Detective Billnitzer's death came only a few minutes after he left Chief Morrison's office, where he had been questioned in the narcotics investigation.

The shooting was obviously a deep shock to Chief Morrison, "It was completely uncalled-for," the chief said.

"Billnitzer was a good man – a good, clean, decent, Christian man," Chief Morrison said. "That I am positive of. He's been under a strain and worried. He was completely honest and wouldn't steal anything."

> The chief said Detective Billnitzer, a well-liked officer with a distinguished career in narcotics cases, was "guilty of a technical violation and has been a little sloppy in his work"…he "failed to properly tag evidence and dispose of it. It could have been carelessness, or it could have been improper disposal."
>
> By "improper disposal" the chief may have meant using narcotics to pry information from stool-pigeons, reportedly one of his main points of interest in the narcotics investigation.
>
> Detective Billnitzer, using his .38 caliber service revolver, shot himself twice in the left side of his chest about 11:30 a.m. He died a few minutes later…
>
> "He (Billnitzer) went to a file cabinet in the outer office and then walked into room 310A and closed the door. After about a minute, I (Officer George H. LaRue) heard a gunshot in that office and then I heard a thud. I got up and rushed to the door, and as I took hold of the doorknob, I heard another gunshot"…
>
> Meanwhile, Mrs. Huston had gone to the vice squad office in an effort to help Officer LaRue find Capt Melton. She opened the inner office door - - it was not locked - - and saw Detective Billnitzer's body… "lying on the floor with his head toward the door that I had opened. His shirt was covered with blood, and he was gasping for breath."

Though the article went on, Patsy couldn't read another word. Overcome with shock and utter disbelief, she crumpled up the newspaper, sat down on a street bench and sobbed. In that moment, she realized that at the time she had been waiting for Billnitzer to arrive yesterday at their designated meeting point at 12 noon, he was lying on his office floor bleeding to death.

In a few moments, Patsy pulled herself together and headed straight for Michael. With every step she realized that without Billnitzer alive, Michael and she were a little less safe. The arrangement that they had for many months was like a shield that deflected a fear that could totally smother a person.

It wasn't that long ago that she had mentioned to Billnitzer that she felt compromised; watched by dangerous hidden eyes. Her mind raced as she silently repeated the nightmare she had just read. Something was not right. Why would a man like Billnitzer shoot himself in the heart…twice? Patsy wondered if that was even possible?

"It's all horseshit," mumbled Patsy to herself. "Absolute horseshit."

~

For the next few days, Patsy's sleep was fitful. Her head ached with questions. She needed answers. At this point, her only source of information was an occasional television news program and Houston-based rag headlines. Every day, she searched the pages for new details about Billnitzer's "suicide" and the government's clandestine investigation of corruption within the Houston PD.

Daily update articles filled major area papers: "Houston Vice Squad Officer Found Fatally Shot in Office," "City Detective, Former FBI Man, Probe Targets," and "Houston Pushing Probe of Police."

And, the word was out that federal agents had extended the drug scandal investigations to San Antonio and the Dallas-Fort Worth areas.

Above this mental storm lay Patsy's realization that she needed to escape downtown Houston. One way or the other she had to get Michael and herself to a safe place until this all blew over. As badly as she hated to admit it, she only had two choices; New Orleans or back home with her parents. Neither place seemed perfect. Either way, she knew that there was no such thing as permanently walking away from her habits.

Home?

New Orleans?

When it came time to leave the city, Patsy – now morphing back into Crit – decided to head home first by cab. Her parents' door was always open to her and Michael, but not her lies, drug use and drinking. Crit knew that eventually she would make her way back to New Orleans; the Veteran's Boulevard Marcades house was an easy berth. Besides, Eddie would never turn them away and Jenny, his mother, almost meant more to her than her own mother. But for now, she headed to her parents; 145 Dipping Lane on the outskirts of Houston. Home; for now.

~

Crit was thankful for the loving way her parents welcomed them home. More often than not, they did not know the exact location of their wayward daughter and young grandson. Crit was determined to do life her own way. In her weakest moments, she lived as if she needed no one.

As the cab pulled into the driveway, Crit saw her daddy sitting in a lawn chair on the front porch. It did not take him long to recognize her face, bobbing blonde curls and infectious smile. It had been months since he had last seen her.

"Mama, it's Crit!" Papa hollered loudly to his wife who was inside the house. Within seconds, the two of them were walking toward their daughter who was climbing out of the Yellow Cab; she was holding little Michael in her arms.

As Crit hugged and greeted her parents, her mother spoke first.

"Oh, my Lord. Crit, we didn't even know you were coming. Give me that precious baby boy." The warmness in her mother's voice was reassuring to Crit. Honestly, she had wondered if all would be well on arrival. Only on rare occasions had she taken time to call home.

Although Michael did not fully recognize his grandparents, he smiled and went to them. Papa helped get Crit's luggage out of the cab trunk, and paid the fare.

Casually, Crit surveyed the small frame home which was located on a corner lot with a huge cottonwood tree in the front corner. After everyone greeted each other, Crit and Michael followed Mama and Papa into the house. As always, her mother's house was spick and span; everything neatly in place. It looked starkly different than her recent rundown apartment; quite a change.

Out back was a large fenced back yard, a perfect playground for Michael. Immediately, her Mama and Papa began setting up the second bedroom for their wayward daughter and their young grandson. A warm bed, food, and familiar voices were just what Crit needed for the moment.

After her daddy finished lugging all the luggage into the bedroom, everyone assembled at the kitchen table; Michael was the center of massive, loving attention. Then, the conversation started.

"Crit, how long are you here?" Mama was the first to inquire as Papa sat quietly, ears alert.

"Well, I don't know for sure; downtown Houston is a little scary these days. I guess you read about the Houston PD scandal in the paper. Unbelievable. I knew the detective who shot himself in the heart, two times. Papa, you know that dog don't hunt." Papa nodded.

"Anyway, can we stay for a while?" asked Crit.

"Of course, you can. But, Crit, we're not going to put up with the drinking. And, as much as we would like to do so, we can't cover everything that you and that boy need. You're gonna have find and keep a job," said Papa.

Papa struggled to not sound accusatory, but he had seen this many times before. Crit's declarations about making changes and heading in a new, healthy direction had always been thwarted by her demons. For a moment, he thought back to the month when Crit contracted acute encephalitis.

Even now, he could hear the doctor's warnings regarding how the prolonged fever and swollen brain would probably take a toll on his daughter as she grew into and beyond puberty. Years later, they were living that nightmarish prediction.

"I know, Papa. I promise, I'll find work. I just don't know what to do about Michael," admitted Crit.

"Sure you do! You know we'll help," offered her mother. Mama wasn't about to let her grandson go unattended. One way or the other, he would be cared for. God only knew what horrible situations he'd been through in recent months.

Then Mama blurted out something that took Crit by complete surprise.

"Eddie wrote me; sent the letter to the Fulton Street house before we moved here. He was pretty frustrated. He said that he'd sent you money and other things for Michael. Did he try to help you? You never told us. We just assumed he had done nothing." Mama's comment was sobering.

"What do you mean he wrote you? Do you have the letter? Show me, please," requested Crit.

Mama went straight to her bedroom and retrieved Eddie's letter from a small cardboard box; she had a habit of keeping things like that. Shortly she returned to the kitchen table, handed the letter to Crit and said: "Read it for yourself."

The letter was labelled: 2/26/54 N. O. La.

> *Dear Mrs. Youngblood,*
>
> *Seeing as how you never answered my letters to you, I will let this be my*

last letter. As for the checks, I am going to send my son's money into a trust fund. The latest news I have from either my son or your daughter is that she called my mother's house on the night of the 24th of Feb. She was drunk – screaming and cursing. God bless my boy but what will really be done of him God only knows.

Chris has sold the high chair and many things I had sent my son – which I know he is still young enough to use. I don't intend for my hard earned money to go to waste in such a manner.

I personally think if you and Mr. Youngblood have any kind of understanding as parents and human beings, you will be kind and polite enough to at least consider this letter and answer me. If not, let your conscience be your guide every day henceforth.

Sincerely, Eddie

Crit was stunned; she never told her parents that Michael's father regularly sent her money and other things that he knew his son needed. And now, there was no denying it.

"Is this true?" asked Papa.

"Yes, daddy. He sent money and some other things. Half the stuff I didn't even need." Crit struggled to recover from the exposure.

"And what about the money? What did you do with the money?" pressed Papa.

"Daddy, do you really want to know? Sometimes food or clothes, other times I just needed a drink. You know how I am sometimes." Oddly, Crit told the truth.

"Alright. Here it is, girl. No drinking here; period. Stay sober and you can stay. You've got a chance to start over. Do what's right for Michael…and you." Crit's father was emphatically clear. Crit wondered how she would adhere.

With that settled, the five of them went about the day. Michael's presence broke the awkwardness. Chatter was constant as Michael toddled through the house; his little hands struggled to grab every nick nack within his sight. Mama didn't seem to mind; having that little boy with her mattered more.

As for Crit being home, Mama and Papa cautiously celebrated it all.

As the hours passed, Crit struggled. She needed a drink and even more. She'd planned for this. Hidden deep within her suitcase was a small stash of white. She knew it was wrong and dangerous to bring it into her parent's house, but her demons reigned. She wondered where and how she could find some beer.

Over the next few weeks, Crit secured some small jobs, some of which included E. V. Kennedy Estate and the *Houston Chronicle*. That entire year, she only earned $438.82. This did not meet the criteria of taking care of Michael and adding to the household income, and it certainly did not show that she was trying to make an honest life for herself and her son.

Yet, even with this limited income, Crit always dressed well and made sure every other detail about her appearance was stunning. Of course, as in the past, her appearance and flirtatious nature always attracted the attention of men; that was something Crit always managed to turn to her advantage.

As the months passed, Crit went through ups and downs with her parents. Most of the time, she felt fenced in, unable to run as she wished. Nevertheless, some days her demons got the best of her and she came home drunk and seemingly high or never came home at all. Mama and Papa fought to protect Michael from the chaos and tried to figure out ways to help their daughter.

"We can't do this; Crit must stop this behavior," grumbled Papa. "She has a son and right now she's using the security of having him with us as a reason to raise hell." Mama listened intently; she recognized her husband's urgent tone.

"All we can do is try to talk some sense into her and pray that God will help us survive these days. I just pray that she doesn't get arrested, hurt herself, or get hurt by some asshole. And God help us if she gets arrested." At times like this, Mama never minced words.

Amid the chaos, Christmas came to Dipping Lane. Since Mike's birth, Crit had not been home for one single Christmas; most holidays were spent in New Orleans. But this year was different. Aunts, uncles and cousins came to Houston from across the state and country. All crowded in the small frame house. Laughter and chatter was everywhere.

During the day, the women focused on food preparations, gift wrapping and gossip. The men, free of almost any responsibilities, fiddled around outside. While Minnie took care of Michael, Crit sprawled out on the living room floor and played various games with Jaxie, Dennis and Dianne, her nieces and nephew. Giggling and worry-free fun permeated the room. Scarcely a moment passed that Crit was not enveloped by the children; how they adored their "Aunt Pippy."

That year, Christmas morning was uniquely joyous. Everyone received and shared gifts. And Michael had a most extravagant Christmas morning; black cowboy boots, a chalkboard desk, a bicycle, more wrapped presents than he could count, and a stocking stuffed with candy. No one said a word about it being too much; Michael was finally home for Christmas.

Christmas passed; 1956 arrived, and it did not take long for things to get back to "normal." By early February, Crit had digressed into alarming behaviors. Increased alcohol and drug consumption away from the watchful eyes at home, often sent her into physical states that were painful to watch and almost impossible to manage. It was not unusual for her to simply not go home; often, she simply hitch-hiked to places where she could find alcohol and drugs.

On February 11, just two days before her son's third birthday, Crit headed to Galveston. In the early morning hours, police found her in an awful state; she was beating her head against the sidewalk, acting like a "wild" woman. Immediately, the beat cop called for assistance. As the black and white pulled up, the two policemen worked to gain control of Crit.

"What the hell are you doing? Get your hands off me you son-of-a-bitch!" Crit's tone left no doubt that she was out of her mind with pain. For years now, she had a curious love-hate relationship with cops. Sometimes she was batting her eye and tossing curls in an effort to avoid jail. But at the moment, she was livid and hurting.

With seasoned calm, the police worked to stand her up, put on cuffs and move her in the direction of the car. One of the cops leaned down and retrieved her small purse. Finally, they were headed to John Sealy/Galveston Psychopathic Hospital. One of the cops had already radioed ahead; attendants were waiting as they drove up.

It took several people to get Crit into the wheelchair, into the ER and onto an examination bed. The attending physician immediately ordered a sedative and within a couple of minutes Crit settled down enough to respond to questions.

"Ma'am, please, try to relax; the sedative should offer some relief. Can you tell us who you are and what's hurting you?"

"Rita Lane…Rita!' screamed Crit. "And my damn head is pounding!" Then, Crit's head rolled forward as she leaned over the edge of the bed and vomited. Personnel recognized the symptoms of heroin withdrawal; dilated pupils, vomiting, sweating, agitation and more.

"Purse! Where's my damn purse?" demanded Crit.

"It's right here, ma'am. No one has taken it," reassured a nurse.

Even under the sedative and other counteractive drugs, Crit was hard to control. Further examination revealed that her hair had smatterings of blood from the small wounds created by her pounding the sidewalk. The nurses and attending doctor worked together to get her bandaged. Off to the side, medical personnel fumbled through Crit's purse hoping to find some identification and a phone number to call. Most of the time, Crit never carried identification, but today was an exception. Inside her purse was a small black address book. Several names and exchanges were listed: John Paul, Bill, Viola, and others. And, on the inside cover the attendant saw: Property of Melba Christine Marcades.

"Rita Lane my ass," mumbled the attendant.

Then, out of nowhere, Crit yelled, "Hillcrest 7-3633…sister!"

~

"Yes, good morning. This is the Galveston Psychiatric Hospital calling on behalf Mrs. Melba Christine Marcades. With whom am I speaking, please?"

"Mozelle Wall; my Lord, what's happened to my sister." Mozelle and her husband Morris had received many such phone calls across the years but it never failed to be a shock.

"Yes, Mrs. Wall, this is Dr. Ashya calling on behalf of the John Sealy Hospital system. We have your sister in ER; she was found on the street, apparently suffering from heroine withdrawal. Police brought her to us and we have administered care for the past couple of hours."

"God bless you for helping her," whimpered Mozelle.

"Ma'am, has your sister had a history of heroin use?"

The question covered Mozelle with sadness. She struggled to answer the doctor. "Yes, sir, she has."

"Well, fortunately, she told us how to reach you. So, we needed to let you know that she is in our care. We are not releasing her at the present time; she is being admitted to the Galveston Psychiatric portion of the Sealy complex. Is there anyone else you need to notify? Husband? Parents?" asked Dr. Ashya.

"Yes, sir," answered Mozelle as she fought back tears. "I will notify her mother and father and I am certain that they will be in touch. How can they reach you?" After writing down the number for the psychiatric hospital, the two hung up and Mozelle wept in Morris' arms. After she pulled herself together, she called Tom and Minnie with the sad news.

~

Thirteen days passed before Crit was in any condition to be released. Once notified, Tom drove from Dipping Lane to Galveston to retrieve his daughter. Minnie remained at home with Michael; praying.

Crit was sent home with two prescriptions to assist with her continued recovery; Dilantin, Phenobarbital and orders to stay away from the heroin. Tom, even in his brokenness and confusion, deeply wanted to help his daughter. Most of the time, he had no idea what to do with her.

The days that followed were difficult. Crit became even more high-tempered and irresponsible than before. She behaved as if she had lost all respect for her parents and struggled to give Michael necessary care. Her demons reigned over her.

~

Then, that which her parents prayed would not return, came. In less than two weeks after her Sealy release, she was again taken into custody in Houston for public intoxication, cursing and swearing, and disturbing the peace. This time, the court took firm action in response to her repeated behavior.

Within a matter of days, she was in the hands of the State of Texas court system, undergoing psychiatric evaluation. On February 29, attending physicians, Dominick C. Adamo, M.D. and Mylie E. Durham, Jr., M.D., appeared in court before a Harris

County judge. As testified, Melba Christine Youngblood Marcades was diagnosed with Sociopathic Personality Disturbance and Alcoholism.

Early the next morning, March 1, 1956, Harris County Judge Bob Casey committed Crit to a period of time not to exceed 90 days in the State Hospital, Austin, Texas. For the first time in Crit's life, she was headed to a facility authorized by law to treat mentally ill persons. By 11:00 a.m., she had been transported to Austin and processed into Ward D at the hospital.

Official notification of her court-ordered, 90-day commitment reached her parents within hours of admission. A blanket of sadness filled the house as they went about their lives caring for Michael and praying for their daughter. Their worst nightmares had come true.

Days turned into weeks as Tom and Minnie tended to Michael and juggled responsibilities in their own lives. As they expected, they did not hear anything from Crit during those first weeks. Though they had never been to the Austin State Hospital, or any other mental care facility, they could only imagine the conditions. All they could do was hope against hope for the best.

Michael never gave them an ounce of trouble. His sweet disposition provided momentary relief from the weighty burden they carried about Crit. Each Sunday, as was their practice, they went to church with Michael in tow. Their pastor and closest friends, who were somewhat familiar with the difficult roads they had traveled with Crit, greeted them with kindness and empathy. However, there were others whose whispers and stares communicated the complete opposite. Nevertheless, Tom and Minnie held their heads high; Youngblood pride ran deep.

Then, out of the blue, came a phone call for Tom, who was listed as the official correspondent on Crit's commitment papers. Evidently, she had exceeded expectations in terms of progress at the State Hospital. As of mid-April, her attending physicians diagnosed her condition as "without psychosis" and set her discharge for April 17.

Tom and Minnie were astounded; only six weeks had passed since Crit was committed.

"Are you telling me that six weeks was all it took to straighten her out," said Tom in utter disbelief.

"Aw Papa, maybe Crit has come to her senses. After all, she has a son to raise. Just maybe this treatment and separation from her son was exactly what she needed."

Minnie struggled to sound hopeful. "So what are we supposed to do? Do we need to drive to Austin?"

"Yep; You keep Michael. I'll take off work and go get her," declared Tom. Already, he was thinking about what he was going to say to his daughter on the long ride from Austin to Houston; plenty of time for Tom to get some things off his chest.

~

On the morning of April 17, Tom got up early; he needed to be in Austin by noon. As he backed out of the driveway, Minnie stood on the front porch holding Michael as she waved good-bye. At this point, she knew full well that Tom had seen enough.

As Tom drove to Austin, he smoked one cigarette after the other. In his best moments, he prayed; in his worst, he railed at God for what he had endured for years with his middle daughter. Mile after mile, he recalled the many times Crit and he butted heads; and, he fully expected that today would not be any different.

After about four hours on the road, Tom pulled into downtown Austin. He stopped at a gas station and asked for directions to 4110 Guadalupe Street. Closer to the hospital grounds, he drove past the tall beige brick and black wrought iron fence that surrounded the facility; patient escape looked highly improbable.

Tom drove straight through the main entrance and proceeded to the security gate. Once he identified himself and the reason he was in Austin, the guard gave him instructions to the main administration building where he would retrieve Crit.

Everywhere on campus, Tom saw white-coated nurses attending patients; some in wheel chairs, some sitting motionless on benches. After he parked his Ford Fairlane, he walked in the front door of the administration building and right up to the receptionist who was encased behind glass and bars. Tom removed his hat, leaned forward and spoke into the small opening in the glass.

"Afternoon, ma'am. I'm T. J. Youngblood and I'm here to pick up my daughter Melba Christine Youngblood Marcades."

"Yes, Mr. Youngblood. We've been expecting you. I'll notify attending personnel that you are here. It will just take a few minutes to process the release papers and you will be on your way. Would you please have a seat," offered the woman as she motioned to the nearby reception seating.

Tom took a seat and waited; he did not know exactly what he would say to his daughter. He just wanted to get it over with and head home. Then, Tom heard the elevator open and out walked someone who appeared to be a doctor; Tom stood up.

"Mr. Youngblood?" said the doctor as he extended his hand. "I'm Dr. Adamo, one of the doctors who has treated your daughter. Before Christine arrives, I thought it would be good for us to have a few minutes together; I'll let you know about her time with us and give you a chance to ask questions."

Tom nodded in agreement.

"If you'd follow me down the hall, we can have some privacy in one of our conference rooms." Dr. Adamo motioned for Tom to follow. Once in the conference room, the doctor closed the door.

"Mr. Youngblood, I am sure you are aware that six weeks ago we received your daughter by direct order from Judge Casey in Harris County. At that time, she was diagnosed as one suffering from sociopathic personality disturbance and acute alcoholism."

"Yes, sir," answered Tom.

"Christine's court-ordered commitment allowed us 90 days to treat your daughter. Surprisingly, our treatments – which primarily consisted of initial isolation and rest, careful administration of antipsychotics and psychotherapy sessions – were effective far sooner than originally anticipated," reported Dr. Adamo.

While Tom was well-educated for a man of his life stature, most of Dr. Adamo's explanation was confusing; however, he did understand that his daughter had been given drugs to redirect her thinking and behavior. In his heart, he just wanted his daughter to get well.

After a few minutes of further discussion, Dr. Adamo escorted Tom back to the reception area and told him that Christine would be down in just a few minutes.

Tom waited anxiously; a mixture of worry, frustration and anger rushed through his body. Then, again, the elevator opened and there was Crit, sitting calmly in a wheel chair. Uncharacteristically, her appearance was somewhat plain and her clothes, which had been stored for six weeks, were wrinkled.

Tom greeted Crit, signed her discharge papers, and headed to the door. As the attendant rolled the wheel chair outside toward the Fairlane, Tom struggled to remain calm. His gate was long and his head drooped downward. Crit was all-to-familiar with her daddy's behaviors; she knew he was in a state and braced herself for the onslaught.

Tom cranked the car, exited the State Hospital campus and headed for Houston. Initially, neither one of them had much to say to each other. Once on the main highway, Tom broached all the issues that were running through his mind.

"Crit, how are you? What happened to you in there?" Papa had heard horror stories about how the hospitals treated mental patients. He wondered how his daughter had been treated.

"I'm okay, Papa. What a hell hole and a complete waste of my time. Drugs and bullshit talking sessions. Can't tell you how badly I want a drink." Her comments went all over her daddy.

"What? Your mama and I have taken care of your son for over six weeks, worried ourselves sick about what to do with you, and all you can say to me is you want a drink. Hell, Crit. You beat everything." Tom's tone grew more coarse with each word.

Wisely, for once, Crit kept her mouth shut. In the silence, Tom drove faster and faster. Mile after mile, Crit stared out the window, body angled away from her daddy, and watching the flickering scenery fly like an old-timey picture show. Everything was blurred, indistinguishable, all jumbled, just like Crit's life. As far as she was concerned, they could not get home soon enough. She wanted to hold her son, see her mama…and figure out a way to have a beer.

~

At Dipping Lane, Minnie walked the floor clutching Michael. By all her reasoning, Tom and Crit were due back anytime. Then, she heard the Fairlane turn into the driveway and come to an abrupt stop. As she walked to the front door, she could hear car doors slamming shut.

In an instant, Crit was on the front porch in search of her son.

"Where's my boy?" asked Crit as she smiled wryly at her mother. Michael came running as Crit held out her arms. Suddenly, a river of tears flowed from her eyes. In her mind, she believed that the only thing she ever got right in this world was Michael; all else was an endless list of "almosts."

"Crit, thank God you are home. Come here," pleaded Minnie. "We have been so worried; are you okay?"

"Hell, I guess. Six weeks…"

As Papa entered the front door, Crit, with Michael in her arms, headed for the bedroom. She was not really in the mood for being reminded of her failures. She just wanted her son.

That evening, the tension in house was stifling. As everyone sat down for supper, Mama took the lead questioning Crit.

"Crit, are you better? Do you feel like you're going to be able to make some changes, get and keep a job, stay sober, and be a mother to that precious boy?" Mama wanted some answers from her troubled child.

"Who knows. What difference does it make? I can't do anything right anyway. Everywhere I step, shit." Clearly, Crit was agitated. "I sure as hell can't stay here." Her blatant honesty cut deeply.

"Don't tell me you're going back to New Orleans; he's had it with you," argued Papa.

"Eddie would never turn me away, and neither would Jenny; certainly not with Michael in my arms. I'll go there, find work, save some money and figure out what to do next." As soon as those words passed her lips, she wondered silently what it would feel like to be back in New Orleans; Bourbon Street, the top of the world.

The next morning, Crit rose early. After everyone else went to bed last night, she packed her suitcase, make-up kit, and as much of Michael's belongings as possible. Then, she retrieved fifty-two dollars that she had hidden beneath the suitcase liner; bus tickets to New Orleans.

As she walked toward the kitchen with Michael, she heard her Mama and Papa talking softly; every morning, coffee and cigarettes.

"Morning, Crit," whispered Mama as she noticed that her daughter and grandson were already dressed as if they were leaving.

Crit smiled as she bounced into the kitchen table chair.

"Goin' somewhere?" asked her daddy.

"Yeah, I can't stay here. I'm grateful for what you did for Michael while I was laid up in Austin. But I gotta go; things to do, people to see in big 'Nawlins.'" Crit knew that Eddie and Jenny would watch Michael, which would give her time to call John Paul about work.

"Crit, does Eddie know you're comin'?" asked Papa.

"No, but it doesn't matter; he'll take me." And with that, Crit got up and called a Yellow Cab. It was not long before the cab pulled into the driveway. The three of them looked at each other, knowing full well what was coming.

Without hesitation, Papa gathered all Crit's belongings and placed them in the trunk. By that time, Crit, Michael and Mama were saying good-bye to each other. Crit walked over to her daddy, kissed his cheek and told him that she loved him. Mama and Papa cradled little Mike in their arms one last minute, and then Crit and he crawled into the backseat. Michael stood on little toddler legs to see "Mama," the woman who had become his security. In frustration, Crit pulled Michael into her lap, out of their sight, as the cab backed out of the driveway.

As the cab pulled away, Mama and Papa stood speechless and broken-hearted in the driveway. Mama wiped her eyes. Then, they were gone.

~

Once in New Orleans, Crit and Michael would make their way, completely unannounced, to the Veteran's Boulevard house. Traveling by bus meant that they were facing a long day. As best as possible, Crit took care of her young son. About ten hours later, they finally pulled into the bus depot. As soon as they unloaded, Crit waved for a cab and headed to Eddie and Jenny's.

Shortly, the cab pulled up to the house, a place she knew well. From all outside appearances, nothing had changed. As she and Michael exited the cab, she saw Eddie near the back of the property, playing with his dogs; Jenny was standing near the shed. Eddie could not believe his eyes, yet in another way, he was not surprised at all. Being unpredictable was one of Crit's most consistent personality traits.

"My God, it's Christine," hollered Eddie to his mother Jenny. She watched in total disbelief. There was a time when she would have done anything for Crit, but those days waned; too many drunken arguments, run-ins with the law on Bourbon Street, and difficult conversations with her son. She shook her head as Eddie walked directly towards his son.

"Christine, why didn't you call me?" Eddie imagined that Crit probably did not call for fear that she would be turned away; after all, they had been divorced since the summer of '55. And, neither he nor his mother had heard from her in months. Off to the side, Jenny kindly smiled at Crit.

An awkwardness loomed over the reunion. Michael clutched at his mother. It had been too long; he no longer recognized his own daddy. Instinctively, Jenny walked closer and coaxed her little grandson into her arms. Unlike Eddie, she realized that Michael was scared.

Eddie wondered, "What now?" Once the divorce was finalized, he went on with his personal life and certainly had not reported those details to Crit. For now, he decided to simply talk to Crit about her unexpected arrival and plans.

"I know you don't want me here, and I don't want to be her either, but, I have a job possibility and Michael needs a place to stay while I secure it." Crit quickly offered an explanation for her coming back to Eddie's house.

"Michael is welcome here. You're not!" Eddie struggled to not raise his voice. "I don't give a damn where you go or who you go to; you aren't staying here." Eddie was still fuming about everything that transpired between him and Crit's parents. They had not even bothered to answer his letters.

"Look, I've been sick." Crit dared not fully explain that she had been committed to the Austin State Hospital. "I wasn't even feeling well enough to write and explain what I was doing and that I was headed here." Crit hoped that the yarn she was spinning was enough to placate Eddie.

"Jenny, I know there was a time that you would do anything for me. Would you help me one more time? Please, keep Michael while I 'secure a job' downtown." Crit glanced back and forth between Eddie and Jenny, hoping to convince them to help.

"I'd never turn away my son," answered Eddie. Crit noticed that Eddie left her out of his comment. "You have one day to find somewhere to go."

~

As nightfall came, things got quiet in the house. Jenny fussed over Michael; fed him and tucked him in bed. Crit had just returned to the house and Eddie realized that he had to talk to her.

Bluntly, Eddie told Crit to sit down at the kitchen table. Things had changed in his life and she needed to know about it now.

"Christine, I need to tell you some things. After the divorce, I went on with my life. I never really knew if I would see you or Michael again; and God knows it's wonderful to see him now," confessed Eddie as Crit listened intently.

"What do you mean, different? You still live here with your mother and I don't see another woman," asked Crit with a slight sense of impatience in her voice.

"Well, I've met someone, Christine; I met Barbara."

"Where'd you meet her, Bourdon Street?" Crit wondered if Eddie has fallen in love with someone at the Blue Angel, the place where they met long ago.

"No, I didn't meet her in the Quarter," answered Eddie.

"Well, then she certainly won't be able to keep you happy Edward Joseph Marcades," snarled Crit. "I know what you need, always have."

"Crit, it's over. Do whatever you have to do to finalize your job. Michael can stay here as long as he wants. But like I said, not you. Not anymore." Eddie addressed his former wife emphatically. "Barbara and I are engaged and have taken steps to buy a little house of our own in Metairie over on Phosphor Street. No way in hell is Barbara going to put up with you being here. We'll find somewhere for you to stay. Maybe you can stay with Malcolm."

Crit was stunned; this was not exactly what she had expected. Then, without warning, she stood up, walked into the bedroom and grabbed her purse. Eddie followed.

"Eddie, I gotta get out of here; I need some time to think about all this. And, more than anything, I need a drink. Watch Michael; I'll be back soon."

"Crit, don't." Eddie pleaded. Then, before he knew it, Crit spun around and was out the door in search of a cab. Unlike years passed, Eddie did not chase her.

~

The next morning, Crit awoke to the smell of bacon and eggs; it made her want to vomit. She stumbled into the bathroom and washed her face. Her hair was a mess. She could hear the chatter between Jenny and Eddie. Jenny had Michael seated at a small table; she had already served him breakfast. Crit mustered up her courage and quietly slipped into a chair at the main table.

For a moment, no one spoke a word. Then, Jenny broke the silence.

"Coffee?" asked Jenny in a rather flat tone. It was all she could do to keep from pouncing on Crit.

"Please," responded Crit. As she put sugar in her coffee, Eddie chimed in.

"Crit, what in the hell were you thinking last night? Left Michael here in my mother's hands. All so you could go out and carouse. Have you lost your mind? You sure as hell better have something to say for yourself."

Crit had heard that tone before; she knew that Eddie was beside himself with anger.

"No, I haven't lost my mind! I wasn't prepared for your news; I just had to get out," answered Crit.

"You can't do that; you have Michael! Let me make it clear; you ain't every pullin' that shit on me, hell on us, again. Do you hear me?" Eddie made clear his orders.

"You're damn right! I ain't doin' it again cause I'm never come back here, at least not to this house. Only God knows when you'll see me or your son again." Before Eddie or Jenny could even respond, Crit shot out of the kitchen with Michael in tow. In the bedroom, she packed up her belongings and dressed Michael.

Eddie stepped into bedroom and picked up Michael.

"Give me my son!" yelled Crit as she struggled to take Michael away from Eddie. In an instant, Crit and Eddie were yelling at each other and pulling at Michael. He became frightened and started to cry.

Against her strongest instincts, Jenny stayed out of it.

"Call me a cab, Eddie," pleaded Crit through tears of her own.

Taking pity on the child, Eddie backed off. Though broken-hearted, he did not try to stop Crit. As the cab drove away from the Veteran's house, Eddie wondered if this was the last time he'd ever see his son.

Crit purchased bus tickets to take her to the only place she knew to go; Houston, but certainly not to her parent's home. She figured that she would track down some old friends who would help her get settled. As the bus pulled out to head west, Crit could not help but remember the panic that led her away from downtown Houston just a few years ago. Even now, it felt like Billnitzer's "suicide" was just yesterday.

Once in Houston, Crit hauled Michael in and out several temporary living situations, none of which were well furnished. She stayed around in different places in Houston that were not child friendly. One thing she did correctly was register Michael at a fairly clean nursery: Miss Connie's Playland. One way or the other, she had to be free to do as she willed during the day and night.

Quickly sliding back into the lifestyle that would not let her go, she frequented night spots picking up men, or letting men pick her up, who would pay her expenses and give her money for sexual favors. She was once again plunged fully into drugs, alcohol and men, a mantra of her life.

Ultimately, Miss Connie would no longer keep Michael because Crit rarely came to pick him up when promised, and she was greatly behind with the required fees. "Ms. Marcades, you need to straighten yourself up and tend to your child. You are neglecting him!"

Crit flew into a rage and cursed the lady with words that only a woman of the street would use. Part of the display was so she could dash away without making the final payment for Michael's childcare; as always, she was broke.

"Dear God, please bless and look over that precious little boy," Miss Connie prayed softly as she shook her head and watched Crit and Michael leave.

Minnie Bell and Tom sat at the kitchen table where the faithful old clock was still ticking away as they shared morning coffee. The sameness of life had melded them together like concrete. They shared everything: church going, grocery shopping, rocking on the front porch, visiting neighbors and relatives, and most of all, any event that pertained to their children and grandchildren. They did even more together now that no one lived at home and it was just the two of them. Months passed; seldom any communication from Crit and certainly not a chance to see Michael. Although Crit never told her parents exactly where she was in Houston, she did call and let them know that she was nearby. Crit had a way of keeping her location and identity secret.

"Wonder where Crit is now?" Minnie Bell sat with her elbow on the table; holding her chin in her left hand and her coffee up to her lips with the right. Tom shrugged and scooted his chair back. "Only God knows that."

They sat silently. Tick-tock. Tick-tock. Tom lit up a cigarette, blowing a smoke ring.

"I can't get little Mike out of my mind this morning. We ain't seen him hardly at all since he started walkin', and he's somewhere right out there in Houston," Minnie answered hoarsely.

"How old is he gettin' to be?" A sad pall fell over the twosome.

"Nearly five." Minnie Bell lit herself a cigarette; it went with her morning coffee.

"Pore little feller. He could be dead by now with a no-good mother like Crit."

"Oh, Tom, don't say that." She slid the lighter back over to Tom.

Tom looked straight ahead, muttering, "You know it's the truth, Minnie Bell. We must have messed up with that child somehow."

She sat still and quiet; listening to the clock. "I heard somethin' I ain't been able to tell you, Tom."

He looked at Minnie Bell with his stoic face. He knew from experience if it was about Crit, it would be something bad. "What's that?"

Minnie's face paled. "Amanda Crow's son told her he seen Crit in downtown Houston a couple of weeks ago."

"That's so?" Tom took a sip of coffee. "What part of Houston?"

"He saw her once on one of the main streets, and another time down there on skid row where all the bums and drunks lay out."

"What was she doin' down there?"

Minnie Bell lifted her chin and took a deep breath, trying to be courageous. "He said she was sellin' dope, and, I can't hardly say it; she was a prostitute, Tom. I just can't get a'hold of knowing a daughter of ours is a street walker and doing such awful things."

"How did Amanda's son know that for sure?" Tom never rushed to judgment.

"Crit walked up to his car window and told him how much it cost. He knew for sure it was her because he met her a few years back. He told his mother she looked terrible and was so doped up she hardly knew where she was. That's why I'm worried about little Michael."

"Well, what are you thinkin'?"

"I'm thinkin' that God wants us to go see about our grandson, Mike. You know, Tom, for all of the trouble and heartache Crit has caused us throughout her life, even back when she turned up with syphilis, and even when she went to prison, we lived through the shame and didn't turn our back on her. Now, I know it's too late for us to save her, but maybe it's not too late for us to save Mike." Minnie Bell reached up under her glasses to wipe away the silent tears, as she stubbed out her cigarette.

Tom looked away and then put his cigarette out also. He then stood up abruptly and picked up his hat, taking the car keys out of his pocket.

"Where are you goin', Tom?"

"Minnie Bell, if God told you that we should go find Mike, then we better do it!"

With a smile for her husband, she quickly took her sweater off of a peg and got her pocketbook from the bedroom. They closed and locked the back door before getting into their silver-grey Ford Fairlane. With the trade of his old car and money he saved ahead, it was free and clear. Tom was proud of that.

Following the uneasy feelings they both were experiencing, they headed for the large, inner city of Houston, without a clue as to how they might be able to find Crit and Michael.

~

Tom and Minnie Bell lived out on the edge of Houston and didn't like to drive in the inner city traffic. He was acquainted with all of the major streets from the years when he worked there as a younger man, which made it a little easier.

Tom clenched the steering wheel and looked over at Minnie. "I don't think there is any hope in looking for them on these main streets. We wouldn't see them anyway. I'm gonna edge on over to the older, run-down part of Houston. It's gotten real seedy through the years. Sounds like what that Crow boy was talking about."

Minnie Bell nervously clutched her pocketbook. "How will we find them in all of this, Tom?"

"Since you said God sent us, we'll just have to depend on that, but it does sound nigh impossible."

Tom and Minnie saw life differently since they experienced the glowing light shining from the crib of their sick and dying first baby, Harvey Lee, moments before his last breath. They believed there was a heavenly presence over the crib and since that day, they began to look for a sign, or a feeling from God to direct them to make the right choices and decisions. They both believed in strong leadings from God and respected it in one another, but especially if it came from Minnie Bell.

Tom drove slowly as he and Minnie Bell looked up and down the sidewalks. The deeper they drove into the bowels of the old section, the more dilapidated it became. Deserted shops and stores with plywood nailed across the fronts were innumerable. Weeds grew in every place there was a little dirt, and up through cracks in the concrete.

The people they saw were mostly vagrants, homeless, and mentally ill, pushing purloined baskets from grocery stores, filled with junk and their belongings. Drunks were sprawled in a state of stupor against walls. A blind man strummed a guitar, begging for money while his cur sat dutifully beside him. Young thugs hung around the corners, buying, selling and preying.

"This is just pitiful, Tom. If Crit is down here with Mike, oh my dear God." Minnie could not face that her daughter had lived a depraved life since she was a young teen. It was too painful to admit, though she knew it in her heart.

"Try not to get upset." Tom was looking and driving, wanting to keep them safe at the same time.

"Listen to me, Tom. If we find Mike, we're takin' him home with us for good. He is an innocent child and has got to be taken away from Crit forever. We've got to fight for him; and I will, until my last breath! We're gonna love him and raise him right, just like he was our own baby. God's got a plan for Mike, or he would not have sent us for him."

Tom glanced over at her determined face. Seldom did he hear his wife speak with such fervor and determination; the fire in her eyes was undeniable. He slowed down at a corner to stop for a red light. Women in garish makeup and skimpy clothes loitered about; a walking advertisement for their trade.

Then, Tom and Minnie heard Crit yelling. "Mama! Wait Papa, wait!" Suddenly, the back car door opened and a breathless Crit jumped into the back seat. "I was afraid you would leave me! I saw you drive by. What are you doin' here?"

The shocked parents looked back at her. "We were lookin' for you. Where's Mike?" Minnie blurted. "Where's that baby? We want to see him now."

"Oh, okay. Turn right here at this corner, Papa. It's not far."

"Who's got him?" Minnie pressed.

"I've got a room where we stay."

"Who's with him?" Tom asked, astounded that Crit was in the car. He gripped the steering wheel tighter, still driving slowly to avoid an accident.

"He's there by hisself."

"Alone?" Minnie almost screamed. "My God, Crit! Have you lost your mind?"

"I've been kinda sick. I need some medicine." Crit's hands were shaking, her face was pale, and she smelled dirty. "Or maybe you could buy me a drink."

She seemed removed and out of control, almost unaware of herself. "Do you have a cigarette, Papa?"

Furious, Tom shouted, "Not now. What's wrong with you, Crit?"

Crit giggled. "Oh, you know. Just stuff. It's that building up ahead. It ought to be pretty safe to leave the car in front since it's daytime." Her speech slurred.

Minnie and Tom clung to one another as they followed Crit up two sets of stairs in a dimly lit stairwell. Debris and trash cluttered their path. Their lost, prodigal, black sheep of a daughter stopped in front of a door with the word "whore" spray painted on it, amongst other types of graffiti.

"This is my room," Crit said, with no emotion in her voice. The threesome stood there together, waiting.

Tom tried to turn the doorknob. "Don't you have a key, Crit?"

She giggled insanely. "Oh yeah, a key." Reaching down into her bosom, she found it and handed it to her father.

Tom turned the lock and slowly pushed open the door. The single room was dimly lit by a tattered, half-raised window shade. A little boy with big eyes sat huddled fearfully in a corner. He was clutching a toy truck, and an empty bread wrapper. The room smelled of urine and filth and cockroaches scurried about without fear.

Minnie Bell knelt down and held out her arms. "It's me, Mike. It's your Grandmama. Come here, you sweet boy."

He looked at her hesitantly, then stood up and ran into her arms, as Minnie sobbed and enfolded him, holding him close.

Tom looked at the scene with a broken heart of horror and disbelief. His brain could not accept the unbelievable reality.

Crit began to sob uncontrollably as if she too was forced to face who she was, and the horrible circumstances her baby, Michael, had to endure because of her. "I can't do this anymore. I can't take care of him. You better take him home with you." Crit looked at the disgusted, shocked faces of the couple who had given her life and nurtured her the best they could.

Tom took Michael from Minnie Bell. The little boy leaned back to look at his face, as if in remembrance, then hugged Tom's neck so tightly it was impossible to loosen his arms. He was not letting go and neither was Tom.

Michael sat in Minnie Bell's lap while Tom drove home. Knowing they might never see their daughter again, they took solace in the fact they had rescued their young grandson. Soon, they would have him settled in their house and enrolled in first grade. There was no doubt it was God's plan, or they would not have found Michael. It was a miracle, a story they would share with him when he became a man.

~

Back in the filthy room, Melba Christine Youngblood Marcades looked around, as if searching for Michael. She saw his box of baby clothes in the open leather bag she still dragged around. Picking up the box, she clutched it to her breast. Staggering forward, she fell down on the bare mattress on the floor, before slipping into a momentary silent rage against the loss of Michael and every dead end road she had traveled up to this point in her life. Prison. Jails. Crazy hospitals. Court rooms. Crit could not resist the litany that defined her failed existence.

"Shit! That's all I am, a worthless piece of shit that can't be enough for any man, at least nothing more than a good screw on command. Not for Eddie. Nor for any man I've known; not even my own daddy. Hell, I used to be on top of the damn world. People fell all over themselves when I glanced their way, cooed and flipped my hair. I used to be somebody. Now, I ain't shit. I can't do anything right, at least not on the right side of the law." The confession did little to lift Crit.

"I don't know why I just don't kill myself; I know how. Hell, who'd miss me? Surely not my parents or sisters. The only people who'd miss me send me up and down the damn highways hockin' crotch and heroin. And, I can't stay away from the stuff. Hell, I don't want to stay away from it."

Then, as she stood up, the rage exited her body. "AHHHHH!!!!!!" Crit's agonizing verbal explosion surely permeated the paper-thin walls of her dilapidated apartment. Then immediately, her tone became sullen.

"And now, I've lost the only thing I ever did right…my boy." With those words, Crit sobbed silently, collapsed on the hard floor and slipped into a stupor of unawareness.

~

The following months were some of Crit's darkest. Morning, noon and night, she indulged the worst side of her humanity. She was constantly at the beck and call of her pimps and lords; one highway after the other, in cars stolen specifically for the surreptitious, cross-state journeys. And when alone, she tried to drown out reality with a deadly combination of heroin and alcohol.

Arrests came, one right after the other, often only days apart. New Orleans. Houston. Dallas. Most of the time, these three cities served as her primary points of connection with those running drugs. Of course, her contacts were with those somewhere down the power chain. Nevertheless, these men were serious assholes; not to be toyed with. The only thing that mattered was the delivery and the money.

"So, tell me again your instructions," ordered one of Crit's handlers.

"Pick up the car at the vacant warehouse, powder is already loaded, keep my mouth shut. If I get stopped, play stupid. If I get arrested, don't panic. Make my one phone call and wait." Crit knew the routine like the back of her hand.

"And when you're done, your cut will be given to you. You don't need to know who, when and where. It'll be there." And with those words, her handler slipped a small flask of white powder into her hand and kissed her on the cheek; clearly, she was owned.

~

In mid-1957, Crit was assigned several trafficking trips, all in New Mexico. Turned out, she was not too lucky in the Land of Enchantment. She wound up getting arrested twice in New Mexico under her given name. The drugs had been delivered but she was stopped for driving a stolen vehicle across state lines: Dyer Act – a major federal crime.

Both times, Crit appeared before the US District Court the District of New Mexico under the prosecutorial scrutiny of James Borland, US Attorney. After being issued guilty verdicts on Criminal Account Nos. 19366 and 19367 (car theft), Crit was further declared as having Sociopathic Personality Disturbance and Antisocial Reaction (alcoholism)…and the court labeled her mentally incompetent, unable to stand trial.

When the verdicts came down, Crit stood motionless next to her public defender.

"Ma'am, sorry we didn't get better results. Good luck on your rehabilitation." Crit figured the attorney had spoken those words dozens of times to his clients.

These verdicts sent Crit halfway across the country to St. Elizabeth's Hospital, Washington, D. C. She was ordered to stay there until such time that she had recovered from her illnesses and was able to understand the difference between right and wrong.

"What the hell? Washington, D. C.?" Crit spoke under her breath; she could not believe her ears. As she was taken out of the court room, she wondered how long this commitment would last and what she would have to endure.

"Damn hot cars. F'n assholes; they better get me out." At the moment, Crit had forgotten that there was no quick answer to this situation. Like it or not, she was headed to St. Elizabeth's…the thought was staggering.

~

On September 20, 1957, Crit arrived and was admitted to St. Elizabeth's Hospital. As she arrived at the hospital under the supervision of designated court officials, she remained silent with eyes looking everywhere. The hospital campus was far larger than she had anticipated, several hundred acres. What she saw from the main gatehouse entrance was a rather plain, albeit expansive, three-story building, adorned in areas by green vines attached to the brick structure. Almost without exception, the windows were covered up with attachments that seemed to block all light of day. The exterior stair cases were lined with fencing and the landings were encaged. For the most part, all the buildings looked prison-like and drab. Only the center court, with sidewalks lined with trees, offered feelings of life.

Court officials escorted Crit into a side door labelled: Admissions. Once inside, she was directed to the admissions desk where she began the arduous check-in process.

"Dr. Moya to Admissions; Dr. Moya to Admissions." The announcement rang down the cement floors, lined with flat tile. Crit did not know it yet, but Moya was to be her psychiatric supervisor during the hospitalization. As he arrived, he greeted her politely.

"Good afternoon, Melba," offered Dr. Moya.

Crit nodded and said, "I prefer Christine, or even better, Crit."

"I'll make a note, Christine. Now, let's get down to business and get all these admissions logistics behind us. The next hour or so seemed laborious to Crit; question after question reminded her of many life mistakes. And at the end, Dr. Moya punctuated the list by affirming that she was sent here by the District Court of New Mexico as suffering from sociopathic personality disturbance and alcoholism.

Again, Crit simply nodded as the doctor went on and on.

"Okay, so if you would, please, hop up onto the examination table. We need to check your vitals, go over a couple of things on your medical record and then I'll send you over for some basic x-rays." It was obvious, Moya was not going to neglect any aspect of Crit's admission examination.

As Moya checked Crit's vitals, he probed for medical record clarifications.

"So, Christine, I see here that you have had some issues with your kidneys in the past," inquired the doctor.

"Yes, sir. Off and on."

"I'm certain you are aware that your affinity for alcohol has certainly contributed to your kidney issues, right?"

"Uh, yes. I've been told that. But sometimes you gotta have what you gotta have, doc." Moya did not chuckle at Crit's comment.

"And, I also see that you had a run-in with an STD when you were in your early twenties; syphilis. Is that correct?"

"Yeah, I was a little wild and didn't really pay much attention to protecting myself. Besides, it was always a possibility, given my vocation." Crit glanced at the doctor with eyebrows raised and a mischievous smile on her face.

Dr. Moya continued.

"Christine, just one additional question before I release you to one of our nurses. Have ever taken a serious fall or been hit in any way that might have injured your skull? I'm seeing something a little abnormal on your scan," declared the doctor.

"My skull? Hell, it's pretty hard, doc," joked Crit. "But, yeah, I've taken a few falls, especially when I was a teenager. Hell, I'd do anything," confessed Crit.

"Well, it looks as if you might have done some damage to the skull structure; nothing major, I just noted it here in your records." Moya carefully underlined the printed comment: "skull defect in left temporoparietal area; age 16."

Crit wondered: "Skull fracture?"

"Okay, Christine, that's it for today. You and I will be seeing a lot of each other. If you need something, just ask. We're here to help you get healthier."

"Nurse, Christine is ready to be taken to her room," instructed the doctor.

Immediately, Crit was led to a room that she was to share with one other patient.

As she followed the nurse through the winding maze of halls, she mumbled under her breath, "Damn, these people look crazy." And with that, her first day at St. Elizabeth's was underway.

⁓

Evening came and Crit crawled into bed and tried to go to sleep. It seemed that night hours at St. Elizabeth's were similar to those in other hospitals, but there were thousands of patients. Never before had Crit been committed to a facility of this magnitude. As she closed her eyes, her mind raced. At all hours, people up and down the ward hall called out for help; it made sleeping difficult. But finally, her fatigue took over and she drifted off.

As morning came, Crit opened her eyes and glanced around; no sunlight. The windows simply did not allow the sunlight to enter.

"How can I get better if I can't even see the damn sun in the morning," thought Crit. Then, following the lead of her roomie, she got up, dressed in the provided patient clothing and shuffled to breakfast. The hall was cluttered with dozens of patients, all fumbling toward the cafeteria.

As Crit picked up her breakfast tray, she constantly looked left and right, kept her ears open and smiled at anyone she thought might be a potential friend. So far, St. Elizabeth's life did not look too complicated; besides, Crit was seasoned at adapting. In most situations, she learned the ropes fast.

"Hey blondie," said a patient at her table. "I'm Viola; what's your name?"

Before responding, Crit noticed Viola's pleasant appearance and rather infectious smile.

"Gosh, I've had lots of names," offered Crit playfully. "How about Christine for starters?"

"Beautiful name, Christine," answered Viola. "You're new, right? First day?"

"Yep," said Crit as she ate her breakfast.

"Well, hey, it ain't as bad as it looks. But you're gonna need some friends. Otherwise, you'll go…crazy, girl!"

Crit found the bantering fun. Only time would tell if she could trust Viola.

"Look," continued Viola. "If you play your cards right, you can get out of this building pretty often, walk around the inner grounds, feel the sun and just breathe fresh air away from the crazies!" That sounded good to Crit.

In the coming days, Crit and Viola spent a considerable amount of time together. As it turns out, Viola had quite a bit in common with Crit; she, too, missed her drugs and alcohol.

Months passed and Crit never heard a word from her family; not even a letter from her mother. Feelings of isolation and insignificance dominated her thoughts. Plus, her body ached for a drop of booze or a quick shot.

Many days, Crit lived in dark, desperate places. Some days her demons got the best of her, resulting in combative outbursts against St. Elizabeth's staff. During private therapy sessions, Dr. Moya and others probed for answers regarding such behaviors.

"Hell, it wasn't me. It was my 'other self.' Sometimes, I just can't control that person." Crit spoke as if she simply had no control over her actions.

When she behaved like this, the result was isolation. Conversely, when she acted well and showed signs of mental health progress, she earned privileges, including the freedom to be outside unattended, and the opportunity to attend entertainment events. At times, Crit was even off medications.

Then, out of the blue, a breath of fresh air rushed into Crit's world.

"Christine Marcades, please report to the nurse's station." The announcement was repeated several times. Quickly, Crit complied. The words she heard shocked her: "You have visitors."

"Visitors, who?" asked Crit.

"A Colonel Jack Stewart, his wife and their daughter," responded the nurse. It was common knowledge that Crit never had visitors. The staff was equally shocked.

Crit raced into the bathroom to check her appearance, then headed outside, down the security steps and out the landing cage into the courtyard where she was told to wait for her visitors.

As she waited on a bench, she saw her sister Grace and family walking toward her. Jaxie, their precocious, brilliant daughter, was a young teenager at the time. She, like the rest of her first cousins, absolutely adored her Aunt Pippy.

Crit stood in anticipation of hugging her family; it had been about a year since she had heard from anyone.

"Aunt Pippy! Aunt Pippy!" Jaxie shouted as she ran gleefully toward Crit.

Instinctively, Crit held out her arms to receive her niece.

"Oh, Jaxie girl, you're all grown up. Look at you. You're beautiful," offered Crit.

"Never as beautiful as you, Aunt Pippy," whispered Jaxie so her parents could not hear.

Crit looked up; there before stood her sister and the ever-distinct Colonel Jackson W. Stewart, her brother-in-law. As the two sisters hugged for the first time in years, Jack watched through his horn-rimmed, government-issued glasses. He was dressed impeccably in his highly-decorated uniform.

Crit smiled at her sister and motioned for everyone to have a seat on the nearby benches. For the first several minutes, superfluous dialogue dominated their conversations. Then…

"Aunt Pippy, when are you getting out? How are you feeling? Have you heard from Mama and Papa?" Jaxie's list of questions rushed out of her mouth.

"Honey, let Aunt Pippy relax," encouraged Grace.

"Hell, Grace. Let her speak. She's not a child anymore." Crit's retort took Grace by surprise and made Jaxie's chest swell.

Meanwhile, Jack stood near everyone, almost at attention. As the three talked, his eyes scanned the grounds as if he were on a battlefield, a place that he knew all too well.

"Are you getting good care, here?" asked Jack.

"I guess," said Crit. "I know that out here it doesn't look like a prison, but it is…At least, I have a friend." Jack nodded and smiled.

As they chatted, Jaxie scrutinized every aspect of her aunt's persona; to Jaxie, Crit seemed hollow…almost asleep. But even without make-up, Jaxie still thought her aunt was stunningly beautiful and she wanted to be just like her. Of course, Jaxie was not privy to all that her aunt had done or experienced in the past and she certainly was not familiar with what it meant for her to be at St. Elizabeth's. None of that mattered to Jaxie.

The allotted visitation time passed quickly. Soon, the four of them were saying their good-byes. Slowly, they released hugs. Crit remained as her family started walking away. "Chin-up" smiles covered their faces. The further they got away from Crit, the more Jaxie kept looking back and waving at her aunt.

Once the family was out of sight, Crit walked to the stairs that led back to her ward. The entire visit was bitter-sweet.

"Mommy, when will we see Aunt Pippy again?" asked Jaxie. "I miss her so much. Please, can we come back?"

Grace and Jack did what they could to pacify Jaxie, but it was not enough for their inquisitive daughter. Jaxie would remember this day for the rest of her life. Sisters who seldom saw each other; it did not make much sense to Jaxie. Her love, even at this age, was different.

~

In the coming weeks, Crit struggled. Without warning, her state of mind fluctuated between irrational and cooperative, belligerent and tranquil. Some days it was impossible to keep the lid on her worst self. Periodically, she suffered grand mal seizures accompanied by incontinence. Other times, she was uncontrollably restless; her lifelong need to break free of all confinement manifested itself each and every time Viola and she escaped the grounds for a good time off-campus. Usually, they headed into the city with nothing but alcohol consumption on their minds. Strangely, when such escapades had run their course, they instinctively headed back to St. Elizabeth's, intoxicated and combative. Neither of them seemed concerned that their rebellious actions would have serious consequences; namely, lengthy, punishing isolations.

~

By early 1959, Crit turned a corner at St. Elizabeth's; the medications, therapy sessions, and expert work of Dr. Moya, and others, brought her to a place of relative peace. At the end of her hospitalization, Crit — as chairperson of the Hospital Federation, an organization that served as a liaison between patients and administration — did what she could to represent and speak for those who could not do so for themselves.

Additionally, after two long years at St. Elizabeth's, Crit's legal status and medical diagnosis improved. First, the New Mexico Court System declared that there was no need for her to return for further prosecution. And secondly, the hospital altered her formal diagnosis from psychoneurotic reaction/disassociate reaction to sociopathic personality disturbance and antisocial reaction (alcoholism). This improved status facilitated her release from St. Elizabeth's. As required by law, the hospital provided Tom and Minnie Youngblood written notification about their daughter's pending release date.

At the appointed time, it did not take Crit long to gather her belongings and dress in something other than patient clothing. Before departing, she took time to locate and say good-bye to Viola, her one true friend and partner-in-crime at St. Elizabeth's.

"Now what?" Viola's voice quivered as she spoke to Crit for the last time.

"Hell, freedom," answered Crit as she hugged Viola. "I won't forget you, Viola. You helped me stay sane in here. And…we raised a little hell together, didn't we?"

Viola smiled and nodded through a gentle flow of tears. Then, Crit turned and walked away without looking back.

That day, January 31, 1959, Crit left the hospital with $47.50 in her pocket. In the minds of her physicians, she was headed home to her parents. Only Viola knew Crit's plan to head straight to New Orleans; the only place where she ever felt like she was "on top of the world."

As Crit hopped off the bus in New Orleans, she felt hopeful. Finally, she was back in the only city that ever brought her happiness; the Blue Angel and the power of its erotic center stage, the best memories of her time with Eddie, and of course, getting pregnant with Michael.

Crit bounced down the street and tapped on the rear door window the first cab she saw. The driver tossed her single suit case into the trunk as Crit crawled in the back seat and slammed the door shut.

"Where to ma'am," asked the driver.

Without hesitation, Crit responded, "The Senator Hotel, Dauphine Street."

"Yes, ma'am. I'll have you there in a jiffy."

During the ride, Crit realized that she had just enough cash left to cover the first week or so. As soon as possible, she would have to get busy looking for work.

Once checked-in and settled in her room, Crit touched up her make-up and hair. Then, she headed out to grab a quick bite to eat at The Potpourri right next to the hotel. This all brought back good memories. Every breath of fresh freedom was invigorating.

"Seat for one?"

Crit nodded to the restaurant attendant. As she slid into the small curved booth, Crit noticed that the restaurant was brimming with customers. All the chatter and bustling business was music to Crit's ears. She ordered quickly and sat drinking some iced tea. What she really wanted was a beer.

"Excuse me, room for another?" asked the uniformed stranger.

Crit was completely startled by the interruption. Then she tilted her head up and fumbled for a nonchalant response. His penetrating eyes never looked away from Crit's; the entire scene captured her full attention. It had been months since she had been with a man. Certainly, none of St. Elizabeth's male patients ever caught her eye; but this man was captivating.

"Uh, sure. It's a free country. Have a seat." As the man sat on the other side of the booth, Crit noticed that he was wearing a wedding ring. Nevertheless, Crit flirtatiously tossed her curls. It was all she could do to resist peppering the man with questions. In a way, the stranger reminded her of Jack, her sister's Army husband; tall, distinguished, handsome and seemingly completely in command. Crit found these early moments strangely erotic; for certain, she was not dead. She was still a woman.

"Thank you for letting me sit down. I couldn't help but notice as you came into The Potpourri. I don't remember seeing you before. I come here at least twice a week; one of my favorite places to eat," continued the man.

"Oh, hell. What's the matter with me? You'd think I had no manners." Then the stranger extended his right hand toward Crit and spoke kindly. "I'm Frank Fontaine,

Fire Marshall here in New Orleans. If you're ever on fire, I'll come runnin'." Both chuckled.

"Christine is my name, but you can call me 'Crit'."

"Nice to meet you, Crit. Today's clearly my lucky day."

Conversation continued as Crit ate her meal as the Fire Marshall sipped sweet tea. As Crit finished eating, she motioned for the waiter.

"Check please," asked Crit. Dutifully, the waiter brought the check and placed it on the booth table. Immediately, Frank reached over and grabbed it before Crit could even react.

"It'd be my pleasure, Crit." She smiled and nodded politely; after all, she had very little money left in her pocket.

"So where you stayin', if you don't mind my asking," inquired Frank.

Clearly, Crit did not mind.

"Senator; Room 306. If you want, give me a call sometime. It's been a while since I've been in New Orleans. Maybe you could show me around. Things have changed a bit." Of course, Crit knew everything about New Orleans. She was simply looking for a way to see Frank again.

Crit smiled as she flipped around and headed out the restaurant, the Fire Marshall in-tow. Before heading to the hotel, she shook Frank's hand and offered appreciation for the meal. As she bounced toward The Senator, she paused long enough to look back over her shoulder; Frank was still watching.

~

It did not take long for the Fire Marshall to reconnect with Crit. Of course, everyone recognized him as he repeatedly entered The Senator and proceeded to Room 306. Because he was the N. O. Fire Marshall, everything was simply kept quiet. For months, when Crit was not reconnecting with those who could supply her with drugs or give her chances to work again as a courier, Frank and she met off and on at her hotel room; without much conversation. As were most men who connected with Crit, Frank was mesmerized by her. On the other hand, Crit seemed content to simply use Frank for her own purposes; usually, she was the one who felt used.

As the months passed, Frank offered to leave his wife so he could marry Crit. He even dangled the hope of having a trailer house of their own off the North Shore of Lake Ponchartrain.

Eventually, Crit became bored with Frank. Over the phone, in November 1960, she informed him that it was over. Crit had decided to leave him. Immediately, Frank made way from his Poydras Street office to The Senator, Room 306. An argument ensued and eventually, Frank stormed off. Shortly thereafter, he returned to Crit's room drunk, smoking non-stop, and spouting off. After a few minutes, he passed out on the bed, lit cigarette in hand. Once Frank fell asleep, Crit dozed in a chair.

Minutes later, Crit woke to the smell of smoke and the crackling sound of flames. Evidently, Frank's cigarette had caught the bedspread on fire and it spread to the window curtains.

"Damn it, Frank, you asshole!" Crit raced across the hall and knocked on a door; she knew the two Norwegian seamen who stayed there. The local fire department and police were called and when they arrived, Frank — the Fire Marshall — was nowhere to be found. Only Crit remained.

"Are you responsible for this?" demanded the Fire Chief.

"I didn't do a damn thing; someone else started that fire," insisted Crit.

"Who?" asked the chief.

"Frank Fontaine!" declared Crit.

"Fontaine? You're out of your mind, lady! And don't you even think about leaving here. Do you understand?" And with that, Crit knew that she was in trouble. Once the police arrived on the scene, the Chief issued instructions to Crit and the officers.

"You're gonna pay for this young lady!" the Chief towered over Crit as he yelled.

Then he turned and barked orders to attending police officers. "Get her downtown, book her for setting fire to a public building, and lock her up 'til I get there."

Crit knew she was being railroaded; no doubt, her lover – Mr. Fontaine the Fire Marshall – had friends and was untouchable.

"This is f'n bullshit! I didn't do a goddamn thing! And who the hell is gonna take care of my nine-month-old baby?" Crit protested as the officers hauled her out of the building and down to the police station. She was booked for aggravated arson (LA, R.S. 14:51), finger printed, and jailed. Crit could not believe it; her head raced in rage and defiance. Complaining about having a baby to care for did nothing to help her; besides, Crit knew everything she said about the baby was a lie. Michael was far away from New Orleans in the loving care of Tom and Minnie.

And, she really did not realize what she was facing. In Louisiana, convicted persons could be in jail for years.

Thanksgiving and Christmas passed.

By the end of December, Crit had gone through several preliminary hearings. At the turn of the new year, defense counsel made a motion on January 11, 1961 before the court requesting that the matter be continued and counsel reassigned. The very next day, the court appointed a Lunacy Commission tasked with the purpose of determining Crit's mental condition. Assigned physicians included Dr. Nicholas J. Chetta and Dr. Andrew J. Sanchez, Jr.

About thirty days later, Drs. Chetta and Sanchez, Jr. notified the court in writing that Melba Christine Youngblood Marcades was at the present time insane. Then, on February 21, after considering the law and the evidence, Section "G" Judge Shirley G. Wimberly, of the Criminal District Court, declared Christine as insane and formally "committed to East Louisiana State Hospital until restored to her sound mind or otherwise delivered by due process of law."

Again, Crit was headed to a mental hospital; now declared mentally insane. About one month later, Crit was admitted to East Louisiana State. The hospital was located in Jackson, a rather small, insignificant town approximately 100 miles from New Orleans. Crit found a very different environment at East Louisiana. Often, staff seemed harsh and patients were crowded into extremely limited spaces.

"Another shithole, and for what?" mumbled Crit. Every time she thought life was getting better, it fell apart again. "That f'n ass Fontaine; screwed me in every possible way. Damn it all to hell." Crit dared not speak her raging out loud.

While at the Jackson facility, Crit was subjected to all kinds of medications and associated psychotic treatments, all designed to "make her sane." During initial consultations with Dr. John Trice, Dr. Sturm, and Dr. Curtis A. Steele, she was informed that the hospital already secured written permission from her mother in regard to the administration of Electro-Shock Therapy (EST).

PERMISSION FOR ELECTRIC SHOCK THERAPY Date: 3-21-1961

> *I, Mrs. T. J. Youngblood, do hereby give permission to the East Louisiana State Hospital to administer Electric Shock Therapy if indicated for treatment to my daughter, Melba Christine Youngblood Marcades w/f #45862 as necessary. I hereby relieve the East Louisiana State Hospital and the attending physicians of all responsibility in case of unforeseen accident or complications.*
>
> *Signed: Mrs. T. J. Youngblood*

While at St. Elizabeth's, Crit observed patients who had been subjected to EST. She remembered what she saw; the people looked as if they had been "erased" and left to do little more than stare off in the distance for hours on end or shuffle along as if they were zombies. The thought that she was going to be subjected to this treatment, under the approval of her own mother, terrified her. Never would Crit believe that her mother understood what she signed.

"Damn, doctors. They don't give a shit; it's all a game. And, now I can't stop it." Again, Crit felt completely powerless.

In the coming weeks, Crit settled into an all-too-familiar pattern of life; wake up, take prescribed medicines including Thorazine and Stelazine, talk to doctors over and over, and attend group and individual therapy sessions. The one stark difference at this hospital was the administration of shock treatments. At times, Crit begged that she not be forced to do EST's. Her objections were ignored.

Initially, Crit did not respond well to this treatment combination. Periodically, Crit's physicians communicated with Judge Wimberly that her prognosis was poor, resulting in the Judge ordering additional hospitalization. Then in July, less than six months after her admission, things changed for the better.

Following a lengthy psychological interview by Dr. Trice, Dr. Steele, Dr. Bishop and Miss Palmer, Crit was reclassified as Sociopathic Personality Disturbance, Antisocial Type – without Psychosis. Once the court was notified, Crit was released from East Louisiana, held in a Parish Prison and returned to court.

Crit wondered what would happen next. Never could she have anticipated what developed. Now that she was no longer deemed insane, she was relieved of further negative consequences related to The Senator Hotel incident and she was released from the court and Parish Prison on her own recognizance.

Crit was stunned. Immediately, she returned to New Orleans. Once settled, again in squalid circumstances, her life consisted of one prostitution drug tour after another. She could be anywhere in the country; Galveston, Los Angeles, Tucson, Deming, Albuquerque, Oklahoma City, Dallas, Montgomery or Houston. Daily, she lived among the lawless and fully understood how one could be used as a puppet by them, as they pulled strings for their own profit.

CHAPTER 9

Dead End Roads: Touching Home and Becoming Rose Cherami (Late 1960 - 1963)

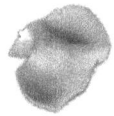

When Michael had been with Crit, there was some restraint to her actions. During this time, his presence had been the catalyst to bring her home. Even if she left for a couple of days or a week, there was the need to return. Her son needed her.

Though Crit found regular work here and there, like becoming a bookkeeper for a short period, she continued to be ruled by the life she had already created. She saw herself as the victim of circumstances while in reality she was the victim of her choices and places.

Her unstable life put her in unbelievable situations. One Mardi Gras night, she was run down by young thugs in an automobile after rebuffing their overt advances. They left her bleeding on the sidewalk. In another incident, she sped through the Vieux Carré, known as the French Quarter, in the middle of the afternoon in a car she had borrowed. She careened down four blocks, damaging three automobiles, flattening a parking sign and smashing a garbage can.

The car finally came to a stop on Ursuline. Police took her to Charity Hospital where she scratched and clawed at her attending nurse. And a third time, after being arrested, booked and jailed for being drunk and attacking a policeman, she stripped and set her clothes on fire. After burning her clothes, she told the police she was going to kill herself and began beating her head against the jail cell wall.

Fortunately, Crit was not prosecuted in any way for such. Of course, similar past behaviors landed her in multiple mental hospitals. Nothing changed. Her life had hit the bottom.

Periodically, Crit managed to step away from the New Orleans madness and go to Dallas. It made sense for her to retreat momentarily to Dallas; she knew people there. One way or the other she would be closer to Michael, even if she couldn't see him. Her Mama, Papa and Michael, with the help of Grace and Jack, made a transitional move to Richardson, Texas where they lived less than a year. Eventually, and with financial assistance from family, Tom, Minnie and Michael moved to the small town of Duncanville, southwest of Dallas.

By the early 1960's, Dallas had become a hot bed of criminal activity. Jack Rubenstein, known as Jack Ruby, owned a nightclub in downtown Dallas. It is claimed that Mafia bosses ordered him out of Chicago for running drugs. Now relocated to Dallas, he established connections with profitable clientele, including members of Dallas' wealthiest and most powerful. Ruby's Carousel Club became known as the most popular place in Big D for those wanting a fast nightlife of booze, beautiful women, and free-flowing access to drugs.

Policemen, lawyers, city and state level politicians, and some of the world's most infamous mafia figures frequented the establishment. Ruby made sure he slighted no one, working the club and winning over the clientele, no matter who or what they were.

Ruby also bought a partnership in another club called the Pink Door. It was there that Crit was able to find work as a stripper. Even at her age and with a rough life showing, she was still stunning and seductive. Shrewdly, Ruby, and those like him, used dependent women like Crit as a disposable commodity. Before long, she was placed on a route from Florida to Texas as a seasonal prostitute and drug courier. Her new bosses quickly saw more in Crit than her erotic stage presence. She was trainable and hungry for more money in her pockets.

This expanded responsibility put her in the company of some of the underworld's worst criminals. These men organized and processed major drug shipments from all over the world. Crit traveled from Dallas to Miami, then to New Orleans and Houston. She would receive heroin shipments from cargo vessels coming into major ports of call. And along the route, she was expected to "earn her keep" at established roadside brothels. This scenario replayed itself day after day and week after week.

~

The late August morning broke warm and beautiful as Crit rolled over, closing her eyes tightly against the sun pouring through her open window. It was still early, as the Texas sun wasted no time in rising to hammer the day. She heard very few cars passing this Saturday morning, a sharp contrast to the weekdays when people were on their way to work.

With a sigh, Crit rolled over, swinging her legs over the side of the bed. She got up slowly and shuffled to the bathroom where she turned on the faucet to splash her face with cold water.

"Just a little," she thought, reaching for the compact containing the white powder that had become her lifeline. Opening the lid, she stared down into the small case, willing it to go away. Oddly, her mind wandered to Mama. Mama was fixing breakfast right now for Michael and Papa. There were fried eggs and plenty of bacon. She was popping a can of Mike's favorite cinnamon rolls to put in the oven.

Crit could smell the coffee perking on the stove.

Turning from the sink, she walked to the phone and dialed Mama's number. It didn't take long for Minnie Bell to pick up the phone.

"Hello?" Minnie Bell spoke in a distracted tone.

"Hey, Mama."

"Crit! Hello! Where are you?" Minnie responded in surprise.

"Please, don't worry about where I am. I was wondering if you would be home today. Thought I'd come by." Crit lifted her voice as if it were a question.

There was a short pause on the other end, "For sure. We're home. Papa and Mike are outside finishing some chores in the yard, and I'm getting some breakfast ready. But, come on, we'll all be glad to see you!"

"Thank you, Mama. I'll be there soon."

Crit hung up the phone and went to the bathroom to hurriedly dress. She pulled the pin curls from her hair and smoothed it with a brush. Again, even without thinking, she opened the compact and inhaled more white dust just to keep her head on straight. Dressing nicely in order to make a positive arrival impression, Crit put on one of her best outfits and made sure that her hair and make-up was perfect before calling a cab. It didn't take long for it to arrive and she was on her way to Duncanville. Home.

When she pulled up, nobody was outside. Crit reached into her bag for the cab fare, paid the driver, took a deep breath and got out. Though small, the little house was well kept. Thanks to her father's immaculate touch, the grass was mowed in perfect rows, the shrubbery trimmed in perfect order, and the Alberta peach tree on the side of the house had a few knotty peaches still hanging. The entire peaceful scene was a stark contrast to the way she now lived her life.

The front door opened quickly as Tom and Minnie Bell came onto the porch smiling. Walking down the steps, they met Crit in the yard and gave her a big hug. Unknown to them, Mike was watching everything from the living room window. As the trio turned to come into the house, he quickly retreated to the safety of his small bedroom.

After visiting for a few minutes in the living room, Crit asked about Mike. Minnie nodded and walked back to his room.

"Mike, your mother is here and wants to see you," she spoke with a gentle tone, understanding that her grandson was most probably filled with a mixture of joy and fear. She reached for his hand, leading him to the living room. As Michael walked into the room, Crit felt tears rising in her eyes and fought valiantly to overcome them. Fighting against a lump in her throat, she spoke to her son.

"Hello, Michael! My…just let me look at you. You are so big." She stood to go to him.

Mike stopped in his tracks. Crit, resisting the urge to sweep her son into her arms, knelt down in front of him and asked, "Can I have a hug?"

Obediently, Mike walked over to her, opened his arms, and wrapped them around Crit's neck. Mother and son timidly hugged each other. By now, Mike had come to feel a strange mixture of emotion when it came to his mother. He'd always been taught to be on guard, and never to allow her to take him away. Nevertheless, he was taken with her beauty, eyes, soft arms, and sweet voice.

As Mama and Papa watched, both wished that life had been different, but it wasn't. In an attempt to lighten the mood, Minnie shared the plans for the day. "When you called, we decided to call Mo and the family and let them know you were coming. We all thought a day at Sandy Lake would do us good. Is that okay with you?"

As Crit continued hugging Michael, she nodded in agreement. "Mama, that sounds like fun," Crit replied happily. "And it will give me some special time with my son."

There was a smile in Minnie's voice as she said, "There is still some bacon and cinnamon rolls left from breakfast if you want some."

"I sure do," Crit replied. "I can smell it from here. And it smells like home."

It wasn't long before they heard the sound of Mozelle and Morris' new Chevy Impala pulling up. Crit took Mike's hand and led him outside to greet her sister's family. Dennis and Dianne bounded out of the car and ran straight to their Aunt Pippy, the name Dianne had given Crit years before. The kids jumped into her arms laughing and giggling. "Hi, Aunt Pippy!" they hollered.

Crit laughed. It was her first real laugh in a long time. She watched as Morris helped Mozelle out of the car. In the moment, Crit wished for that kind of love, though she would never voice it aloud to her baby sister.

The two sisters greeted each other in the yard with a hug, as if all was right with the world. Together, they walked back to the house which was abuzz with family chatter and picnic preparations. Pretty soon, everyone was loaded up, headed for Sandy Lake.

It was a perfect day as the two cars traversed the little winding road leading to the lake. Towering pine trees overhead only allowed fingers of sunlight to filter through; protecting them from the rest of the world in their private get away. As they looked for the perfect place to stop, Crit felt transported from the daily chaos of the life she had come to despise. The ecstasy and joy she was feeling in this simple outing with her family and her precious Michael reminded her of what real love was.

Papa and Morris pulled the vehicles into a pine straw softened clearing. The kids tumbled out of the cars before the engines could stop. For the next hour, they ran around and played games with Aunt Pippy; any game requested by them found a willing companion. They played chase, hide and seek, and climbed trees. All the while, Minnie Bell and Mo prepared lunch for the happy crew and took pictures every possible chance they had. When lunch was ready, the children didn't want to quit playing, but they were also ready to eat. Everyone gathered around the picnic table to scarf down sandwiches and all the trimmings. The family group relaxed lazily in the lawn chairs; talking and laughing.

After lunch, and after waiting their prescribed thirty minutes before being allowed to swim after eating, the kids started begging to be allowed in the water. "You have to let us put this stuff back in the car so we can go with you," Mozelle advised. The women got all of the picnic items together, and Morris helped carry them to the trunk of his car. At the same time, he pulled out the bags holding the towels. The children could no longer contain themselves as they ran down to the edge of the water and waded in, splashing one another and laughing.

Minnie Bell, in a wide straw hat to keep the sun off her face, pulled a lawn chair to the edge of the lake to watch the fun. Mozelle waded in knee deep, watching every little bobbing head. Tom and Morris sat in chairs talking about the news, what was going on with their jobs, and other matters of importance.

"You guys keep an eye on the children for a while." They nodded affirmatively.

Mo walked over to sit on the edge of the beach with Crit. The two sisters sat quietly for a few minutes until Crit finally broke the silence. "Mo, I want to thank you for all you have done for Mike."

"He's a sweet boy. Smart. Talented. Polite," Mo responded.

"I have Mama and Papa and I guess you and Morris to thank for that," Crit said quietly.

Mo smiled tenderly as she lit a cigarette. "I love him, Crit. I love Mama and Papa too." She paused a moment.

"And believe it or not, I also love you. We're all family."

Crit couldn't speak for a minute. How long had it been since she heard those words? "And I love you, Mo."

Minnie Bell watched her girls from the lawn chair, wondering where it all went wrong, but thankful for the day. She offered a silent prayer for her girls; now fully grown women.

Tom got up, folded his chair, walked over to where Minnie sat and looked down at her intently. Something in his demeanor told Minnie that he understood her thoughts. After all these years, no words were necessary.

He put his hand on her shoulder. "Let's go, Mama. It's gettin' late."

"Yep, Papa, it is. Let's go home."

The kids reluctantly left the water and dried off. Mo made sure they had a towel around them for the short ride home. After all was loaded into the car, they were on their way back up the shady road leading away from the lake.

The children grew quiet on the trip back; it wouldn't take much for them to go to sleep that night. Their two-car caravan pulled into the driveway, and the kids tumbled out, dragging their towels. After the picnic supplies had been sorted and separated, Tom took what belonged to them back to the kitchen. Mo, Morris, and their kids said their good-byes and climbed back into the Impala.

Crit stood in the driveway waving good-bye. She watched as the car headed down Millar and faded out of sight. Minnie viewed all this from the doorway after telling Michael to get his bath. When Crit turned to the house, Mama met her tenderly on the little front porch and put an arm around her daughter.

"Crit, how long are you here?"

"Probably a couple of days, if that's okay?"

Mama smiled, "Let's have a Coke on the porch."

For the next few days, except for the occasional trip to the bathroom with her compact, Crit was the perfect mother. She ironed, cooked, washed clothes, and spent as much time as possible with Mike. It was no surprise to anyone, except Mike, that she soon grew restless and knew it was time to return to her world.

"Mama, I need to get back." Crit announced, with a hint of dread in her voice. Looking at her daughter, Mama said, "It has been real good to see you."

"You too, Mama." Crit lowered her head, looking down at the floor. "Mama. Thank you. Mike looks great and happy. Wish I coulda' done that for him."

"He's a good boy and a joy for your Papa and me," she responded. "He'll be fine."

"I know, Mama. And I want to tell you something. I know you won't believe me, but when we're all lined up in front of the Pearly Gates, turn your head around and look way back to the very end of the line. Look for my blonde curls. I'll be there."

And with that, they walked into the house for Crit to call a cab. Then, as suddenly as she had appeared, she was gone.

As Crit hopped in the cab, a wave of dread covered her. Then, she mumbled instructions to the driver. "Carousel Club, downtown, and make it quick."

"Yes, ma'am," responded the driver.

Immediately, Crit shifted her mind away from the serene lakeside setting where she spent time with Michael; sadly, he barely recognized her and was quite reluctant to spend much time close. As Crit stared out the window, her heart sank as she realized, more clearly than ever before, that her life was in utter shambles and there was nothing she could do to fix any of it.

One scene after the other passed by the window; but Crit did not seem to notice anything. It was as if she was in and out of awareness. Then, the cab came to a halt.

"Here you go, miss. Carousel Club, downtown 'Big D.'" The driver smiled at Crit somewhat flirtatiously as she handed him cash. As the cab door slammed, the driver lingered just a moment in order to catch a final glimpse of his exited passenger.

As she had done many times before, Crit sauntered into the Club and went directly to the back office where she was to meet with John Paul and others. The monotonous merry-go-round was again about to spin full speed. Crit took a big breath.

"Rose…come here. It's great to see you," responded John Paul as he walked toward

Rose, arms open wide for a hug.

Rose smiled and flashed her big blues his direction while the club owner watched with envy.

"How was the quick break? See your kid?" asked John Paul trying to pretend that he actually gave a damn.

"Yeah; I saw him and some family. It was nice but I'm ready to get back to work. Need some money and I'm runnin' low on white. What's the plan?" Crit fought against all the feelings she felt during the cab ride. It was 'show time' and she realized that her time off in her make-believe family world was over. Besides, Michael seemed different and her family simply did not understand her struggles.

"Have a seat, babe. Let's talk. Lots on the table and we don't want any screw-ups." Rose recognized John Paul's 'all-business' tone.

"Where now?" asked Rose. She did not waste time asking the silent owner for input; she knew he was just a pawn.

"Mainly Oklahoma City, with a little while in Norman and Dallas."

"Sounds like a long haul," inquired Rose.

"Yeah, it'll take a few months to cover it all. You'll earn a wad of cash and get whatever booze and 'h' you want; only the best for our best." John Paul knew well that Rose was one of the system's most reliable. He did whatever the system allowed to take good care of her. And periodically, he took her for himself.

"I'm gonna need some new clothes." John Paul gave her the once-over and nodded in approval.

"What am I drivin' and is it hot?" Rose knew the answers but asked anyway. Getting stopped by the cops in stolen vehicles was getting a little old.

"Fast Chevy, V-8, looks all family-like." For a split second, Rose had a flashback to Mozelle and Morris' new Impala that they drove to the lake just hours earlier.

John Paul continued: "And, we've got cash to cover hotels, food and gas. You should be all set."

"Where and when does all this happen," asked Rose.

"You leave tomorrow. Go check-in at the 'dolphus. Everything is set under Rose Cherami. Enjoy the night; tomorrow, you're on the road, babe. Later this evening, I'll drop by for some dinner." Rose knew what that meant. At least she would get an expensive meal out of it.

Then, John Paul walked over to the owner's desk, opened the bottom left drawer, pulled out a cash-filled envelope and handed it to Rose. "Tomorrow morning we'll have your car keys and route schedule waiting for you at the front desk. Car'll be in the parking garage. Clear?" John Paul did not have any doubts that Rose would produce as she did so many times in the past.

"What if I get pinched," asked Rose. "The damn cars…"

"You know my number; call me with your one call and we'll get you out."

Rose heard that line repeatedly over the years. She knew it was pure bullshit. If trouble arose, she would have to fend for herself.

"Here, babe. I'll walk you out," offered John Paul as he glanced at the club owner. "Later, Jack." And with that, John Paul escorted Rose through the club and out the front door. Once outside, John Paul spoke more intimately than in the club. "Rose, be careful on this one. Lots of pot holes."

"Just like always, right John Paul?" Rose smiled softly. "I'll do what I can to dodge 'em."

"That's right, babe. Just like always," whispered John Paul as he inched closer to Rose and gently slid the back of his fingers across her covered breasts. "Go on, now. I'll see you later." Then John Paul kissed Rose on the cheek and sent her away. As Rose walked away, John Paul said, "You know I love you."

Rose turned back and smiled. As she walked up the sidewalk toward the Adolphus, she imagined what it would be like to have John Paul all to herself, away from their present, shit-filled lives. For a moment, she thought that it could happen; almost.

The Adolphus was Dallas' finest; Rose took in every amenity for she knew that come tomorrow, the luxury ended. Miles and miles and constantly being on alert for anything questionable. She was seasoned and knew the ropes, but she also knew what it meant to be caught.

Later that night, while soaking in a hot bath, Rose heard a knock on her door. Quickly, she threw on one of the provided terry-cloth robes and scampered to the door. "Who is it?" asked Rose hoping that it was John Paul.

"It's me, babe." Instantly, Rose cracked open the door and peered out.

"I'd know that voice anywhere," answered Rose as her wet hair dripped onto the floor in front of John Paul. "Wanna come in?" teased Rose. Then Paul gently pushed back the door and slipped into the room.

"Caught you at a bad time, huh, babe?"

"Oh, my hair's wet, but the rest of me is just fine." Rose smiled sensuously as she unwrapped her robe and let it fall to the floor. He picked her up in his arms and gently laid her on the cushy bed. Instinctively, Rose seductively leaned back on the pillows and purred at John Paul. "So, have you missed me?"

Rose had all she needed at the moment; John Paul. Hours passed and when it was over, he had dinner delivered by room service. When the meal arrived at the door, he carefully opened the door just enough to take the tray; his left foot blocked the door opening any wider. "Put it on the tab," instructed John Paul. "Add 15% for yourself." The server smiled and nodded in gratitude.

John Paul walked to the small table and placed down the tray. Rose noticed that he had only ordered one meal.

"You're leaving?" asked Rose in a sad tone.

"Yep, gotta run. Things to do. I'll make sure your car keys are at the front desk. The stuff will already be loaded. Just get in, drive off, and Rose…be careful. Call me if you need me."

"Well, I guess I'll be calling a lot."

"How much do you want for tonight?" John Paul never presumed that having Rose was free. Yet Rose found the question disturbing. It was never that way with John Paul.

"Why can't I just have you?" asked Rose; she already knew the answer.

"Babe, you know how it is." And with that, John Paul handed Rose a familiar looking, clear vial of white powder, tossed some bills on the night stand, and started for the door. With his hand on the doorknob, he looked back to Rose, still perched on the bed. "Enjoy it. And, remember I love you." As the door closed, Rose broke into tears and eventually fell asleep without eating.

Morning came; Rose dressed, gathered her possessions and headed downstairs. As she approached the reception desk, the man behind the counter recognized her. John Paul had set up everything for her. Rose did not even have to speak.

"Miss Evans," – one of the many sir names invented by Rose – "here's your keys and the car's already out front waiting for you. We've watched it carefully. And, don't forget this envelope." Rose reached forward for the envelope; no doubt, it contained instructions from John Paul.

"That's sweet," answered Rose. As she spoke, the receptionist snapped his fingers for a bellman to collect and load Rose's suitcase and make-up kit into the front seat of the parked Chevy. He knew to not open the trunk.

Once settled in the car, Rose cranked the engine and headed out onto US Hwy 77 / I-35. First stop, Oklahoma City.

The monotonous hum of the V-8 made it hard for Rose to stay awake as she crossed the state line into Oklahoma. Her mind wandered beyond her assigned duties. Twenty-four hours ago, she had her last hit and booze. And, she was hungry. As she neared Ardmore, she decided to stop at a roadside restaurant-bar. When she walked in, heads turned as she glided into a booth.

"What'll it be, honey," asked the waitress.

"Oh, hell, I'll have a Schlitz for starters…in the bottle." Rose simply could not resist drinking. "And bring me a cheese burger, everything on it, and fries."

"Comin' right up." In a few seconds, the waitress returned to Rose's table, Schlitz in hand. Without hesitation, Rose took the bottle in her hand and turned it upward. A familiar satisfaction fell over her, so much so that she almost did not even hear the waitress speak to her. "Burger's comin'," offered the waitress. Rose did not even answer.

As the waitress returned with her meal, Rose immediately asked for another Schlitz, and another. Countless times, she had driven under the influence; why should today be any different. Now just a little tipsy, Rose called for the check, handed cash to the waitress and slithered out to the car. Before she pulled onto the highway, Rose reached into her purse and pulled out the small vial that John Paul gave her. In a few seconds, the vial was empty and she tossed it out the window into high grass along the highway. As Rose headed up the highway toward Oklahoma City, by way of Norman, her accelerator foot got heavier and heavier; the combined effects of alcohol and pure white caused her to speed faster and faster up the highway. Shortly thereafter, Rose saw red lights flashing behind her.

"Shit…damn it all," mumbled Rose. "F'n cops." Although her mind was fuzzy, she still had the wherewithal to remember what was hidden deep within the car fenders. It was all she could do to hold herself together as she pulled the car onto the shoulder and came to a screeching hault. Thinking that she could dazzle her way out of this, Rose checked her make-up in the rearview mirror and tossed her curls with both hands. Then, she braced herself for what was coming.

"Uh, yeah. This is OHP-22 on north I-35 just south of Norman; be advised I got a 10-70 in process." As required, the highway patrolman notified dispatch before approaching Rose's vehicle.

The officer surveyed the inside of the car as he motioned for Rose to roll down the driver side window. "Ma'am, can I see your driver's license?" Immediately, the officer noticed that Rose seemed to be under the influence.

Rose fumbled through her purse, knowing full well that there was not a license to retrieve. After a few seconds of frantic searching, she looked up at the policeman and said, "Officer, I am so sorry. I seem to have left home without my license. And, I don't have any other ID with me. How stupid of me," said Rose hoping to flirt her way out of the situation.

"Ma'am, I'm gonna have to ask you to step out of the car."

As Rose searched for door handle, the officer stepped back slightly; he could tell that something was not right. Once Rose was out of the car, the officer spoke firmly, "Turn around, put your hand on the hood and don't move." Immediately, Rose complied, but not before the officer smelled alcohol on her breath.

Rose stood quietly as the officer walked the perimeter of the car and jotted down some notes in his notebook. Although the officer did not recognize the car tag as a stolen vehicle, he had been briefed earlier in the day about a hot car that matched the color, make and model of Rose's vehicle. As he finished circling the car, the officer did not hesitate. "Ma'am, I'm gonna have to ask you to stand still while I cuff you."

"What the hell for? You son-of-a-bitch." Clearly, Rose was out of it.

"Well, we'll just have to see little lady." Now in cuffs, Rose was led to the police car and placed in the back seat behind a security divider that kept the officer safe. As the officer slammed the back door, Rose kicked the back of the front seat in frustration.

"Uh, yeah. OHP-22 follow-up; I've got a 10-38; unidentified driver under the influence in custody; possible 10-29."

"Go ahead 22; what's your 10-20?" responded dispatch.

"About two miles south of Norman, I-35 north; possible 10-65; tow needed asap." Although Rose listened intently, she did not have a clue what the officer reported to dispatch.

"10-4 OHP 22; tow enroute."

Rose, still dazed by the white and alcohol, sat surprisingly still as the officer continued writing in his notebook. Shortly, the tow truck arrived, hooked up the car and headed for Norman; and OHP-22 headed to his station to investigate and possibly jail Rose.

Seldom did Rose make such stupid errors; only when she was under the illogical control of booze and drugs.

Once Rose arrived at the OHP station, she was expertly interrogated. It did not take long for investigators to uncover her present assumed name – Rose Evans – plus other assorted aliases and her legal given name. Furthermore, her past record of arrests and hospitalizations, the fact that the car was indeed stolen, and…the heroin sequestered in the Chevy fenders, all landed her behind bars waiting for arraignment. Rose wondered if the OHP was as "well organized" as the Houston PD.

No time was wasted by the authorities; in just a few hours, Rose stood in court under the full and harsh analytical scrutiny of an Oklahoma county judge. On April 5, 1963, Rose received yet another order of detention. Three days later, she was committed by court order to Central State Mental Hospital in Norman for psychiatric evaluation and associated treatments as deemed necessary by attending physicians. Again, Rose's life turned hellish and there was no one to rescue her.

Without delay, Rose was transported to Central State Mental Hospital courtesy of the Oklahoma HP. As the patrol car entered the exterior hospital grounds, Rose noticed the beautiful trees that lined the street, the manicured lawn and a formidable fence that surrounded the facility. Off in the distance was an attractive, two-story administration building; therein, Rose went through a familiar admission process. At that moment, all she saw appeared benign, even for a mental hospital. Never could Rose have imagined the hell that lay beyond the hospital's initial visual impression.

Probably unknown to Rose, Central State was one of Oklahoma's most deplorable mental care facilities. For almost fifty years, the facility was "managed…by superintendent Dr. D. W. Griffin, considered as a pioneer in the development of state institutions for the mentally ill. Nevertheless, and in spite of Griffin's best efforts, Central State had a long history throughout the 1940's and early 1950's as a facility with barbaric patient conditions that violated modern psychiatric conditions. Many factors contributed to this reality. Unlike many other states, Oklahoma legislators allocated an exceptionally low annual state per patient expenditure of only $168.52. Also, there existed an insufficient number of doctors, nurses and attendants in relation to the patient population; it was not unusual for staff to be responsible for several hundred patients. Ward conditions were horrible; overcrowded, poorly ventilated, and shockingly unsanitary."

By the time Rose was committed to Central State, April 1963, such conditions were minimally improved, but there were other issues. Allegedly, Central State's deplorable environment was fertile ground for an "illicit, clandestine Central Intelligence Agency behavior-modification/mind-control program called MK/ULTRA. Such therapeutic experimentations included various forms of electro-shock therapy, with and without anesthesia, and in conjunction with LSD (lysergic acid diethylamide). These painful experiments, often described as psychologically tortuous, were performed on selective patients, sometimes without their consent."

Once admitted, Rose was escorted to Hope Hall, a multi-floored building that housed hundreds of patients. Unlike St. Elizabeth's, she was not assigned to an actual room with a roommate. Rather, she was initially directed to one of many beds lined against hall walls. Rose looked up and down the hall; she could hardly believe what she saw; patients clad in thin cotton attire without underwear, some sitting or lying on the floor all but motionless, others propped up in a corner, staring off into space as if no one "was home." Although Rose had seen worse in Angola, she winced at her first exposure to the horror of Central State.

"Where the hell am I?" thought Rose. "And how in God's name am I gonna get out of here?"

Rose continued her survey of the hospital population and remembered how Viola helped her survive the long months at St. Elizabeth's. "Who the hell am I gonna talk to here?"

"Evans…Rose Evans?" Immediately, Rose turned around in response to the attendant's voice. "I'm Rose," she answered as she raised her hand and waved through the patient crowd. The attendant motioned for Rose to come toward him to an area away from the other patients.

"Rose, there's been a mistake," offered the attendant as he directed her to the elevator.

Rose thought: "You're damn right there's been a mistake. Get me out of here."

"If you will follow me, I've been told that you should be on the third floor of Hope, not down here with these patients," clarified the attendant. "We'll need to get off on the second floor and shift over to a set of stairs that lead to the third floor. You might want to stay close; the next floor up is reserved for some of our most disturbed patients." In actuality, the attendant did not have any business revealing anything about those patients. Regardless, Rose made a mental note: "Poor crazy people on floor two."

As the elevator doors opened on the second floor, Rose's senses were bombarded with a mixture of repulsive odors; and visually, she could hardly believe her eyes.

"This way," instructed the attendant. Rose followed as she saw some unattended younger people "writhing and groveling" on the floor; most of the others were much older and sitting in wheel chairs, frozen in place.

As they walked down a hall, Rose noticed a door with a large, barred window labelled:

SECLUSION. STAFF ONLY. Curiosity would not let her walk by without looking inside. What she saw was horrific; hard cement flooring, a single jail-like window at the end of the space. On the left and right were sheet metal doors that appeared to lead to a kind of stall that "housed" humans. On the floor, Rose saw several scantily dressed patients; some staring off in space, others rolled up into balls and rocking back and forth.

"Hey, this way! That space isn't for you! Don't you see that it says: STAFF ONLY!" The attendant was clear; reluctantly, Rose followed to the stairs.

As the two entered the third floor space, Rose noticed that it was completely different from the lower floors. There seemed to be smaller rooms that housed one or two patients, plus a double door entrance into an area marked TREATMENT, NO ADMITTANCE.

"Evans, this is where you are supposed to be," said the attendant as he pointed to one of the rooms. "Go ahead and get settled; one of the doctors will be in to see you in a few minutes."

Rose walked into the small room; two beds covered with sheets that look as if they have not been laundered in weeks, a small table with chairs, and a sink and exposed toilet. Compared to the first floor, the room looked like the Adolphus.

Rose wondered who would be her roommate; she prayed for a "Viola." Then, she walked over to the window and peered out at the rest of the grounds and other smaller buildings. During her stay at Central State, Rose learned that conditions in the outlying buildings were even worse than Hope Hall. "When a patient is transferred from Hope hall, in a very literal sense he leaves all hope behind."

"Rose Evans?" asked one of the doctors as he entered the room. Curiously, the doctor never identified himself. Rose found that odd but resisted asking questions at this point in her confinement.

"Yes, I'm Rose Evans."

"Rose, we've studied your record. Looks like you've been hospitalized all over the place, even St. Elizabeth's. Coincidentally, some of the Central State physicians worked at St. Elizabeth's in the past."

Rose nodded and clarified. "Yep, I've been in a few hospitals here and there."

"Well, we here at Central State offer our patients a variety of contemporary treatments; hopefully, you'll respond well, make some progress and be released to continue your life outside these walls." Rose pondered the doctor's comments. Her instincts told her to take his words with a grain of salt.

"Stage 1 of your treatment will include some of the newest advances in shock therapies in coordination with complimentary oral and intravenous medications."

"Oh, I get it. You're gonna shock the hell out of my brain." Rose did not mince words with the doctor.

"Well, that's one way of looking at it. We consider this therapy combination as a means to 'reset' your thought processes and recondition your behavior." Rose found the doctor's jargon questionable. "And, we'd like to start first thing in the morning, right after breakfast. For your convenience, all your treatments will be right here on the third floor. So, rest well tonight and I'll see you in the morning." Before Rose could even respond, the doctor turned and walked out of the room.

That night, Rose avoided contact with other patients. In her self-made isolation, she waged war against her prevailing hopeless feelings.

~

The next morning, Rose awakened early in anticipation of her first Central State treatments. Breakfast, both the food and the experience, was horrendous. When she got back to her sleeping space, a nurse and an attendant were waiting for her. In just a few short minutes, Rose was in one of the treatment rooms, a place she would see many times during her stay.

"Rose, right here." The attendant motioned for her to lie down on the treatment gurney. Once in place, the nurse and attendant secured Rose with leather straps for her arms and legs.

"What the hell are you doing to me!? I've done ECT before and I was never strapped down for any of those treatments!" As Rose raised her voice, two "white coats" entered the treatment room. She recognized one of them as the doctor who never communicated his name during the admission process; the other, she saw for the first time. Again, no introductions were offered.

"Rose," said the admissions doctor. "You remember that I told you yesterday about our advanced, combined therapies…the restraints are merely for your own protection;

nothing more. Now, relax and let us do our jobs as ordered by the court." Resignation covered Rose as the doctors closed the treatment room doors.

Then, the nurse approached Rose with what appeared to be three sugar cubes. As experienced as Rose was with heroin, she did not recognize what was being administered. Each cube consisted of 100ug LSD. Both physicians anticipated that Rose would experience a rather calm, but somewhat deep psychological, hallucinogenic response to 300ug LSD. Once the drug had taken full effect, they would proceed with ECT, the passing of electrical current through the brain.

"Rose, take those cubes and let them melt under your tongue; no need to rush the process," said the admissions doctor. He continued, "And, the nurse has some water to help you dissolve the cubes. In a little while, you should feel quite calm and relaxed. Once you reach that state, we'll continue with the other aspect of your treatment."

Rose knew what that meant; ECT.

With some trepidation, Rose allowed the nurse to place the three cubes inside her mouth. Slowly, as they started melting, Rose washed down the sweet liquid with water. Less than an hour later, the drug altered her complete perception of reality.

Once Rose was lost in the LSD world, both doctors and the nurse connected her to the electroshock machine. Electrodes were attached to Rose's scalp and on command of the doctors, electric current was applied. Immediately, Rose's body convulsed in reaction to the current as it "broke through the blood-brain barrier, allowing toxins to flow into an area that normally is protected…the greater the shock, the greater the brain damage."

~

Half the daylight hours passed before Rose returned to her "normal" state. As she did, it was as if a small part of her had been erased, forever.

Over the next two weeks, Rose was subjected to several similar processes. With each passing treatment, she loss a small piece of herself as the ECT treatment eradicated more and more neurons. Her external demeanor was less aggressive and her attitude more compliant.

Much to her surprise, Rose's treatments were terminated after the authorities deemed her "healed." On April 23, two weeks after being committed to Central State, Rose was released. She exited the hospital campus by cab with a small amount of provided cash in her pocket.

Less than twelve hours later, Rose – who had just been deemed "healed" of her demons by Central State physicians – was arrested in Oklahoma City for drunkenness and potential, complicating charges with the State of Oklahoma. At this point in life, Rose had just about seen "it all." But she could have never anticipated what transpired in just a matter of hours. Once sober, she was notified by her assigned public defender that all state charges were dropped. The only thing that stood between her and freedom was a $12 fine.

"Rose Elaine Evans, all former charges against you by the State of Oklahoma are dismissed. Furthermore, associated fines have been covered on your behalf by an outside source. Miss Evans, you are free to go. Bailiff, escort the defendant to processing. This court is adjourned," barked the judge as he slammed his gavel on the bench.

"All rise," slurred the bailiff.

The entire process stunned Rose; then, she thought…"John Paul or…"

~

Rose spent late spring and summer 1963 back on the heroin treadmill. Seldom was she assigned "pleasure runs." Now under a new boss, Rose felt like a used-up commodity. Her "employers" directed every day of her life. She was expendable.

By order of the new boss, Rose's trafficking assignments bounced back and forth between Oklahoma City, Houston, Norman…and Dallas. During those times when she was in and around Big D, Rose dared not contact her family in North Dallas or Duncanville. At times, she worried about what might happen to Michael, her parents or other family members were she to end up on the wrong side of her handlers.

Day and night, even while "working," Rose turned more and more to her habits as a way to temporarily escape or soften her harsh reality. With regularity, she found herself behind bars for public drunkenness, vagrancy by prostitution, lewd behaviors under the influence of heroin, and more. Strangely, Rose was seldom subjected to punishments beyond limited jail time or low level fines that usually got paid by anonymous outside sources.

~

Summer gave way to fall. Crit, now consistently known as Rose Cherami, was fully immersed into the world from which she could never break free. By November of 1963, as one who was "unseen" and rarely consulted, Rose heard plenty. The boss, as Rose thought of him in her head, and his associates spoke freely in her presence, as if she were nothing more than a desk or chair; just a tool to be used and discarded when they finished a task.

Talk of Kennedy's trip to Dallas escalated among those who owned her. Political parties were vehemently outspoken, but particularly the Republicans opposing Democrats in power. And, Rose never missed any of it. She heard news and talk of rising political discontent against America's young President. Even loyal Republicans were warning President Kennedy not to travel to Texas that fall. Nevertheless, nothing she heard interrupted her merry-go-round existence on the road and at the Club.

In mid-November, Rose walked into the Pink Door to get her next assignment. Discretely, she noticed two men of Latin descent coming from the direction of the boss' office at the back of the club. She eyed them as they passed, faintly remembering them from past drug runs. They were men who regularly subcontracted women in the boss' employ for drug runs and white slavery.

As she walked by the boss' office, he called for her to come in, motioning toward the chair across from his desk. "Rose," he said, barely looking up from what he was doing, "I'm sending you to Miami." He handed her an envelope containing explicit instructions for the run.

"You'll get your cut when it's all done."

"How much is the take?"

"8G's."

The boss continued. "You have several stops to make, so you'll be gone for a few days. Get your stuff and meet back here in an hour. Your ride will be waiting for you." His comment was a dismissal, as she nodded her acknowledgment and turned to leave.

"Oh, and Rose, make sure you take a couple of real special dresses; you know, sexy. You'll need 'em," he said, with a slight smirk.

"Ok, boss man. Thanks." She attempted a pleasant smile, but her amiable spirit had died long ago. Rose knew this was just another way for the boss to make money on his investments.

Once again, Rose went back to her room to get a few things together, including a couple of sexy dresses, as requested. She pulled her suitcase and the small box of baby clothes out of the closet. She opened the case and gently laid the box with her keepsakes on the bottom. This time, it brought back good memories of her recent brief summer visit to Duncanville and Sandy Lake.

After making sure she had everything, Rose left the apartment and walked the short distance to the club. Upon entering, she was met by the two men she had passed earlier in the day. Very little was spoken between them as the trio walked back outside and got into the parked car. Rose was once again on the road.

The tires made the familiar "thu-thump, thu-thump," as they rolled down the highway leading to Houston. Rose dozed in the back seat, half listening to the talk coming from the front seat. She was nothing and was ignored by the men anyway.

"It's goin' down," said one of them in a thick accent. "I heard talk they gon' do it in Dallas."

The other answered, "Yeah. We gotta be there by the twenty-first, so let's keep this business on track."

Talk continued even after their drug pick-up in Galveston. Stop after stop from Texas to Florida, Rose heard bits and pieces of the plot that would change America's history forever. It was surreal. "Could this be true? Are they serious?" But because she ran with dangerous characters from Dallas to Miami, she had little doubt that it was probably true.

On the return trip from Miami back to Dallas, Rose became increasingly agitated. These guys were low-life types in the worst sort of way. Rose knew she had a job to do and was under no illusion that she was a model citizen. Yet, this was something entirely different. Living a life in shadows, she knew she had to keep her mouth shut, finish the job, collect her money and keep her son protected.

On Wednesday, November 20, 1963, Rose and her companions, traveling on Louisiana State Highway 190, stopped at the Silver Slipper Lounge, a seedy bar locally known to be a brothel. They got out of the car and the two men hurried Rose through the front door. She knew why she was there. She had done this before; but this time, her conscience rose up. Now in need of a fix, the men ushered her into a secluded back corner booth, completely out of view. They took out a small box containing "smack" and helped Rose shoot up. In a matter of seconds, the warm, familiar flush began to wrap her body. Her limbs were heavy, and she began to nod.

They left her there while they went over to the bar. Mac Manual, the local proprietor and bartender, glanced at Rose in the corner and then at the two men walking toward him. He continued drying his glass and asked, "Whatcha' drinkin'?"

"Capt'n," one of them said. Manual poured him a shot of rum.

"Same," the other said, and it was done. The men sat at the bar for a while, talking to the bartender and just shooting off their mouths. Pretty soon they were joined by another man. The conversation continued, interrupted once in a while by a glance in Rose's direction.

The trio didn't notice when she had gotten out of the booth; still in a state of euphoria with a loss of all inhibitions. "Whiskey," she said, with an air of haughty carelessness as she approached the bar.

"Yes, ma'am," Mac responded sarcastically.

Rose took the glass and drank it down in one gulp. "Another, Mr. Bar Man," she said, sensuously. Manual complied. Now that the drugs and alcohol "had spoken to her," Rose pushed her way into the conversation. In a few minutes, it was apparent she had consumed more than enough as she began talking louder and louder.

"Shut up, bitch!" quipped one of the "Italians."

Rose lost her temper, exploding. "Aren't you two a couple of dark-skinned bastards?" Then, Rose spat at them. Her attitude and gestures heightened as she hurled one insult after another. Fed up with her mouth, one of the men reached over and slapped her, while the other restrained her from behind. At that moment, Manual realized it could get worse; fearing a barroom brawl.

"Get that bitch out'ta here!" he yelled, as the two men continued struggling with her. Immediately, one of the Italians grabbed her by the hair, dragging her to the front door. He tossed her outside into the dust of the unpaved parking lot, screaming — "Get back to Dallas by yourself, ya' bitch!" Again, Rose cursed, spat, and threw handfuls of dirt and rocks at them.

Greatly angered, the men stormed over to her, slapping her around. Then, one of them hit her with a full fist. Rose, falling to the ground from the punch, kicked and screamed. One of the men put his foot on her back while the other opened the trunk and tossed her suitcase out onto the parking lot.

"Get the hell outta' here, ya worthless whore!" They scoffed as they picked her up, hands and feet, and threw her toward the highway. The men continued to walk, glancing back and laughing at her.

Once the men were back in the Silver Slipper, Rose tried to gather herself. As she straightened her clothes, she noticed a tear on the front of her skirt. She looked up to see bar patrons staring at her, scoffing and shaking their heads.

"What the hell are you lookin' at?" she snarled. Rose turned and walked to the edge of the highway. Determined to get to Dallas, she began hitchhiking.

~

Frank Odom was traveling down Highway 190 on his way to Eunice, Louisiana. He was exhausted and just wanted to get home. About five miles outside of Eunice, he glanced down at his watch, estimating when he would arrive.

Thump! "God what was that!" he said aloud.

Looking back, Odom saw a woman lying beside the road. She was trying to get up. "Oh, no," he said under his breath.

Quickly, he turned around and hurried back. Pulling beside her, he jumped out of the car. "I'm so sorry. Are you all right?" Odom was genuinely shaken.

"You son-of-a-bitch! You hit me!" Rose screamed at him. He couldn't tell how much of her emotion was anger and how much was fear.

"Ma'am, let me get you to a hospital," he said politely, while gathering her suitcase.

Rose was still ranting long after he put her in his car. She fussed and cursed all the way to the hospital. When Frank Odom asked where she was going, she mumbled something about being thrown from a car and left stranded. Then, out of the blue, Rose paused long enough to ask him for a cigarette.

"Uh…yes, ma'am." Odom was already disgusted with this woman as he handed her a cigarette. "I'm taking you where you can get some help. You're really banged up."

When they arrived at Moosa Memorial Hospital, Odom placed her in the care of emergency room personnel. Shortly after that, emergency room attendants checked Rose's vitals and began cleaning her scrapes and cuts, while Odom explained the situation and relayed Rose's story. He waited at the hospital until the Louisiana State Police was contacted. Convinced that Rose was in good hands, he left the hospital and headed home.

Trooper Ardoin from Troop K in Opelousas responded to the Moosa Hospital call. When he arrived, he entered the ER area and heard Rose arguing with the staff about what had transpired. Ardoin approached the attending physician and asked if he could talk to the patient. Reluctantly, the doctor agreed, noting that she was rather uncooperative and nothing she said made sense.

Ardoin found Rose on an exam bed and introduced himself. She was visibly defiant. "Hello, Ms. Cherami. My name is Trooper Ardoin. I understand you were involved in a car incident and physically assaulted. May I ask you some questions?"

Rose haltingly agreed. She was unsure as to how she would relay the events or even if she should. If she told him the whole truth, she ran the risk of her traveling companions finding her, because she knew the trooper would have to investigate the Silver Slipper. But, she didn't want to appear to be uncooperative.

For a while, the trooper questioned her, getting very little usable information. She couldn't tell him the make and model of the vehicle or even exactly where the assault had occurred. Fully confident that Rose was receiving adequate medical attention, the trooper wrapped up his interview, leaving the hospital to return to his regular duties.

Rose became more and more volatile. It had been too long since the fix at the Silver Slipper, and she was coming down hard. Hoping to allay the symptoms of withdrawal, she demanded drugs and loudly ranted about using heroin and that she was involved in transporting drugs. For a mainline heroin user such as Rose, surviving time between hits is critical. It was apparent to all that she was a user who was in desperate need of a fix.

Because her injuries did not warrant hospital admittance, the hospital staff initiated release procedures. All the while, Rose continued to be disruptive and increasingly louder. As was standard procedure, Mrs. Louis Guillory, the hospital administrator, was made aware of the chaos going on in the emergency room. Guillory went to investigate and immediately recognized that Rose was an addict.

With the assistance of attending nurses, she analyzed Rose's records, injuries, and financial status. Rose was considered to be indigent. Guillory couldn't keep her, and couldn't release her. She could not knowingly release a patient that could cause harm, purposely or inadvertently, into the small community of decent, law-abiding citizens in Eunice.

As if a gift from God, a face flashed in her mind. Lieutenant Francis Frugé, Louisiana State Police, narcotics specialist.

Immediately, she went to a telephone and called the state police in search of Frugé.

When the dispatch answered on the other end, she said, "Yes, I am Louise Guillory, administrator of Moosa Hospital. I need to speak to Lt. Francis Frugé immediately."

"Ma'am. He is at the annual ball."

"I understand. I wouldn't interrupt if it weren't absolutely necessary."

"Yes, ma'am. Let me get him on another line and see if he can talk to you."

The police dispatch located Lt. Frugé at the ball and had him call Mrs. Guillory at Moosa Hospital. "Yes, ma'am. How can I help you?" He said politely.

"Lieutenant? I am sorry to interrupt your evening. I have a patient who is obviously a severe drug user. I can't keep her, and I am sure it isn't wise to release her. Can you come down?" Mrs. Guillory requested.

"Yes, ma'am. I'll come right now." Lt. Frugé, a good officer, and a good man, made his apologies to his family and friends and dismissed himself. Making the short drive over to the hospital, he entered the emergency room and found Rose in an adjoining waiting room with an attendant.

Assessing the situation quickly, Frugé saw that she was incoherent and quite boisterous. He arranged her release from the hospital and escorted her back to the Eunice city jail where he placed her in a cell himself. Although Rose was an obvious addict, Frugé didn't book her. There were no arrest records, fingerprints, or mugshots. Rather, he went straight to the phone and called his friend, Dr. F. J. DeRouin, the St. Landry Parrish Assistant Coroner.

"Hey Doc…Yeah…Fun party…Yeah…I was sorry I had to leave. But listen, I got a girl down here at the jail, an obvious doper. Can you come and give her a sedative? Ok…Yeah…Thanks…I'll be here."

Frugé hung up the phone and went back to the cell to see how Rose was doing. She was still fuming about being locked up and complaining about feeling cold and then hot. Frugé assured her that he was getting her some help.

It didn't take long for the assistant coroner to arrive; Frugé showed him to the cell. Rose began to relax as the doctor injected the calming sedative into her vein. She closed her eyes and leaned against the wall. The two men carefully laid her down on the cell bed, hoping the sedative would give her relief until morning.

Frugé left the jail and returned to the ball. He was glad he hadn't missed the whole evening. But, it wasn't to be. About an hour later, a young police officer approached him at his table.

"Sir, may I speak to you?"

Giving a slight sigh, Frugé stood and moved to the edge of the banquet hall. "Yeah?"

"Lieutenant? The woman you brought in earlier has gone crazy. She's screaming and cuttin' herself. We're tryin' to stop her, but…well…can you come back?"

"Yeah. I'm coming." Frugé went back to the table and kissed his wife, Jamie. "Honey, I'm sorry, but, I gotta go back to the jail. I'll see you at home." Looking at their table companions, he apologized again and made sure his wife would get safely home. Kissing her again, he left.

Returning to the jail, he stepped into the back holding area. He could hear Rose screaming before he got there. When he got to her cell, he was stunned. Rose was naked. She had stripped off all of her clothes and was clawing at her skin. She thrashed about, sweating profusely and complaining of chills. She was bleeding from cuts to her ankle from a razor blade. Frugé wondered how in the hell Rose had access to a razor blade.

He quickly recognized her actions as major signs of withdrawal. Many times, he had observed mainline heroin users in withdrawal. Often, addicts struggle with decision making, memory loss and can lose all ability to maintain self-control. In the dire cases, they experience intense skin itching, which invokes scratching and clawing, along with possible nausea, vomiting and decreased pain response. He hurried to a phone to call Dr. DeRouin.

It was near midnight when Dr. DeRouin returned to the jail. Together, he and Frugé entered Rose's cell and gave her a second sedative. Against Rose's objections, the two men struggled with her in order to bandage her cuts. Eventually, Rose calmed, and the doctor questioned her about her drug use, asking when she had last used.

She tried to answer. "Uuuhmmm…" she stammered. "I…uh…uh…nine years. Nine years, uhmm, chasin' the dragon."

"When did you use last, Rose? Tell me again," DeRouin asked kindly.

"Uuuhhh…2:00. I think. Yeah, two today."

Once out of the cell, DeRouin said, "Francis, she needs a hospital, and not here, and certainly not a jail cell. She's in heavy withdrawal and clinical shock."

"Guillory told me that she's indigent. Let's get her to Jackson."

Lt. Frugé began the task of making the arrangements for her transfer. He needed a court order, but it was after midnight. Getting a judge's signature would be difficult. DeRouin, realizing the urgency of the situation, called East Louisiana State Hospital and arranged for Rose to be accepted. Crit had been there once before.

They called Charity Hospital in Lafayette to supply an ambulance and a straight jacket. It was an hour drive from Lafayette to Eunice. Frugé was able to find a Special Commissioned Officer, Elza Fontenot, assigned as the local dog catcher, to accompany Cherami and him to Jackson. Fontenot had a relative who worked at East Louisiana.

By the time the ambulance arrived, the injection had calmed Rose enough for DeRouin and Frugé to get her partially dressed and into the straight jacket.

Attendants placed her on a stretcher and rolled her into the ambulance. Frugé elected to ride with Rose, and they were on their way.

Rose was docile during the almost two-hour drive to Jackson. She dozed off and on.

After about an hour, Frugé noticed she was slightly awake.

Frugé smiled and said."Hey there. How ya' doin'?"

"Feel like shit," she said weakly.

"Yeah. I guess you do," he responded kindly. "So, what were you doin' in Eunice?"

"On my way through."

"Through to where? From where?"

"I was comin' from Miami on a drug run with two guys. They looked like Italians. We stopped at the Silver Slipper and had a few drinks. Got in an argument. It got rough. Then the manager threw me out. I had to get to Dallas, so, I started hitchhiking. Hadn't got far when a car hit me." She was a little more coherent and working to stay focused.

Frugé knew the place. It was a local roadhouse. Drugs. Prostitution. He continued his questioning. "So what were you doing with those guys?"

Her next statement shocked him. "Number one, pick up some money, pick up my baby, and kill Kennedy when he comes to Dallas in a few days."

"Whoa. What did she just say?" he thought. He didn't ask her anything else about it. It had to be the drugs talking. She continued to vacillate between periods of alertness and periods that were trance-like. So, Frugé shifted the focus.

"What's your baby's name?"

"Michael. My baby, Michael." She answered as she again drifted off.

When they finally arrived at East Louisiana State Hospital, it was very late or very early, depending on your vantage point. The Eunice Police Officer's relative met them in the admitting area and recognized Rose as having been a former patient, her most recent release being August 10, 1961. Dr. M. Peyton Russell officially admitted her at 6:00 a.m. on August 21. Rose was now, once again, a patient in a State Hospital.

After she was admitted, Frugé left with the young officer who had accompanied them. Both of the men were tired; it had been a long day.

Rose was taken to a ward with several other patients and given another sedative. Again, she moved in and out of consciousness; her mouth so dry it felt like cotton. The effects of withdrawal wracked her body as she felt hot, then cold, with subsequent sweats and chills.

Tossing constantly, she moaned about her baby, her family, and some strange need to be in Dallas.

Later that morning, Dr. Victor J. Weiss, Psychiatrist and East Louisiana's Clinical Director, and his nurse assistant checked on "Melba" during their morning rounds. As was their custom, they entered the ward and kindly greeted several of the patients.

Weiss had already checked her records and realized this was not her first stay at Jackson, thus he called her by her name of record. "Morning, Melba," he said, approaching her bed. "How are you feeling this morning?"

He looked down at her medication orders.

Moaning softly, Rose looked up at him. "They're going to kill the President." With a pleading look, she reached for his arm.

Dr. Weiss raised his eyebrow slightly with a questioning look and glanced at his nurse assistant. He gently patted Rose's hand and tucked it under the covers. "Ok, then." he said. "Try to rest. I'll be back later." Turning away, he and the nurse looked at each other shaking their heads.

"No, no." Rose pleaded as they left. "Kennedy. They're going to kill him. These are some mean ass-holes." The only ones left to hear her were patients lost in their own hazy worlds.

As the morning wore on, Rose struggled through withdrawal. She had moments of lucidity, moments when her body couldn't decide what temperature to hold, and moments when she just floated away in her mind. Her body was trying to rid itself of the poison that had become its mainstay.

Later, the nurse came by to adjust her IV. Rose moaned and tossed. Looking up at the nurse, she said again, "They are goin' to kill Kennedy. Please…somebody…listen." The nurse patted her arm and tried to make her comfortable.

This behavior continued through the morning. Dr. Weiss returned later to check on Melba. "How is she?" he asked, as he picked up her records.

"She's still in withdrawal. Keeps babbling about somebody killing Kennedy."

"Hmmm. Really?" he said calmly as he looked up from the medical chart. "Let's see her."

Dr. Weiss and the floor nurse went into the ward. The nurse moved to the opposite side of the bed to take Rose's vital signs. Though still uncomfortable, she sounded more coherent.

"Hello there. You look like you're feeling better? You look more awake. How are you?" Weiss inquired.

Rose looked up at him with worry and fear. "They are going to kill the President," she warned.

"Who wants to kill the President?"

Dr. Weiss understood that he needed to offer Rose an outlet. Many times he had heard patients speak about impossible things, strange people no one else saw and other equally implausible happenings. He knew she had been declared criminally insane, which made her rantings all the more implausible. But, Weiss allowed Rose to continue.

"They are really bad men."

"How do you know this?"

"I've been a stripper in Dallas. I've heard things. They wanna kill him." She was more coherent, but definitely foggy.

Dr. Weiss was polite and listened intently.

Moaning slightly, she tried to make herself more comfortable in the bed. "Like I said, I'm a stripper and run drugs. I hear 'em talking at the club and on some runs. I've seen things. People."

"What things, Melba?" He continued questioning her.

"Things. You know. I was comin' from Miami with two real mean guys. I think they are going to Dallas to kill the President."

"Ok, Melba. Let me see what I can do. You just get some rest." And with that dismissal, Weiss made note of her status and medication as he left the ward.

Hours later, the effects of the narcotics continued to lose their hold on Rose. She became more and more lucid throughout the day. She stayed the rest of the day in her bed in the ward, still tossing and turning. Incessantly, Rose spoke in whispers about needing her baby and killing the President.

The next morning, Rose woke more rested and less controlled by her demons. She had spent the night kicking her habit, and though she wasn't through the ordeal, she was better. After the morning nurse checked on her, she was taken to the ward common room to eat, and sit with patients and staff.

Dr. Wayne Owen, a young intern from Louisiana State University, was in the common room attending to patients and doing rounds. East Louisiana Hospital offered good training in many areas of medicine for young doctors at the University. Young interns, such as Owen, worked in tandem with and under the supervision of directing physicians.

The television in the common room was on daily, if there was something to watch. It offered a distraction for those patients who had the ability to focus. With the assistance of a nurse, Rose made her way to a chair and sat down. She still felt rotten, but at least she could get up and move.

The last few days and weeks were a blur, one flowing into the other. Rose seldom had any idea of the day or time. She sat absent-mindedly in front of the television, as there was nothing else to command her attention. But, then, there hadn't been anything to get her attention for a while. In an instant, that changed.

"And other news," the television interjected. "President Kennedy and his wife, Jacqueline Kennedy have arrived in Dallas." There was more to follow, but no one heard it as Melba Christine Marcades began shouting to all in the room.

"Oh…Oh no, no…they're gonna kill the President!" Now alert, Rose pointed at the television as she turned toward anybody in the room who would listen.

Other patients watching with her, looked up at her with little interest. Nevertheless, Rose became more animated in response to the announcement about Kennedy in Dallas. Charlie Wilbans, a male nurse on duty in the common room, approached and tried to calm Rose as he changed the subject. It took a little effort, but Rose finally relaxed.

Charlie led Rose over to a table and asked if she'd like something to eat.

"No, no thank you." Rose mumbled. She sat for a while longer glancing periodically at the television.

"Here; let's turn to something else." The nurse went back to the television and turned the station to "As the World Turns," a popular soap opera. Things had finally calmed down in the common room when suddenly there came an urgent news bulletin.

"We interrupt this program with an important announcement. In Dallas, Texas, three shots were fired at President Kennedy's motorcade in downtown Dallas. The first reports say that Kennedy has been seriously wounded by this shooting."

The newscaster's words broke the humdrum activity in the patient common area.

Silence blanketed the room. Everything stopped. Those who were in their right minds looked one to another in utter disbelief, and then…at Rose. She knew. How did she know? Aside from the shock of the attack on the President, patients and nurses alike were staring in disbelief at the woman sitting in the room with them.

Other doctors and nurses came into the room, pulled up chairs and listened for any other news coming from Dallas. Rose sat almost motionless.

The CBS New Report came back. "Apparently, three bullets were fired. Governor Connolly also appears to have been hit. The President was rushed to Parkland Memorial Hospital four miles from Dealey Plaza. We are told the bullet entered the base of the throat and came out the backside, but there is no confirmation. Blood transfusions are being given. A priest has administered the last rites."

By this time, Dr. Weiss entered and looked around. He saw Rose sitting in her chair, her mouth slightly open. All turned to look at him and then at her. What had occurred was unbelievable.

Shortly after 1:30 Central Time, Walter Cronkite was back on the air. Cronkite struggled to report the gruesome developments. With a slight catch in his throat, he spoke, "President Kennedy died at one p.m. Central Standard Time… that's 2:00 Eastern Standard Time… some thirty-eight minutes ago."

There was a pause as Mr. Cronkite wiped his eyes and tried not to show the emotion that filled his voice. "Vice President Lyndon Johnson has left the hospital. Presumably, he will be taking the oath of office shortly and become the 36th President of the United States."

The air was super-charged. No one could believe their ears. Rose sat shaking her head slightly, trying to hold back the tears. Everyone else joined the rest of the nation with exclamations of grief and disbelief.

Dr. Weiss turned to his nurse and said, "Get Mrs. Marcades back to her ward."

For the rest of the afternoon and the next day, Rose talked with many people, the relative of the Eunice police officer Fontenot, several nurses and physicians, and others about the people she knew, including Ruby and Oswald.

Lt. Frugé was at home watching television when he heard the devastating news. His first thought, "Rose Cherami!"

Going to the phone, he dialed East Louisiana Hospital and asked for the administrator, Dr. Charles Armistead. When Dr. Armistead answered, Frugé asked if Rose Cherami was still a patient at the hospital. After confirming that she was, Frugé stated that in no uncertain terms she was not to be released.

"Mrs. Marcades is in no condition to be questioned," the doctor responded. "We will call you when she has completed her withdrawal. The next time you talk to her, she will be in better condition."

Early Sunday morning, November 24, shots could be heard in the wetlands around Jackson. Dr. Weiss and several companions had chosen the beautiful fall morning for some dove hunting. After bagging a few birds, the men went back to their lodgings. After unloading and feeding the bird dogs, they turned to the chore of cleaning the birds.

Hunting provided these men with a welcomed distraction from the business and stress of the hospital. But, today was different. Weiss was plagued with nagging concerns about Kennedy's assassination and Mrs. Marcades' unheeded warning. The idea that the nation's president was dead and a drug-crazed woman under his care told him about it the day before frightened him.

The discussion around the cleaning table ranged from the hunt to the recent assassination of President Kennedy.

Weiss, unable to contain his thoughts, interjected, "Let me tell you some things you won't believe and if anyone asks me about it later, I'll deny it." They looked at Weiss in disbelief. "I have a patient at the hospital who told me Kennedy would be assassinated the day before he was killed."

He continued. "She said it again in the common room the morning of the shooting." His hunting friends stopped what they were doing and became totally quiet. Weiss relayed the sensational events at the hospital and the tale of Rose Cherami.

And it wasn't over, not by a long shot. Within hours of Weiss' startling revelation, news came that Lee Harvey Oswald, Kennedy's alleged assassin, had been murdered at the hands of Jack Ruby in the basement of the Dallas police department.

On Monday, November 25, Lt. Frugé got the call that Rose was well enough to talk. As he drove the two hours to Jackson, he tried to imagine the conversation he was going to have with Melba Christine, aka Rose Cherami. The whole situation was unimaginable and astounding.

Arriving at the hospital, Frugé parked his car and went to the front desk. He flashed his badge as he asked for Dr. Weiss. As the two men walked together toward the common room where Rose would be sitting, Weiss shared that since Friday the entire hospital had been electrified with talk of Friday's events.

"No one can talk of anything else." Weiss paused to look at Frugé. "She knew. How could she know?"

"I don't know. But, we'll get some answers." Frugé was determined.

The Lieutenant found Rose sitting in the common room. Physically, she looked much better than she did when he rode with her to the hospital. Rose looked up and gave him a weary smile.

"Hello, Rose," he said, holding out his hand to her. "I'm Lieutenant Francis Frugé."

"Yeah. I remember you." She returned his greeting, but ignored his hand.

"You look better," Frugé complimented her.

"Feel better. But, I 'spec you didn't come to talk about my health," she stated matter-of-factly.

"No, I guess not," he confessed. "Rose? Oh uh…Melba? What would you like for me to call you?"

"Rose is fine."

"Ok. Rose." Frugé launched his questions, hoping not to place her on the defensive.

"Now, Rose, when we helped you back in Eunice, you told us you were on a drug run from Miami to Dallas with two men. Can you tell me what you were doing on that run?"

Piece by piece, Rose relayed her story. She had been on a drug run going from Miami to Dallas. They were then going to someone's house in Dallas, pick up her baby, and $8,000. Then, they were to drive to Houston and check into the Rice Hotel with reservations already made under an assumed name. "We were meeting this seaman coming into Galveston on the 'Mary Etta' with eight kilos of heroin. He was to meet us at the hotel, and we would make the exchange…money for the China White." She was quite coherent and remembering a lot of details.

"Then, me, my boy, and these two guys were going to Mexico." She finished her tale with Frugé looking at her incredulously.

"Excuse me. I'll be back." He got up and went to find a phone.

He called his superior, Lt. Col. Ben Morgan, who was located about an hour away in Baton Rouge. He needed to give him this information. Morgan stated that he would come to Jackson. Morgan arrived as planned and Frugé updated him on all levels. Morgan then sat down with Rose and asked her to repeat her story.

"Look. If I tell you all this, I want a deal. I wanna get back to Dallas and get my son, Michael."

It is forever unknown why she would have had such dramatic action stuck in her mind since Michael was happy and safe with his grandparents, unless there had been a threat to use him as a pawn.

Morgan nodded and said, "Ok. I'll do what I can."

Rose told him everything exactly as she had said to Frugé, Weiss, and anyone else listening. She added the information about the drug shipment into Galveston.

Late that afternoon, Frugé and Morgan left her at the hospital, drove to Baton Rouge and met with Superintendent Colonel Thomas Burbank, who ordered the two men to follow up on the information Rose had given them.

In an effort to confirm facets of the story, they called Nathan Durham, Chief of Customs Agent in Port Authur, Texas. Durham confirmed the ship SS Maturata, which sounded like the name 'Mary Etta' that Rose had given them. Durham confirmed when the ship was to dock and that the named seaman was indeed on the manifest list. Next, they called the Rice Hotel and confirmed Rose's assumed reservation. It, too, was accurate. It seemed that Rose Cherami had provided correct and valuable information.

The three men looked at each other, speechless.

Col. Burbank broke the silence. "Give her what she wants. I'm authorizing a private plane. Take her to Houston and follow up on this information." He turned towards Morgan and added, "Call Fritz in Dallas and let him know what we have."

Morgan called Captain Will Fritz of the Dallas Police to share the information.

"Hello, Captain Fritz. I'm Lieutenant Colonel Ben Morgan of the Louisiana State Police. My officer in Eunice, Louisiana, picked up a woman with prior information about the assassination of President Kennedy. We're making arrangements to fly to Houston to follow up on some other leads. Would you like to see her first?"

There was a temporary silence on the other end. "No, thank you. We have our man."

Stunned by Fritz's disinterest, Morgan continued to explain Rose's prior knowledge. Again, Fritz made it clear that he wasn't interested, after all, the White House had ordered Dallas Police Chief Jesse Curry to turn over all the evidence collected by the Dallas Police to the FBI on November 22, the night of the assassination. Things had moved out of Dallas Law Enforcement's hands.

In surprise, Morgan hung up the phone. "I guess we aren't going to Dallas."

"Well, follow up on the Houston information," Burbank finished.

Headed back to Eunice, Frugé collected Rose's suitcase which was still in his possession. Briefly, he rifled through the contents in search of additional pieces of information. In the suitcase, he found two cardboard boxes. One of them contained baby clothes.

On Wednesday, November 27, Rose was released from East Louisiana State Hospital by Dr. Malcom Gray Pierson and into the care of Lt. Frugé and Trooper Moran. The trio drove to Baton Rouge to board a private plane to Houston.

They helped Rose climb into the back of the small Cessna 180 and told her to get comfortable. The engine sparked and they were taxiing down the runway. Frugé sat in the seat next to her. As he took his seat, Rose noticed a newspaper lying between the seats. The headlines alluded to the fact that investigators had not been able to establish any relationship between Jack Ruby and Lee Harvey Oswald.

Giggling, Rose pointed to the article. "How do you like that?" she scoffed.

"What do you mean?" Frugé had to shout over the roar of the engine.

"Them two queer sons-of-bitches. They been shackin' up for years."

Frugé asked her how she knew. "Hell, I worked for Pinky...You know, Ruby, remember? I was the dancer at the Pink Door in Dallas. Those two had a thing, if you know what I'm sayin'," she shouted back.

Once in Houston, Rose, Frugé, and Morgan met with Customs Agents Nathan Durham and Agent Bob Woody. Together, they checked into a Holiday Inn, giving Rose a chance to freshen up in her room. They relaxed until she joined them.

Now that they were in Texas, Agents Woody and Durham took over the investigation. Rose repeated her assertion that Ruby knew Oswald. Everyone in the room witnessed as Agent Durham called Dallas and advised them of the fact that Rose had worked for Ruby-Rubinstein, and had stated that Oswald and Ruby knew each other intimately. They got the same response, as before. Not interested.

The next day, Agent Woody and Rose checked into the Rice Hotel to wait for the seaman who was bringing the heroin. However, the seaman never showed. US Customs put a tail on the man when he left the boat, but they lost him, purportedly.

It was over. No case, no investigation, no resolution. US Customs released her.

Shortly thereafter, Rose, Frugé, and Morgan checked out of the hotel. As they headed to the front revolving door, Frugé realized that this might be the last time that he would see Rose. Then, following his instincts, he motioned for Rose to step aside as Morgan continued outside.

Rose did not know quite what to think; she wondered if Frugé was going to detain her. His words shocked her.

"Look, Rose, I can't let you leave without making sure that you understand what you're facing out there." Rose listened intently. "What's your plan? How are you going to explain this to the mob guys who own you? You didn't get it done; some questions are going to be asked. And honestly, you might be in serious danger," whispered Frugé.

Uncharacteristically, Rose let down her guard and spoke honestly. "Let me get this straight…you're worried about me?" Rose smiled.

"Yes! God knows I'm concerned. Rose…you know too much and they aren't going to forget about you." Rose was shaken by Frugé's emphatic comments. He continued. "Don't forget, you have options. Your life would change drastically. Never again would you be allowed to contact anyone; not family, not a friend, no one. But… you'd be safe. All it would take is one phone call to the FBI; one call."

"No. I don't want any more to do with it," Rose said, quietly. "Not callin' anyone."

Frugé sighed as he pulled a card from inside his coat and handed it to Rose. "Take this. Call this number if you need help or change your mind." Rose glanced at the number and stuck it in her pocket.

As the two made their way to the door, Frugé grunted and shook his head. "We almost got 'em, Rose." Frugé's voice was filled with regret.

"Yeah…, 'almost; story of my life.'" Rose turned and walked away.

Frugé and Morgan returned to Louisiana.

CHAPTER 10

Florida: "A Merry Go 'Round"
Montgomery: Tours, Drugs and the FBI
(1964 - 1965)

Sadly, Rose seldom heeded the warnings of others; not at home, not at school, not in a hospital, and sometimes not even within the powerful circle that owned her. It was as if doing so reflected a situational illogic and a lack of fortitude on her part. Most of the time, she simply did not have ears to hear; even Frugé's well-intentioned words of warning momentarily fell silent. "I can take care of myself; hell, I always have," thought Rose as she casually reviewed the information listed on the card that Frugé gave her. "Besides, if I need help, I can certainly wiggle my way into some man's life, if only for his billfold." Rose scoffed, "Most men are such easy prey." Sensual confidence was never something Rose lacked.

Hours later, Rose left Houston by way of her thumb; exact destination unknown. She did not have enough money in her purse to even consider traveling another way. About the only thing Rose could control at the moment was the initial "where" of her post-Frugé saga. She knew the ropes and the contacts. "Work" awaited.

Traffic was heavy on the newly constructed interstate that connected Houston with all points north; all the way to Minnesota, if necessary. Traffic was heavy; eighteen-wheelers saturated the highway.

Gingerly, Rose walked up the highway; small suitcase, make-up kit, and purse in hand. Her blonde curls bounced left and right with every step. Eventually, she stopped walking, stacked her belongings on the shoulder, propped a leg on the suitcase and turned her eyes and smile toward oncoming traffic. Even now, one hard life knock after another, she still "had it." Her petite beauty was unquenchable. Less than a minute later, a big truck slowed and pulled onto the shoulder. Once parked, the driver climbed out of the Peterbilt cab and waved as he made his way back to Rose.

"Hey, there!" shouted the handsome driver. "Need a lift?"

"Of course, I do. Not out here for my health," quipped Rose as she flashed her big blues at the driver.

"Where you headed?" asked the driver as he picked up Rose's cases.

"Anywhere but here, honey," as she followed the driver back to the bright red tractor cab. Familiar diesel odor filled air as black smoke exited the dual stacks.

"Here, let me get that door for you," offered the driver. Then, Rose, clad in her flats, pedal pushers, blouse and warm jacket, stepped upward, grabbed the cab handle and plopped into the spacious passenger seat. Once he had stored Rose's belongings, the driver took his place in the driver's seat, slammed his cab door, and offered his hand to Rose. "Hi, I'm Michael Russo; been drivin' this rig up and down this interstate for months; never seen you before," flirted Michael.

As Rose shook hands and introduced herself to the driver, she could not help but wonder about her own Michael. Now ten, he was little more than an imagined image. Rose had not seen her son for quite some time now; not since the lake. Next month he would turn eleven years old. Rose struggled to conjure up a true picture of how he looked now. She knew better than to let her thoughts override the moment.

"Sorry, I'm Rose; Rose Elaine Cherami."

"French Cajun girl, huh? I know New Orleans; love Bourbon Street." Just the mere mention of that street brought back pleasant memories for Rose. "Rose…well, darlin', it's nice to meet you. Let's get this rig movin'," said Michael as he shifted his truck into the first of many available gears and pulled back onto the highway.

Mile after mile, Rose and the driver engaged in normal chit chat. For Rose, the conversation was replete with lies. She dare not speak the truth about her capricious life. She needed the ride.

"Oklahoma State Line – 2 miles," read the sign now visible to Rose; her mind flashed back to the hell she experienced at Central State. "Not ever goin' back there," declared Rose silently. "Never." Unknown to the truck driver, Rose had her eye on Oklahoma City; lots of work there and all the contacts she needed were listed neatly in her address book; something she kept up with meticulously.

"Hey, I sure appreciate the ride," offered Rose. "I need to get out near downtown Oklahoma City; anywhere near downtown works."

"Sure thing, Cajun Rose," quipped the driver. "I gotta get gas anyway; we'll pull in at a big truck stop right on the edge of the city."

Moments later, Rose crawled out of the rig that had taken her miles and miles away from Houston. In her usual flirty way, she thanked Michael for the ride, collected her items and headed straight for a pay phone. As Michael walked away, he turned back his head and mumbled to himself, "Anytime, Cajun Rose; anytime."

~

As anticipated, Rose made quick, careful contact with the out-of-sight prostitution and heroin bosses based in Oklahoma City. Shortly, a big Cadillac pulled into the truck stop; she knew that was her ride. As she approached the car, a man hopped out of the front seat, loaded her luggage into the massive trunk, and helped Rose into the back seat.

"Long time no see, Rose. How's life?" asked the driver whom she recognized.

Determined to put on a good face, Rose lied to the driver. "Never better; ready to work. But it's been days since I had a hit…and God knows I can always use a drink and a good night's rest, and in that order."

As the driver rolled the big Cadillac onto the highway, he smiled and responded to Rose, "All in good time, Rose…all in good time. We got lots of work; we'll set you up tonight and get on the road tomorrow. The boss'll give you the details later."

Rose knew better than to press for answers now. She was back to following orders.

~

Oddly, the night went without complications. No one showed up at her hotel door expecting free "favors." And, Rose received what she was told; food, a soft bed in a decent hotel, a little "white" to tide her over and the keys to a car that was not hot. Long ago, Rose lost track of the number of times she had been arrested for driving a stolen vehicle; for once, things were different for the next run.

Late the night before, the boss filled her in on logistics that included a run to Altus, a tiny city in West Oklahoma, and then back down to Fort Worth, all with three other "professionals" in tow.

The next morning, Rose and three other pros loaded up the late model Impala and headed out. "Should be an easy tour; seasoned pros up against men in uniform away from their wives. Candy from a baby," whispered Rose.

While the others slept, the Impala's isolated hum made the miles down I-44 South and US Highway 62 West lonely and boring. Once they arrived in Altus, the four women proceeded to the designated motel on North 7th Street, just west of the Altus Air Force Base. After Rose and the others checked into the motel, they organized their rooms and belongings and took naps; it was going to be a busy night.

One after the other, men in uniform showed up at the motel in the middle of the night. None of the women asked questions about how the soldiers got there; granted, some may have been on 24-hour passes into Altus. Rose was fairly certain that some of them simply had connections that allowed them an occasional midnight jaunt.

About 2 a.m., business slowed down and the four of them decided to head into town for a drink and some early breakfast. As they entered town, they stopped at one of the first bars they saw, Hideout Bar on South Hudson. The place was still hopping and of course, Rose and the others turned some heads as they came in.

Several beers later, mood at the table shifted as Rose started mouthing off about the bad food and piss poor beer. In spite of their best efforts, the other three could not get Rose to pull herself together; the booze was talkin'. Without warning, the local blues showed up at the bar; someone must have called the station and reported the commotion.

"Hey, officers…we can handle this," pleaded Rose's girls.

"Not this time, honey. Step back, and you," instructed the policeman as he pointed directly at Rose, "are comin' with us." As the officers cuffed Rose and led her out of the bar, she shouted back to the girls, "My purse; keys; get me in the morning. Call 'em." The girls knew exactly what to do.

The next morning happened exactly as Rose knew it would. Although she had been arrested for public intoxication, and suspected prostitution and drug trafficking, she walked free and was released into the hands of her three companions. Once the four were outside, Rose spoke up about what transpired. "Piece o'cake, girls. And we got connections, ladies; powerful connections. Let's hit the road for Fort Worth. Work to do." Rose's arrogance and flippant attitude was soon enveloped by the girl's infectious laughter. For the moment, they were walking between the rain drops.

When Rose pulled the Impala into Fort Worth, she was just minutes away from her son Michael; he now lived in Duncanville, just southeast of Cow Town. Of course, for many reasons, she was not free to visit him. The threat of potential harm to him always hoovered over her head.

Seldom had Rose worked the hotels in Fort Worth, but one large city was pretty much like the other. However, Fort Worth's finest, under orders from vice detectives, stayed on top of suspicious, high-dollar prostitution activities, particularly those located with increasing regularity within the lobbies, bars and halls of major hotels. More and more, vice – with the full cooperation of hotel management – posed as plain clothes johns; their stakeouts were effective and discrete.

While in Fort Worth, Rose and her companions lodged at the historic Ashton Hotel. During mid-to-late evening, the pro quartet dispersed throughout the hotel's many posh venues. It was not unusual for men, interested in sexual favors, to casually approach one of them. That evening, Rose – meticulously dressed and groomed – dined alone. She always attracted attention and that night nothing was different, except that she was approached by a well-groomed, slick undercover vice squad detective. Unknown to Rose, the Fort Worth vice squad had lots of information on women with recorded, repeated arrests for prostitution and drug distribution. Tonight, Rose was recognized.

Once the detective talked his way into sitting down with Rose, he listened carefully for any slight or overt sexual offer, but none came. However, he already knew about Rose's past and was not about to miss the chance to question her at length down at the station. He preceded with care so as to not alarm hotel guests.

"Miss Cherami, at least I believe that is one of your current aliases…" said the detective. Rose was stunned.

"How do you know my name?" asked Rose.

"Well, ma'am, I'd much rather discuss that with you outside this setting. Your name isn't all we know about you, Rose, or whatever your name is at the moment." The detective paused in anticipation of Rose breaking into a tirade. Atypically, Rose sat silent.

"Now, we can do this the easy way or the hard way; my preference is the former, but it's all up to you. I have assisting detectives stationed in the lobby. If required, we'll take you by force." The detective spoke rather softly so others nearby could not discern the conversation. "Forget about the bill; we'll cover it. But, I'd like to get out of here. What's it gonna be? I just want to ask you some questions. You may or may not be held overnight. I give you my word. Just questioning." Of course, Rose had little choice but to go with the detective, but she learned long ago, with the exception of Billnitzer, never believe a cop. Then, Rose stood up, grabbed her purse and nodded for the detective to follow her to the lobby. Once there, Rose turned and waited for instructions.

"What now?" asked Rose in a non-threatening tone.

"This way, ma'am," said the detective as he motioned for her to exit the hotel.

What followed was indeed as stated by the detective; nothing but questions and a thorough review of her lengthy rap sheet. Of course, Rose was pumped for names, locations, phone numbers and other. She'd been in similar situations before, but seldom sober. This time, she held out. Granted, she lied creatively here and there but managed to convince the police that it was mostly truth. Ironically, she was released after a few hours later and allowed to return to the Ashton with explicit instructions: "Get out of Fort Worth and don't come back. Next time, things won't go as well." It was impossible for Rose to not get the clear message.

As soon as she returned to the Ashton, she checked in with her companions, but more importantly, with her boss. Once he understood what transpired that evening, he issued orders for Rose and the others to disperse away from Fort Worth.

"Rose, take the car to Florida; the Pensacola safe house. You know where, right?" asked her boss.

"Got it," answered Rose.

"Look, I'll leave some cash at the checkout desk. Just ask for your mail. And before you go to bed tonight, tell the other girls to lay low in Dallas; the usual locations. I'll be in touch."

"Will do; will call from Pensacola." Rose reassured her boss that she understood the instructions. Then, the call just went dead.

As ordered, Rose presented the plan to the others.

"Girls, tonight I was lucky. I don't understand how, but I was. Tomorrow, I'm gone and I advise you to do the same." Rose continued, "The three of you should head to Dallas and lay low until further instructions. Get there however you can. I'm takin' the Impala, as ordered."

Reluctantly, one of the girls asked what all three wanted to know about their organizer, "Where you headed, Rose?"

"None of your damn business. Now go," responded Rose with a slight smile across her face. With that, the girls headed to their rooms, relieved that Rose avoided jail.

That night, Rose slept very little. Long before sun-up, she dressed and gathered her sparse belongings, keys and purse. As soon as it was daylight, she went straight to the hotel desk, gathered her "mail," and left the Ashton, headed for Florida. Shortly after getting onto I-35 South, Rose saw a turn-off sign: "Duncanville 21 miles." She kept driving to Florida.

~

Very late that evening, Rose pulled into Pensacola. People at "the house" had been notified of her pending arrival. No questions were asked. Rose was simply shown to her room.

The next day, Rose received word that she was to get a couple weeks rest in Pensacola, stay out of trouble, and stretch the cash; more would be provided later. When the time was right, she would be notified of upcoming work assignments and future connections.

~

Several weeks passed; more than the original implied two. Miraculously, Rose stayed clear of trouble as if she were an entirely different person. By late spring, Rose's life took a seemingly positive turn for the better. During her hiatus, she met and established some kind of relationship with a man named J. E. Crawford (Gene). Surprisingly, and perhaps against her best intuition, Rose decided to write her parents, something she had not done in months. The handwritten letter, sent without a return address, left Tom and Minnie shaking their heads in confusion; very little rang true.

May 13, 1964 (excerpts)
Letter Postmarked: Cape Canaveral, Florida
No return address provided.

Minnie read aloud to Tom.

> *Hello there,*
>
> *Well like the old saying goes, the bad penny has turned up again. But it isn't quite like it was before, this time I am married; and that's the truth. Was married the 5 of April in Pensacola…*

"Good, God. Married? How many is that? And all the way over in Pensacola? Hell, the letter is postmarked Cape Canaveral," groaned Tom.

"Now, Tom, let's see what the letter says," requested Minnie.

> *…he is 44 yrs old, a retired Navy man and is working out here at Cape Canaveral…Gene bought us a house trailer…just enough room for us too. Our checks pay most of the payment, 86.40 a month and we will receive checks the rest of our life even if Gene stops working. He gets $168.40 and I get 73.20…*

"Checks? What checks and for the rest of their lives? How can that be? Neither one of them is old enough for Social Security. Besides, it wouldn't be that much. That's good money," said Tom in disbelief.

> *…You should see how brown I am. I just have to step out my door and walk down to the beach. I love it here and you can be sure this is a fisherman's Paradise, every way you look are places to fish. There's the Ocean, Banana River, Indian River and a million other places…When Gene comes in and eats, we head for the rods and reels and fish until dark…So, we are putting quite a bit away for the rainy day. This is the first time, with all the husbands I've had that I've got a home, security and a good man…*

"This is ridiculous! It sounds like she has gone from being an alcoholic, drug addict and mental hospital patient to completely being completely normal and on a life-long paid vacation. What in the world is this?" Tom, who had seen about everything when it came to his wayward, problem-infused daughter, simply could not believe what Minnie was reading.

Minnie continued:

> *...How's my big boy? Would he love it here . . Guess he is really getting to be a grown boy. Tell him I love him very much and would love to see him but don't know when that will be. So to always be the fine boy that I know he is and no matter what comes or goes to always know that some where in this world is his Mother that will always love him...we are moving the trailer out to Merritt Island...will let you know how to write us...*
>
> *Will close for now. Love to you three, Crit*

By the time Minnie finished reading the complete, six-page letter, she was all but in tears. Her head struggled to take it all in, and if the truth be known, it all sounded like a fairy-tale, an impossibility. "Cape Canaveral? Two thousand dollars a year guaranteed income...for life?!" And, how dare she tell us to let her son know that she may never see him again?" Minnie was clearly overwhelmed.

Within minutes, Minnie telephoned Mozelle and Morris. Maybe they could help Tom and her make sense of this madness. Some days, Tom and Minnie just wanted it all to go away. Their years-long burden and pain about Crit had taken a great toll.

~

Several weeks later, Tom and Minnie received communication that Crit was living at 14 West Belmont...Pensacola...but moving to Merritt Island. In the end, they did not know any more than they did weeks ago. Their daughter failed to provide any kind of Merritt Island address update. Tom and Minnie recognized the pattern; their daughter simply did not want them to know where to find her.

~

If indeed, during the first few months of 1964, Rose discovered a positive, "Camelot-like," life-changing formula that successfully exorcised the alcohol demon from her being, it returned with a vengeance in June and July. Within six weeks, she was arrested five times for public intoxication, all under the assumed names, Roselle Jeanne Crawford and Roselle Jeanne Cherami. Additional violations included resisting arrest, and general investigation detentions. Oddly, only one of those arrests landed Rose in jail for any extended length of time.

~

By mid-fall, Rose relocated to New Orleans, her personal mecca, where she had some connections and could get a fix when she needed it. In this city there was always a steady stream of work. And, Gene Crawford was no longer in the picture.

Rose continued down familiar roads; heroin addiction, trafficking, and prostitution tours. Nothing changed. In the process, she connected with J. B. Hill, who ran a prostitution ring from Oklahoma City to Pensacola. It did not take her long before she was leading a group of girls and running drugs for a group out of the Seaman's International Union. She was back in and this time, there was no getting out.

~

Rose was still sleeping as the rays of the sun fell across Lake Pontchartrain and along the Rigolets. The night had been rowdy and long, with incessant drinking, and a hit now and then to keep her going so she could turn one high-dollar trick after the other. That was how she made her living; that and running drugs. Her mind and mouth both fuzzy, she squinted through her slightly parted eyelids protecting her eyes from the shock of the bright light.

Blinking slowly, Rose tried to remember where she was, and which name she was using now; she had so many. Sometimes she forgot her real name, having lost her sense of self.

The bedside phone rang. Rose put her hands on her throbbing head, the sound unbearable. She knew there would be hell to pay if she didn't answer it, as she rolled over in bed, fumbled with the receiver, and put it to her ear.

"Yeah?"

"Get the girls together; heading to Montgomery. Meet me out front at noon and don't be late!" The male voice on the other end of the line was gruff and demanding.

"Okay, J.B., I got it," Rose answered.

She knew she had no choice, no matter how rotten she felt. Choice had been eliminated from her life for a long time now. The big bosses made all of the decisions for everybody. It had been almost two years since President Kennedy's assassination, and she was still in New Orleans. Her growing disappointment with life coupled with her age had slowed her down.

She sat up in bed and moaned, looking around the room. Clothes were strewn about in a disorderly mess. She didn't remember seeing some of the items before. Fumbling around on the bedside table, she tried to find a cigarette, but the pack was empty.

"Oh, damn it to hell!" She wadded up the empty package, throwing it on the floor.

Looking down at herself, she was still fully clothed in a provocative black satin cocktail dress slit up the side to reveal the red lace garter belt holding up her fishnet stockings.

"Oh, God," she complained, as she stood up, swaying slightly while holding on to the wrought iron foot piece of the bed.

She had stumbled into her room in the early morning hours, at the decadent Jung Hotel, and fallen into the bed, completely wasted. For decades, The Jung, located on Canal Street in the heart of New Orleans, was the place to be. Nearby, the shabby, sensual and sleazy side of the French Quarter lured hotel guests, offering exotic experiences, unlike any other place. The hotel provided expansive ballrooms, rooftop dancing, formal seated dining, and high-rise rooms with a view. Guests who had the money could buy whatever met their desires and party-goers always found satisfaction without boundaries at The Jung Hotel.

Shuffling toward the bathroom, Rose caught a glimpse of herself in the full-length mirror. The image startled her. Her curly blonde hair, a tangled mess, smelled of marijuana. The dark circles under her eyes competed with the smeared black mascara, and her bright red lipstick was crooked, running into the creases at the corners of her mouth. The wear and tear of the way she lived her life was indisputably displayed on her face.

"Damn. I've gotta get myself together in a hurry." She knew that running late wouldn't be a good idea, as she still had to get the other girls up and moving. Leaving the light off as she entered the bathroom caused her to stumble and stump her toe on the toilet.

"Damn it, damn it, damn it!! That's all I need."

Still, in the dark, she leaned over the sink and splashed her face with cold water from the faucet. Flipping on the light switch, the glare of light shot stars through her headache. No matter how bad she felt, she had to get ready for the trip to Montgomery. Rose picked up a small compact from the glass shelf under the mirror. Hesitating for a second, she flipped it open and took a small pinch of white power, sniffing it up her nose. Closing the compact with a snap, she paused, reopened it, and took another snort.

After a quick shower, she fixed her hair and put on makeup, while intermittently racing around the hotel room picking up her personal belongings and throwing them into a suitcase. She was still an attractive woman, after all.

Foundation, mascara, eyeliner, lipstick, hair spray, curlers, hairbrush and hand mirror were crammed into her makeup kit, all necessities for a woman who had sex for sale. There was a certain sensual look required for the trade. It was a must. A man didn't want a woman who looked like the one he had left at home. There was no excitement in that. He wanted a temptress who brought fantasy into his life.

It took more time now for Rose to create that image, more teasing, and spraying of her hair, more make up. Middle age was a long way from sixteen. After more than twenty years of drinking, smoking, drug use, incarceration and rough living, she was shopworn, but Rose was still alluring to men. Perhaps the embodiment of her numerous dark experiences is what lured them.

Inwardly, Crit, the young girl, had died. Rose was jaded, no longer aroused when a strange man fondled her. There was no sparkle in her smile or her eyes. It was just a job, and she was a pro, so she faked it, all of it. That was how she made her living. It was impersonal.

"I've got to get some coffee before I do another thing." At the sound of the service cart, she opened the door of her room to look out into the hall. The waiter, in a white jacket, paused to look at her.

"Hey, cutie. How about giving me that pot of coffee with a cup, lots of sugar and cream."

"Uh, ma'am, it's part of this breakfast order." He was young, and blushed as she walked sensually into his space, her dressing gown partially open.

"I know, honey. Just tell them the coffee was left off of the cart and you'll bring up some more in a minute. I really need it right now. I promise I'll make it worth your time the next time I see you…but I'm in a hurry right now."

"Hmm, sure, okay." He hurriedly put the things she wanted on a serving tray and started to lift it up with one hand to take into her room.

"I can carry it, honey. You are just a sweetheart," she said provocatively. "Put a piece of that toast on the tray, too."

Still blushing, he quickly complied. Rose kissed him on the cheek before stepping back into her room and kicking the door closed.

Men, she thought, young or old, they are all alike.

~

Throughout the late 1950's and into the 60's, Montgomery was a city where emotions were ablaze over the issue of civil rights. As Rose sat in the lobby waiting for Walker, she was thinking about the problems surrounding those events, since she and her traveling companions would soon be headed that way. She and the girls had to steer clear of all of that, or anything else that might result in publicity.

Rose knew about the bus boycott by blacks in 1956; that was when her son, Michael, was just three years old. She had also kept up with the things Governor George Wallace had done to thwart federally mandated desegregation efforts. She knew blacks were not treated fairly and faced a lot of meanness from many whites. Her Papa was openly prejudiced and blatantly critical of black people, as if they were sub-human. That was something Rose could never understand. One thing she had learned from experience, all people weren't treated equally in this world, not by a long shot.

Dexter Avenue Baptist Church, where the man of visionary dreams, Martin Luther King, Jr., pastored, was located right next to the state capitol building in Montgomery. Rose used to work the streets around there, plying her trade. She had better assignments now when she went to Montgomery. It was an odd memory, considering the symbolism of the location. The church on one side, the state on the other, and a drug using whore in the middle.

Rose knew it was to her advantage to keep up with what was going on. She often read the newspapers left at the doors of the hotel rooms where she was working, and also watched some news on television when she could. Sometimes, she knew more about the actual truth of crime, vice, and murder than the news reported. The mob that employed her ran most of the prostitution and drug industry. Rose kept her mouth shut and did as she was told. That did not mean she didn't know.

"Hey, Rose come on! The wagon's here," one of the girls shouted while pounding on the door.

"Comin'." Her reverie broken, she headed half-heartedly in that direction. Glancing around the room one more time to make sure she had everything, she placed the box of baby clothes in the suitcase and closed it. Sighing, she picked up the old case and walked to the elevator.

As Rose exited the hotel lobby through the revolving door, she was surprised to see her driver; Walker wasn't in charge of the group as he usually was. Loading her belongings into the station wagon, she saw Whity Shultz sitting behind the steering wheel. He was slumped over against the window with his head propped up on his hand; taking a cat nap.

"Where the hell is George?" Rose asked one of the working girls next to her. The girl shrugged.

Rose wondered why Walker wasn't driving, and if something was coming down that she didn't know about. Things just seemed a little odd. On top of that, Whity was one of her least favorite people. His mouth was always running; mostly lewd comments accompanied by verbal and physical advances toward the girls. He also had a hot temper. Rose had seen him fly off the handle many times, taking his anger out on anyone near him. The girls were always tense around him, never knowing what to expect.

He roused as Rose and the other girls began to get into the station wagon. Rose didn't want to upset him needlessly. She smiled in his direction as he looked over at her when she sat in the front seat beside him.

"Hey, Whity, what's up today? Where's Walker?"

"He ain't drivin'. I got a last minute call to take his place. Is that a problem with you, nosey Rosie?" Whity asked, sarcastically.

"Hell, no. No problem with me!" Rose replied cheerfully, while the other girls listened intently. They, too, were quite familiar with Whity and his quirky mood swings. The less said to him the better. "I'm not particular who drives me to Montgomery, or any other place."

Whity revved the motor and scratched off with a jerk. "He'll meet us there," Whity said, as he looked for traffic out the side window of the car.

The girls began bantering back and forth, laughing and joking with one another, with Whity joining in with some obscene comment from time to time. Though Walker was usually at the steering wheel, this wasn't the first time Whity had taken over the responsibility of transporting the call girls from New Orleans to Montgomery, as well as a number of other cities from Florida to Texas. They were the elite prostitutes and pure heroin divas who sometimes sold drugs to their Johns.

The process was managed like a business. Because of her years of experience, and street savvy, Rose had her own designated New Orleans-based duties. Those responsibilities reached far beyond the routine acts of prostitution. Men in the top echelon of the organization made efficient use of people like Rose in multiple areas of vice and crime.

The bosses had connections in Miami, New Orleans, Birmingham, Montgomery, Mobile, Houston, Dallas, San Antonio and beyond. Such connections made it possible to put people in jobs and other points of observation throughout the cities, for the recruitment of experienced women as seasoned prostitutes, and for the acquisition of high-grade heroin.

The drugs were most often brought into the expansive, deep-water port of New Orleans, with the alleged assistance of Seaman's International Union (SIU) employees. At one time, Rose was employed as a bookkeeper with River Terminals Corporation, placed there so she would know about the shipments. She was in constant contact with seedy segments of the SIU and had direct access to scheduled arrivals and departures of hundreds of ships from Latin America, West Africa, Asia and Europe, all through the Port of New Orleans. Many of those vessels brought in pure heroin, cocaine, opium, and other drugs. The illegal drug trade flourished in New Orleans and many who were on the inside loop became wealthy because of it.

The station wagon on the way to Montgomery was transporting cargo far more valuable than a load of female prostitutes. Whity and Rose were privy to the car's hidden cache that included about $30,000 worth of pure heroin. It had arrived earlier that morning with the assistance of Louis G. at the SIU. Louis had secured the illegal heroin distribution off the ship, JOHN B. WATERMAN, and had delivered the package to Whity for storage inside the customized door panels of the station wagon.

Throughout the trip to Montgomery, they made various stops along the highway. At each stop, Rose deftly removed a designated number of small, plastic packets from the supply in the secret panel of her side door, slipping them into a small duffle bag. At each location, Rose exited the car with the bag and walked toward a designated drop off such as a store, a garage or a service station. Once inside, she exchanged the packets for payment given to her in a paper bag for predetermined amounts of heroin. Rose would then casually return to the station wagon to remove the payoff from the duffle bag. She carefully put each initialed paper sack containing cash into the door panel and placed the empty duffle bag under her feet. Such drops, though risky, meant an additional bonus for Rose, who needed the money to support her habits. The girls in the car pretended they saw nothing. They were prostitutes, nothing else.

The station wagon had grown quiet as some of the girls took naps anticipating a long night of work ahead of them. Occasionally, someone would make a comment or ask a question, but there wasn't much conversation. This wasn't a joy ride; after all, it was a car full of people on their way to work.

Connections in the underworld of crime had begun to keep a close eye on Rose. She had been privy to loose conversation while hanging out around the men as a call girl, or when picking up and delivering drugs. Rose knew many of the men intimately, and about some of their criminal activity in detail. She knew names and places. They liked to brag about their illegal escapades and the amount of money they made from them while lighting their cigars with hundred dollar bills to show off.

Rose knew more than she should know. That was especially true considering her loss of control around drugs and liquor, and her increasing number of arrests. She had become a possible liability. It was troublesome to those who ran the system.

As the station wagon entered Montgomery, the girls were dropped off at their designated hotels. In each of the locations there were people on the inside track to guide them discreetly to their pre-arranged encounters for a few hours, or for the evening. The girls preferred an evening with one man, but sometimes had several, whatever the market demanded and the client was willing to pay. Money mattered.

The girls considered themselves fortunate to be elite prostitutes, which usually meant dinner and dancing, gifts, elegant suites, wine and caviar, and often a call-back through their booking agent at the hotel. They weren't streetwalkers.

Rose found herself daydreaming about home, her son, her family…her former husband, Eddie. What had happened? How did she get here? She was so tired. Maybe, it was time.

"Rozella?" Whity looked in her direction. His voice had startled her.

"Yeah?"

"Is everyone square on aliases for this job?"

Rose answered with a smile, "I think so." Dressed sharply with her hair and makeup just so, Rose had become "Room Mother" for the other women.

"Girls, you know the names we are all going to use on this trip, not just yours but everyone in this car, in case you need backup? That will be critical on the chance you get picked up. We've got good coverage, but sometimes things don't go as planned. If something happens, just keep your cool until we get help to you."

They all nodded. One of the girls said, "We know you'll take care of us, Rose. You always do."

Whity looked over at Rose with a smirk. "And, Rozella, or whoever the hell you are on this trip, you know the routine, right?"

"No, Whity I have no idea. I'm just an innocent little lamb," Rose said in a testy, sarcastic tone.

Whity chortled. Sometimes he liked Rose because she was such an ass. "Kiddin' aside, what's goin' on with Walker? Is he my contact on this trip?"

"Both you and him are already registered for cover at The Jefferson Davis, Room #408. He should be meetin' you in the front lobby. Get into The Exchange and then walk over to The Jefferson. He'll meet you there. Keep your head on straight, Blondie. And remember, if you or any of the girls end up in the slammer, contact the other 'Rose,' you know, the older bitch at the Montgomery jail. Hell, lots to keep up with, gettin' girls to all these different places. Let's not mess this up," Whity ordered.

"I think I can handle it, Whity. I was handlin' it a long time before you ever came on the scene. I don't need your sorry ass mouth tellin' me how to do my business!" Rose took a second to regain her composure.

With so much hanging in the balance, they both knew this was not the time to get into a fight. Everything was too serious right now, too much money on the line to blow it over a personal conflict. With that, Rose, soon to be "Mrs. Walker" at The Jefferson Davis Hotel, and "Maria Evans" at The Exchange, began barking her last minute instructions to the girls.

"Remember, cover your asses and don't be buggin' me with your petty problems. I got problems of my own. But, if you really need me, you know how to find me, and it better be for a good reason. Girls, let's make 'em happy and beggin' for more!" exhorted Rose.

Return business meant more money for the girls, and their bosses. It was a must.

After all the girls had been secured in their locations, Rose exited the station wagon in front of the main entrance to the historic Exchange Hotel, her home for the next few days.

"See ya' later, Whity." Rose spoke in a kindly manner, attempting to smooth down any ruffled feathers from their earlier conversation. He set her bags on the curb.

"Yep. Happy tricks!" Whity drove away as if this was a normal life. The other girls were to meet Walker at his address.

As Rose entered the hotel, she went directly to the front desk. The Exchange was a fashionable hotel conveniently located near the Alabama River. As she gazed around the familiar front lobby, she thought of the recent news publicity surrounding Martin Luther King, Jr., his powerful speeches, and the four-day freedom march a few months earlier. Hundreds of people had come from Selma to the capitol city, under the protection of military forces ordered in by President Johnson. People were still talking about it.

"Yes, ma'am, how may I help you?" The desk clerk had the reservation book open in front of him.

"Maria Evans. I have a reservation," Rose answered as if she owned the place.

"Uh yes, ma'am. You've been assigned Room #422, Miss Evans. And your room has been prepaid. Here's your keys and your bags will be sent up right away. It's a pleasure to have you both with us, and I hope you enjoy your stay." The desk clerk smiled at her.

"Wonderful. I sure do thank you for your assistance. By the way," Rose spoke with charm and held herself like the lady she was pretending to be. "Would this room be havin' 'aiuh' conditioning?"

"Hmmm…No ma'am. It doesn't. Would you like for me to make a change?"

"Please do," she answered.

"Room #612 is available with air. Is that acceptable?"

"Yes. Thank you."

With the proper set of keys in her hand, Rose headed through the lobby to the elevator and noticed a black bellhop employed at the hotel. Though she fully recognized the man, and he her, she kept walking briskly toward the elevator, ignoring him. In no way was she willing to compromise her cover. She had seen him before and knew the black man as the syndicate's contact man at the hotel. It was impossible not to recognize him with his one blind eye and scarred cheek. He "walked between the raindrops," so to speak, as did Rose — both were employed by the same underworld bosses.

"Wonder what he's doing here? Rose felt uneasy. Maybe to keep an eye on me?" He continued to watch her as she left the lobby.

Shortly after getting situated in her room, the room phone rang. "Hello?" she said cautiously.

"Miss Evans?" It was the clerk from the front desk. "There is a gentleman here at the desk, asking for you. A Mr. Walker?"

"Not now," Rose spouted at him. She hung up the phone abruptly and continued to unpack her things. "I'm not going to have him here and there, too."

As she walked through the lobby later, Rose was stopped by the desk clerk who informed her that the gentleman had made quite a scene at being rebuffed and then tried to check into another room. The desk clerk had refused this request for her protection.

"There will be a tip on my bill payment for you and your excellent service." The clerk smiled politely.

Rose sighed, as she knew she would see him shortly and have to explain her actions. She didn't care. There was no way she would be continually available at his discretion.

As she stepped out the door, Rose saw Walker waiting for her on the sidewalk, leaning against a pillar as he guarded two suitcases.

"What was that?" George asked with a tone of impatience. "I don't know what you're talking about. I was dressing."

"Since when does that matter?" he asked, picking up the luggage and leading her down the sidewalk toward the corner. Together, they walked the few blocks to The

Jefferson Davis Hotel, one of Montgomery's most prestigious lodgings. They made their way to the front door where the bellhop graciously opened the door and spoke a word of greeting.

Though the hotel remained segregated into the 1960's, it had accommodated famous preachers such as Dr. Martin Luther King, Jr. and Ralph David Abernathy. In the 1930's, it was home to WSFA radio where Hank Williams, Sr. had performed.

George and Rose exchanged pleasantries with the bellhop as he picked up their luggage and took it to the front desk for them to check into the hotel.

For the next two nights, well-to-do "Johns" came and went from Room #612 at The Exchange. Rose carried out the same familiar charade. By mid-morning, with the bulk of her duties behind her, she moved through the hotel and out onto the city streets like any visitor to Montgomery, as free as any person could be who felt they were under constant surveillance.

For the past two years, Rose had grown increasingly wary and frightened. Ever since Kennedy's assassination, it seemed she had been treated with more scrutiny. The days since then were almost always filled with an overshadowing uneasiness. Rose felt she was being followed, watched and stalked. Out of the corner of her eye she had frequently seen strange men jump back out of sight, or start reading a newspaper while watching her whenever she sat down for coffee or on a park bench. She often wondered if this was an overactive imagination, but today she had again seen their man at the hotel where she was booked. He was out of context and a notorious hit man.

That, plus the frequency of other sightings, led her to know she was right. Rose had already made up her mind on the drive to Montgomery that it was time for her to take action. Whity taking the place of George Walker as driver was the cincher. He was a sneaky low life in a place of authority and not to be trusted.

With the intense feeling her life was at risk, Rose knew she needed to act while she still could. If miraculously possible, it was time to call in her chips for all of the information she had provided. On her second night at The Exchange, Rose felt a growing need to call her sister. She knew it put her and her family at risk, but she couldn't hold her feelings back anymore.

Picking up the phone in her room, she asked the hotel operator to place a call to Dallas, Texas. Waiting nervously, Rose almost broke into sobs when she heard the familiar sound of Mozelle's voice on the other end. Even after years of accumulated resentment and hurt between them, Rose loved her family; blood was blood.

"Hello?"

"Mo? This is Crit. How are you?" Crit spoke with controlled emotion.

"Crit? Where are you?"

"Oh, Mo, I'm fine. I just wanted to say hello. How's Michael? Mama? Papa?"

"They're all fine. Michael's growing. Had a good summer playing baseball. Papa took him to practices. 'Come on, Son, hit that ball,'" Mozelle said, trying to sound like their Papa. They both laughed. "And Crit, you should hear him play his cornet… beautiful."

"Really? How marvelous." Crit was happy to hear all the news about the family and especially Michael. They talked for a little while longer until Crit realized she needed to get off the phone. "Mo?"

"Yea, Crit?"

"I'd really like to come home." Her voice broke in tired whispers.

"Then come home, Crit," Mozelle said softly.

"I'll let you know when."

"I'll be listening for you."

With pleasant good-byes, they hung up. As she spoke with her baby sister, Rose determined that she had come to the end of her running.

~

On her third morning in Montgomery, Rose took a stroll to the Dixie Drugstore, a beloved hangout for longtime Montgomery residents. She ordered a cherry Coke and sat on a stool at the soda fountain. The old overhead fan turned slowly with a comfortable creaking sound, and the gentle breeze felt good against the ruthless muggy heat outside. The Coke picture calendar hanging on the wall showed August 3, 1965.

Looking cautiously around, Crit was now Rozella, or Rose, two of multiple other aliases. She walked over to the old wooden telephone booth in the back corner of the drugstore. Sitting on the small built-in seat, she quickly pulled the folding door closed and braced it shut with her knee. There, she placed a direct call to the RA, the Resident Agent of the FBI. She had memorized the number when it was first secretly given to her. It was her lifeline. The ace she had kept to play as a last resort.

As she dialed the number, she was completely unaware of the man discretely watching her from the sidewalk through the drugstore front window. He had followed Rose from the hotel so he could report what she was doing and had noted her secluded phone call.

The phone rang. On the other end, a woman answered quickly. "Federal Bureau of Investigation, Montgomery. How can I direct your call?"

"Yes. I'm Rozella Clinkscales. I need to talk to whoever is the agent in charge."

"Yes ma'am. Are you in danger in any way?"

"Hell yeah! I wouldn't be callin' if I wasn't."

In a minute, Special Agent James Morgan took the phone and said, "Ma'am, this is Agent Morgan. Where are you?"

"I'm in a phone booth at the Dixie Drugstore near the capitol building," Rose spoke with trepidation. "I don't want to leave here. Can you come downtown?"

"Stay put. We'll be there in about ten minutes."

Rose hung up the phone and sat back in the booth. For the first time in all her years of working for the underworld, she had never been so gripped with fear. Her failed life flashed through her mind. Her son, her family, her marriages, and her big dreams were all lost. She had blown all of it because of the choices she had made. Sitting in the cubicle of the phone booth, she would have given her last breath for one final look at her son.

When Agents James P. Morgan, Jr. and Philip P. Snodgrass arrived at the Dixie Drugstore, they found Rose still sitting in the phone booth. When they tapped lightly on the glass door pane, Crit held her breath as she pressed her head back in the booth with fear. They showed her their badges, motioning for her to open the door. Crit's hand and knees were shaking as she opened the door and stood up.

They led her from the phone booth to sit at a table near the soda fountain. "Miss Clinkscales? I'm Agent Morgan, and this is Agent Snodgrass."

Before Rose spoke, her eyes darted around the drugstore looking for anything or anyone suspicious. "Okay. Do we have to stay here?"

"No ma'am. Come on, we'll take you someplace you will feel safe."

The two men led Rose out to their parked car. As they drove away, Rose allowed herself to slide down into the back seat and relax, something she had not done for days.

In less than ten minutes they pulled into the Resident Agency parking lot. Agent Snodgrass got out of the car and opened the door for Rose, quickly escorting her through the rear entrance and into a first-floor office.

Agent Morgan had preceded them and pulled out a chair for Rose to sit down. She was grateful the chair had arms as it made her feel more secure. "Can I get you anything? Water? Coffee?"

"A cup of coffee would be nice."

"Be right back," he said, returning quickly with a mug of coffee. "I didn't know what you used." He put some cubes of sugar, powdered cream, and a plastic spoon on the table.

"Sugar is fine. Can I have a cigarette?" Rose hoped that a cigarette would help her calm down.

Agent Snodgrass reached into his pocket taking out a pack of Lucky Strikes and put the cigarettes in front of her. Rose took one with trembling fingers. "Here, let me light that for you." He flipped open a lighter and held it to the cigarette. The agent waited until she took a couple of drags, giving her time to recover from her perilous day. "Ms. Clinkscales, you called to say you were in trouble. Could you tell us about that?"

Rose started off slowly. "Look. I'm a junkie with a $40 a day habit. I've been working both sides of the fence, and now I know I can't do that anymore." She began telling them the story of how she came to be in Montgomery and said she was a call girl from a ring out of New Orleans. She was recruited out of The Jung Hotel by J.B. Hill, a railroad employee living in Montgomery and known to the Montgomery Police Department. On the side, he was running a string of prostitutes from Pensacola to Oklahoma City. Rose was one of the several girls who regularly made that trip. She pulled a black book out of her purse and quickly read aloud the names of girls, but refused to let the agents look at it.

Rose continued with the story that she and seven other girls were brought to Montgomery by Whity Shultz. Rose described him as being in the 5th Police District in New Orleans and said he returned to New Orleans after dropping them off in Montgomery.

"I was left at The Exchange Hotel to register as Maria Evans. I was supposed to be in Room #412, but I had them move me to an air-conditioned room. They put me in #612." Agent Snodgrass was writing everything down as she spoke.

"I know I recognized one of the syndicate's guys when I checked in. He's real tough and looks like he had just as soon kill you as look at you. He's a bellhop at the hotel, but I think he was just put there to watch me."

Morgan asked, "Could you identify him from some pictures?"

"Yeah, sure."

Morgan got up and went to the door. He spoke to an assistant in the office before closing the door behind him.

"I met George Walker outside the hotel, and we walked to The Jefferson Davis. We had a room there under the names of Mr. and Mrs. Walker. Several girls and I shared the room, but it was mostly for me. Some of the other girls who came with me also used an apartment in Montgomery that Walker owned."

Rose paused for a sip of coffee and a drag on the cigarette. "When we left New Orleans, we stopped at the port and picked up $30,000 of 'China White' from Louis Guardino at the Seaman's International Union. He gave it to us in the wagon, and we dropped it off at places along the way from there to here. Next place on the circuit is Birmingham." Still nervous, she took another puff of the cigarette and stared up at the ceiling.

"Take your time, you're doing great." Snodgrass glanced over his notes.

"April and May, I worked as hostess on a ship for the SIU. I do that some."

Rose was getting tired of trying to keep everything straight in her confused mind. "I just want to get out of here. This is too much!"

Agent Morgan broke into her thoughts. "Ms. Clinkscales, are there any others involved?" It had been a little difficult to follow all that she was saying as the story shifted at times.

"Yeah." Her manner and attitude changed as she abruptly snuffed out her cigarette in the ashtray and took another from the open pack on the table. After Snodgrass lit the new one, she opened her little black book again and read several names of call girls and others she would contact as needed.

"Also, there is a Norwell Thompson who has a group of girls out of New Orleans, but he is here sometimes. Some of his drivers are slick Jimmy King and Joe E. Brisas. Thompson and J.B. said if we ever got into trouble, they have a contact in the Montgomery jail. Her name is Rose, like my name; she's the head matron. She'd take care of things for us."

By now Rose had become quite agitated. Suddenly standing up, she began pacing around the small office. "Look. I had to go along with this 'cause the syndicate is holding my 6-year-old boy, Mike." Once again she raised the spectre of danger for her son.

"Where?" Agent Morgan was now concerned about possible child abduction. He also thought Rose seemed to be shifting off of center, and he would need to get the FBI to verify that statement.

"They've got him either at 824 Royal Street or 731 Conti in New Orleans. I have to make $3,000 for them or they will hurt him."

"Who?"

"No way am I tellin' you that!" Rose grabbed her purse and headed for the door. She was in need of a hit and had to get to her things from The Exchange. One way or another, she was getting out of town.

"Look. I've said too much. I gotta get my fix. J.B. will make sure I get it. I've got to go back to The Exchange."

"You said you'd identify the Exchange bell hop. Will you take a minute to look at some pictures?" Morgan hoped to distract her.

"Ok. Yeah."

Morgan went to the door and spoke to the assistant. She brought in a large book and laid it on the table. Rose continued to smoke her cigarette from the safety of the other side of the table. Agent Snodgrass opened the book at the beginning and showed her the first page.

"Ms. Clinkscales, this is a collection of all the bellhops in Montgomery. Would you like to take a seat and look through it? Just point out who you think it is, as you can." Snodgrass spoke cheerfully, hoping to keep her from leaving. They needed to get as much out of her as they possibly could.

Rose looked through the first two or three pages while standing over the table. She calmed down a little and perched on the chair, carefully studying each picture.

"That's him." She pointed to a one-eyed black man in a picture.

Agent Morgan looked down and saw that she was pointing to Jimmy Knox, a known syndicate informant and hit man. If what she said was true, this woman was in trouble.

Looking at each other, Agents Morgan and Snodgrass considered what to do next. Rose took the decision from them by jumping up and once again grabbing her purse.

"I gotta go right now!" She darted for the door. Since there was nothing to hold her there, the agents searched for a way to maintain contact. "Here," Morgan said, "take this card. If you need to get in touch with us, call that number, day or night."

Rose took the card and almost ran from the building.

After she left, Agents Morgan and Snodgrass began making phone calls.

Rose started walking swiftly toward The Exchange. She looked down at the card in her hand. "Where did I get that?" she thought, slipping the card into a side pocket of her purse. By now Rose was in a complete state of desperation for her "fix" and wanted to get her things out of the room. As she arrived at the front door, she looked for Jimmy Knox and didn't see him. "Good," she thought.

Going directly to the elevator, she told the operator the floor. When Rose arrived at her room, she fumbled in her purse for the room key to unlock the door and hurried inside. She did not want to be observed. Closing the door behind her, she pulled clothes out of the drawers, and reached tenderly for her precious little box of baby clothes. Giving the box a kiss, she carefully placed it in the bottom of her suitcase, putting everything else on top.

Rose then went into the bathroom to collect her toiletries. While she was finishing, she heard someone at the door. In a panic, she slammed the case lid closed and slid it under the bed. The sound of a key in the lock made her heart pound; then the door opened to reveal J.B.'s stoic face.

"J.B.! You're here," Rose said, with a nervous smile.

"Yeah, honey. How's my girl?" His voice was big, like him.

"Oh, fine. I had breakfast at that cute drugstore down the street and walked around the city for a while. I've never actually seen Montgomery." She lied.

"Hmmm. Really?"

"Of course." Rose acted indignantly. "I never do anything, but what you say. I wanted to get out and see something."

"Just wondering. You didn't make a phone call?" He spoke with an accusatory tone.

"Sure, I did." Venom was now spewing from her lips as she found her courage. "I have a son, remember? I just wanted to check on him. Is that okay with you?"

"Yeah, yeah. Check on your son. But, I want you to get yourself together. We leave tomorrow for Birmingham. Jimmy King will be here to collect all you girls, so be ready." He moved close enough to Rose for his body to touch hers, as he reached up to stroke her blonde hair. Rose cringed at his touch.

"And Melba, you know you're my favorite. It'd be real disappointing to lose you."

Rose coyly moved away from him. "Why J.B., what makes you think that? I'm your girl. It's what I do. I just remember about my boy sometimes, but that doesn't mean I don't think of my big boy, too." She had to play the role. J.B. got the fixes for her that she desperately needed, but he could also hurt Mike, or have her killed if he suspected anything.

J.B. chuckled at her comment. "Don't worry, your boy is safe in New Orleans," he lied. "We'll see to it that you see him when you get back."

Rose gave him a beautiful smile, but was thinking, "Liar."

J.B moved around to the desk and pulled some paraphernalia from his briefcase. He mixed a drink for both of them, giving her a glass and taking one for himself. Raising his glass for a toast, he said, "To a profitable business." They both drank down their drinks and J.B then held her face in his hands, looking intently into her eyes. "I wish I had more time to do what I want to do to you," he said with ardor. "I've got to go now." He picked up his briefcase and gave her a slap on the rear as he left the room.

Rose knew from experience he wasn't as macho as he tried to sound.

With J.B. gone, Rose continued with her plans. She waited a while to make sure he had time to leave the hotel, before opening the door a crack to check the hallway. After being certain no one was there, Rose picked up her suitcases and crept cautiously toward the back stairs. Every landing of the stairs brought a renewed fear that she would run into Jimmy Knox, but that didn't happen. She didn't see him, but that doesn't mean he didn't see her.

She decided to go out the back of the hotel and avoid the front entrance, which would be more heavily watched. Going down the back hallway, she finally found the service door to the outside.

Rose became terrified that her "drink" might have been more than a "drink." The term "hotshot" kept coming to her mind. "They are trying to kill me," she thought. Though a "hotshot" is frequently given as an injection, she considered J.B. wasn't above doing anything if he thought she was a threat.

She walked back to the Dixie Drugstore and went up to the counter to ask for the druggist. Waiting nervously, she shifted back and forth from foot to foot. "How can I help you?" asked the druggist in a concerned tone.

"I…I…I need some help," she stammered. "Just some paregoric. I think I have had too much of a drug. I…I just want to get rid of it."

"Ma'am, we need a doctor's order for that. Do you need a doctor?"

"No!" She all but yelled. Rose stomped over to sit in the phone booth. The confines made her feel safe.

Rose stayed in the phone booth with the door open as she kept begging the druggist for paregoric. Looking in her purse, she discovered the card Agents Morgan and Snodgrass had given her. "Call anytime," she mumbled. "They said to call anytime. I bet they can get paregoric." She called the number, gave her name and asked that they come to the drugstore.

The pharmacist met the agents at the door. "She has been asking me for paregoric and saying she's had a 'hotshot,' but frankly, if that were the case, she'd be in a coma by now." The concerned druggist shared the information.

Agent Morgan decided then that she should be taken to the hospital. They picked up her bags and purse, holding Rose steady as they helped her to the car. In route to the hospital, Rose admitted she might have not been given a "hotshot," but still felt afraid and threatened.

"I haven't had my fix and just…uh, I just…needed the paregoric." She became increasingly agitated the closer they came to the hospital.

When she saw where the agents were taking her, she tried to open the door and jump out, but her back door was on safety lock. "I've done this before. I WILL NOT let them keep me. Hell, NO!!"

Pulling their car into the ER entrance, they struggled to get Rose out of the car. She continued resisting as they walked her toward the door. The closer they got to the entrance, the more she dug in her heels and would not cooperate with them. So they started dragging her as the toes of her shoes scraped across the concrete. When the ER door opened, the agents called for help. Rose raised her voice, as she screamed, "I don't need your help!" She began to fight the agents. The nurse on duty called for a male attendant to give assistance. Before he got there, Rose lashed out wildly to keep the nurse away, striking her in the face.

Agent Morgan fought to restrain Rose with handcuffs as Agent Snodgrass held her arms in place. At the same time, they turned their heads to avoid her spitting in their faces. Wrestling her into a chair they finally tied her in place with a sheet, so she could not hit or kick them. Exhausted from the struggle, she was gasping for air like a cornered animal.

Agent Morgan turned to Snodgrass and whispered, "Philip, I agree with the druggist. If she'd had a 'hotshot,' she'd be out by now. I don't think she's had her fix. Let's get her out of here and down to the police station. This is out of our category."

Snodgrass agreed and called the police station from the nurses' desk.

Soon, the police arrived and took Rose to the squad car. She slumped in the back seat on the trip downtown. She was spent. Hopeless. Again, she felt totally isolated and alone. At least they didn't put her in a hospital.

Once at the police station, she was placed in a holding room, but they did not book her. That was different. They brought her some water and posted a guard in the chamber for her protection. Her case had been turned over to Detective D. Terry of the Montgomery Police Department.

Having gotten her bags at the hospital, Detective Terry and the two agents began searching her bags for any clues to this wild, worn, out of control woman. As they searched through the suitcase, Morgan noticed the black book that Rose had guarded in their earlier interview. It was lying on top of a small box at the bottom of the suitcase. "This is it," he said. "The book she was reading earlier in the office."

They opened the book and found a full list of names, phone numbers, and places. It also included the name of the ship that she had mentioned serving as a hostess; the SS Angelo Petri. It would later be revealed that this ship was, in actuality, a cargo ship and had been under a narcotics investigation by the Coast Guard.

They went back to the room where she was being held and continued to question Rose about the contents of the book. "Look, I've said enough. You have what you need. I just want to get out of here and go home." Rose's voice was filled with exhaustion.

Reluctantly, and with nothing to hold her, Rose was released and escorted to The Jefferson Davis hotel to get the rest of her things, as was her request. With everything she owned in hand, she called a cab and went back to the drugstore. The pharmacist gave her a BC powder and a Coke to make her more comfortable while she waited. Rose had told him Detective Terry was going to come get her. The pharmacist didn't know whether to believe her or not, but he felt sorry for Rose.

Det. Terry looked concerned as he walked into the drug store. Rose smiled at him. "I'm ok. I had my fix."

The detective doubted this. Either way, he put her in the car and drove west to the edge of town, where he pulled to the side of the road. She had called and asked him to help her get out of town.

"Can I call anyone for you?"

"No, thank you." Rose sounded weak and tired.

She got out of the car, gathered her things, and walked a little farther down the road. Det. Terry turned his vehicle around and headed back to town. In his rear view mirror, there she was…hitchhiking.

The next day they made calls to The Exchange and The Jefferson Davis, verifying the information Rose had given them. They learned she had placed phone calls from The Exchange to Dallas, one to someone in Montgomery, and another to Florida. She had sent a cable to S.R. Clinkscales — Calico M.V.S. — 22, Venice, Louisiana, asking that lover call her at The Exchange on Thursday.

Several of the other pieces of information checked out. Instead of a J.B. Hill that she had mentioned, they found a J.B. Hitson, who worked for the Louisville and Nashville railroad out of Montgomery. This man had done a little bit of everything, including pimping and gambling.

For the next three days, they followed her leads, each one uncovering something new coming out of New Orleans and filtering into Montgomery. During that time period, the informant, Rozella Clinkscales, had disappeared.

CHAPTER 11

The Final Highway: Pathway to Truth (September 4, 1965)

It was September 4, 1965, when the Chevy sped down the familiar stretch of East Texas Highway 80 on the way to Dallas. Rose was physically exhausted.

She leaned her head back against the padded headrest in the front seat; staring ahead as the headlights cut through the heavy night mist. Though she frequently stayed up all night, the constant hum of the engine made it hard for her to stay awake.

Rose glanced over at the driver. He had driven her on other late night excursions, but she didn't know much about him. She could sense he was not interested in carrying on a conversation. If she said anything to him, he would reply with one or two words or a shrug. That made her uncomfortable because men always wanted to talk to her as Rose's mature sensuality drew out the maleness in them.

Not a kid anymore, Rose had experienced everything anyone could imagine about the dark side of life. After all of these years, the things that she used to think were dangerously exciting and fun were just a job now. Rose was in her forties; used up and worn out ahead of her time. She had tried it all, done it all, had it all and lost it all.

Rose was riding along, mesmerized by monotony while thinking about her life. By the time she reached twelve years of age back on the farm where everyone called her "Crit," she had started throwing away and destroying anything that tied her down, or tried to set a boundary. Rules did not apply to her. Fences could be climbed and restrictions trampled. Freedom to do as she pleased was the lodestone that continually lured her, no matter the outcome.

"What a dumb ass I have been. I threw away everything. My son, my family, my life…Michael…That's the only good thing I ever did. He was a little doll, those dark eyes, and wavy hair, right from the day he was born." Rose wiped a tear from the corner of her eye. "What is he now…twelve years old?"

"I pray to God this is my last job working both sides of the trafficking fence. I know I'm playing with fire and have got to get out while I still can before one side or the other takes me out. Maybe I will have a chance to set things right back at home, and be a real, honest to goodness mother to Mike…if it's not too late."

Rose tried to think about something else, as she stared out the window on her side of the car. The litany of the towns ahead seemed endless: Gladewater, Mineola, Terrell, Forney and Mesquite, before they would reach Dallas. She planned to get a few hours of sleep there in a reserved hotel room before making her assigned drug delivery the next day. Once that was done, they would tell her what to do next before being taken quickly out of Dallas. Runners like Rose were kept on the move and as low profile as possible.

Gladewater was only a couple of miles away as she succumbed to sleep. When they neared the edge of town, the car slowed slightly. Suddenly the driver made a hard right turn off of Highway 80; on to North FM 155.

Partially awakened by the quick change of direction, Rose lifted her chin and looked around at the darkness of the area. "What…where are we going? Why did you leave the highway? This isn't the road to Dallas!" Suddenly wide awake, she sat up in the seat, trying to see where they were going.

"Shortcut," the driver said, without emotion.

"Shortcut, my ass! Where in the hell are you taking me? Stop now, damn you, stop!" Rose screamed. Her heart pounding, she tried to grab the steering wheel while clawing at the driver with her long fingernails.

He roughly hit her under the chin with his elbow, deftly warding off her attacks and brutally throwing her against the far side of the car. With engulfing fear, Rose knew this was life or death.

The driver was apparently well acquainted with this dark patch of road as he turned off the headlights, then veered off of the pavement across a bumpy patch of land and into a secluded patch of trees. It was all done so quickly, and Rose couldn't process what was happening as her assailant slammed on the brakes, threw the car into park, and turned off the ignition.

Rose tried to find the door handle to escape, but just at that moment both of them could hear a car coming down the old Farm to Market Road 155. She tried to scream, but her captor pressed her down on the floorboard where he lay on top of her head and shoulders until the car passed. As the taillights faded away, he jerked her back up onto the seat as he took a pistol out of the door pocket. Her fear escalating, Rose gasped for breath as she tried not to faint.

As he kicked open the car door, he pulled her across the seat by her blouse and threw her down on the ground face up. "Please…oh please don't shoot me," she begged hoarsely. She could barely see him in the darkness, but she could see the silhouette of the gun.

"Shut up." There was no pity in his manner.

"I'll just go away. No one will ever see me or hear from me again, just don't kill me. Please!"

He roughly grabbed Rose by the hair and dragged her around to the back of the car into a patch of tall grass. When he let go of her hair, she managed to regain her footing. "Why?" Rose was beginning to sob. "Why can't we just make a deal? Why do you need to do this?" She held out her hands in supplication.

"Shut up, Bitch." He slapped her across the face; hard. As Rose fell to the ground, her assailant leaned over, pressed the barrel of the gun against her head, and pulled the trigger. The report of the pistol was muffled by the closeness of the barrel to her hair and skull, the silence of the night broken for only a moment. The smoky odor of gunfire surrounded both of them briefly before moving away in wisps.

Not one to leave things unfinished, the assassin began to lay out the scene he had in mind. Rose's legs were numb, and she was growing cold all over, unable to feel the rough stones as he dragged her onto the shoulder of the road. "Got to stay alive. See Michael…my baby. Mama, Papa, help me!" Crit's thoughts were growing dim.

The assailant positioned her body; head on the edge of the pavement, eyes to the north, arms nestled around the head, body out flat on the rocky shoulder, legs slightly into the grass and weeds.

Placing the pistol between his back and belt, he walked back to the reddish maroon Chevy still hidden among the trees and brush. Starting the engine and turning on the parking lights, he proceeded to the highway a short distance south of the body.

Turning the car around toward the north, he accelerated, eyes fixed on Rose. While gaining speed, he flipped on his high beams and zeroed in on the head of his victim; her flowing blond curls plainly visible. As cruel and calloused as he was, he still grimaced at the sound the right front side of the car made as it raised and lowered with a dual thud when the tire ran over Rose's left arm, and then her head. He made a quick U-turn in the middle of the road to see in the headlights if the scene looked like an accident. Perfect. Just as he intended.

Moving the car beyond where she was laying, he yanked Rose's three suitcases from the trunk; the sum of her worldly possessions. He stopped to look down at her motionless, ruined body, before he began to scatter her belongings.

He threw the first suitcase as hard as he could a short distance from her head. It popped open as he had hoped. Cosmetics, curlers, all sorts of make-up items tumbled out, the hand mirror shattered to pieces.

The second suitcase was tossed a little further away in the middle of the lane with some of the clothes scattered. The box that had been carried so carefully for so long popped open and baby clothes gently spilled over the side.

The biggest case, farther away still, was opened and placed right on the broken middle line separating the two lanes. This placement assured that a car would have to swerve right toward the shoulder to avoid the cases. In the darkness, Rose's body would not be visible until it was too late for an unsuspecting driver to avoid running over her.

After placing the luggage, just to be safe, he drove the car back into the partial cover of the trees. The assassin then walked nonchalantly back over to look at his handiwork. He then returned to the car, got in and started the ignition. Hearing a car in the distance, he drove into the edge of the trees, parked, and turned off the ignition to watch and wait.

Off in the distance, Jerry Don Moore was running late, making the return trip from dropping off his girlfriend after a fun evening of drinking and dancing at the local Roundup Club. He was a little bleary eyed from drinks and the late hour, but not too impaired to drive. It would be unusual to see another car on FM 155 after midnight. It was the road that would take him and his faithful old Dodge home. He knew it like the back of his hand.

Unknown to the shooter, Rose was still alive, but barely conscious and unable to move. Breathing a few shallow breaths; she was hanging on to a thread of life. Within minutes, the old Dodge could be seen coming up the road, with headlights slightly askew. It was the same car that went by earlier before the unknown man had dragged Rose out of the car. He knew whoever it was would run over Rose and be blamed for the death. Having no choice, he would have to stay hidden where he was until the driver either went for help or left the scene of the accident. He didn't want to shoot him as that would ruin the plan.

Unexpectedly, Jerry Don saw debris scattered in the middle of the road and began veering to the right. Clothes were lying everywhere. Suddenly there was a suitcase! "What the hell is that?? A woman!" Moore yelled into the night. His brakes screeched as he slammed the brake pedal to the floor. There was a sickening thud as the car came to a shuddering halt.

"Oh, my God! Damn it all! Tell me I didn't," he said aloud.

Jerry Don Moore jumped out of the front seat of the old Dodge and ran around to the back of his car to see a woman lying partially in the road, and part way out. His bald tires had come close, but did he hit her? Or was the thud noise of his worn out brake pads slamming against the drums?

The woman's head and arm were a bloody mess, and she wasn't moving. Looking around in the darkness, he desperately hoped for help. Noticing the maroon Chevy in the trees, he wondered if there was anybody in the car. "I don't see nobody in it, maybe it belongs to this lady?" he asked himself.

Moore was sure he saw that same car parked over on the layby when he went to take his girlfriend home. He thought it was strange, but didn't pay too much attention to it then. "Who is this woman and what's she doin' out on a road like this in the dark, tryin' to carry all of these suitcases at this time of the mornin'? It don't make no sense a'tall."

As Moore walked cautiously toward the body, he began to see features dimly lit by the taillights of his car. There lay a woman with curly blonde hair, arms and legs askew, clothing disheveled, torn and bloody. Looking around, he saw the hubcaps of the reddish maroon Chevy parked over in the layby reflect his headlights. He had an uneasy feeling that someone was watching him.

Kneeling on one knee, he leaned down close to the bloody head. "Lady?" Rose was unconscious; breathing with a shallow, occasional gasp for air. "Ma'am, can you hear me?"

He could see blood spots on the road, and tire tread marks on her left arm. There were wounds on her forehead and the side of her skull, as if she had suffered a hard blow of some type. Though distressed, he was also relieved to see that the tread marks could not have come from his bald tires, and he had not run over her. Thankfully, he had been able to stop in time.

Just as Moore stood up, a car heading north was coming up the road toward the scene. Stumbling out into the road, he started waving his arms frantically, and the car pulled up slowly beside him.

"Thank god you showed up! Please help me," Moore pleaded. "This lady is hurt bad, but I didn't do it. She needs help now. She's barely alive. Hurry!" The decrepit old car was full of Negro men, women and children. They looked at one another, concerned about what they saw, and what this strange man was asking of them.

One of the older men blurted, "Lawd, naw'sir, we ain't gettin' out o' this car," shaking his head as he spoke. "We's not 'bout to touch no white lady!"

"Naw'sir; don't mean no disrespect mister, but we don't want no trouble!" said another. All of the adults were nodding in agreement. The children were big eyed and totally silent.

"Well, you two men don't know what trouble is if you don't get your tails out here and help me put her in my car. I've got to get this woman to a doctor, or she's gonna die, and it'll be your fault! You don't want the blame for that, do you? Come on and help me get her in the backseat."

Reluctantly, one of the men got out and opened the back door of Moore's car. "Now, you get her feet and pull her into the backseat while I hold her arms," he said, as they struggled with the limp body. "You standin' over there, come give us a hand. Be easy with her, I'm pretty sure she's still alive, and we don't want to make her worse."

The unlikely trio of unwilling good Samaritans hurried; sweating with fear that they might be seen, or accused of causing all this mayhem.

"I want you to follow me as witnesses to all of this. There's a doc outside of Hawkins; over t'ward Big Sandy. I know he'll help us. No time to go to a hospital. Come on!"

Fearing they would be implicated, the two men looked knowingly at one another before running to their car and driving away, leaving Moore standing alone on the road.

"Damn cowards!" Moore said as he looked at their fading taillights. He gently lifted Rose's arm, placing it across her chest. Before he closed the back door, he thought he heard her make a noise, like a gasp for breath.

Glancing once again at the car parked in the layby, he had the same eerie feeling of being watched. Jerry Don Moore slid quickly under the steering wheel and drove away from the scene that was to haunt him for the rest of his life. As he gained speed, driving faster and faster, he stared straight ahead while listening for any sound from the mysterious passenger in the back seat.

As Moore pulled up to the only red light in Hawkins, a Texas State patrolman was parked at the corner of the intersection. Moore jumped out of the car, leaving the door opened and the motor running, as he rushed toward him.

"Officer, help me, please!! I got a girl in the back seat of my car; she's hurt bad. I got to get her to the doctor right away!"

"Follow me! Come on!" answered the patrolman.

In tandem, the two vehicles sped through the little town of Hawkins, headed northwest to the doctor's house, out in the middle of nowhere. As the two cars pulled rapidly up the gravel driveway, lights came on in the house and also on the front porch. After so many years of experience, the country doctor recognized the sound of urgency in the middle of the night. After tying his robe around his waist, the doctor sprang out the front door, carrying his medical bag.

Seeing the patrol car, he called out, "Are we staying or going?"

"Staying," the patrolman yelled. "Sorry to wake you up, Doc, but I've got a man out here with a girl in his car that's hurt real bad and needs your help."

Moore opened his back door for the doctor and pointed to Rose, her hair dangling out the door well. He started frantically trying to explain, "On Highway 155, Doc. Just lyin' there in the road. My God, I thought I might have hit her. I was drivin' a little fast, but…"

"Quiet! Get her out of the car so I can examine her; do it now!" the doctor said, acting out of reflex.

Moore began getting Rose out of the car, cradling her head and lifting underneath her shoulders. He motioned for the patrolman to lift her at the waist and legs.

"Bring her up here on the porch in the light and be careful with her." The doctor instructed the two men, as he took a stethoscope out of his bag. "Good, now lay her down."

Deftly, the doctor placed his stethoscope near her heart. Placing two fingers directly on her neck, he found a faint pulse. Reaching into his bag, he took out a vial and syringe to prepare an injection, then administered it with a sense of caring so as not to hurt her, though not sure if she could feel it at all.

He then began to make observations. Broken arm. Black, deep tire tread marks. Torn clothes and scrapes on exposed skin. Her head had a curious injury, as Moore had also noticed, and it was bleeding from the temple and back of the skull. All of his observations saw her condition to be crucial. One after the other the list flew through his mind: "BP high, signs of crepitation, probable fracture of the left forearm, apparent punctuate stellate laceration over the right temple and scalp, extending down to the underlying cranium."

"Call an ambulance. Quick!" the doctor said urgently to the patrol officer, who hurried to his car to call for emergency transport. Moore stood off to the side just watching and listening, anxious to go home to explain things to his wife. That was going to take some doing. But he felt the right thing to do was to stay with this helpless woman until she got some help, and in case the police wanted to talk to him.

The doctor took another look at the wound on Rose's temple. "God, no!" he uttered under his breath, as the stunning meaning rushed through his mind. He wrote, "punctuate stellate laceration." That would mean a gunshot wound; barrel flush against the victim's skin, in this case, skull; upon discharge, gasses from the weapon's barrel would have been trapped between the thin skin and the underlying bone. Resulting effect: expansion and bursting of surrounding flesh. This would mean a serious investigation.

The ambulance, owned by Malcolm Stone Funeral Home out of nearby Gladewater, arrived quickly at the doctor's house. "Get this woman back to the hospital in Gladewater as fast as you can," the doctor urged the two attendants, as they picked Rose up off of the porch and put her on a stretcher. The county nurse had come with them, carrying her medical bag. She hurriedly climbed in back beside Rose. Within seconds they were on the way to the hospital, with Jerry Don Moore following in his Dodge, and Texas State Trooper Andrews bringing up the rear in the patrol car.

As the ambulance pulled up at the Emergency Room entrance to Gladewater Hospital, a nurse and two male attendants hurried out the doors. They quickly opened the back of the ambulance and pulled out the stretcher holding Rose's motionless body.

The county nurse needed help getting out of the vehicle as she began rattling off Rose's vitals. "BP 90 over 60, erratic breathing; comatose" she said, panting for breath while rushing along beside the stretcher. The hospital personnel hurriedly took Rose into the emergency care unit.

Moore was following behind until a nurse pointed him toward the waiting room as the doors swung shut behind Rose and the medical team. The sign on the door said, "NO ADMISSION." Standing out in the hall, Jerry Don gave some cursory information and identification to the state trooper who then left to resume his duties for the night. The team from Stone Funeral Home waited in the ambulance until the county nurse hurried out to ride back to the funeral home with them. Behind closed doors, nurses and the attending ER physician, Dr. C. B. McKenzie, provided lengthy, documented medical care for Rose who was struggling to stay alive.

No one approached Jerry Don about anything as he sat alone in the quiet waiting room. Feeling useless and restless, Moore decided to jump into his car and go back to where he had found Rose. He could at least gather up her suitcases and things scattered all over the road and bring them back to the poor girl. Maybe that would help the police find out something about her. She had to belong somewhere, to somebody.

He hurried back to the scene and began picking up the half broken suitcases, filling them with scattered items. As he picked up a crushed cardboard box, he saw baby clothes inside. Hmm, that's strange. Jerry Don hurriedly crammed them in with everything else.

He made the round trip back to the hospital in Gladewater in a little over an hour. It had been an emotional experience for him as he gathered up the things at the scene of the accident. In the pale early light, he had seen blood where Rose's head had been laying and shuddered to think of it. He also noticed that the reddish maroon car wasn't up in the layby, thinking the police had probably towed it off.

Jerry Don had come upon a horrible scene on the road and was barely getting some help to put Rose in his car and get her to a doctor. He had gone to the hospital with her, but everyone walked by him as if he was invisible. Now he had these suitcases crammed with clothes, trinkets, and several letters from family members. He finally convinced the woman at admissions to take the things and put Rose's name on them. He thought the letters might help identify the lady.

What else could he do? He wondered why the police hadn't shown up to question him about all of this. No one had told him to go or stay. Looking down, he saw drops of blood on his shirt. "This is damn crazy," he muttered. "None of it makes any sense."

Hungry, confused and worn out, Moore decided to go back home, but not without first leaving his name and phone number at the admitting desk. He still had the job of trying to explain all of this to his wife, and she probably wasn't going to believe him. This was a no-win situation for Jerry Don Moore.

~

Rose's extensive injury evaluation and intensive ER care continued at Gladewater Hospital. The early observations made by the doctor in Hawkins, out on his front porch, were now being confirmed, expanded and well documented by a staff physician and nursing team.

For the next eight hours, Dr. McKenzie and his assistants did everything possible to care for Rose, including a cast to the left forearm, a diagnostic x-ray, and a cutdown with a venous catheter to the left leg, a urinalysis and a complete blood work up. The laceration on her scalp was sutured and covered with a pressure dressing. Nurses administered a variety of prescribed drugs.

She was then moved from the ER into Room 211, with doctor's orders for extensive bed rest and hour-by-hour monitoring. Rose continued the fight to live, while the staff at Gladewater Hospital did everything they could do to keep her alive.

Every twenty minutes, nurses administered the ordered drugs and recorded BP readings, accompanied by written statements about Rose's overall condition. By now it was 6:30 a.m., her blood pressure was 90 over 60 and her condition remained poor. Though an IV had been ordered by Dr. McKenzie, the nurse was unable to access a vein. A compassionate caregiver, the nurse did everything possible to ensure that Rose was comfortable.

Rose seemed stable for a couple of hours until her blood pressure dropped to 84 over 40. The attending nurse became more watchful as she inserted a much-needed Foley catheter. At 9:00 a.m., things began to change quickly and drastically. The nurse noted on her chart that BP was now 100 over 70, breathing was labored, pupils unresponsive. She was growing increasingly uneasy about her patient.

Then, at 9:45 a.m. the situation worsened. Blood pressure escalated to 140 over 90 and oxygen was administered through a mask. Rose's BP rose to an alarming 190 over 100! By this time the attending nurse never left her alone. At 10:00 a.m., her blood pressure rose to 224 over 140, and Dr. McKenzie was immediately notified. Upon arrival, he ordered 50 mg of Demerol to make her more comfortable. As he left the room, he instructed the nurses that he would be down the hall and to call him immediately with any additional changes.

Though not spoken aloud, the nurses wondered about the Demerol order. Seldom had they found themselves in a similar situation. They realized the administered Demerol would immediately eliminate any source of pain in Rose's body. All hurt would soon vanish, as does light at the flick of an off switch.

A short seven minutes later, her blood pressure dropped to 70 over 0 and her breathing was less noisy, as the nurse stood over her. Then the blood pressure became immeasurable, breath very shallow and cyanosis increased. At 10:20 a.m., no vital signs were observed. When Dr. McKenzie hurried back to the room, he found no vitals, and at 11:00 a.m. on September 4, 1965, Rose Cherami, previously known as Melba Christine Youngblood Marcades, was pronounced dead.

Her body was removed to the morgue, with an autopsy request to the coroner made by the doctor and police. Shortly thereafter, the body, along with the damaged suitcases and possessions, were picked up by Malcolm Stone Funeral Home there in Gladewater.

Authorities began the routine process of trying to notify her family. In the case of Rose, it wasn't routine at all and would have been nearly impossible had it not been for the assorted letters found in her suitcases. As Jerry Don had requested, someone from the hospital gave him a call about the situation.

"Mr. Moore?"

"Uh, yeah. This is Moore."

"I am calling from the hospital in Gladewater. I am sorry to inform you that the woman you brought in last night, or early this morning, has passed away."

Moore took a deep breath. He was still in personal shock over everything that had happened. "She's dead…oh dear God."

"Mr. Moore? Are you okay?"

"I tried to help her, you know. Did everythin' I knew to do. It wasn't me that hit her. I hope nobody thinks I did." His voice was shaky. "Uh, can you tell me how, I mean she was hurt real bad, wasn't she?"

"Well, Mr. Moore, I can't discuss the details with you, sir, but you should know that we did all we could to keep her alive. We took good care of her for over eight hours, but we lost her about two hours ago." There was a tearful sadness in the caller's voice.

"Uh, I see. Well, I 'preciate you callin' me." His voice trailed away.

"Yes, sir. It'll all be okay," the caller reassured, before hanging up.

"Well," Jerry Don Moore, thought, "it ain't gonna be okay for that woman, and I sure ain't okay neither."

~

Jerry Don sat silently staring at nothing. He had a feeling it was all just beginning for him, as he heard the crunch of tires slowly pulling into the graveled area in front of his house. He pulled back the curtain to look out the window and watched the Texas State Trooper getting out of the black and white car.

"Jerry Don, what's all of this about?" asked his wife, as she looked out the window over his shoulder. "Who wuz' you talkin' to 'while ago on the phone?" His late night visits into town made her suspicious that he had a girlfriend. "Are you in some kind of trouble?"

As the state trooper started up the sidewalk, Jerry Don tried to reassure her. "Go sit in the kitchen and let me handle this, honey. You hear? Go on now, and be quiet."

She obediently shuffled to the kitchen and sat at the table with her ears perked up. The trooper was knocking on the door as Moore hurriedly pulled it open.

"Sir, I know this sounds strange, but I have to ask you if your name is Jerry Don Moore, and are you the owner of the Battery Specialty Company? I'm required to ask that for my report even though you've already told me." The officer removed his hat as he entered the house, holding a form pad and a pen.

"That's me, and that's how I make a livin'," he said, pointing him toward a chair. "I've been expectin' somebody from the law to come by. I wasn't sure it would be you, though."

"I'm just following up with you about the accident and the things that involved you last night; or early this morning. Want to be sure we have all of the details possible and make sure it's all correct." The state trooper was in a crisp uniform, attentive and professional. "I didn't have time to ask you much at the hospital."

Jerry Don saw the trooper's nametag, "Andrews." He didn't remember seeing it before. "Regarding the accident, I want you to tell me everything about it."

"I sure will." Moore sat down in a cane bottom, straight back chair.

"Well, it was real early this morning on old FM Road 155, involving a woman; never seen her before in my life."

"Yes, sir. She has now been identified as Rose Cherami or Melba Christine Youngblood Marcades. I guess you did hear that she died?"

"Yep. They called me from the hospital a bit ago. Real sad. How come she has all those names? Strange sounding, ain't they?"

"Well, right now, we're not exactly sure what name is legal and what name is assumed, or an alias. Anyway, you were the first person present at the scene. Right, Mr. Moore?" The officer was filling out a routine form and also making notes.

"Yeah, that's right," he pursed his lips, "unless there was somebody up in the layby that I couldn't see."

"Mr. Moore, for my report, could you just tell me what happened?"

"Okay." He lowered his voice, pulling his chair slightly toward the trooper so as not to be heard by his wife in the kitchen. He wanted to be able to tell her about all of it himself when they were alone and could talk, so he could tell her his side of the story.

Jerry Don began, "I was headin' home last night, pretty late. I know it was after midnight. I had just made the trip south down 155. I was takin' a lady home. We, uh, I had been over at The Roundup for some fun. And, yeah, I had been drinkin' a little." He paused and looked at the trooper with assurance. "I didn't need nobody to take me home. I could drive fine and was headed north back up FM 155."

"I got it, go on."

"Well, earlier, when I was headin' south, I saw somethin' odd near the layby. You know where I mean?" Moore looked questioningly at the young man.

"Yes sir, I do. I know the very spot, a few trees and bushes clumped off to the side."

"That's it. Well, the first time I went by, goin' south, I saw a reddish-maroon Chevy parked over by the trees, but there wasn't nobody around on the road that time of night. Hell, there never is, so the parked car surprised me a little." Moore paused to catch his breath.

"Yes sir, the Chevy?" responded the officer. "Take your time because I have to get all of this down in writing."

"Heck, like I said, I was runnin' way late, so I just let go of seein' the car and didn't give it no more thought. Then, about thirty minutes or so later, when I came flyin' back north toward home, not sure how fast I was goin' cause my spuh'dometer don't work right, I run up on all this stuff scattered out ever'where."

"Hmmm...interesting. Go on."

"Well, there was three suitcases; first one smack dab in the middle of the road and when I swerved right to miss it, there was another one, and then a third one. Clothes was layin' in the road everywhere."

"Uh huh," the trooper nodded.

"My lights wasn't workin' great, but I could still see real good. One by one, I dodged them cases and ended up veerin' right toward the shoulder." He paused a moment. "Then, Lord have mercy, there she was, just layin' on the road, half on and half off. I could see her long curls in my lights. Scared that I was gonna hit her, I slammed on my old brakes and swerved back to the left so I wouldn't! Then, I heard a loud thud. Scared the hell out of me. I thought I had hit her for sure!" Jerry Don had grown agitated as he relived the experience.

"Take your time, Mr. Moore. You're doing fine," the trooper said, to reassure him.

"I know. It's just so fresh and bothersome in my brain." He shook his head. "Anyway, like I was sayin', once I got the car stopped, I ran back to see what happened, and it was like a nightmare seein' that woman like that. She wasn't movin', and I didn't think she was breathin' either. I was afraid to touch her, but I did get down on my knees and tried to talk to her. I thought I heard somethin' like a little breath."

Moore paused to catch his breath.

"I went to the front of my car, lookin' all around and trying to decide what to do next. Then, a car full of Negroes come along, and two of them helped me pick that poor lady up and get her in the backseat of my old Dodge, out there. Then, they ran off as fast as they could go. Skeered, I guess. You know the rest when I ran up on you at the crossroads in Hawkins and you led me to the doc's house." The officer was diligently writing down Moore's report of the event.

The trooper looked up in a minute. "Anything else?"

"I got a little restless sittin' around in the hospital by myself, after I talked to you and you left. After a while, I decided to head back to where I found the lady and get her stuff, you know, the cases and all the clothes spilled out. And, that's exactly what I did. Then, I took them right back to the hospital and handed everthin' over to the woman at the receivin' desk. I gave her my name and number, too, when I decided to head on home. The sun was up and I was wore out."

Moore paused again, trying to get a clear read on the officer's response to his tale. He was telling the truth, but it was all so crazy he didn't know if the officer would believe him or not. He hardly believed it himself.

"Did the police get that reddish maroon car towed off that was sittin' up in the layby when I found the lady? It was gone when I went back to get the suitcases and stuff. You know I saw it there when I went by the first time to take my friend home."

The trooper's head jerked up as he looked at Jerry Don with a startled expression.

"Who did it belong to? I think there was somethin' fishy goin' on with that car, like there was somebody sittin' up there just watchin' everythin'," Jerry Don said.

"I'm writing this all down, Mr. Moore. I will need to check that out. You said reddish maroon in color?"

"Yes sir. I think it was a late model Chevy from what I could tell from the hubcaps, but I'm not sure."

"Well," the officer said, "you've been a big help to everybody, Mr. Moore. Without those suit cases, you went back to get, the hospital would have had no option but to label that lady a 'Jane Doe.'"

Jerry Don Moore hoped his wife was listening from the kitchen.

"Oh, I didn't know that. I did see some letters when I was picking up the stuff, but I didn't read any of that. It wasn't any of my business. Besides, it was too dark. I just turned everything over to the hospital people, or the police, to look through."

"Good thing you did."

"She died afore noon?" Moore blew his nose, avoiding eye contact with Andrews.

"The report says eleven this morning. I need to ask you a few more questions, especially about your car."

"Alright." Jerry Don looked down at the clean shirt he had put on in place of the one with blood on it.

"I understand, sir, that your car, the one involved in the accident, is a 1957 Dodge Coach with '65 Texas plates, tag number JHM-626. Is that correct, sir?"

"Uh-huh. That's my car and tag number."

"Well, Mr. Moore, I'd like to have your permission to take a look at the car. Is it the one outside?"

"Sure is. Right out there in front of the house."

The trooper picked up his hat, and the two of them walked outside together to the

Dodge. Interested in what the trooper wanted to see, Moore followed him as he looked the vehicle over from top to bottom. Getting on his hands and knees, and rolling over on his back, the trooper looked carefully underneath the carriage, and at the bald tires, making notes as he checked each thing. Looking everywhere, there was no blood, no hair, nothing questionable was found underneath or on the car. Content with his inspection under the car, the police officer scooted out and pulled himself up on the door handle. There were some signs in the back seat where Rose had been placed, which the officer understood, having helped get her out of the back seat at the doctor's house.

"Well?" Moore asked.

"Mr. Moore, I don't see any reason for further questions. Everything is as you said. I sure appreciate your help last night and today," he said, patting Jerry Don on the shoulder. The trooper touched the brim of his hat and headed for the patrol car.

Moore watched as the trooper backed up and pulled out onto the road. Taking a deep breath, he walked slowly back to the humble house where his wife was standing at the screen door, looking at him with a distressed expression on her face.

The patrolman drove slowly from the white frame house, thinking about all he had just heard, and the sincerity of Jerry Don. This wasn't the first time he had seen bizarre facts that related to an unusual death, but this set of circumstances was way out there. He knew a pile of paperwork awaited him about this case when he got back to his desk. Not only everything he had hand written and other forms but also paperwork from the hospital and the coroner would be included in a formal file to be sent on up to the state. It would take a while to get it all together.

He was thinking of all the aspects of evidence: isolated location of the accident, the bald tires, no blood or hair, no evidence pointing to negligent homicide on the part of Jerry Don Moore. And what was the deal with that car up in the layby?

~

As the patrolman arrived at his office, all of the details were swirling around in his head. He was talking to himself, trying to sort everything out as he read the report:

MELBA CHRISTINE MARCADES, alias ROSE CHERAMI, white female, d.o.b. 11-14-23, Louisiana State Penitentiary #256-375; FBI #234-2922, apparently died of automobile accident injuries on FM Road 155, 1.7 miles East of Big Sandy, Upshur County, Texas, between 2:00- 3:00 a.m.. September 4, 1965, subject expired at the

Gladewater Hospital, subsequent inquest by Justice of the Peace Ross Delay (who was also the Coroner), Precinct #3, Gregg County, Texas

"Hell, 155 is just a back road, runs parallel to 271 and 80. Why would that woman be hitchhiking on a farm to market back road in the middle of the night instead of out on the main highway? Where would she be going?"

He walked around in the office, trying to make the details fit together. The preliminary death certification data had been placed on his desk, waiting for him. He picked it up.

It read: "D.O.A. as result of traumatic head wound and hemorrhage to the brain caused by being struck by auto."

"D.O.A.!" He looked at it again. "What the hell is this? Dead on arrival, as in not breathing when she got to the damn hospital! Then why does the data show eight hours of medical attention after admission to the Gladewater Hospital? Were they taking care of a corpse!!?" He kicked over the wastebasket. "Eight hours! Hell, she wasn't dead when she got to the hospital!"

"I smell something rotten going on here. Somebody doctored the report somewhere along the line. Who, and why? And why would a woman like that have an alias, and a FBI number?" Officer Andrews knew there was nothing ordinary about this event, and he was in over his head. This was no accident.

He was obligated to duplicate all paperwork as presented and to include it in his report. His good common sense, and his designated duty to the state of Texas as a State Trooper were painfully at odds as he dealt with the conflicting information.

The next responsibility for Officer Andrews was to contact the family of Rose Cherami or Melba Christine Youngblood Marcades, however she was known. Had Jerry Don Moore not gone back to get her belongings with the letters included, the officer would not be making this call. There was no other identification on her, or in her things.

The trooper had never processed a death report wherein the victim had no identification, nothing in a purse or wallet to say who they were. All Melba Christine Youngblood had in her possession were some letters from her family. Attached to her alias as Rose Cherami was an assigned FBI number. Apparently, the Federal Bureau of Investigation knew who she was.

The officer sat weighing the options as he went through his notes. He had phone numbers for two relatives, both in the Dallas area: Mozelle Wall, sister, and Minnie Youngblood, mother.

"Which should I call? I think I'll call the sister and let her get in touch with her mother," Andrews determined. With the decision made, he picked up the phone to make his call. Quickly, the connection rang, and a woman answered the phone.

"Hello?" The woman answered pleasantly.

"Yes, ma'am. Mrs. Wall, Mrs. Mozelle Wall?" inquired the patrolman.

Her tone changed to one of concern. "Yes, I am. Who is this calling, please?"

Mozelle and her husband, Morris, had received many calls like this in the past. She immediately recognized the formal, legal way of speaking on the end of the line. It would have to be about Crit, so that would mean it was some kind of trouble.

Crit had called her just a few days earlier saying she was on her way home to Dallas and would be hitching a ride with three sailors based in New Orleans. Mozelle and Morris, along with the whole family, knew they couldn't put stock in anything Crit said. She might show up and she might not.

"Are you there, ma'am?"

"Uh, sorry, yes."

"Ma'am, I am Texas Highway patrolman Andrews; J. A. Andrews of Gilmer, Texas. I regret to have to inform you of the death of your sister, Melba Christine Youngblood Marcades."

The line was silent for a moment. The young patrolman waited, before adding, "Also known as Rose Cherami."

EPILOGUE

He Who Loves the Rose: A Son's Reflections

It is strange to see my mother's name in print, or portrayed as a character in movies. The internet also makes it possible for thousands of interested or curious persons to learn more about her and the many facets of her life. She is an intriguing figure who emerged from nowhere and innocently became entangled in the events surrounding espionage and the deaths of two publicly prominent people. This would consequently lead to her early, lonely and tragic demise.

Unlike others, her story is personal to me. My interest goes far beyond the speculation and conjecture about who she might have been, or what she might have done. My name is Michael Glenn Marcades, and I am the son of Melba Christine Youngblood Marcades. She is my mother. I am the result of a short marriage to Edward Joseph Marcades that ended in disaster, along with almost all of her life experiences.

When I look at my baby pictures with my young mother cradling me in her arms, I feel robbed. I have no memories of what it felt like to be held by those caring arms. I am told she was present at my second birthday party, and I was also photographed with her on Easter Sunday in 1959 beneath a large cottonwood tree where I then lived. There are other black and white photos of her with me. I vaguely remember those experiences.

I have only one clear memory of seeing my mother alive. I was about ten years old. Her mother and father, my grandparents, were my legal guardians. A Yellow Cab pulled up in front of their house in Duncanville, Texas, where we lived. My grandparents seemed surprised to see my mother in the backseat, and I expect they had no clue she was coming to see us as they went out on the porch to meet her. I later learned they would go long stretches of time without knowing where she was or what she was doing.

I vividly remember the moment as I looked out the living room window. I saw my mother lean forward to pay the cab fare. She gathered up her purse and make-up case while the driver retrieved a small suitcase from the trunk. Seconds later, she climbed legs first out of the rear seat, took the suitcase from the driver and started walking up the driveway, with a dazzling smile on her face.

She was magnificent to see, wearing high heels and hose, a close fitting dress, meticulous make-up and a head full of blonde curls bouncing in all directions. I remember thinking that she was so pretty.

Filled with a curious mixture of apprehension and gladness, I ran to my tiny bedroom at the back of the house. What would I say to her? Should I hug her? Would she hug me? In the back of my mind I was remembering that my grandparents had told me to always be careful around my mother, and never allow her to take me away from home.

Then my grandmother, "Mama" to me, called me to the living room. I couldn't move. She came to my room. "Mike, come with me. Your mother is here to see you." Mama's voice and face were filled with gentleness and understanding. Now I know she could tell that I was scared and confused.

I remember that for several days there was laughter and happiness in the house, as my mother joined in with domestic chores, cooking and ironing. I don't remember her sweeping me up into her arms or hugging me. She was probably aware that though she was my biological mother, we were relative strangers. She didn't know me at all, nor I her.

Then, with no advance warning, mother was gone just as quickly as she had arrived. Though I feel certain she told me good-bye, I don't remember it.

Almost two years passed before I heard anything more about my mother, then came September 4, 1965. Unfortunately, the occasion was not nearly as pleasant as the day she had arrived in the Yellow Cab. Though the details surrounding the situation were sketchy, the bottom line was totally clear. Mother was dead.

It is very hard for a twelve-year-old boy to process an experience like that, and the feelings live with me until this very day. I recall the funeral, hugs and condolences, struggling to walk close to her as she lay in the casket. Although I had some pictures, and knew she existed, I had learned to live without her. Now she was dead. I should have known her, but I didn't. Other children knew their mothers.

By the time I was old enough to retain and internalize such memories, mother had already been gone for a long time. For decades, my deep evolving feelings about her premature passing, and her mysterious death, were overshadowed by my own self-involvement. My grandparents, aunts, uncles and cousins, supported me while reaching my life goals: high school, college, marriage, fatherhood, graduate school, ordination, church music ministry and reaching a long-range goal of a PhD, followed by a university level choral conducting career.

Through my early years, immediate family members and others had made limited comments in the outside world. I heard whispers about my mother's years of mysterious absences, and hints that she was an unsettled soul who chose the wrong road in life and had always been in trouble.

Somewhere in my late thirties, I felt an increasing desire to seek my own legitimate answers. For a goodly portion of the next twenty-plus years, I devoted large amounts of time to related research. Who was this woman who gave me life, the beautiful girl holding me in her arms? Who was Mother, in reality?

Initially, I found my relatives to be tight-lipped about her as their sibling, in-law, or daughter. After many years of curiosity seekers plying them for personal information about Melba Christine Youngblood Marcades, they simply wanted to let the past stay in the past. Years later, I came to understand that preference as an outward manifestation of their protracted inner pain and emotional exhaustion. Nevertheless, and probably solely for my personal benefit, my grandparents, aunts, uncles and cousins provided periodic glimpses into my mother's convoluted short life.

As I dug deeper into her past in a more concise manner, I began to discover information far beyond what I hoped to find, and in greater detail. Much of this detailed information came to me through a large number of carefully preserved letters written in my mother's own hand. These letters introduced me to the private thoughts of a young woman who struggled with a myriad of desires, hardships, disappointments and addictions. Many of these facts and issues were confirmed when I, as a thirty-eight year old man, located, contacted and visited my father Edward Joseph Marcades for the first time in my life. I will never forget the tenderness in his eyes as we talked about Mother. Sadly, he knew nothing of her mysterious, untimely death. It was through him that I learned more about Mother's private New Orleans life and the hard-to-understand specifics of their divorce; particularly, his being excluded from my life. Additionally, I learned about a formerly unknown extended Marcades family, including Barbara, my father's second wife of over twenty years, and three half-brothers, Terry, Dean and Barry. All welcomed me with open arms.

As the years passed, my research intensified. With every new discovery, I became convinced that Mother's story had to be told, her real story, without suppression of the truth. I had to tell it for my own peace and satisfaction.

To that end, I have written this book. Every penned word has drawn me closer to her. In the process, layers of discovery have emerged. At moments I have cried out in anger against those who hurt her in her short life. And, I have marveled at those who loved her through every winding turn in the treacherous road she had chosen.

I know, in the eyes of many, she was a woman of questionable character who lived a bizarre life. Nevertheless, she gave me life, and in spite of her absence, or perhaps because of her absence, I have done my best to live it well. Though I was disenfranchised from her presence, a fact that caused me much confusion and pain over the years, I have morphed into moments of forgiveness, compassion, and the mature understanding love of an older son.

What I would give for just one hug and a glimpse of her face. Though I can't return to the past, or change it in any way, it brings me some degree of peace to have shared the experiences of my life with others who perhaps are looking for the same peace and acceptance within their own ambivalent lives.

Soli Dei Gloria

Michael with his Mother, Melba Christine "Crit"
Photo Copyright Michael Marcades

No man is an island, entire of itself;
every man is a piece of the continent, a part of the main.

JOHN DONNE (1573-1631)

Acknowledgements

Contrary to what many may imagine about my growing up as the sole son of Rose Cherami (Melba Christine Youngblood Marcades), I never felt abandoned during my childhood. As a young boy, and even into my early teenage years, I was constantly surrounded by genuine, sacrificial love. This blanket of reassurance came to me in many forms, especially during those years when my mother was unable or incapable of providing such.

To this day, I recall the security of sitting on the floor in front of my maternal grandmother (Mama) as she sat in her favorite chair; there, I knew love and peace. Long before those days, as documented by photographs of my infancy in and out of New Orleans, I was offered peace in the arms of many others, including my paternal grandmother (Jenny), my father (Edward Joseph Marcades), and his extended family. Once divorce separated my parents, my mother's life became such that providing adequate care for me was all but impossible. At the age of five, my grandparents, Tom and Minnie Bell Youngblood, rescued me from Rose's chaotic and increasingly unsafe world. From that day forward, Tom and Minnie assumed full-time responsibility for me as my legal guardians. They loved and cared for me as their own son. This sacrificial love was augmented by that of maternal aunts and uncles, cousins, friends, and eventually, mentors within the Church and public education.

Together, when my mother was incapable of doing so, these persons held me under their close, loving care and guidance. I acknowledge this great love.

As a young boy, teenager, and young adult, I learned many things about my mother: her wild, troubled lifestyle and her almost complete absence from my life. It wasn't until I was a full grown man that an inextricable, "to be expected" pain surfaced within me. For the first time, I associated this pain with my mother's unexplainable absence from my life, the mysterious events surrounding her death, and the "never discussed" absence of my father. I acknowledge this pain.

ROSE CHERAMI: GATHERING FALLEN PETALS represents my lifelong efforts to uncover and face any and every fact or event that would take me closer to my knowing and understanding Rose as daughter, sister, wife and mother. After almost thirty years of research, I learned how honest discovery and thought gives rise to perspective. I acknowledge this long, tedious, painful journey.

To J. Gary Shaw and Joe West (now deceased), I offer deep gratitude for introducing me and an inner circle of family to the staggering "tip of the iceberg" regarding Mother's life of drugs, prostitution, incarceration, mysterious death, and unbelievable connection to the assassination of President John F. Kennedy. Today, decades after this introduction, I acknowledge J. Gary Shaw as treasured friend.

To my maternal grandparents, aunts and uncles, who preserved a grocery sack of Mother's handwritten letters, legal documents, pictures, newspaper clippings, and more, I offer appreciation. The items in that sack served as the launching pad for my research and an invaluable connection to Mother's thoughts, prayers, joys and regrets. I acknowledge the gift and value of this treasure trove.

To my father, Edward Joseph Marcades and my half-brothers, I offer love and gratitude for welcoming me without question into their lives. Sadly, my father died just six months after our reunion. How I wish I had known you years earlier. I acknowledge this miraculous connection with my Marcades family.

To my loving wife Kelly, I offer my deep love and appreciation for insisting that I document and accurately record Mother's story, the sacrifices of family and others for my benefit, and the impact of all on my life. Many times, the weight and massive scope of this multi-edition project left me with feelings of inadequacy and despair. I acknowledge the love and encouragement offered me by Kelly throughout the entire, painfully confusing, yet exhilarating journey.

To Dr. Arch Mayfield, lifetime friend and initial manuscript consultant, I offer my appreciation for wading through page after page, kindly correcting grammatical errors and offering sincere encouragement. I acknowledge this selfless investment.

Acknowledgements

To Norma J. Kirkpatrick, who miraculously entered my life almost ten years ago, I offer deepest appreciation for falling in love with Mother's story and for standing beside me as genuine friend and co-author/editor. Her indispensable female perspective, masterful writing skills, and tireless commitment to this project allowed me to walk across the First Edition finish line. I acknowledge Norma's sacrificial contribution to this journey.

To Chris Gallop, treasured friend, I offer gratitude for providing me with my first opportunity to speak publicly about my lifelong research and resultant manuscript. Thereafter, Chris provided research assistance and enthusiastically introduced my work to JFK Lancer. I acknowledge Chris' sincere and insistent support.

To Debra Conway, President of JFK Lancer Productions & Publications, I offer gratitude for publishing the First Edition. She believed in the importance and value of the story within these pages and confirmed all associated research.

To Robert Hartline and Matthew Halsey, my Christian brothers, I offer my sincere appreciation for bringing to life PENIEL UNLIMITED, LLC and the Revised Second Edition vision and implementation. I appreciate their belief in and dedication to the promotion, distribution and worldwide importance of this story. And finally, I acknowledge them as treasured Christian brothers.

To Daniel Whisnant, Colorado-based graphic artist, I express appreciation for designing all associated graphics for both the first and second editions of this book. I acknowledge Daniel's gifted artistic talent.

To John C. Tripp, gifted Georgia-based professional formatter, I offer genuine gratitude for transforming the Revised Second Edition manuscript into a stunning final product. Furthermore, I thank him for endless patience with me, a rookie formatting client. I acknowledge John's "above and beyond" contributions to this edition.

To an anonymous couple, who helped me discover and better understand many associated detailed facts about my mother, Rose Cherami, I acknowledge their sacrificial research and gifting.

And most importantly, I give thanks to my Savior Jesus Christ who has carried me through the entire journey. He has whispered reassuring, saving love in my heart's ear and carried me when I could no longer stand. At the end of this journey, more than ever before in my life, I realized that I am nothing at all without Him; absolutely nothing. I acknowledge my Lord and Savior, Jesus Christ.

Dr. Michael Glenn Marcades, January 2020

References

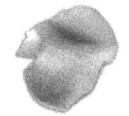

PUBLISHED BOOKS, NEWSPAPER ARTICLES, PERIODICALS

Albarelli Jr., H. P. *A Secret Order: Investigating the High Strangeness and Synchronicity in the JFK Assassination Volume One*. Chicago: Trine Day LLC, 2013. Print.

Anonymous. "2 Relieved of Duty As officer Kills Self: Melton Out in Big Police Shakeup; Suicide Blows Probe Wide Open." Houston Post, June 4, 1954.

Anonymous. "City Detective, Former FBI Man, Probe Target." Houston Post, June 3, 1954, front page.

Anonymous. "Houston Pushing Probe of Police." Austin American, June 5, 1954.

Anonymous. "Houston Vice Squad Officer Found Fatally Shot in Office." Austin American, June 4, 1954, p. A-10.

Anonymous. 1953-1964: "Operation Midnight Climax – CIA's lurid ventures into sex, hookers, and LSD." Alliance for Human Research Protection, 18 January 2015, www: ahrp.org/1953-1964-operation-midnight-climax-cias-lurid-ventures-into-sex-hookers-and-lsd. Accessed 21 October 2019.

David, Alex. "Shock Treatment." FREEDOM MAGAZINE, Florida Edition, Vol. 46, Issue 4, 2019.

Delaup, Rick. "Vintage Bourbon Street Burlesque," The History of the New Orleans French Quarter

DiEugenio, Jim. "Rose Cheramie: How She Predicted the JFK Assassination." PROBE, Monday, 16 August 1999.

Elliott, Todd C. A Rose by Many Other Names and the JFK Assassination. Walterville: Trine Day LLC, 2013.

Fehrerbach, T. R. "San Antonio, TX," Handbook of Texas Online, Published by the Texas State Historical Association

Fisher, Jaxie. "Re: pictures." Received by Michael Marcades, 11 April 2008. Subject: St. Elizabeth's visitation.

Goodwin, Sue. 1940-1949. "American Cultural History," Lone Star College Kingwood Library, 1999.

Gorman, Mike. "Misery Rules in State Shadowland." Daily Oklahoman, September 30, 1946.

Haney, Craig. "From Prison to Home: The Effect of Incarceration and Reentry on Children, Families, and Communities, The Psychological Impact of Incarceration"

Helen Harrison Courtney, "Fairfield, TX, Handbook of Texas Online," Published by the Texas State Historical Association

Haney, Craig. The Psychological Impact of Incarceration: Implications for Post-Prison Adjustment," University of California, Santa Cruz, December 2001 (research paper).

Jones, Sloane. Houston In The 1920s and 1930s, Images of America Story, Arcadia Publishing, 2009.

Lee, Martin A., Bruce Shlain. Acid Dreams: The Complete Social History of LSD, the CIA, the Sixties, and Beyond. New York: Grove Press, 1985.

Marrs, Jim. Crossfire: The Plot that Killed Kennedy. Revised and Updated Edition. New York: Basic Books, 2013. Print.

Mellen, Joan. A Farewell to Justice: Jim Garrison, JFK's Assassination, and the Case That Should Have Changed History. University of Nebraska Press, 2011. Project MUSE muse.jhu.edu/book/41084.

Mills, Chris. "Rambling Rose." Received by DES3MILLSCC@NTU.AC.UK, 22 August 1996. Subject: Rose Cheramie.

Rideau, Wilbert. In the Place of Justice: A Study of Punishment and Deliverance"

Sanders, L. H. "Eleven Tips on Getting More Efficiency Out of Women," Mass Transportation Magazine, July 1943.

Shaw, J. Gary with Larry Ray Harris. Cover-Up. Second Edition. Austin: Thomas Publications, 1992. Print.

Shaw, J. Gary. "The Rose Cheramie Affair." The Continuing Inquiry Newsletter, Issue 5 February 1994.

Stagg, Edward with John Lear, "America's Worse Prison," Colliers, November 22, 1953 http://www.unz.org/Pub/Colliers-1952nov22

Stein, Joel. "Angola, La.: The Lessons of Cain," TIME Magazine, July 10, 2000

Wood, Amy Louise. "Violence" Volume 19 of The New Encyclopedia Of Southern Culture

HSCA Documentation and Associated Memoranda

Francis Frugé Report, April 4, 1967 ("Officer J. A. Andrews, Texas Highway Patrol, interview relative to the death of Melba Christine Youngblood Marcades, alias Rose Cheramie).

HSCA File Number 005003 MO 166-98, pp. 1-14.

HSCA File Number 180 10106 10014, pp. 1-17, Frugé interview 1978 Subjects Rose Cheramie, Frank Odom, Francis Louis Frugé, Nathan Durham.

Memorandum to FBI from SA James P. Morgan, Jr. (Mobile office), November 23, 1965 (Re: George H. Walker; Rozzella Clinkscales – Victim / Interstate Transportation in Aid of Racketeering – Prostitution).

Memorandum to G. Robert Blakey, Chief Counsel from S. Jonathan Blackmer, Staff Counsel, JFK, May 17, 1978 (Re: Deposition of Francis Louis Frugé taken on April 18, 1978 in Baton Rouge, Louisiana).

Memorandum to Jim Garrison, District Attorney from Andrew J. Sciambra, Assistant District Attorney, February 2, 1968 (Re: Rose Cheramie).

Memorandum to Jim Garrison, District Attorney from Det. Frank Meloche and Sgt. Fenner Sedgebeer, February 23, 1967 (Re: Statement of Mr. A. H. Magruder).

Memorandum to Jim Garrison, District Attorney from Detective Frank E. Meloche, February 25, 1967 (Re: Statement of Mr. A. H. Magruder).

Memorandum to Louis Ivon, Chief Investigator, May 22, 1967.

Certified Medical Records

Austin State Hospital, Austin, Texas, Medical Record confirming March 1, 1956 court ordered admission and April 17, 1956 discharge of Mrs. Melba C. Marcades. Certified October, 2019.

East Louisiana State Hospital, Jackson, Louisiana, Medical Records confirming two admissions and treatments of Rose Cheramie (aka Melba Christine Youngblood Marcades). Admission and discharge dates: 3.23.61 to 8.10.61 with John Trice, M. D. and Curtis A. Steele, M. D. attending physicians; and 11.21.63 to 11.27.63 with T. M. Armistead, M. D. attending physician.

Gladewater Municipal Hospital, Gladewater, Texas, Medical Record confirming 9.4.65 admission and treatment of Rozelle Cherami (aka Mrs. Melba Christine Youngblood Marcades). C. B. McKenzie, M. D. attending physician.

Griffin Memorial Hospital (formerly Central State Mental Hospital), Norman, Oklahoma, Medical record confirming 4.5.63 court ordered admission and 4.23.63 discharge of Rose Evans (aka Melba Marcades). Certified via Rene Maricle, Griffin Memorial Hospital, October 18, 2019.

John Sealy Hospital (Galveston Psychiatric Hospital), Galveston, Texas, Medical Record confirming 2.11.56 admission and 2.24.56 discharge of Rita Lane (aka Melba Christine Youngblood Marcades). Dr. Ashya attending physician.

St. Elizabeth's Hospital, Washington, D. C., Medical Record confirming court ordered 9.20.57 admission and treatment of 1.31.59 discharge of Melba C. Marcades. Medical Officer Clara Moya, M. D. attending physician.

Internet Sources

"Angola Museum," Louisiana State Penitentiary Museum Foundation http://www.angolamuseum.org

Bourbon Street http://en.wikipedia.org/wiki/BourbonStreet

Cottonseed Industry / Cotton in East Texas / Texas in the 1920's http://www.tshaonline.org

Dănut, Incrosnatu. "How to Take LSD – Beginners Guide for Safe Use LSD," October 10, 2016, https://www.sociedelic.com/how-to-take-lsd/.

Economy of Texas http://www.wikepedia.org

Editors. "CIA: Project MK-Ultra," August 21, 2018, https://www.history.com/topics/us-government/history-of-the-cia/.

Houston and the Great Depression http://www.history.uh.edu/cph/tobearfruit/story 1927-1954 section04.html

Kays, John. "News Blaze: Rose Cheramie Knew in Advance That John Kennedy Would be Killed in Dallas," July 19, 2010, http://newsblaze.com/business/legal/rose-cheramie-knew-in-advance-that-john-kenney-would-be-killed-in-dallas_14669/.

Kleiner, Diana J. Aldine, TX (Harris County), "Handbook of Texas Online," Published by the Texas State Historical Association http://www.tshaonline.org/handbook/online/articles/hna18

Lackland Air Force Base http://en.wikipedia.org/wiki/Lackland_Air_Force_Base#References

Lee, Martin A. 1953-1964: "Operation Midnight Climax – CIA's lurid ventures into sex, hookers, and LSD." Alliance for Human Research Protection, 18 January 2015, www: ahrp.org/1953-1964-operation-midnight-climax-cias-lurid-ventures-into-sex-hookers-and-lsd. Accessed 21 October 2019.

McComb, David G. Houston, TX, "Handbook of Texas Online," Published by the Texas State Historical Association. http://www.tshaonline.org/handbook/online/articles/hdh03

Texas Almanac 1941-1942, 1941, University of North Texas Libraries, "The Portal to Texas History," crediting Texas State Historical Association, Denton, Texas. http://texashistory.unt.edu

Texas State Historical Association http://www.tshaonline. org/handbook/online/articles/hgf02

Texas State Historical Association http://www.tshaonline.org/handbook/online/articles/hds02

Tunica Hill WMA / July 10, 2000 http://www.wlf Louisiana..gov/wma/2752

Vintage Burlesque http://www.frenchquarter. com/history/vintageburlesque.php

William Sadler, "Wooden Ear, Hell On Angola" http://www.kairosangola.net

World of the Tenant Farmer (http://www.texasbeyondhistory.net/osborn/world.html)

World War I http://ask.com/wiki/World War I

Cinematography and Other

General Manager (name withheld on request). (2012, October) Onsite research interview at Larry Flynn's Hustler Club (formerly The Blue Angel), 225 Bourbon Street French Quarter, New Orleans, LA.

JFK. Directed by Oliver Stone. Producers: A. Kitman Ho and Oliver Stone, December 20, 1991.

The American Trap. Directed by Charles Binamé. Producers: Fabienne Larouche, Michel Trudeau, May 16, 2008.

The Farm: Angola (USA). Directed by Liz Garbus, Wilbert Rideau, Jonathan Stack. Producers: Liz Garbus, Jonathan Stack, 1998.

Additional Records

Rose Cherami was a crucial witness who was overlooked by the Dallas Police Department, the Federal Bureau of Investigation, and also the Warren Commission Investigation. It was not until Jim Garrison, District Attorney of Orleans Parish, Louisiana, initiated the investigation and the subsequent trial of businessman Clay Shaw for his alleged involvement in the assassination of President Kennedy, that Rose's story was first brought to light. Lt. Francis Frugé, the officer who encountered Rose Cherami on her fateful trip to Dallas, and heard her warnings first-hand, was assigned to the District Attorney's office to substantiate Cherami's statements and investigate other Louisiana witnesses' claims.

Later, in 1976, the House Select Committee on Assassinations finally acknowledged the existence of Rose Cherami. Thanks to Oliver Stone's 1993 movie "JFK," Rose Cherami's story was given new life, as the film opened with her ominous warnings of President's Kennedy's impending death. The end of the movie informed the general public of the thousands of assassination- related records still withheld by the US government. Consequentially, 1992, a law was passed to review and release these documents. The JFK Act was enforced by the Assassination Records Review Board from 1994-1998, and those records are still being released as of today. The JFK Record's Act mandates that all governmental assassination records be publicly available by October 26, 2017.

- Research Collection of Chris Gallop, generously shared with JFK Lancer.
- US Department of Justice, FBI, Known names of Melba Christine Youngblood, Record Number 2 347 922
- Rose Cherami Investigatory Notes from Anne Dischler, assistant investigator to Lt. Francis Frugé for District Attorney Jim Garrison of Orleans Parish, LA, the investigation into the assassination of President John F. Kennedy, 1967
- Gladewater Municipal Hospital, Gladewater, TX, Emergency Room Records, Roselle Cherami, Melba Christine Youngblood Marcades, September 7, 1964; Accident and Death Records
- East Louisiana State Hospital, Melba Christine Marcades
- John Sealy Hospital Records, Melba Christine Marcades
- Papers and Documents referencing the account of Dr. Wayne Owens, East Louisiana State Hospital
- Memorandum to Jim Garrison from Frank E. Meloche, March 13, 1967 (On February 25, 1967, I had occasion to investigate one ROSE CHERAMI" ; "WEISS stated that during her stay at Jackson, ROSE had told him that she knew both RUBY and OSWALD

and had seen them sitting together on occasions at Ruby's club. When asked about the statement that MR. A. H. MAGRUDER had given to me he (MAGRUDER) states that she told DR. WEISS that the President and other Texas public officials were going to be killed on their visit to Dallas. DR. WEISS states that he doesn't recall whether this was told to him before or after the assassination" ; "On March 6, 1967, I met LT. FRUGE in Houston and continued a search for ROSE CHERAMI.")

- JFK Lancer Productions & Publications, Inc.http://www.jfklancer.com
- Debra Conway, Study of Rose Cherami Documents, Records of Witnesses, and Related Events to the Assassination of President John F. Kennedy
- Sherry Fiester, Forensic Evaluation of Rose Cherami Medical and Death Records and also Anne Dischler Investigatory Notes
- November in Dallas Conference 2003 Speaker Robert Dorff, Letter from Dr. Donn E. Bowers regarding Dr. Victor Weiss' Statements
- November In Dallas Conference 2003, 2006, Speaker Jim Olivier, Rose Cherami, Jim Garrison investigation of the John F. Kennedy assassination
- November In Dallas Conference 2006, Speaker Anne Dischler, Garrison Investigator, Garrison investigation of the John F. Kennedy assassination
- Mary Ferrell Foundation http://www.maryferrell.org
- Staff Report of the Select Committee on Assassinations, Appendix X, March 1979, "Rose Cheramie," pp. 199-205
- Robert Dorff, Rose Cherami Documents and Correspondence, including the HSCA Staff Interview with Lt. Francis Frugé
- "The Rose Cheramie Affair," J. Gary Shaw, "The Continuing Inquiry" Newsletter, Issue 5, Feb. 1994
- "Rose Cheramie: How She Predicted the JFK Assassination," Jim DiEugenio, PROBE July-August 1999 (particularly Dr. Owens' statement to A. H. Magruder)
- David Reitzes, Rose Cherami Files at http://www.jfk-online.com/cherfile.html
- Statement of A. H. Magruder, February 23, 1967 (Dr. Owen: "During the Christmas holidays, that date being Christmas of 1963 to New Year's [sic] of 1964, I returned from a hunting trip with DR. VICTOR J. WEISS")
- Francis Frugé Report, April 4, 1967 ("Officer J. A. ANDREWS, Texas Highway Patrol, was interviewed by us, relative to the death of one MELBA CHRISTINE MARCADES, alias ROSE CHERAMIE")
- Memorandum to Louis Ivon, Chief Investigator from Frank Meloche, May 22, 1967 ("nurses had told several people of this incident")
- John Kays, "News Blaze: Rose Cherami Knew in Advance That John Kennedy Would be Killed in Dallas," July 19, 2010, http://newsblaze.com/business/legal/rose-cheramie-knew-in-advance-that-john-kennedy-would-be-killed-in-dallas_14669/
- Joan Mellen, "A Farewell to Justice: Jim Garrison, JFK's Assassination, and the Case That Should Have Changed History" Potomac Books, Inc, 2005
- p. 207, Jim Garrison called Frugé on February 25, 1967: Notes of Anne Dischler
- p. 208, direct knowledge of the assassination plot: "Comment CaVa" by Matt Vernon, Eunice News, July 18, 1967

M E M O R A N D U M

February 23, 1967

TO: JIM GARRISON, DISTRICT ATTORNEY

FROM: DET. FRANK MELOCHE and SGT. FENNER SEDGEBEER RE: STATEMENT OF MR. A. H. MAGRUDER

My name is A. H. MAGRUDER and I live at 4312 Duplessis Street, Parkchester Apartments. My phone number is 282-7542, answering service 947-2181. I am 47 years old and self-employed as a manufacture representative.

During the Christmas holidays, that date being Christmas of 1963 to New Years [sic] of 1964, I returned from a hunting trip with DR. VICTOR J. WEISS who at the time was Clinical Director of East Louisiana State Hospital in Jackson, Louisiana. We were sitting at my home near St. Francisville, Louisiana, just having a big bull session and he related the story that I am going to tell you. This is in connection with the KENNEDY assassination.

DR. WEISS said that prior to the KENNEDY assassination by several days, that the Louisiana State Police had picked up a woman on Highway 190 near Eunice, Louisiana, and that she had apparently been thrown out of an automobile from her physical appearance. The police thought that she was psychic [sic] so they took her to the East Louisiana State Hospital.

DR. WEISS gave her a thorough physical and psychiatric examination and determined that she was a narcotic addict and was having withdrawal symptoms. She told him that she worked as a dope runner for JACK RUBY. I believe she also mentioned that she worked in the night club for RUBY and that she was forced to go to Florida with another man whom she did not name to pick up a shipment of dope to take back to Dallas, that she didn't want to do this thing but she had a young child and that they would hurt her child if she didn't. She and this male companion of hers got into some kind of argument or fight and he beat her up and pushed her out of the car.

She also told DR. WEISS that the President and other Texas Public officials were going to be killed on their visit to Dallas. Dr. Weiss said that he didn't really pay much attention to a woman of this type until after the assassination occurred at which time he went back to this woman who was still in the hospital and had further conversation with her.

Now this was also after RUBY had killed OSWALD and she did say that she had seen OSWALD sitting at the same table at RUBY's club but didn't elaborate any further. About two nights later the FBI [sic] came to East Louisiana State Hospital and picked this woman up and DR. WEISS had to sign the papers for her release at that time.

That's about all. I've given you DR. WEISS' address and phone number.

VICTOR J. WEISS, MD
Psychiatrist Medical Arts Bldg. San Antonio, Texas
Phone 512 / CA-5403
Res. 234 Weather Cock Rd. Phone OL 5-0089

February 23, 1967, Memo to District Attorney Jim Garrison from A. H. Magruder, confirming that Dr. Weiss told Magruder, his hunting guest, of Rose Cherami's statements regarding her knowledge of the planned assassination of President Kennedy.

July 18, 1967, Matt Vernon, writer for the Eunice News "Comment CaVa Column," interviewed Lt. Frugé where he confirmed Cherami told him she had been a performer in Jack Ruby's Club. (In 2006, Ann Dishler, Frugé's investigatory partner, confirmed Frugé had sources to this claim who wished to remain unidentified.)

Reference copy, JFK Collection: HSCA (RG 233)

by the name of the Silver Slipper.

MR. BLACKMER: Do you know who manages that lounge?

MR. FRUGE: The manager at the time was a fellow by the name of Manual, Mac Manuel.

MR. BLACKMER: Now, after you were traveling -- while you were traveling to Jackson from Eunice, and I understand that's a drive of approximately one to two hours?

MR. FRUGE: Yes, at least.

MR. BLACKMER: Could you relate to us then anything further Rose Cheramie told you?

MR. FRUGE: Yes. I asked her what she was going to do in Dallas. She said she was going to, number one, pick up some money, pick up her baby, and to kill Kennedy.

MR. BLACKMER: And after you heard this, did you question her further about those statements?

MR. FRUGE: No, because the answers she'd come out with were -- in other words, to start with when she came out with the Kennedy business, I just said, wait a minute, wait a minute, something wrong here somewhere.

Now, bear in mind that she talked; she'd talk for a while, looks like the shots would have effect on her again and she'd go to, you know, she'd just get numb, and after a while she'd start talking again. I was more or less

Lt. Frank Fruge interview with the staff of the House Select Committe on Assassinations, April 18, 1978.
"She said she was going to, number one, pick up some money, pick up her baby, and to kill Kennedy."

Reference copy, JTK Collection: SSCA (RG 233)

1 letting her do most of the talking.
2 MR. BLACKMER: Now, after -- when you first saw
3 Rose Cheramie, did you go through any possessions that she
4 had with her?
5 MR. FRUGE: The only possessions she had with
6 her were two cardboard boxes.
7 MR. BLACKMER: Did you have occasion to go through
8 these cardboard boxes?
9 MR. FRUGE: No, I did not go through them.
10 MR. BLACKMER: You do not know what were the contents
11 of either of the boxes?
12 MR. FRUGE: Not at that time.
13 MR. BLACKMER: Did you ever have occasion to go
14 through any boxes in her possession?
15 MR. FRUGE: Yes, yes.
16 MR. BLACKMER: And when was that?
17 MR. FRUGE: When I went back to interview
18 her at the hospital.
19 MR. BLACKMER: And when you went through those
20 boxes, what did you discover they contained?
21 MR. FRUGE: Some of her clothes, and some baby
22 clothes.
23 MR. BLACKMER: All right. If we can now
24 go back to the trip to the East Louisiana State Hospital
25 in Jackson. After you arrived in Jackson, what did you then

-10-

Lt. Frank Fruge interview with the staff of the House Select Committe on Assassinations, April 18, 1978.
"And when you went through those boxes, what did you discover they contained?"
"Some of her clothes, and some baby clothes."

Reference copy, JFK Collection: HSCA (RG 233)

1   MR. FRUGE: I came on back home.
2   MR. BLACKMER: This, _____, was a day or so
3   before the Kennedy assassination?
4   MR. FRUGE: Yes.
5   MR. BLACKMER: On Friday, November 22,
6   President Kennedy was assassinated. When did you learn
7   of the assassination?
8   MR. FRUGE: I was watching it on TV. I was
9   home.
10 MR. BLACKMER: And as a result of hearing of the
11 president's assassination, did you do anything with respect
12 to Rose Cheramie?
13 MR. FRUGE: Immediately got on the phone and
14 called that hospital up in Jackson and told them by no way
15 in the world to turn her loose until I could get my
16 hands on her. And I talked to Dr. Armistead, and he
17 said that she was still kicking pretty hard, and he said
18 as soon as she gets the monkey off her back, he said, I'll
19 call you.
20 MR. BLACKMER: And did you later receive a call
21 from anyone at the East Louisiana Hospital?
22 MR. FRUGE: Yes, the following Monday morning.
23 MR. BLACKMER: And who called you?
24 MR. FRUGE: I believe it was Dr. Armistead.
25   I'm not positive.

-11-

Lt. Frank Fruge interview with the staff of the House Select Committe on Assassinations, April 18, 1978. "Immediately got on the phone and called that hospital up in Jackson and told them by no way in the world to turn her loose until I could get my hands on her."

Reference copy, JFK Collection: HSCA (RG 233)

MR. BLACKMER:	And as a result of your conversation with Dr. Armistead, did you then go back to the East Louisiana State Hospital?
MR. FRUGE:	Right.
MR. BLACKMER:	And at that time, did you interview Rose Cherami?
MR. FRUGE:	Right.
MR. BLACKMER:	How did you find her condition the next time you went back to the hospital?
MR. FRUGE:	Very normal.
MR. BLACKMER:	And this would have been on what day, sir?
MR. FRUGE:	It would have been on the Monday after the assassination, the first Monday after the assassination.
MR. BLACKMER:	That would have been November 25th. What did you learn from this next conversation you had with Rose Cherami?
MR. FRUGE:	She gave me -- she went more in details. They had to go to Dallas. The president was going to be killed; they were going to kill him.
MR. BLACKMER:	Excuse me, sir; they, you mean -- was she indicating the men that she was traveling with from Miami?
MR. FRUGE:	That's correct.

-13-

Lt. Frank Fruge interview with the staff of the House Select Committe on Assassinations, April 18, 1978.
"Excuse me, sir; they, you mean - was she indicating the men that she was traveling with from Miami?"
"That's correct."

Re: Rose Cherami and East Louisiana State Hospital

Dear Bob,

This letter is intended to set the record straight regarding my alleged statements concerning Rose Cherami in conjunction with her November 1963 stay at East Louisiana State Hospital in Jackson, Louisiana. You and I discussed this quite extensively during a series of telephone calls in early 2002. At that time you read a section on page 200 and 201 of Appendix 10 to the House Select Committee on Assassinations, which stated, quote:

"The commission [sic] interviewed one of the doctors on staff at the East Louisiana State Hospital who had seen Cheramie during her stay there at the time of the Kennedy assassination. The doctor corroborated aspects of [the Cheramie allegations]. Dr. Victor Weiss verified that he was employed as a resident physician at the hospital in 1963. He recalled that on Monday, November 25, 1963, he was asked by another physician, Dr. Bowers, to see a patient who had been committed November 20 or 21. Dr. Bowers allegedly told Weiss that the patient, Rose Cheramie, had stated before the assassination that President Kennedy was going to be killed."

Dr. Weiss's statement is untrue. I was not at the hospital on Monday, November the 25th. I spent that day working at my regular job at the Baptist Hospital in New Orleans, Louisiana. My regular tenure at East Louisiana State Hospital ended in July, 1963, when I moved to New Orleans and commenced work at the Baptist Hospital in that city. I worked weekdays Monday through Friday. On weekends I would drive to Jackson to earn extra money working in the medical division at the East Louisiana State Hospital.

I never saw Rose Cherami and only found out about her allegations on Sunday, November the 24th, 1963, during a dove hunting engagement with Dr. Weiss. It was he who told me what she allegedly told Weiss and possibly others. I was never contacted by anyone from the House Select Committee on Assassinations.

When I began getting telephone calls from assassination researchers informing me about the statements attributed to me, as memorialized [in Weiss's HSCA testimony], I called Dr. Weiss and asked him why he had said these things. Weiss rebuffed my inquiry and flatly refused to discuss it. I found that very odd as I had known and respected him for many years. I still cannot understand why he made those statements.

On mature reflection I recalled that, during our dove hunting foray on Sunday, November the 24th, Dr. Weiss told me about Cherami's allegations. That was the first time I heard any of this. I remember that incident because, while driving back to New Orleans that day, I heard on the radio that Oswald had been shot in the basement of the Dallas Police Department. Years later I personally reviewed Rose Cherami's hospital records at the East Louisiana State Hospital and was unable to find any reference to her alleged remarks about an impending assassination of President Kennedy.

I'm sorry I was unable to attend the JFK Lancers forum in Dallas and hope this letter makes clear that I had no contact with Rose Cherami.

Sincerely,

Donn E. Bowers, MD

Author/researcher Robert Dorff interviewed Dr. Donn E. Bowers in 2002 regarding the claims of Dr. Viector Weiss. Several persons have stated Dr. Weiss told them of Rose Cherami's statement regarding the killing of President Kennedy before the assassination was carried out. The above letter from Dr. Bowers was read by Dorff at the JFK Lancer's November in Dallas 2003 Conference.

MEMO:

RESOLVING THE WEISS SAYS BOWERS TOLD HIM ISSUE:

The HSCA "Outside Contact Report" (via telephone) is the genesis of their inaccurate information contained on p.200 of APPENDIX X.

1. Dr. Bowers was in THE MEDICAL DIVISION therefore would have no reason to see ROSE CHERAMIE who was A PSYCHIATRIC PATIENT.
2. Dr. Bowers told me he could prove that his employment during the relevant period was at BAPTIST HOSPITAL IN NEW ORLEANS. It was however his custom to travel to ELSH (in Clinton) "on weekends to make extra money." He could not have seen anyone on Nov. 21-22 because these were weekdays – when he would have been at work in NEW ORLEANS. He mentioned having learned later about someone at the hospital making statement about Kennedy being killed prior to the events of November 22nd, but has no independent recollection of who told him this.
3. BOWERS categorically denied ever seeing this patient nor does he recall having contemporaneous discussions with WEISS on this subject. Years later, when the info surfaced in the HSCA APPENDIX, BOWERS called his friend DR. WEISS and confronted him with his specious allegations. WEISS continually ignored him and changed the subject.
4. On p.46 of Lt. Frances Fruge's testimony to the HSCA he was asked about WEISS. He said it was his recollection that this may have been the doctor who telephoned GIM GARRISON to relate the ROSE CHERAMIE incident at ELSH.
5. Dorff was unable to detect the name DR. WEISS on any of the hospital records. The doctor who first saw her was MALCOLM GRAY PIERSON who died in March 1989 in Hillsborough, Flordia

UPDATE: Aug. 11th 2002

In telcon with DR. BOWERS, he remembered Dr. Cecil G. Edwards as being in the MEDICAL DIVISON, at ELSH. He feels if Edwards is alive he'd probably be the doctor who saw CHERAMIE first, or very early on, therefore might be the best bet for resolving what statements CHERAMIE actually made to him. Dorff is mailing some documents to BOWERS, in hopes he might be able to puzzle some of them out. Says records may have been put on MICROFILM by ELSH, but fifty odd pages was not what he saw when he checked file on CHERAMIE at the hospital. BOWERS further recalled having hunted doves with DR. WEISS the Sunday Ruby Shot LHO, having heard that news in his car while returning to N.O. Now thinks he and WEISS may have discussed CHERAMIE during this outing. She was of course still at the ELSH.

Author/researcher Robert Dorff interviewed Dr. Donn E. Bowers on August 11, 2002 regarding the false claim of Dr. Victor Weiss to the HSCA

March 13, 1967

TO: JIM GARRISON, DISTRICT ATTORNEY

FROM: FRANK MELOCHE, INVESTIGATOR

RE: ROSE CHERAMI

On February 25, 1967, I had occasion to investigate one ROSE CHERAMI, a white female. On November 20, 1963, ROSE CHERAMI was picked up by LT. FRANCIS FRUGE of the Louisiana State Police on Highway 190 near Eunice, Louisiana. Subject was suppose to have been thrown from a vehicle by two white males. ROSE CHERAMI was brought to the Moosa Hospital in Eunice, Louisiana, for treatment and then returned to the Eunice jail where she was suspected of having narcotic withdrawals. Assistant Coroner of St. Landry Parish, DR. F. J. DeROUEN, was called in and he gave ROSE a sedative and later had to be called again when she became violent, stripped herself of her clothing, and cut her ankles. DR. DeROUEN agreed to commit ROSE to Jackson (East Louisiana State Hospital) ROSE was brought to Jackson in an ambulance from Charity Hospital in Lafayette accompanied by a Eunice Police Officer. ROSE remained in confinement until November 26, 1963. It was during this time between the 20th and 26th of November, 1963, that DR. VICTOR J. WEISS, JR., of San Antonio, Texas, was house psychiatrist in Jackson. WEISS stated that during her stay at Jackson, ROSE had told him that she knew both RUBY and OSWALD and had seen them sitting together on occasions at Ruby's Club. When asked about the statement that MR. A. H. MAGRUDER had given to me he (MAGRUDER) states that she told DR. WEISS that the President and other Texas public officials were going to be killed on their visit to Dallas. DR. WEISS states that he doesn't recall whether this was told to him before or after the assassination.

On November 26, 1963, LT. FRUGE was notified by DR. WEISS that ROSE CHERAMI had completed her withdrawals and he could now talk with her. She gave LT. FRUGE some information about a narcotic ring working between Louisiana and Houston. ROSE CHERAMI was released to CAPTAIN BEN MORGAN and LT. FRUGE of the State Police and ANNE DISCHLER of the Revenue Division, and flew to Houston for further investigation of narcotics. While in flight, ROSE CHERAMI picked up a newspaper with headlines of RUBY killing OSWALD and further on down in the newspaper it stated where RUBY denied ever knowing or seeing OSWALD in his life. ROSE CHERAMI laughed and stated to LT. FRUGE that RUBY AND OSWALD were very good friends. They had been in the Club (RUBY'S) together and also stated that RUBY AND OSWALD were bed partners. Upon arrival at Houston she again repeated this story to CAPTAIN MORGAN. When asked to talk to the Federal authorities about this, she refused and stated that she did not want to get involved in this mess. All information on narcotic ring that was given to

-2-

...FRUGE by ROSE CHERAMI was true and good information. ROSE ... left in Houston and LT. FRUGE reported back to Louisiana.

On March 6, 1967, I met LT. FRUGE in Houston and continued a search for ROSE CHERAMI. A thorough search was made of Houston and Dallas, checking first on her mother, MRS. THOMAS J. YOUNGBLOOD, residing at 125 Carby Road, Houston, Texas. Subject, MRS. YOUNGBLOOD, had moved from there to places unknown about two years ago. A further check revealed that MRS. MORRIS WALL, 3626 La Joya Drive, Dallas, Texas, is the sister of ROSE CHERAMI. I contacted MRS. WALL and was informed that on September 4, 1965, ROSE was hit by a car and killed outside of Gladewater, Texas, while walking on Highway 155 approximately one and one-half miles East of Big Sandy, Texas, at about 2:00 A.M. Under Texas law I was unable to obtain a copy of the accident report. I verified the above accident and death through LT. SHAWLS of the State Police. The investigator officer was Texas State Trooper J. A. ANDREWS, 918 Sucess Street, Gilmer, Texas, telephone TI 3-2654. The driver of the vehicle was JERRY DON MOORE, 1425 E. Erwin Street, Tyler, Texas.

March 13, 1967, Memo to District Attorney Jim Garrison from Frank Meloche, concerning Rose Cherami's statements of regarding the assassination of President Kennedy. Page 2

MEMORANDUM

February 1, 1968

TO: ANDREW SCIAMBRA, Assistant D. A.

FROM: TOM BETHELL

RE: DR. WAYNE OWEN

* * * * * ***************** * * * ** * * * * * * * * *

   Today I received a telephone call from DAVE SWEIFEL, a reporter from the Capital Times in Madison, Wisconsin, and he advised that they had just run a story about a DR. WAYNE OWNE, who in the Fall of 1963 was an intern at the Jackson Memorial Mental Institute near New Orleans. DR. OWEN is himself from New Orleans, but is currently practicing medicine in Madison, Wisconsin.

   DR. OWEN and ten other interns were making the rounds at the hospital when three people were brought in, one who died from a gunshot wound, and two others who recovered from a motor accident.

   One of these two then warned of a plot to kill JFK in which one JACK RUBENSTEIN was supposedly involved. This warning occurred on approximately November 18, 1963.

   After the assassination, DR. OWEN tried to locate these two patients, but they had been discharged and their hospital records were missing.

   DR. OWEN said that he warned the authorities before the assassination of this alleged plot. DR. OWEN also said that the 10 other interns were present when the patients warned of the impending plot to kill the President.

   According to the reporter, DAVE SWEIFEL, two of these interns were recently subpoenaed by Garrison and told him of the above incident.

February 01, 1968, from Tom Bethel to Andrew Sciambra, Assistant DA, referencing Dr. Wayne Owen regarding an interview with Dr. Wayne Owen by "Capital Times" reporter, Dave Sweifel. This warning was on approximately November 18, 1963 at Jackson Memorial Mental Institute near New Orleans (East Louisiana State Hospital)

MEMORANDUM

February 2, 1968

TO: JIM GARRISON, District Attorney

FROM: ANDREW J. SCIAMBRA, Assistant District Attorney

RE: ROSE CHERAMIE

I talked to DAVE SWEIFEL of the Capitol Times Newspaper in Madison, Wisconsin, and he informed me that DR. OWEN had completely changed his story according to an account that was printed today in the Wisconsin State Journal. It seems that OWEN now says that the event did not come about as he had told SWEIFEL in the presence of Circuit Judge BARDWELL but that he was only recounting what had been told to him in a psychology discussion session by a doctor teaching classes in New Orleans. DR. OWEN cannot be reached by telephone and the hospital has given instructions that he will not comment on this any more and that he has taken a week's vacation. I gave SWEIFEL some background information on ROSE CHERAMIE and DR. WEISS and he said that he would pursue this matter for us and report his findings to us.

February 02, 1968 from Andrew Sciambra, Assistant DA, to Jim Garrison, referencing Dr. Wayne Owen "completely changing his story," to "Capitol Times" (Wisconsin State Journal) reporter Dave Sweifel regarding statements made by Rose Cheramie.

APRIL 4, 1967

STATE OF LOUISIANA PARISH OF ST. LANDRY

CITY OF EUNICE

Officer J. A. ANDREWS, Texas Highway Patrol, was interviewed by us, relative to the death of one MELBA CHRISTINE MARCADES, alias ROSE CHERAMIE [sic], w/fm, d.o.b. 11-14-23, LSP #256-375, FBI #234-7922.

Officer ANDREWS stated that subject died of injuries received from an automobile accident on Hwy. #155, 1.7 miles East of Big Sandy, Upshur County, Texas, at 3:00 AM, on Sept. 4, 1965. Subject died at the hospital in Gladewater, Gregg County, Texas. The inquest was held by Justice of the Peace ROSS DELAY, Prec. #3, Gregg County, Texas.

The accident was reported to Officer ANDREWS by the operator of the car, after he had taken the subject to the hospital. ANDREWS stated that the operator related that the victim was apparrently [sic] lying on the roadway with her head and upper part of her body resting on the traffic lane, and although he had attempted to avoid running ove[r] her, he ran over the top part of her skull, causing fatal injuries. An investigation of the physical evidence at the scene of the accident was unable to contradict this statement. Officer ANDREWS stated that due to the unusual circumstances, mainly time, location, injuries received and lack of prominent physical evidence, he attempted to establish a relationship between the operator of the vehicle and the victim to determine if any foul play was involved. This resulted negative.

It should be noted that Hwy. #155 is a Farm to Market Road, running parallel to US Hwys. #271 and #80. It is our opinion, from experience, that if a subject was hitch-hiking, as this report wants to indicate, that this DOES NOT run true to form. It is our opinion that the subject would have been on one of the US Highways.

ANDREWS stated that although he had some doubt as to the authenticity of the information received, due to the fact that the relatives of the victim did not pursue the investigation, he closed it as accidental death. We wish to further state that fingerprint identification shows that deceased subject, MELBA CHRISTINE MARCADES, is the same person as subject ROSE CHERAMIE [sic], who was in custody, by us, from November 21, 1963, through November 28, 1963, at which time she stated that she once worked for JACK RUBY as a stripper, which was verified, and that RUBY and LEE HARVEY OSWOLD [sic] were definitely associated and known to be, as she stated, "bed partners." She further referred to RUBY as alias "PINKEY."

Other statements made by subject, relative to your inquiry, are hear-say, but are available, upon your request.

(signed) Lt. F. L. Frugé

LT. F. L. FRUGÉ, LA. STATE POLICE

Record of interview with by, Lt. F. L. Frugé with Officer J. A. Andrews, Texas Highway Patrol, "...relative to the death of one MELBA CHRISTINE MARCADES, alias ROSE CHERAMIE."

MEMORANDUM

May 22, 1967

TO: LOUIS IVON, CHIEF INVESTIGATOR

FROM: FRANK MELOCHE, INVESTIGATOR

I received information from LT. FRANCES [sic] FRUGE, State Police, on May 22, 1967, that we should talk with one MARY YOUNG who is manager of the business office at Charity Hospital. MARY YOUNG was recruited by LEE HARVEY OSWALD to join some type of women's club while OSWALD was in New Orleans. Also, there is an operator of a computer, name unknown, now employed by Charity Hospital who has been with them about a week who also was an operator of a computer at Standard Coffee Company while OSWALD was employed there.

Information was also received that several nurses employed at Jackson Mental Hospital who were watching television along with ROSE CHERAMI the day Kennedy was assassinated stated that during the telecast moments before Kennedy was shot ROSE CHERAMI stated to them, "This is when it is going to happen," and at that moment Kennedy was assassinated. Information states that these nurses had told several people of this incident.

FRUGE said that he will drive to Jackson, Louisiana, to investigate this matter further and will contact us on Tuesday, May 23, 1967.

Memo to Louis Ivon, Chief Investigator for District Attorney Jim Garrison, from Frank Meloche, Investigator regarding "several nurses watching television along with Rose Cherami the day Kennedy was assassinated. stated Cherami said, 'This is when it is going to happen.'"

Second Edition Documentation

1a. Austin State Hospital Medical Record
1b. Austin State Hospital Medical Record
1c. Austin State Hospital Medical Record
2.   Edward Joseph Marcades' and Rose's Marriage Certificate
3.   Letter from Edward Joseph Marcades to Mrs. T. J. Youngblood
4a. John Sealy Hospital / Galveston Psychiatric Hospital Medical Record
4b. John Sealy Hospital / Galveston Psychiatric Hospital Medical Record
4c. John Sealy Hospital and Galveston Psychiatric Hospital Medical Record
4d. John Sealy Hospital and Galveston Psychiatric Hospital Medical Record
5a. 1955 Tax Return
5b. 1958 TaxReturn
6a. Saint Elizabeth's Hospital Medical Record
6b. Saint Elizabeth's Hospital Medical Record
6c. Saint Elizabeth's Hospital Medical Record
7a. East Louisiana State Hospital Medical Record
7b. East Louisiana State Hospital Medical Record
7c. East Louisiana Stare Hospital Medical Record
8.   Electroshock Therapy Permission Form signed by Mrs. T. J. Youngblood
9a. East Louisiana State Hospital Medical Record
9b. East Louisiana State Hospital Medical Record
9c. East Louisiana State Hospital Medical Record
9d. East Louisiana State Hospital Medical Record
9e. East Louisiana State Hospital Medical Record
9f. East Louisiana State Hospital Medical Record
9g. East Louisiana State Hospital Medical Record
9h. East Louisiana Seate Hospital Medical Record
9i. East Louisiana State Hospital Medical Record
9j. Rose Cherami signature, ER Register, ELSH, November 20, 1963

(courtesy of T. C. Elliott)
10a. Central State Mental Hospital Medical Record
10b. Albarelli, H. P. A SECRET ORDER, The End of Road for Rose, p. 216
11. Handwritten Letter and envelope from Melba Christine Youngblood Marcades to Mrs. T. J. Youngblood, May 1964, p. 1 of 6
12a. Gladewater Municipal Hospital Medical Record
12b. Gladewater Municipal Hospital Medical Record
12c. Gladewater Municipal Hospital Medical Record
12d. Gladewater Municipal Hospital Medical Record
12e. Gladewater Municipal Hospital Medical Record
12f. Gladewater Municipal Hospital Medical Record
12g. Gladewater Municipal Hospital Medical Record
12h. Gladewater Municipal Hospital Medical Record
12i. Gladewater Municipal Hospital Medical Record
13. Death Certificate Melba Christine Youngblood Marcades
14a. HSCA File Number 005003 MO 166-98, pp. 1-2 of 14
14b. HSCA File Number 005003 MO 166-98, pp. 1-2 of 14
15a. HSCA File Number 180 10106 10014, pp. 1-17
Frugé interview 1978 Subjects Rose Cheramie, Frank Odom, Francis Louis Frugé, Nathan Durham
15b. HSCA File Number 180 10106 10014, pp. 1-17
Frugé interview 1978 Subjects Rose Cheramie, Frank Odom, Francis Louis Frugé, Nathan Durham
15c. HSCA File Number 180 10106 10014, pp. 1-17
Frugé interview 1978 Subjects Rose Cheramie, Frank Odom, Francis Louis Frugé, Nathan Durham
15d. HSCA File Number 180 10106 10014, pp. 1-17
Frugé interview 1978 Subjects Rose Cheramie, Frank Odom, Francis Louis Frugé, Nathan Durham
15e. HSCA File Number 180 10106 10014, pp. 1-17
Frugé interview 1978 Subjects Rose Cheramie, Frank Odom, Francis Louis Frugé, Nathan Durham
15f. HSCA File Number 180 10106 10014, pp. 1-17
Frugé interview 1978 Subjects Rose Cheramie, Frank Odom, Francis Louis Frugé, Nathan Durham
15g. HSCA File Number 180 10106 10014, pp. 1-17
Frugé interview 1978 Subjects Rose Cheramie, Frank Odom, Francis Louis Frugé, Nathan Durham

15h. HSCA File Number 180 10106 10014, pp. 1-17
Frugé interview 1978 Subjects Rose Cheramie, Frank Odom, Francis Louis Frugé, Nathan Durham
15i. HSCA File Number 180 10106 10014, pp. 1-17
Frugé interview 1978 Subjects Rose Cheramie, Frank Odom, Francis Louis Frugé, Nathan Durham
15j. HSCA File Number 180 10106 10014, pp. 1-17
Frugé interview 1978 Subjects Rose Cheramie, Frank Odom, Francis Louis Frugé, Nathan Durham
15k. HSCA File Number 180 10106 10014, pp. 1-17
Frugé interview 1978 Subjects Rose Cheramie, Frank Odom, Francis Louis Frugé, Nathan Durham
15l. HSCA File Number 180 10106 10014, pp. 1-17
Frugé interview 1978 Subjects Rose Cheramie, Frank Odom, Francis Louis Frugé, Nathan Durham
15m. HSCA File Number 180 10106 10014, pp. 1-17
Frugé interview 1978 Subjects Rose Cheramie, Frank Odom, Francis Louis Frugé, Nathan Durham
15n. HSCA File Number 180 10106 10014, pp. 1-17
Frugé interview 1978 Subjects Rose Cheramie, Frank Odom, Francis Louis Frugé, Nathan Durham
15o. HSCA File Number 180 10106 10014, pp. 1-17
Frugé interview 1978 Subjects Rose Cheramie, Frank Odom, Francis Louis Frugé, Nathan Durham
15p. HSCA File Number 180 10106 10014, pp. 1-17
Frugé interview 1978 Subjects Rose Cheramie, Frank Odom, Francis Louis Frugé, Nathan Durham
15q. HSCA File Number 180 10106 10014, pp. 1-17
Frugé interview 1978 Subjects Rose Cheramie, Frank Odom, Francis Louis Frugé, Nathan Durham

```
MARCADES, MRS. MELBA C. AGE:33 CASE NO. 33240
         (Wht-female)

Admitted: March 1, 1956, Harris County
         (90 Day Commitment)
Diagnosis: Sociopathic Personality Disturbance
           Alcoholism
Discharged: April 17, 1956, Condition Without
                           Psychosis

              Official Correspondent

              T. J. Youngblood (father)
              145 Dipping Lane
              Houston, Texas.
```

1a. Austin State Hospital Medical Record

#58179

THE STATE OF TEXAS   In the County Court of
COUNTY OF __Harris_____   __Harris_____ County, Texas.

This the __29th__ day of __February__, 19__6__, came on to be heard the question of the mental illness of __Melba Christine Mercades__ and said __Melba Christine Mercades__ appearing in open Court in person and the Court having heard evidence in said matter and the testimony of Doctor __Dominick C. Adamo, M. D.__, whose address is __411 W. 20th St. Houston, Texas__ and Doctor __Mylie E. Durham, Jr. M. D.__, whose address is " " " ", being two reputable physicians, authorized by law to practice medicine in the State of Texas, and neither of whom is on the staff of any Texas State hospital, as to the mental illness of said person, and as to the welfare of ___her__self, and others, finds that such person is not charged with a criminal offense, is neither feeble minded, an idiot, an imbecile, nor an epileptic, is mentally ill and the court finds that the welfare of said person and/or others requires that such person should be temporarily committed for observation and/or treatment to a Hospital authorized by law to care for and treat mentally ill persons, as provided by law, for a period of not to exceed ninety (90) days.

IT IS THEREFORE ORDERED that the said __Melba Christine Mercades__ be and she is hereby temporarily committed to __Austin State Hospital__ as provided by law, being a hospital authorized by law to receive, care for and treat mentally ill persons, for a period of not to exceed ninety (90) days from and after the date hereof, for observation and or treatment, and at the expiration of which said ninety (90) day period this order shall be and become of no further force and effect

BOB CASEY   County Judge,

Harris   County, Texas

1b. Austin State Hospital Medical Record

FIRST ADMISSION (90 DAY COMMITMENT)   FEMALE (WHT)
AUSTIN STATE HOSPITAL

Name __MARCADES, MRS. MELBA CHRIST__ fnr No. __33240__ Committed ___ Voluntary ___
Psychosis—No. __52.D__ Group __Sociopathic Personality Disturbance, Alcoholism__
Age on admission __33__ yrs. Marital condition—Single married widowed __divorced__ separated No. of children ___
Nativity (State or Country) of patient __Texas__ of father __Texas__ of mother __Texas__ Year of arrival in U. S. ___
Citizenship—of patient __American__ foreign of father __American__ foreign Race ___
Education—None reads only reads and writes __common school__ high school collegiate
Occupation __Office work__ Religion (denomination) __Baptist__
Environment—__Urban__ rural Economic condition—Dependent __marginal__ comfortable
Actual residence—County __Harris__ P. O. ___
Time in State __Lifetime__ (Time of last residence) (Total time)
Etiological factors other than heredity
Mental make-up { Temperamentally normal, abnormal (specify)
                { Intellectually normal, abnormal, (specify)
Family history of mental diseases
Family history of nervous diseases
Family history of mental deficiency
Family history of inebriety (alcohol or drugs) (specify)
Alcoholic habits of patient { Abstainer
                            { Temperate (specify)
                            { Intemperate (specify) __alcohol__
Accompanying physical diseases not an integral part of the psychosis
Duration of present attack before admission __3__ yrs mos days
No. of previous attacks __First__
DATE OF ADMISSION __March 1, 1956__ 19
Presented at staff meeting ___ 19 by Dr. ___
                                        Hospital No. for the year __668__

1c. Austin State Hospital Medical Record

This Certifies

That on the __8th__ day of __April__
in the Year of Our Lord __1952__
__Edward Joseph Marcades__
of __New Orleans, La__
and __Miss Christine (melba) Youngblood__
of __Houston__
were united in

Holy Matrimony,

at __Houston__
in __Harris Co__
According to the Ordinance of God and
the laws of __Texas__
by __D E Sloan - minister__

Witnesses:

_____

_____

2. Edward Joseph Marcades' and Rose's Marriage Certificate

2/26/64
N.O., La.

Dear Mrs. Youngblood:

Seeing as how you never answered my letters to you, I will let this be my last letter. As for the checks, I am going to send my son's money into a trust fund. The latest news I have from either my son or your daughter is that she called my mother's house on the night of the 24th of Feb. She was drunk — screaming & cursing. God bless my boy, but what will really be done of him God only knows. Chris has sold the high chair & many things I had sent my son — which I know he is still young enough to use. I don't intend for my hard earned money to go to waste in such a manner.

I personally think if you & Mr. Youngblood have any kind of understanding, as parents & human beings, you will be kind & polite enough to at least consider this letter & answer me. If not, let your conscience be your guide every day henceforth.

Sincerely
Eddie

3. Letter from Edward Joseph Marcades to Mrs. T. J. Youngblood

JOHN SEALY HOSPITAL

Name: Mercado, Mrs. Melba Christine   Age: 33
Unit History No.: 217466-M   Dr. Rango
Admitted: 2-11-56   Dis. Date: 3-10-56

CASE HISTORY

A. **Present Illness**

This thirty-three year old white divorced female was admitted to the Galveston Psychopathic Hospital under the name of Rita Lane. She was transferred from the Emergency Room where she was brought in by the police on 2-11-56, early in the morning, after having been found beating her head against a side wall. She was absolutely "wild". No physical or neurological abnormalities were found at the time of examination. In the Emergency Room she was given sedation, being transferred under barbiturate narcosis.

In the beginning the patient demonstrated uncooperative and hostile attitudes, rejecting and refusing all kinds of relationships with the medical personnel. She seemed to be well oriented in all aspects, complained of memory trouble, and crying a lot because she was being placed in the hospital. Later on her behavior changed; she became friendly, cooperative, obviously manipulating the environment, and adopting a submissive attitude.

She related a history about her illness, which changed during each interview, and with special fabrications and confabulations, wanting to appear as an innocent girl, and so forth.

At a later date, we had the opportunity to talk with the patient's mother, and she related the following: The first pathological manifestation the patient had was when she was about twelve years old. At that time she was suffering of kidney trouble, unilateral pyelitis, and a few days later had an encephalitic complication manifested by high fever, somnolence, headaches and other serious symptoms. This picture lasted twenty-three days, later obtaining remission after intensive medical therapy.

Weeks after, the patient totally recuperated from the physical point of view, but she began changing completely in her personality. She became irresponsible, high-tempered, childish, stubborn, disobedient, destructive and making precocious sexual acts, loosing all respect for her parents, being a positive problem. A few months after getting the above symptoms, she left home without her parent's permission and went to Houston. The parents picked her up there, returned to Dallas, where she in turn was placed under psychiatric care. Extensive medical evaluation was done with physical negative results, after which psychotherapy was given, apparently successfully, still in this condition for about one year. Later, she kept the same misbehavior and psychopathic attitude, was placed in different school, with mediocre results.

Her personality was described by the mother as follows: She is

Name: Marcades, Mrs. Melba Christine   page   2

a very nice, friendly, temperamental and attractive girl. She is extremely irresponsible, coquette, amoral and unstable. Some periods she demonstrates very good behavior, at other times she presents episodically psychopathic behavior.

Melba has been working in several different places with good adjustment, but frequently left her jobs without any apparent reason. For the most part of the time she has lived with her parents, but has left home several times and then returns again, as though nothing had happened.

When she was fifteen years old she was admitted to the hospital in Dallas, receiving unknown treatment to the informant.

During the past few years the mother has had very poor contact with the patient, but she does know that Melba has been in psychopathic hospitals, jails, prostitution houses, night clubs, et cetera. Last year Melba was in the state hospital in Louisiana, at which time she received electroshock treatment. The informant gave a vague history in regard to the patient's delirium, drugs, etcetera as she has not had much contact with her within the past few years.

I. Personal History:

Personal History is all very vague and not accurate as the patient was not very cooperative. We do know however, that Melba married twelve years ago for the first time, and divorced after two years of marital life. She married again four years ago, lived with her husband for only three or four months. One child resulted of this union, who is living with the husband's mother.   No other information was obtained at this time.

III. Examinations:

The physical and neurological examinations were essentially negative at the time of her admission.

IV. Laboratory Studies:

Hematology: Hemoglobin was 12.9 grams %, 5,800 leukocytes, 66% neutrophiles, 13% lymphocytes, 2% monocytes.

Urinalysis: Specific gravity was 1.009, reaction acid, negative for albumin, sugar, acetone, and RBC's and microscopy.

Blood Chemistry: Glucose fasting 90 milligrams percent, NPN 35 milligrams percent, chlorides as sodium chloride 550 milligrams percent.

Electrocardiogram: reported a ventricular rate of 100, rhythm

4b. John Sealy Hospital / Galveston Psychiatric Hospital Medical Record

JOHN SEALY HOSPITAL

Name: Mercades, Mrs. Melba Christine   page 3

of regular, definite evidence of myocardial damage with posterior ischemia.

Electroencephalogram was interpreted as a normal tracing.

Radiology: Films of the skull show a normal calvarium in size and shape. The convolutional markings, vascular markings and sutures are normal. The pineal is not visualized, the petrous ridges, sphenoidal ridges and sella turcica are normal. Impression: Negative skull in the plain films.

Chest x-ray reported the heart and great vessels to be normal. The lungs are clear.

Hospital Course and Treatment:

At the time of her admission the patient was in a hypersomnolence state because of sedation which she had received in the Emergency Room. When she cleared up, she showed an extremely hostile attitude toward the medical personnel, rejecting and refusing to talk, in regard to her illness. However, later on she had crying spells, protesting because of her hospitalization. From the beginning she stated she did not want to receive anymore Shock. She stated she had been hospitalized in Louisiana in a mental hospital and had received electroshock treatment.

Two or three days after her admission Melba became very friendly, cooperative, well oriented in all aspects, socialized well with the other patients, trying to help them. Apparently, she did not have any preoccupations in her life and adjusted well to the hospital environment.

During her hospital stay Melba developed some spells with convulsive disorder characteristics. She stated she has had spells of unconsciousness before, and received treatment in Louisiana for that. Actually, the patient adapted to her new environment, and she was considered as being a very nice and empathetic person by the other patients. Since her admission and after all physical evaluation was completed she was placed on Dilantin and Phenobarbital, and some medication at bedtime with apparent good results. She also received visitors, demonstrating good behavior. Thirteen days after her hospital admission the patient discharged herself. She was instructed to continue anticonvulsant medications.

Etiology:

Questionable encephalitis.

JOHN SEALY HOSPITAL

Name: Mercados, Mrs. Melba Christine   page 4

VII. **Impression:**

000-x60 Sociopathic personality disturbance (320.?).
930-x90 Convulsive disorder.

VIII. **Prognosis:**

Poor.

IX. **Recommendations for further therapy:**

The patient was advised to continue taking anticonvulsant medication because we felt that she had some diffuse abnormality suggestive of convulsive disorder.

MA/mrv

1955 Tax Return

FORM 1040 — U.S. INDIVIDUAL INCOME TAX RETURN
For Calendar Year
U.S. Treasury Department / Internal Revenue Service
or other taxable year beginning _____, 1955, and ending _____, 195___

1955

NAME: Melba Christine Morcades

HOME ADDRESS: 145 Dipping Lane

(CITY OR POST OFFICE): Houston (COUNTY): Harris (STATE): Texas

YOUR SOCIAL SECURITY NO. AND OCCUPATION: 455-26-9098 / Unemployed

Exemptions
1. Check blocks which apply. Regular $600 exemption — ☒ Yourself ☐ Wife — Enter number of boxes checked: 1
2. List names of your children who qualify as dependents...
3. Enter number of exemptions claimed for other persons listed at top of page 2.
4. Enter the total number of exemptions claimed on lines 1, 2, and 3 1

Income
5. Enter all wages, salaries, bonuses, commissions, and other compensation received in 1955, before payroll deductions.

Employer's Name	Where Employed (City and State)	Wages, etc.	Income Tax Withheld
E. V. Kennedy	1101 Scanlan Bldg	$116.17	$2.70
Houston Chronicle		322.65	25.90
	Enter totals here →	$438.82	$28.60

6. Less: Excludable "Sick Pay" in line 5
7. Balance (line 5 less line 6)
8. Profit (or loss) from business (from separate Schedule C)
9. Profit (or loss) from farming (from separate Schedule F)
10. Other income (or loss) from page 3
11. ADJUSTED GROSS INCOME (sum of lines 7, 8, 9, and 10) $438.82

Tax due or refund
12. Enter tax from the Tax Table, or from line 9, page 2 .... $0.00
13. (a) Dividends received credit (line 5 of Schedule J)
    (b) Retirement income credit (line 12 of Schedule K)
14. Balance (line 12 less line 13)
15. Enter your self-employment tax from separate Schedule C or F
16. Sum of lines 14 and 15
17. (a) Tax withheld (line 5 above). Attach Forms W-2 (Copy B) $28.60
    (b) Payments and credits on 1955 Declaration of Estimated Tax
18. If your tax (line 12 or 16) is larger than your payments (line 17), enter the balance here →
19. If your payments (line 17) are larger than your tax (line 12 or 16), enter the overpayment here → $28.60 / 28.60

Refunded: $28.60

5a. 1955 Tax Return

354 – Rose Cherami

FORM 1040 U. S. INDIVIDUAL INCOME TAX RETURN—1958
U. S. Treasury Department
Internal Revenue Service — or Other Taxable Year Beginning _____ 1958, Ending _____, 195__

(PLEASE TYPE OR PRINT)

Name MELBA C. MARCADES
(If this is a joint return of husband and wife, use first names and middle initials of both)
Home address 125 CARBY RD
(Number and street or rural route)
HOUSTON 9 TEXAS
(City, town, or post office) (Postal zone number) (State)

Your Social Security Number 455 20 9098 Occupation SALES Wife's Social Security Number ____ Occupation ____

If Income Was All From Salaries and Wages, Use Pages 1 and 2 Only. See Page 3 of the Instructions.

Exemptions
1. Check blocks which apply. Check for wife if she had no income or her income is included in this return.
   (a) Regular $600 exemption........................... ☒ Yourself ☐ Wife
   (b) Additional $600 exemption if 65 or over at end of taxable year... ☐ Yourself ☐ Wife
   (c) Additional $600 exemption if blind at end of taxable year.... ☐ Yourself ☐ Wife
   Enter number of exemptions checked _____
2. List first names of your children who qualify as dependents; give address if different from yours. _____ Enter number of children listed _____
3. Enter number of exemptions claimed for other persons listed at top of page 2 ....
4. Enter the total number of exemptions claimed on lines 1, 2, and 3 1
5. Enter all wages, salaries, bonuses, commissions, tips, and other compensation before payroll deductions (including any excess of expense account or similar allowance paid by your employer over your ordinary and necessary business expenses. See instructions, pp. 5-6.)

Employer's Name	Where Employed (City and State)	(a) Wages, etc.	(b) Income Tax Withheld
HENKE - PILLOT	HOUSTON TEXAS	$1061 19	$147 19
HENRY'S GOOD FOOD CAFE	HOUSTON TEXAS	53 35	1 60
DOROTHY R. WILSON	HOUSTON TEXAS	61 00	4 30

Enter totals here → $1175 54 $153 09

6. Less: Excludable "Sick Pay" in line 5 (See instructions, page 7. Attach required statement.)...
7. Balance (line 5 less line 6)................................ $
8. Profit (or loss) from business from separate Schedule C................
9. Profit (or loss) from farming from separate Schedule F................
10. Other income (or loss) from page 3 (dividends, interest, rents, pensions, etc.)..
11. ADJUSTED GROSS INCOME (sum of lines 7, 8, 9, and 10)......... $ 1175 54

Unmarried or legally separated persons qualifying as "Head of Household," see instructions, page 7, and check here ☐
Widows and widowers with dependent child who are entitled to the special tax computation, see instructions, page 8, and check here ☐

12. Tax on income from line 11. (If line 11 is under $5,000, and you do not itemize deductions, use Tax Table on page 16 of instructions to find your tax and check here ☒. If line 11 is $5,000 or more, or if you itemize deductions, compute your tax on page 2 and enter here the amount from line 9, page 2).. $ 94 00

If income was all from wages, omit lines 13 through 16.
13. (a) Dividends received credit from line 5 of Schedule J.... $
    (b) Retirement income credit from line 12 of Schedule K....
14. Balance (line 12 less line 13).................
15. Enter your self-employment tax from separate Schedule C or F........
16. Sum of lines 14 and 15...........

17. (a) Tax withheld (line 5 above). Attach Forms W-2, Copy B............. $ 153 09
    (b) Payments and credits on 1958 Declaration of Estimated Tax (See page 8, instructions.) ...... $
    District Director's office where paid _____
18. If your tax (line 12 or 16) is larger than your payments (line 17), enter the BALANCE DUE here →
    Pay in full with this return to "Internal Revenue Service." If less than $1.00, file return without payment. $
19. If your payments (line 17) are larger than your tax (line 12 or 16), enter the OVERPAYMENT here → $ 59 09
    If less than $1.00, the overpayment will be refunded only upon application.
20. Amount of line 19 to be: (a) Credited on 1959 estimated tax $_____; (b) Refunded $ 59 09

Did you receive an expense allowance or reimbursement, or charge expenses to your employer? ☐ Yes ☒ No (See page 6, instructions.)
If "Yes," did you submit an itemized accounting of expenses to your employer? ☐ Yes ☐ No

County in which you live HARRIS
Is your wife (husband) filing a separate return for 1958? ☐ Yes ☒ No If "Yes," enter her (his) name. _____
Do you owe any Federal tax for years before 1958? ☐ Yes ☒ No

I declare under the penalties of perjury that this return (including any accompanying schedules and statements) has been examined by me and to the best of my knowledge and belief is a true, correct, and complete return. If the return is prepared by a person other than the taxpayer, his declaration is based on all the information relating to the matters required to be reported in the return of which he has any knowledge.

Sign here ▶ _____
(Taxpayer's signature and date) (If this is a joint return, BOTH HUSBAND AND WIFE MUST SIGN) (Wife's signature and date)

_____
(Signature of preparer other than taxpayer) (Address) (Date)

5b. 1958 Tax Return

| CLINICAL RECORD | Report on |
| | Continuation of S. F. 507 Notes |

January 31, 1959 Dr. Clara L. Hoye (Medical Officer-Psychiatry Supervisor)
CLOSING NOTE AND SUMMARY OF CLINICAL RECORD

Mrs. Marcades, a U. S. prisoner, was officially discharged from Saint Elizabeths Hospital January 31, 1959, after the hospital received word from James A. Borland, U. S. Attorney, District of New Mexico, that the indictments against our patient had been dismissed as of January 26, 1959, and that she need not be returned to New Mexico.

The patient packed up her things and left the hospital with approximately $47.50, with the intention of returning to her mother in Houston, Texas. A letter of notification is being sent to her mother, Mrs. Y. J. Youngblood, 145 Dipping Lane, Houston, Texas.

Melba G. Marcades was admitted to Saint Elizabeths Hospital on September 20, 1957, as mentally incompetent, having been sent here from the U. S. District Court for the District of New Mexico, Criminal Nos. 19366 and 19367 (Miss. 4151). She had a history of numerous previous hospitalizations and asocial and antisocial conduct since the age of eight. Her charge on admission to this hospital was car theft.

During her stay here she was periodically very disturbed, and the course in the various services was extremely stormy. She had been changed to status "C" on several occasions and had had ground parole for short periods, but had always become violently disturbed when she had taken a drink or two. In January 1958 she was placed in category "C" after improvement, and on February 4, 1958, she decided to walk out of the hospital gate to test her strength, as it were. Again she became intoxicated and was returned, disturbed and assaultive. She had another period of improvement and regained her ground privileges in March. On March 18, 1958, she left the grounds again without permission and was not returned until March 20th. At this time she was quite intoxicated and unable to give a clear account of herself. She rationalized and blamed her "other self" for her behavior. In one or two days she was completely clear and normal for her. On May 25, 1958, she fell while mopping the floor and was sent to M & S to rule out fracture of the pelvis. While there she became upset and had a series of "grand mal" seizures, with incontinence but without duskyness, as they stated. It was the opinion of the neurologist that her convulsive disorder was functional. It also was discovered that amytal had had a deleterious effect on her, and that after having it i.m. she convulsed. She then was on her excellent behavior for two months, became chairman of the Patients' Federation, and took a great deal of interest in this organization. Again her prisoner classification was changed from "A" to "B" in July 1958, and she was allowed to have privileges to attend entertainments with

MARCADES Melba G.   75,150   RICHARDSON
                      Report on Continuation of 507 Notes
Saint Elizabeths Hospital

6a. Saint Elizabeth's Hospital Medical Record

```
                                                                              75,180
        CLINICAL RECORD          Report on
                                         of
                                 Continuation of S. F. 507 Notes - 2

(Dr. Hoyo - 1-31-59 - 2)          (Sign and date)

        the group. Finally, on October 10, 1958, she was changed to category "C"
again, and on October 26th was granted ground privileges. At that time she
was receiving no medication whatsoever and had been on her good behavior for
five months.
        In about a week's time she left the grounds with a friend (?),
Viola Gilbert, who immediately encouraged the patient to drink. She came
back the same day, quite intoxicated, and of course lost her privileges and
was changed back to category "A." Since this incident, November 7, 1958,
she had resided on CT1-B and there had adjusted and cooperated very well.
Therefore recommendation was made on January 9, 1959, for her discharge and
certification to return to court for trial, as well as for a change of
diagnosis from 60.1 Psychoneurotic reaction, dissociative reaction (psycho-
pathic traits) to 52.0 Sociopathic personality disturbance, antisocial reac-
tion (alcoholism).
        A letter was addressed to the United States Attorney,
District of New Mexico, Albuquerque, as well as to The Clerk, District Court
of the United States for the District of New Mexico, Albuquerque, New Mexico,
with copy to the Director, Bureau of Prisons, Washington, D. C., stating
that Mrs. Marcades was considered competent to stand trial. On January 29,
1959, a letter was received from James A. Borland, United States Attorney,
District of New Mexico, stating that the indictments against Mrs. Marcades
had been dismissed and advising us that we could proceed to discharge her
here and that it was not necessary to return her to New Mexico.
        Mrs. Marcades left the hospital about 9:30 a.m. Saturday,
January 31st, and at 5:30 p.m. word was received from the Women's Bureau
that she was being held there in a very disturbed and intoxicated state
since she had been discharged from this hospital, she was taken to D. C.
General Hospital.

        DIAGNOSIS:   52.0 SOCIOPATHIC PERSONALITY DISTURBANCE, ANTISOCIAL
                          REACTION. (ALCOHOLISM.)

        CONDITION ON DISCHARGE:   IMPROVED.

        COMPETENCY:   PATIENT IS COMPETENT.

        FOR LISTING OF PHYSICAL DIAGNOSES, REFER TO DIAGNOSTIC SUMMARY FORM 501.


        Clinical Director                        Medical Officer-Psychiatry Supervisor

        MARCADES   Melba  C.                                  75,180          RICHARDSON
                                                                              507 Notes
        Saint Elizabeths Hospital
```

6b. Saint Elizabeth's Hospital Medical Record

75,180

9-20-57   1-31-59

52.0 Sociopathic personality disturbance. Antisocial reaction. (Alcoholism.) (1-9-5?)

9-20-57 Skull defect in left temporoparietal area (history of skull fracture at 15).
9-25-57 Convulsive disorder, etiology undetermined.
4-21-58 Chronic cervicitis.
5-27-58 Convulsive disorder—functional?
         Lumbar muscle strain.
         Contusion, left chest.
6-7-58   Abnormal EEG; diffuse; no focus.

SECTION "D"

STATE OF LOUISIANA
versus
MELBA CHRISTINE PASCALES

INFORMATION FOR
V.O: R.S. 14:51

Filed Nov. 16, 1960

(Sig) H.J.Alexander, Deputy Clerk
Arraigned 12/13, 1960
and pleaded Not Guilty.

(Sig) Clarence Molinario, Dpue Clerk

1/11/61,
    On motion by defense the Court ordered this matter continued to be reassigned.

(Sig) Clarence Molinario,
Min. Clk.

1/12/61,
    Lunacy Commission Appointed by the Court

(Sig) Clarence Molinario,
Min. Clk.

2/21/61,
    After hearing held this day the Court found the defendant to be insane, and ordered her committed to East La. State Hospital.

(Sig) Clarence Molinario,
Min. Clk.

7a. East Louisiana State Hospital Medical Record

STATE OF LOUISIANA : NUMBER 169-075
CRIMINAL DISTRICT COURT
vs. : SECTION "G"
PARISH OF ORLEANS
MELBA CHRISTINE MARCADES : STATE OF LOUISIANA

JUDGMENT

After considering the law and the evidence, the Court finds that the accused Melba Christine Marcades is insane; that she does not understand the proceedings pending against her in this case; that she is unable to consult with counsel and assist him in preparing and making a defense.

IT IS ORDERED that the accused Melba Christine Marcades be held as insane; and that she be committed to the ward for the criminally insane at East Louisiana State Hospital, Jackson, Louisiana, there to be detained as an indigent patient until she be restored to her sound mind or otherwise delivered by due process of law subject to further orders of this Court.

New Orleans, Louisiana
February 21, 1961

(Sig) Shirley G. Wimberly,
Shirley G. Wimberly, Judge
Section "G"

Clerk's Office 4/7/1961
A TRUE COPY.
_____ Deputy Clerk,
Criminal District Court,
Parish of Orleans.

7b. East Louisiana State Hospital Medical Record

DOCTOR'S ORDER SHEET

DATE 3-23-61

PATIENT Marcades Melba Christine # 45,967 age 32
DOCTOR Steele
ORDERS Thorazine 50 mg Q10 Admitting physician
Stellazine 2 mg Q18
Blood Wass + CBC 3-22-61
X Ray of Chest 3-22-61
Eurolysis 3-22-61

4-15-61 Thorazine 50 mg I.M. 6:30 P.M.
         1 oz Gelusil
         2 dram Donnatel

4/18/61 D/C Gelusil + Donnatel
         Milk of Mag 3i h.s. prn

5/15/61 Multitand i cap tid prn
         for headache

6/22/61 Librium 5 mgm

7-25-61 May see attorney

7c. East Louisiana State Hospital Medical Record

PERMISSION FOR ELECTRIC SHOCK THERAPY

Date 1-24-61

I, Mrs. T. J. Youngblood, do hereby give permission to the East Louisiana State Hospital to administer Electric Shock Therapy if indicated for treatment to my daughter, ḇeḏṟa Christine Marcades w/f a 45862 ẉ ṟḍḍḍḵs. I hereby relieve the East Louisiana State Hospital and the attending physician of all responsibility in case of unforeseen accident or complications.

WITNESS:

_____   _____
                                          (Name)

8. Electroshock Therapy Permission Form signed by Mrs. T. J. Youngblood

9a. East Louisiana State Hospital Medical Record

9b. East Louisiana State Hospital Medical Record

9c. East Louisiana State Hospital Medical Record

9d. East Louisiana State Hospital Medical Record

9e. East Louisiana State Hospital Medical Record

ORDER OF RECORDING	Marginal outline is not to be used as check list. Record positive findings in detail and/or specify negative findings.
	Height_____ Weight_____ Age_____ Date_____
	Temp._____ Pulse_____ Resp._____ Blood Pressure_____
1. General	*[illegible handwriting]*
2. Skin	*[illegible handwriting]*
3. Head & Neck	*[illegible handwriting]*
4. EENT	Pupils constricted
5. Respiratory	Clear
6. Cardiovascular	P. Rate 130 ... BP ... *[illegible]*
7. Gastro-Intestinal	*[illegible handwriting]*
8. Genito-urinary	*[illegible handwriting]*
9. Musculo-skeletal	*[illegible handwriting]*
10. Neurological	*[illegible handwriting]*
11. Impression	*[illegible handwriting]* _____ M.D. Examined by _____ M.D. Attending Physician

Name: Charles Rose Hosp. No. 5236
Sex/Color: M Ward: ___

PHYSICAL EXAMINATION

9f. East Louisiana State Hospital Medical Record

Date	
9/27/6_	Released to St. Tangi. of La. State Police a ...dect...
	R.P. M.D.

9g. East Louisiana State Hospital Medical Record

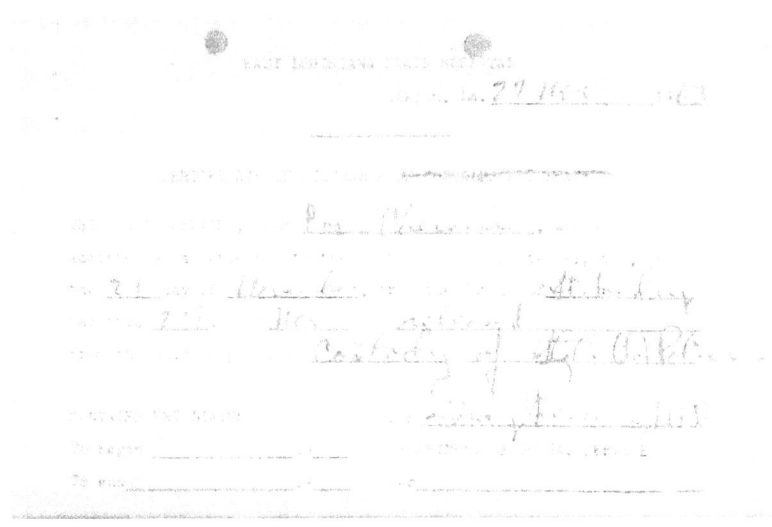

9h. East Louisiana State Hospital Medical Record

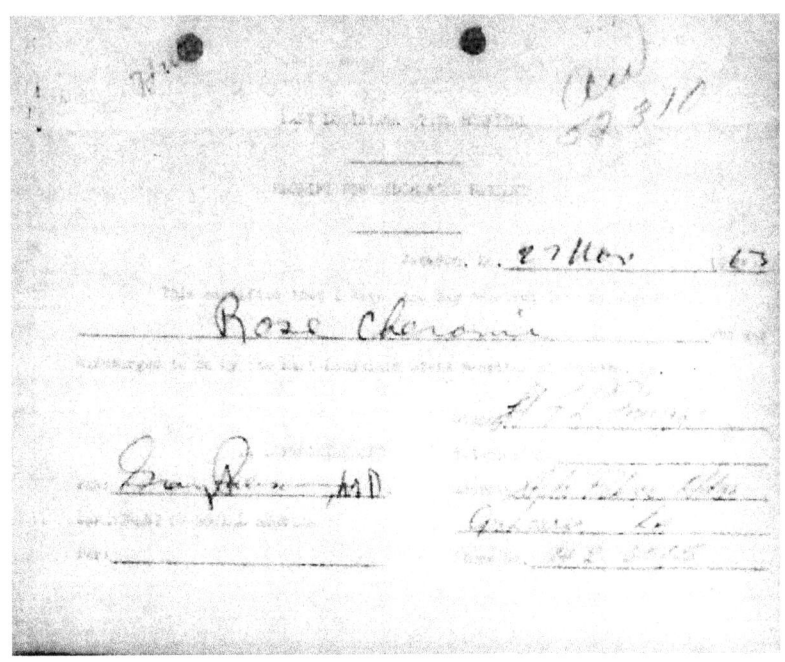

9i. East Louisiana State Hospital Medical Record

9j. Rose Cherami signature, ER Register, ELSH, November 20, 1963
(courtesy of T. C. Elliott)

October 18, 2019

Dr. Michael Marcades,

Enclosed is the only information Griffin Memorial Hospital has of your family member. The records are outside our required retention period and have been destroyed.

Sincerely,

Rene Maricle
Griffin Memorial Hospital
Health Information Coordinator
P. O. Box 151 Norman, OK. 73070
OFFICE: (405) 573-8223
rmaricle@odmhsas.org

```
SAME AS EVANS, Rose
NAME                                    REGISTER #        WARD
MARCADES, Melba                         64096             3A
ADMISSION DATE    SEX    COLOR   MARITAL STATUS
4-5-63            F      W       Divorced
BIRTH PLACE              BIRTHDATE       COUNTY OF COMMITMENT
Louisiana                10-14-32        Oklahoma
CORRESPONDENT
    No relatives known
                                         4-23-63
    Died.

    AKA under various other names
    See FBI Sheet
```

```
NAME                                    REGISTER #        WARD
EVANS, Rose                             64096             5-B
ADMISSION DATE    SEX    COLOR   MARITAL STATUS
4-5-63            F      W       Divorced
BIRTH PLACE              BIRTHDATE       COUNTY OF COMMITMENT
Louisiana                10-14-32        Oklahoma
CORRESPONDENT
    No relatives known
    Discharged                           4-23-63
```

10a. Central State Mental Hospital Medical Record

The End of the Road for Rose

Unfortunately, Rose's story only worsens. In late April 1964, Rose was committed to yet another mental institution, this one in Norman, Oklahoma, where reportedly she had been committed at least twice before. No researcher, to date, has explained what Rose was doing in Oklahoma, but neither has anyone yet been able to explain why Lee Harvey Oswald had "1318 1/2 Garfield Ave., Norman, OK" written in his address book. [For discussion see Notes for this chapter.]

According to CIA documents, it turns out, most likely just by coincidence, that the Oklahoma facility where Rose was confined, Central State Mental Hospital, was being covertly used by the CIA's Project MK/ULTRA, the agency's behavior-modification or mind-control program, at the same time that Rose was confined there. CIA psychologist and Oklahoma native John Gittinger, who oversaw the MK/ULTRA contract with Dr. Ewen Cameron in Montreal, Canada, worked with the agency's Technical Services Section and also monitored the CIA's subproject with the Oklahoma facility, at the same time as Rose's last confinement there. Additionally, Dr. Louis Jolyon West, M.D., professor of psychiatry and head of the psychology department at the University of Oklahoma and a CIA consultant, most likely also saw Rose while she was confined in Oklahoma, but this remains to be verified. What is certain and well documented is that Dr. West, also a long-time CIA consultant and contractor, did professionally visit Lee Harvey Oswald's killer Jack Ruby on April 27, 1964 in Dallas, at the same time that Rose was confined. Of course, Dr. West never revealed to Ruby that he had strong ties to the CIA. Not long after Rose was released from the Oklahoma facility, she was back in the Texas, where she met her ultimate fate.

10b. Albarelli, H. P. A SECRET ORDER, The End of Road for Rose, p. 216

May 12.

Hello there,
Well like the old saying goes, the bad penny has turned up again. But it isn't quite like it was before, this time I am married, & that the truth. Was married the 5 of April in Pensacola. As I told you he is 44 yrs old, a retired Navy man & is now working out here at Cape Canaveral never saw the lil in your life booming gal.

11. Handwritten Letter and envelope from Melba Christine Youngblood Marcades to Mrs. T. J. Youngblood, May 1964, p. 1 of 6

```
                                                      Approved 1952 by the American Hospital Association Code M21-52
Name—Last                          First                Middle                    Hospital No
Marcades, Mrs.  Melba Christine Youngblood                                        20830
Duration in Hospital               Clinic or Service                              Attending Physician
2'1                                Emerg.                                         C. B. McKenzie, M.D.
Address                            City              Zone    State    How Long There    Phone
??  New Orleans, La.                                                   ?
Sex      Color or Race    S. M. W. D.    Citizen of What Country    Military Service    Social Security No
F        Cauc.            Sep. D
Age      Date of Birth                   Birthplace                               Occupation
41       Oct. 14, 1924                   Texas
Employer                                 Address of Employer — Phone
Unemployed
Name of Father                    Living or Dead    Maiden Name of Mother         Living or Dead
T. J. Youngblood                  L                 Minnie B. Stroud              L
Next of Kin                       Address
Mr. Morris Wall                   3633 High Vista, Dallas, Texas                  Brother-in-law
Notify in Case of Emergency                          Address — Phone
Same
Date of Admission                                 Date of Discharge  Expired
9/4/65                 2:40AM                     9/4/65             11:04
```

Final Diagnosis

1) Accident Victim (apparently struck by auto)
   a) Shock
   b) Extensive cerebral contusion + intracranial hemorrhage
   c) Lac. of forehead + scalp
   d) Fx. left forearm
   e) Contusion of chest - pulmonary edema

Complications and/or Secondary Diagnosis:

1) As above

Operation

1) ...
2) ...
3) ...

Result: Recovered ☐ Improved ☐ Unimproved ☐ Not treated ☐ Died ☒ Released Against Advice ☐

SUMMARY

12a. Gladewater Municipal Hospital Medical Record

HISTORY

Family Name	First Name	Attending Physician	Room No.	Hosp. No.
Mercades, Mrs.	Melba Christine	Dr. McKenzie	211	208-30

Information should be recorded on all positive and also relevant negative findings regarding present complaint; present illness; past, family and social histories; and inventory by systems

Date 9/4/65

CC: Accident victim.

PI: This 41 yr. old WF was brought to the ER of the hospital by ambulance. The information given was that the pt. was apparently run over by an automobile near Hawkins and she was carried to a doctor in Hawkins, who examined her superficially and called the ambulance and rushed her to the Gladewater Municipal Hospital. When she arrived in the ER I was summoned. No other history is obtainable on the pt. at the present time. Her identy is not even known at the present time.

PH: No history is available on this pt.

PHYSICAL EXAMINATION

Family Name	First Name	Attending Physician	Room No	Hosp. No.
Marcades, Mrs.	Melba Christine	Dr. McKenzie	211	208-30

Information should be recorded on all positive and also negative findings regarding general condition; skin and lymph glands; eyes, ears, nose and throat; neck; chest; heart and blood vessels; abdomen; genitourinary, rectal and vaginal; muscles bones and joints and neurological findings

GENERAL: Age 41 Temp. _____ Pulse _____ Respiration _____ Blood Pressure _____ Weight _____ Date 9/4/65

This is an adult WF who was brought to the ER of the hospital comatose and unresponsive. She has deep punctate stellate type laceration noted over the right side of the forehead. There is a deep extensive 15+ cm. laceration extending completely around the left posterior scalp area, extending down to the underlying cranium and effectively lifting the scalp from the underlying skull. The external auditory canal on the left is filled with blood and the entire left ear is swollen and contused in appearance. The pupils are large and unresponsive to light. There is blood in the pharynx and mouth. There is the odor of alcohol to the breath. The pt.'s breathing is regular and essentially normal. She is swollen and contused over the entire left side of the face. The neck is supple, but each time the pt.'s head is turned toward the right side she apparently has occlusion of her airway and becomes slightly cyanotic and has vomiting. She has open airway and normal respiratory exchange and no vomiting occurs when she is lying with her head to the left side. She is contused over the left shoulder and there is crepitation of bones in the left forearm with deformity. Portable X-Ray was performed, which revealed fracture of both bones of the forearm. There are scattered rales over both lung fields and markedly impaired breath sounds. The skin is cold and clammy to palpation. The abdomen is soft and flaccid and no specific organomegaly or evidence of internal injury to the abdomen is noted. There are contusions over both lower extremities, but there are no deformities noted. The lacerations of the scalp were cleansed and sutured and dressings applied. There was closed reduction of the left forearm with application of a cast, and there was a cutdown with a venous catheter applied to the left leg, and the pt. is being transeferred to her room in very poor condition.

IMPRESSION: Accident victim apparently struck by an automobile, who is in shock with intracranial damage, lacerations of the forehead and scalp, fracture of the left forearm, and pulmonary edema.

LABORATORY REPORTS

Marcades, Melba Christine Youngblood

Hosp. No. 208-30

URINALYSIS

Name: Meram, Roselle Room: 4 Hosp. No.
Physician: Dr. M. Kerr, Jr. Lab. No.
Color: straw   Character: slightly hazy   Reaction: acc
Specific Gravity: 1.025   W.B.C.: 8-10
Albumin: neg   R.B.C.: 1-3
Sugar: neg   Ep. Cells: occ
Acetone: Casts:
Diacetic Acid: Bacteria: much
Bile: Crystals: uric acid
Urobilinogen: Urobilinogen, quantitative (Normal 1.0–4.0 mg. per 24 hrs.)
*Kolmer

Technician: Tomkin
FORM 30 - MIRROR   Date: 9-4-65

BLOOD (Morphology)

Name: Meram, Roselle   Room: 4   Hosp. No.
Physician: Dr. M. Kerr, Jr.   Lab. No.
R.B.C.: 40%   W.B.C.: 47,100   Hb.: 13.0 gms.
Color Index: Reticulocytes: Platelets:
Coagulation Time: Bleeding Time: Prothrombin Time:

Schilling Differential:

Count	Bands	Eosin.	Myelos.	Juveniles	Stabs	Segs.	Lymph.	Monos.
					5	88	6	1

Neutrophils, immature   mature

Hematocrit:

CBC 7:15 AM   Tomkin Technologist

Mirror No. 42   Date: 9-4-65

GLADEWATER MUNICIPAL HOSPITAL
PROGRESS NOTES

Family Name: Marcades, First Name: Melba Christ[ine], Attending Physician: McKenzie, Room No. 211, Hosp. No. 268-30

Note: Should be Signed by Physician

9/4/65
note of
Expiration
11:00 a.m.

The patient remained unresponsive from admission — had agonal respirations but with effective airway — BP remained very low until blood line [up?] she became markedly elevated then abruptly it dropped again — Vital signs had disappeared — [NVS] tal again noted — pupils unresponsive — no corneal reflex — BP, T, R, absent — patient pronounced dead — Due to the nature of the accident and the fact that the patient is unidentified at present, believe a post mortem examination by Coroner request is indicated — The appropriate Coroner is to be contacted by the Police Officers concerning same.

9/4/65
@ 11:00 AM

EXPIRATION NOTE: This 41 yr. old WF was admitted on 9/4/65 from the ER. The history obtained from the ambulance driver was that the pt. was apparently run over by an automobile near Hawkins and she was taken to a Hawkins doctor. He examined her and had the ambulance bring her on to our hospital in Gladewater. When she was seen in the ER she was comatose and unresponsive. She had a deep punctate stellate laceration over the right side of the forehead and a deep long laceration extending completely around the left posterior scalp, extending down to the underlying cranium. The left external auditory canal was filled with blood and the left side of the face was swollen and contused in appearance. The pupils were large and unresponsive to light. There was blood in the nose and mouth. She

12e. Gladewater Municipal Hospital Medical Record

GLADEWATER MUNICIPAL HOSPITAL
PROGRESS NOTES

Family Name	First Name	Attending Physician	Room No.	Hosp. No.
Marcades, Mrs.	Melba Christine	Dr. McKenzie	211	208-40

Date

9/4/65 — Continuation of Expiration Note: was swollen and contused over the entire left side of the face. The neck was supple, but each time the head was turned to the right side the pt. apparently had occlusion of her airway, because she would become cyanotic and begin to vomit. She had crepitation over the left forearm and evidence of a fracture of this. BP was 90/70 and she was clinically in shock. In the ER a cutdown was performed on the left leg and fluids were started. The lacerations of her scalp were sutured and dressings were applied and then she was taken to her room. She remained cold and clammy and unresponsive for the next several hours and then suddenly had an elevation of BP to an extremely high level and then the BP suddenly dropped and the pt. expired. Due to the nature of the accident, which apparently was responsible for the pt.'s condition. A coroners autopsy was requested. Dr. Jones performed the gross examination at postmortem and I spoke to him over the telephone. Although I have no official report on it he stated that at the time of his gross examination, examination of the brain revealed marked gross areas of contusion but no specific lacerations or specific bleeding points were noted. No specific reason for bleeding from the right ear other than the contusions of the cerebrum were observed by him. The lungs were markedly edematous and heavy and boggy he stated. The abdominal organs did not appear to be lacerated and no specific internal difficulty of that nature was observed by him. These organs were sent to the headquarters in Austin for microscopic evaluation. The impression as to the cause of death was that the pt. was apparently struck by an automobile. She had clinical shock with extensive cerebral contusions and intracranial hemorrhage, lacerations of the forehead and scalp, and a fracture of the left forearm and contusion of the chest with marked pulmonary edema.

12f. Gladewater Municipal Hospital Medical Record

GLADEWATER MUNICIPAL HOSPITAL
PHYSICIAN'S ORDERS

Family Name: Marcades, Melba Christine
First Name: (Cheramie Rosette)
Attending Physician: Dr. McKenzie
Room No: 011
Hosp. No: 208-30

Date Ordered	Date Discontinued	ORDERS
9/4/65		1) Admit to hospital
		2) Dx: Struck by auto a) Cerebral concussion b) Lac. scalp & and possible skull fx — d] fx left forearm & internal injuries etc.
		3) Condition: Very poor —
		4) Bed rest — Keep suctioned well & watch for vomiting & aspirate same — Keep head turned to left side
		5) Catheter to be inserted if not voiding well in 4-6 h — to bed-side drain
		6) Keep legs on cast elevated on pillows
		7) Tetanus tox. #1 ½ cc booster 2 h
		8) Lincocin ii cc I.M. q 8h —
		9) Chymotase ice I.M. bid —
		10) N.P.O. till further advised — CRM
9/4/65		1) If Veni catheter inserted, give Dextrose 5% N/S slow drip & keep IV open with slow drip of Dextrose 5% D/W — Do not let stop up —
		2) If unable to start catheter (venous) give Dextrose 5% D/W 1000 cc by chymo today

12g. Gladewater Municipal Hospital Medical Record

GLADEWATER MUNICIPAL HOSPITAL
NURSES NOTES

Name: Marcades, Melba Christine Dr. McKenzie Room No. 211 Case No. 208-30

Time	T	P	R	Diet	Medications and Treatments	Remarks
9-4-63 5 am		28			BP 70/60	White female - approx 30-32 yrs old. adm. to Room 211 from E.R. c̄ head, scalp wounds, & left arm & possible internal injury.
					T3t Toxoid 1/2cc IM	given on admit.
						Suction throat & nasal passage frequently —
6:30					BP 90/60	Condition remains poor —
					P.S.	D. McKenzie here
7:30		22/12			BP 90/60	unable to start IV — (2) X-
					Terramycin 1cc Chymotrace 1cc Glucose 1000cc 5% [illeg] as above Headache	
8:30		84/24			BP 84/60	
9:00		92/12			BP 88/60	Foley Cath inserted - spec blood
9:15		100/6			BP 100/90	
9:45		10			BP 140/90 — O₂ per mask	difficult breathing
		168/0			BP 190/100	cyanosis neck
10:00		A			BP 224/140	Dr. McKenzie notified
					Demerol 50mg (IM) given	
10:07					BP 70/0	

GLADEWATER MUNICIPAL HOSPITAL
NURSES NOTES

Name: Marcades, Melba Christine Dr. McKen[zie] Room No. 211 Case No. 208-30

Time	T	P	R	Diet	Medications and Treatments	Remarks
9/4/65			5		Cont'd 7-3	Breathing less noisy —
10:15		150			BP ?/?	shallow — cyanosis increasing —
10:25						No vital signs observed — Dr. McKenzie notified — Dr. McKenzie here —
11:00						Pronounced dead —
11:30						Body removed per Stone Funeral Home. Suitcase + personal belongings to Funeral Home c̄ body. — C. Jordan

12i. Gladewater Municipal Hospital Medical Record

CERTIFICATION OF VITAL RECORD

STATE OF TEXAS
COUNTY OF GREGG

CERTIFICATE OF DEATH — STATE FILE NO. 10903

1a. Place of Death — County	Gregg County
1b. City or Town	Gladewater
1c. Length of Stay	1 Day
1d. Name of Hospital or Institution	Gladewater Hospital
1e. Place of Death inside City Limits	Yes
2a. Usual Residence — State	Texas
2b. County	Dallas
2c. City or Town	Duncanville
2d. Street Address	502 Falling Leaves
2e. Residence inside City Limits	Yes
3. Name of Deceased	Melba Christine Marcades
4. Date of Death	September 4, 1965
5. Sex	Female
6. Color or Race	White
7. Married/Never Married/etc.	Divorced
8. Date of Birth	October 14, 1923
9. Age	41
10a. Usual Occupation	Waitress
10b. Kind of Business or Industry	Restaurant
11. Birthplace	Texas
12. Citizen of What Country	U.S.A.
13. Father's Name	Thomas J. Youngblood
14. Mother's Maiden Name	Minnie B. Stroud
15. Was Deceased Ever in U.S. Armed Forces	No
17. Informant	Thomas J. Youngblood

18. Cause of Death:
Part I. Immediate Cause (a): Traumatic Head wound with Subdural & subarachnoid & Petechial Hemorrhage to the brain caused by being struck by auto. — 8 hrs.

20a. Accident
20b. Describe How Injury Occurred: Deceased was lying in the highway and her head was struck by auto.
20c. Time of Injury: 2:00 a.m. 9-4-65
20d. Place of Injury: Highway
20f. City, Town, or Location: Big Sandy, Upshur, Texas

21. D.O.A. — Death occurred at 11:00 A.M.
22c. Date Signed: 9/11/65
22a. Signature: [Coroner signature] Gladewater, Texas

23a. Burial, Cremation, Removal: Removal
23b. Date: September 6, 1965
23c. Cemetery: Wheatland Cemetery
23d. Location: Dallas, Texas
24. Funeral Director: Rogers Funeral Chapel by Rev. F. Rogers

25b. Date Rec'd by Local Registrar: 9/14/65

5116

This is to certify that this is a true and correct copy of the official record placed on file in the office of the Gregg County Clerk.

DATE ISSUED: 11-01-1996

Laurie Woloszyn, County Clerk
Gregg County, Texas

By: _____, Deputy

13. Death Certificate Melba Christine Youngblood Marcades

FD-304 (Rev. 3-3-59)

UNITED STATES DEPARTMENT OF JUSTICE
FEDERAL BUREAU OF INVESTIGATION

Copy to:

Report of: SA JAMES P. MORGAN, JR.   Office: MOBILE
Date: November 23, 1965

Field Office File No.: MO 166-98   Bureau File No.:

Title: GEORGE H. WALKER;
ROZZELLA CLINKSCALES- VICTIM

Character: INTERSTATE TRANSPORTATION IN AID OF
RACKETEERING - PROSTITUTION

Synopsis:

Victim voluntarily appeared at Montgomery, Ala. RA, and advised she had been brought to Montgomery, Ala., on 7/31/65, from New Orleans, La. for purpose of prostitution. Investigation disclosed that GEORGE H. WALKER, FBI No. 2186852, had registered with the victim at the Jefferson Davis Hotel, Montgomery, Ala., 7/31/65. Arrest record for WALKER set out. Investigation continuing.

- P -

DETAILS: AT MONTGOMERY, ALABAMA

On August 3, 1965, a female who identified herself as ROZELLA CLINKSCALES telephonically contacted the Montgomery Resident Agency and advised that she and seven other girls had been brought to Montgomery, Alabama, from New Orleans, Louisiana, by the syndicate for the purpose of prostitution. She asked that an agent come to the drugstore telephone booth from where she was calling and protect her from the syndicate. This same day, Special Agents JAMES P. MORGAN, JR. and PHILIP F. SNODGRASS went to the Dixie Drugstore in Montgomery and accompanied victim to the Resident Agency. At the Resident Agency, victim refused to give definite background information on herself except to state that she was thirty-one years of age. By observation, it was determined that she had red hair and was approximately 5'5" and weighed 140 pounds.

This document contains neither recommendations nor conclusions of the FBI. It is the property of the FBI and is loaned to your agency; it and

FD-302 (Rev. 4-...-64)

FEDERAL BUREAU OF INVESTIGATION

Date August 10, 1965

1

ROZZELLA CLINKSCALES voluntarily furnished the following information during an interview at the Montgomery Resident Agency:

At the outset of the interview, she insisted that she was a "junky" with a $40 a day habit, although there was the smell of alcohol on her breath. She began in a very eratic way to name the people who are responsible for her being in Montgomery. All efforts to have her relate her story in a logical fashion met with her resistance and on several occasions she indicated she was leaving.

At different times, she accused the following men of bringing her or being responsible for her coming to Montgomery: J. B. HILL - allegedly recruited her out of the Jung Hotel in New Orleans. His station wagon was supposedly used to transport her from New Orleans to Montgomery. She further described him as a railroad employee living in Montgomery and known to the Montgomery Police Department.

WHITY SCHULTZ - described as the police chief of the 5th Police District, New Orleans. He allegedly returned to New Orleans immediately after seeing that she and the other girls were delivered to Montgomery.

GEORGE WALKER - an older man who registered with her at the Jefferson Davis Hotel, Montgomery, Alabama, on July 31, 1965, Room 804.

SAM AMAZIO, JOHN CALLAMINE, and LOUIS GUARDINO.

GUARDINO is allegedly an employee of Seaman's International Union and brought $30,000 worth of pure heroin off the ship, JOHN B. WATERMAN at New Orleans, and then gave it to the occupants of the station wagon to be dropped off at various places.

On __8/3/65__ at __Montgomery, Alabama__ File # __MO 166-98__

by __SA PHILIP F. SNODGRASS and SA JAMES P. MORGAN, JR.__ /egp Date dictated __8/7/65__

This document contains neither recommendations nor conclusions of the FBI. It is the property of the FBI and is loaned to your agency; it and its contents are not to be distributed outside your agency.

2

```
                              JFK Assassination System                      Date:   10/6/201
                                Identification Form

                                   Agency Information

              AGENCY :   HSCA
       RECORD NUMBER :   180-10106-10014

       RECORD SERIES :   NUMBERED FILES

   AGENCY FILE NUMBER :  014141

                                  Document Information

           ORIGINATOR :  HSCA
                 FROM:   FRUGE, FRANCIS LOUIS
                   TO :

                TITLE :


                 DATE :  04/07/1978
                PAGES :  16

             SUBJECTS :
                        CHERAMIE, ROSE
                        ODOM, FRANK
                        FRUGE, FRANCIS LOUIS
                        DURHAM, NATHAN
        DOCUMENT TYPE :  SUMMARY
       CLASSIFICATION :  Unclassified
         RESTRICTIONS :  Open in Full
       CURRENT STATUS :  Redact
   DATE OF LAST REVIEW :  08/09/1993

      OPENING CRITERIA :

             COMMENTS :  Box 251.
```

15a. HSCA File Number 180 10106 10014, pp. 1-17
Frugé interview 1978 Subjects Rose Cheramie, Frank Odom, Francis Louis Frugé, Nathan Durham

KENNEDY

014141

INVESTIGATION INTERVIEW SCHEDULE

Identifying Information:

Name **Mr. Francis Louis Fruge** Date **4-7-78**
Address **Rt #1 Box 283** Place **Home**
City/State **Basile, La.** Telephone **318-432-5109**
Date of Birth **8-25-27** M or S **M**
Social Security **437-34-5383** Spouse _____
Children _____

Physical Description:

Height **6 1"** Color Eyes **Brn** Hair **Blk**
Weight **170** Special Characteristics _____
Ethnic Group **White**

1. Personal History:

   a. Present Employment: **Self Employed- Oil Lease Operator**
      Address **Residence**
      Telephone **Above**

   b. Criminal Record
      1. Arrests **None**
      2. Convictions **None**

2. Additional Personal Information:

   a. Relative(s): Name _____
      Address _____

   b. Area frequented: _____
   c. Remarks: **See Attached interview sheet**

   Investigator *Robert C. Buras Jr.* Robert C. Buras Jr.
   Date **4/11/78** Form #4-B

SELECT COMMITTEE ON ASSASSINATIONS - Kennedy

NAME Francis Louis Fruge   Date 4/7/78   Time 10:00 a.m.
Address Rt. 1, Box 283   Place   Residence
         Basile, La.

Interview:

    Investigator Robert Buras met with Mr. Fruge at the above time and date. Mr. Fruge stated that he is self-employed now but he was a lieutenant with the Louisiana State Police from 1947 to 1967. He retired with twenty years' service.

    In 1963 he handled Rose Cheramie in Eunice, La. as a possible mental patient; then as an informant he worked with her and the U.S. Customs from Houston, Texas. This occurred from 11/20/63 through 11/27/63.

    From 1965 through 1967, he assisted New Orleans District Attorney Jim Garrison's investigator, Andy Sciambra, in the Clinton-Jackson area of Louisiana.

    From 1965 through 1967, he was assigned to the Louisiana Sovereignty (State) Commission in Baton Rouge, La.

    On Wednesday, November 20, 1963, at approximately 10:00 p.m., Mr. Fruge was called to the emergency ward of the Moosa Memorial Hospital in Eunice, La. by Mrs. Louise Guillory.

    A patient, Rose Cheramie, was in the ward because she had been struck by an auto on Highway 190 in front of the Silver Slipper Lounge. She had only minor abrasions when she

Interviewer_____
              (Signature)
          Robert Buras
                (Typed)
                        Date Transcribed 4/17/78   /am

Francis Louis Fruge Interview...page 2

was brought into the hospital by the man that hit her, a Mr. Frank Odom. Mr. Odom was known to Mr. Fruge and is a long-time resident of the area. Mrs. Guillory called Lt. Fruge because she thought that the patient was on drugs. She could not be released due to her condition, so Lt. Fruge brought her to the local jail and locked her up for safekeeping until she sobered up. Rose Cheramie had been hitchhiking when she was struck by Mr. Odom. A short while later, Lt. Fruge was called to the local jail because Rose Cheramie had stripped off all of her clothes and was "cutting up" in the cell. He called a Lafayette Charity Hospital ambulance and accompanied the driver as he transported Cheramie to the East Louisiana State Hospital for examination. He took this action on the advice of Dr. Rodney Derouin, who met him at the jail and sedated Cheramie.

The trip took about two hours and during this time Cheramie was calm and asked the usual questions about why she was being held and where she was being taken. During this trip, she was in a straightjacket. Mr. Fruge stated that this procedure was used on any person that showed signs of drug withdrawal to the extent that they needed medical attention. The people would be treated until their withdrawal symptoms stopped and were then released.

Francis Louis Fruge Interview...page 3

During the trip from Eunice to Jackson, Rose Cheramie stated that she was just passing through town from Miami and on her way to Dallas and Houston. She stated: "We're going to kill President Kennedy when he comes to Dallas in a few days." She talked about traveling with a couple of guys, but Lt. Fruge did not take any of the conversation as serious due to her condition. He admitted her to Jackson at about 3:00 a.m. Thursday, November 21, 1963. She was still calm but she was put into a patient sack for her own protection.

On Friday, November 22, 1963, Lt. Fruge was at his home when he heard that the President had been shot in Dallas. He called the Hospital and found out that Cheramie was kicking up again to the extent that he didn't think a trip or talk to her would be fruitful. He asked the doctors at the Hospital to call him when she calmed down. On Monday, November 25, he found out that she was calmed down and he went to Jackson to talk with her. She stated that she was coming from Miami with two men that were either Cubans or Italians and she was going to go to Dallas, then to Houston. The men were going to kill Kennedy and she was going to check into the Rice Hotel, where reservations were already made for her, and pick up 10 kilos of heroin from a seaman coming into Galveston. She was to pick up the money for the dope from a man who was holding her baby. She would then take the dope to Mexico. Mr. Fruge could not remember the name of the seaman that she gave, or the ship's name, or the

Francis Louis Fruge Interview...page 4

name name that she used as an alias at the Hotel. He stated that the U.S. Customs would have this information if anyone checks with them.

Lt. Fruge told Col. Morgan of the State Police and he told Col. Burbank. Col. Burbank was in charge of the State Police at the time Burbank told them to check out the story. Morgan and Fruge called Nathan Durham, Chief Customs Agent in Port Arthur, Texas and gave him the name of the seaman and the ship that Cheramie said the dope was coming in on. Durham called back in about 30 minutes and confirmed that a ship was coming into Galveston by that name and the seaman's name was on the ship's roster. Col. Morgan called Will Fritz of the Dallas Police Department and told him the story about the assassination and the heroin, which had partly checked out. Fritz told Morgan that it was in the hands of the Federal Agents and gave Morgan a name to call. Morgan called the agent and was told that they weren't interested at that time. They made plans to meet with Nathan Durham in Houston to work the heroin. Rose Cheramie, Fruge, Morgan and a State Police Pilot took the LASP plane and flew to Houston on Tuesday. They worked with the Customs people and attempted to get the dope. The Customs people checked the Rice Hotel and reservations were made just as Cheramie had said. The man that allegedly had the money and her baby was checked and his name showed that he was an underworld, suspected narcotics dealer.

Francis Louis Fruge Interview...page 5

While flying to Texas in the plane, one of the men had a daily newspaper and it had a headline or story title that stated that Oswald and Ruby were not connected. Rose Cherami saw the headline and laughed. She told the men in the plane that Oswald and Ruby were "bed partners" when she worked for Ruby as a stripper. She stated that she worked for Ruby, but Fruge does not remember the name of the bar that she said she stripped at. It wasn't the Carousel. It had a name with something like the Pink Door or Red Door. Fruge thinks that this might have been checked later, but they didn't do anything with it at that time.

When Cheramie was first picked up on the highway in Eunice, La., she had two cardboard boxes of clothes and belongings. Fruge looked in one of the two boxes and found baby clothes and shoes. This led him to believe that she at least had a baby, but he didn't check the boxes any further. An Agent named Bob Woody checked into the Rice Hotel with Cheramie and acted as her sugar daddy. An Agent was assigned to follow the seaman. The seaman got onto a bus from Galveston to Houston, but he lost the tail. No one contacted the room at the Hotel and Rose Cheramie missed her time schedule. The whole deal fell through on the dope. The Agent in charge of Customs in Houston called the Agents, probably F.B.I., and asked them if they wanted to talk to Cheramie. They didn't want to speak with her so Fruge, Morgan and the pilot came back to Baton Rouge. They cut Rose Cheramie loose in Houston. Mr. Fruge forgot about the incident.

Francis Louis Fruge Interview...page 6

In 1965 or '66, an investigator for Jim Garrison called and asked about the above information. Lt. Fruge was loaned to the Garrison investigation by the State Police. Lt. Fruge stated that a Dr. Person had somehow heard about the Cheramie case and had called Garrison. Fruge then helped with some of the interviews in Jackson and Clinton, La. He got a set of photos from the Garrison investigation and went to the man who managed the Silver Slipper Lounge, Mack Manuel. Mack Manuel remembered the incident and stated that he had seen Rose Cheramie talk to three men. Two men were with her and a third came in later and talked to the others. Mack Manuel went through the mug shots and other photos and picked out the two men that were with Rose Cheramie the night that she was there. One was Sergio Arcacha Smith and the other was a name like Assanto, unknown if last or first name. The man who came in and talked to them was identified by Manuel as John Paul Jennette. This man, Jennette, might have talked to Assanto previously because he died of a heart attack in Eunice, La. on February 18, 1978. He was born in Worcester, Massachusetts on April 17, 1927. His social security number was [JFK Act 6 (3)] This man, Jennette, might have known Assanto. Mack Manuel stated to Fruge that Assanto (or a name like that) used to bring girls to the Silver Slipper from Miami. The girls would work for a couple of weeks and then go back. The name of the man should be in some reports of Garrison's investigator. Mack Manuel was shot to death in 1974-75 in Villeplatte, La.

Francis Louis Fruge Interview...page 7

Fruge was asked in 1966 to attempt to find Rose Cherami. He learned that she was born in Houston, Texas and she died in a small town in Texas in 1965. She was the victim of an auto hitting her while she was either walking or hitchhiking on a highway. Fruge found that the cause of death was listed as a fractured skull and Jim Garrison wanted the body exhumed. Mr. Fruge stated that the local authorities would not exhume the body and were generally unfriendly. Mr. Fruge stated that he found it unusual that a person would be hit by an auto and only have a fracture of the skull without breaking any other bones in the body.

Mr. Fruge stated that he could not find any other records of the driver that hit and killed Rose Cherami except in the Police Report and at the State Vehicle Office of Registration. He checked the address given and no one at that address had ever heard of the man. He states that someone might have found him later but he (Fruge) doesn't remember hearing about it.

Mr. Fruge touched on a few other points that he remembered. There was a Dr. Silva, who was born in Havana, Cuba, working at the East Louisiana State Hospital in 1963. That is the only year that he worked there and Mr. Fruge does not have information nor does he imply that the doctor was involved in anything illegal. Mr. Fruge only mentions him because he was from Cuba.

Mr. Fruge asked if this Committee had found that diagrams of the sewer system in Dealey Plaza were found in Arcacha Smith's apartment in Texas. He thinks that Captain Will Fritz might have mentioned something about that, but Mr. Fruge was not sure on this point.

Francis Louis Fruge Interview...page 8

Mr. Fruge stated that he had a letter in his possession from Margarette Martens, the mother of Layton Martens, to a Father Toups. The letter (a xerox copy) stated that Mrs. Martens heard talk about killing President Kennedy among Ferrie, Shaw, and Banister in 1963, but she denied that her son, Layton Martens, was involved in the talk. This letter was written, to the best of his memory, after Garrison called her son before the Grand Jury in New Orleans. Mrs. Martens was dating David Ferrie -- or at least was friendly with him. Mr. Fruge remembers checking on Mrs. Martens and learning that Mr. Guy Banister had her committed to Charity Hospital, New Orleans, then to Mandeville, Louisiana on August 16, 1963. She was committed to Charity Hospital, New Orleans again on November 30, 1966 by David Ferrie and Layton Martens. Mr. Fruge and Andy Sciambra talked with her doctor, whose name he doesn't remember. The doctor, a psychiatrist, stated that Mrs. Martens was not insane. He didn't talk with Mrs. Martens. These dates might or might not be significant, but he mentions that in August 1963 Oswald was in New Orleans handing out leaflets and this would be the time that she claims to have heard the talk of killing the President. The 1966 date would be about the time that talk was going around New Orleans that the District Attorney was going to call people before the Grand Jury.

Father Toups is now deceased.

Francis Louis Fruge Interview...page 9

Another point of interest to Mr. Fruge was a statement by one Andy Dunn of Clinton, Louisiana. Mr. Dunn was sitting across the street from the black vehicle that was parked by the voter registration office. He remembered seeing three men in the car -- two in front and one in the rear -- at the time that Oswald was in line to register. That would mean that there is one man that was in the car that has not been identified to this day. Mr. Dunn, who was a local drunk, died in jail in Clinton a short time later. Mr. Fruge does not have the report, but he remembers the story that Mr. Dunn died by hanging himself while lying on his bunk. He had a belt around his neck and around the head of the bunk and he strangled while he was lying there. This has not been verified to his knowledge.

Mr. Henry Sybly of Denin Springs or Hammond, Louisiana was the chairman of the State Sovereignty Commission. Mr. Fruge doesn't remember anything about Mr. Guy Banister's files ever being brought there. It is possible that files were there that he did not know about. Mr. Fruge stated that he never worked with retired Major Russell Willie of the Louisiana State Police while he was with the Commission.

Mr. Francis Louis Fruge   4-7-78
Rt #1 Box 283   Home
    Basile, La.   318-432-5109
    8-25-27   M
    437-34-5383

6& 1"   Brn   Blk
170
    White

            Self Employed- Oil Lease Operator
    Residence
    Above

        None

        None

        See Attached interview sheet
            Robert C. Buras Jr.

Mr. Francis Louis Fruge   4-7-78   10:00AM

Rt 1 Box 283   Residence

Basile, La.

Investigator Robert Buras met with Mr. Fruge on the above time and date. Mr. Fruge stated that he is self employed now but he was a Lieutenant with the Louisiana State Police from 1947 to 1967. He retired with twenty years service.

In 1963 he handled Rose Cheramie in Eunice, La. as a possible mental patient then as an informant he worked with her and the U.S. Customs from Houston, Texas. This occurred from 11-20-63 thru 11-27-63.

In 1965 thru 1967 he assisted New Orleans District Attorney Jim Garrison's investigator Andy Sciambra in the Clinton&Jackson area of Louisiana.

In 1965 thru 1967 he was assigned to the Louisiana Sovereignty (State) Commission in Baton Rouge, La.

On Wednesday Nov. 20, 1963 at approx. 10:00PM Mr. Fruge was called to the Moosa Memorial Hospital in Eunice, La. by Mrs. Louise Guillory, to the emrgency ward. A patient, Rose Cheramie, was in the ward because she had been struck by an auto on highway 190 in front of the Silver Slipper Lounge. She had only minor abrasions when she was brought into the hospital by the man that hit her, a Mr. Frank Odom. Mr. Odom was known to Mr. Fruge and is a long time resident of the area. Mrs. Guillory called Lt. Fruge because she thought that the patient was on drugs. She could not be released due to her condition so Lt. Fruge brought her to the local jail and locked her up for safe keeping until she sobered up. Rose Cheramie had been hitchiking when she was struck by Mr. Odom. A short while later Lt. Fruge was called to the local jail because Rose Cheramie had stripped off all of her clothes and was cutting up in the cell. He called a Lafayette Charity Hospital ambulance and accompanied the driver as he transported Cheramie to the East Louisiana State Hospital for examination. He took this action of the advise of Dr. Rodney Derouin who met him at the jail and sedated Cheramie.

Robert Buras

Page two   Interview Mr. Frank Fruge

The trip took about two hours and during this time Cheramie was calm and asked the usual questions about why she was being held and where she was being taken. During this trip she was in a straight jacket. Mr. Fruge stated that this procedure was used on any person that showed signs of drug withdrawal to the extent that they needed medical attention. The people would be treated until their withdrawal symptoms stopped and released.

During the trip from Eunice to Jackson Rose Cheramie stated that she was just passing through town from Miami and on her way to Dallas and Houston. She stated " We're going to kill President Kennedy when he comes to Dallas in a few days". She talked about traveling with a couple of guys but Lt. Fruge did not take any of the conversation as serious due to her condition. He admitted her to Jackson at about 5:00AM Thursday, Nov. 21, 1963. She was still calm but she was put into a patient sack for her own pretection.

On Friday Nov. 22, 1963 Lt. Fruge was at his home when he heard that the President had been shot in Dallas. He called the hospital and found out that Cheramie was kicking up again to the extent that he didn't think a trip or talk to her would be fruitful. He asked the doctors at the hospital to call him when she calmed down. On Monday Nov. 25 he found out that she was calmed down and he went to Jackson to talk with her. She stated that she was coming from Miami with two men that were either Cubans or Italians and she was going to go to Dallas then to Houston. The men were going to kill Kennedy and she was going to check into the Rice Hotel, where reservations were already made for her, and pick up 10 kilos of herion from a seaman coming into Galveston. She was to pick up the money for the dope from a man that was holding her baby. She would then take to the dope to Mexico. Mr. Fruge could not remember the name of the seaman that she gave, or the ship's name, or the name that she used as an alias at the Hotel. He stated that the U.S. Customs would have this information if anyone checks with them.

Lt. Fruge told Col Morgan of the State Police and he told Col Burbank. Col. Burbank was in charge of the State Police at the time. Burbank told them to check out the story. Morgan and Fruge called Nathan Durham, Chief Customs Agent in Port Arthur Texas and gave him the name of the seaman and the ship that Cheramie said the dope was coming in on. Durham called back in about 30 minutes and confirmed that a ship was coming into Galveston by that name and the seaman's name was on the ships roster. Col. Morgan called Will Fritz of the Dallas Police Department and told him the story about the assassination and the herion which had partly checked out. Fritz told Morgan that it was in the hands of the Federal Agents and gave Morgan a name to call. Morgan called the agent and was told that they weren't

con't

Page three   Interview Mr. Frank Fruge

interested at that time. They made plans to meet with Natan Durham
in Houston to work the herion. Rose Cheramie, Fruge, Morgan and a
State Police Pilot took the LASP plane and flew to Houston on Tuesday.
They worked with the Customs poeple and attempted to get the
dope. The customs people checked the Rice Hotel and reservations
were made just as Cheramie had said. The man that alledgedly had
the money and her baby was checked and his name showed that he was
an underworld, suspected narcotics dealer. While flying to Texas
in the plane one of the men had a daily newspaper and if had a head
line or story title that stated that Oswald and Ruby were not connected.
Rose Cheramie saw the headline and laughed. She told the
men in the plane that Oswald and Ruby were " bed partners W when
she worked for Ruby as a stripper. She stated that she worked for
Ruby but Fruge does not remember the name of the bar that she said
she stripped at. It wasn't the Carousel. It had a name with some
thing like the Pink Door or Red Door. Fruge thinks that this might
have been checked later but they didn't dod anything with it at that
time. When Cheramie was first picked up on the highway in Eunice,
La. she had two cardboard boxes of clothes and belongings. Fruge
looked in one of the two boxes and found baby clothes and shoes. This
led him to believe that she at least had a baby but he didn't check
the boxes any further. An Agent named Bob Woody checked into the
Rice Hotel with Cheramie and acted as her sugar daddy. An Agnet
was assigned to follow the seaman. The seaman got onto a bus from
Galveston to Houston but he lost the tail. No one contacted the room
at the Hotel and Rose Cheramie missed her time schedule. The whole
deal fell through on the dope. The Agent in charge of Customs in
Houston called the Agents, probably F.B.I. and asked them if they
wanted to talk to Cheramie. They didn't want to speak with her aso
Fruge, Morgan and the Pilot came back to Baton Rouge. They cut Rose
Cheramie loose in Houston. Mr. Fruge forgot about the incident.

In 1965 or 66 an investigator for Jim Garrison calls and asks about
the above information. Lt. Fruge was loaned to the Garrison investigation
by the State Police. Lt. Fruge stated that a Dr. Person
had somehow heard about the Cheramie case and had called Garrison.
Fruge thenhelps with some of the interviews in Jackson and Clinton
La. He got a set of photos from the Garrison investigation and went
to the man that managed the Silver Slipper Lounge, Mack Manuel. Mack
Manuel remembered the incident and stated that he had seen Rose
Cheramie talk to three men. Two men were with her and a third came
in later and talked to the others. Mack Manuel went through the
mug shots and other photos and picked out the two men that were with
Rose Cheramie the night that she was there. One was Sergio Areacha
Smith and the other was a name like Assanto, unknown if last or first
name. The man that came in and talked to them was identified by
Manuel as John Paul Jennette. This man Jennette might have talked
to Assanto previously because he died of a heart attack in Eunice, La.

Con't

Page four   Interview Mr. Frank Fruge

2-187878 of a heart attack. He was born in Worcester, Mass. 4-17-27. His social security number was [JFK Act 6 (3)]. This man, Jennette might have known Assanto. Mack Manuel stated to Fruge that Assanto or name like that used to bring girls to the Silver Slipper from Miami. The girls would work for a couple of weeks and then go back. The name of the man should be in some reports of Garrison's investigator. Mack Manuel was shot to death in 1974-5 in Villeplatte, La.

Fruge was asked in 1966 to attempt to find Rose Cheramie. He learned that she was born in Houston Texas and she died in a small town in Texas in 1965. She was the victim of an auto hitting her while she was either walking or hitchiking on a highway. Fruge found that the cause of death was listed as a fractured skull and Jim Garrison wanted the body exhumed. Mr. Fruge stated that the local authorities would not exhume the body and were generally unfriendly. Mr. Fruge stated that he found it unusual that a person could be hit by and auto and only have a fracture of the skull without breaking any other bones in the body.

Mr. Fruge touched on a few other points that he remembered. There was a Dr. Silva that was born in Havana, Cuba working at the East Louisiana State Hospital in 1963. That is the only year that he worked there and Mr. Fruge does not have information nor does he imply that the Dr. is involved in anything illegal. Mr. Fruge only mentions him because he was from Cuba.

Mr. Fruge asked if this Committee had found that diagrams of the sewer system in Dealy Plaza were found in Arcacha Smith's apartment in Texas. He thinks that Captain Will Fritz might have mentioned something about that but Mr. Fruge was not sure on this point.

Mr. Fruge stated that he had a letter in his possession from Margarette Martens, the mother of Layten Martens, to a Father Toups. The letter (a xerox copy) stated that Mrs. Martens heard talk about killing President Kennedy between Ferrie, Shaw, and Banister in 1963 but she denied that her son Layten Martens was involved in the talk. This letter was written, to the best of his memory, after Garrison called her son before the Grand Jury in New Orleans. Mrs. Martens was dating David Ferrie or at least friendly with him. Mr. Fruge remembers checking on Mrs. Martens and learning that Mr. Guy Banister had her committed to Charity Hospital New Orleans then to Mandeville, La. on August 16, 1963. She was committed to Charity Hospital New Orleans again on Nov. 30, 1966 by David Ferrie and Layten Martens. Mr. Fruge and Andy Sciambra talked with her doctor, whose name he doesn't remember. The doctor, a psychiatrist stated that Mrs. Martens was not insane. He didn't talk with Mrs. Martens. These dates might or might not be significant but he mentions that

con't

in August 1963 Oswald is in New Orleans handing out leaflets and this would be the time that she claims to have heard the talk of killing the President. The 1966 date would be about the time that talk is going around New Orleans that the District Attorney is going to call up people before the Grand Jury.

Father Toups is now deceased.

Mr. Fruge stated that he could not find any other records of the driver that hit and killed Rose Cheramie except in the the Police Report and at the State Vehicle Office of Registration. He checked the address given and no one at that address had ever heard of the man. He states that someone might have found him later but he (Fruge) doesn't remember hearing about it.

Another point of interest to Mr. Fruge was a statement by one Andy Dunn of Clinton, La. Mr. Dunn was sitting across the street from the black vehicle that was parked by the voter registration office. He remembered seeing three men in the car. Two in front and one in the rear at the time that Oswald was in line to register. That would mean that there is one man that was in the car that has not been identified to this day. Mr. Dunn who was a local drunk died in jail in Clinton a short time later. Mr. Fruge does not have the report but he remembers the story that Mr. Dunn died by hanging himself while lying on his bunk. He had a belt around his neck and around the head of the bunk and he strangled while he was laying there. This has not been verified to his knowledge.

Mr. ~~Henry S~~ ~~~~ It is possible that files were there that he did not know about. Mr. Fruge stated that he never worked with retired Major Russell Willie of the La. State Police while he was with the Commission.

                 End   Of   Memo

www.ingramcontent.com/pod-product-compliance
Lightning Source LLC
Chambersburg PA
CBHW071229290426
44108CB00013B/1345